ALEXANDER HAMILTON AND THE CONSTITUTION

Books by Clinton Rossiter

CONSTITUTIONAL DICTATORSHIP (*1948*)

THE SUPREME COURT AND THE COMMANDER IN CHIEF (*1951*)

SEEDTIME OF THE REPUBLIC (*1953*)

Part I revised and published as THE FIRST AMERICAN REVOLUTION (*1958*)

Part III revised and published as THE POLITICAL THOUGHT OF THE AMERICAN REVOLUTION (*1963*)

CONSERVATISM IN AMERICA (*1955; revised edition 1962*)

THE AMERICAN PRESIDENCY (*1956; revised edition 1960*)

PARTIES AND POLITICS IN AMERICA (*1960*)

MARXISM: THE VIEW FROM AMERICA (*1960*)

ALEXANDER HAMILTON AND THE CONSTITUTION (*1964*)

Editor, DOCUMENTS IN AMERICAN GOVERNMENT (*1949*)
Editor (with Milton R. Konvitz), ASPECTS OF LIBERTY (*1958*)
Editor, THE FEDERALIST (*1961*)
Editor (with James Lare), THE ESSENTIAL LIPPMANN (*1963*)

ALEXANDER HAMILTON

AND THE

CONSTITUTION

Clinton Rossiter

HARCOURT, BRACE & WORLD, INC.

New York

IN MEMORIAM

Edward S. Corwin, 1878–1963

EXEGIT MONUMENTUM AERE PERENNIUS

PREFACE

THIS is a book about Alexander Hamilton which, like the man himself, spills over into more areas than it probably should. That, I plead in defense, is what usually happens when one wrestles with a giant, and that, I rejoice in retrospect, is what happened in this instance despite the best of scholarly intentions. I say "in retrospect" because this preface, like all proper prefaces, was written after the fact.

It should, in any case, be understood that only one of several themes woven into this book is picked out clearly in the title. While it is, as it was supposed to be, primarily a study of the contributions of Hamilton to the creation of that supple instrument of nation-building, the Constitution of 1801, it is also inevitably a study of the relevance of Hamilton for the interpretation of that venerated symbol of nationhood, the Constitution of 1963. Just as inevitably it includes an exposition of his constitutional law and theory, perhaps not quite so inevitably—yet, in my view, altogether logically—an exposition of the political philosophy that animated his efforts to transform the Constitution into the charter of a republican empire.

The reader should have no trouble identifying any of these themes, since the first is largely concentrated in chapters 2–3, the second in chapter 7, the third in chapter 6, and the fourth in chapters 4–5. He may, however, want to be informed more pointedly that two additional themes or theses will be stated again and again in all these chapters. The first is that, despite some prodigious labors in behalf of his reputation, Alexander Hamilton is still the least known and most misunderstood major figure in American history, a man in plain if not desperate need of a fresh appraisal. Even though this book concentrates on the constitutional Hamilton, I have tried to see the whole public man in the perspective of his time and ours. Lest the reader think me timid or devious, let me say at the outset of this quest for the essential Hamilton that its conclusions will do nothing intentionally to dampen the slowly rising enthusiasm for the man, his ideas, and his achievements. I undertook this study not to celebrate Hamilton but to understand him; I ended with the conviction that to understand him is to celebrate him, if not necessarily to love him. While my feelings about the man are only slightly less ambivalent than they were in the days when I, like all undergraduates of the 1930's, was taught American history by one dedicated Jeffersonian after another, my newly measured opinion of his ideas and achievements is pitched at a high level. Talleyrand, that fox among lions, is supposed to have said: "I consider Napoleon, Pitt and Hamilton as the three greatest men of our age, and if I had to choose among the three, I would without hesitation give the first place to Hamilton." If this judgment was not at the time entirely fair to Napoleon and Pitt, who strode on far more spacious stages (or, for that matter, to such as Metternich, Wellington, Fox, Washington, Jefferson, Franklin, Nelson, Burke, and Frederick the Great), it has made more and more sense to men of fair mind as America has moved in fits and starts toward the glory Hamilton foretold. My hope is that this book may help to explain why Hamilton deserves full membership in this illustrious company.

The second of the recurring themes is that the immensely popular and comforting view of Jefferson as the Child of Light and Hamilton as the Child of Darkness in an endless struggle for the soul of America does small honor to the one and no justice to the other. Even though I may annoy all good Jeffersonians (a legion in these days) without at the same time gratifying all good Hamiltonians (a corporal's guard in any day), I have thought it important to suppress my own urges toward historical Manicheanism and to be as exact and outspoken as possible in indicating the debt of this and every generation of Americans to each of these two great men. If this book is a touch more Hamiltonian than it ought to be, that is because, at least among most of the people with whom I live and work, Hamilton is a man admired only grudgingly and liked not at all, and also because it deals primarily with the two battles he fought with Jefferson that, to our good fortune, came out in his favor. While we have every right to be thankful that Jefferson spoke and wrought so effectively for democracy, we might also be more thankful that Hamilton spoke and wrought so effectively for the Union and the Constitution. This country can aspire to be free in a world of fear and envy because it is first of all united and second of all constitutional. We might all therefore be a little more conscious of the legacy of that faithful servant of a more perfect Union and that imaginative expounder of a Constitution designed to perfect it, Alexander Hamilton.

WITHOUT the help of many kind persons—Jeffersonians, Hamiltonians, Jeffersonian Hamiltonians, and Hamiltonian Jeffersonians—this book could not possibly have been finished. My warmest thanks are owed to Elaine F. Crane, who was my devoted research assistant from the first to the last day of this journey into the past, and to Mary Crane Rossiter, who has always been my most severe and thoughtful critic. I am also indebted for aid, comfort, or criticism (in some instances for all three) to Walter Berns, Ardella Blandford, Stephen Crane, Robert E. Cushman, Janet Forman, Marguerite Gigliello, Anthony Kahn, C. Peter Magrath, David Millar, Broadus Mitchell, Frederick Mosteller, Lawrence Parkus, Leonard Rapport, Hon. Alex H. Sands, Jr., Sara L. Schwarz, Cushing Strout, and Mary K. Tachau, as well as to the staffs of the following institutions: in New York, the New York Public Library, New-York Historical Society, Columbia University Library, New York Law Institute Library, and Association of the Bar of the City of New York; in Albany, the New York State Library; in Troy, the Troy Public Library; in Clinton, the Hamilton College Library; in Portsmouth, the Portsmouth Athenaeum; in Concord, the New Hampshire Historical Society; in Boston, the Massachusetts Historical Society, Boston University Library, and Boston Athenaeum; in Cambridge, the Houghton Library of Harvard University; in Worcester, the American Antiquarian Society; in Hartford, the Connecticut Historical Society; in New Haven, the Yale University Library; in Norwich, the Norwich Public Library; in Newark, the New Jersey Historical Society; in Morristown, the National Historical Park; in Princeton, the Princeton University Library; in New Brunswick, the Rutgers University Library; in Trenton, the New Jersey State Library, Division of Archives and History; in Philadelphia, the Historical Society of Pennsylvania and American Philosophical Society; in Baltimore, the Maryland Historical Society; in Washington, the Library of Congress and National Archives; in Richmond, the Virginia State Library and Virginia Historical Society; in Charlottesville, the Library of the University of Virginia; in Williamsburg, the Institute of Early American History and Culture and William and Mary College Library; in Winchester, the Handley Library; in Charleston, the Charleston Library Society; and in Ithaca, as always and above all, the Cornell University Library. Several of these institutions have granted permission to quote from letters or documents in their keeping.

Finally, to all those who have participated in that splendid project *The Papers of Alexander Hamilton,* and especially to Harold Syrett, Mrs. Harold Syrett, Dorothy Twohig, and Cara Miller, I am grateful with the gratitude of one whose own labors were shortened many months by the labors of others. I am equally grateful to Lashley G. Harvey and his colleagues in Boston University, who, by inviting me to give the Gaspar G. Bacon Lectures on the Constitution of the United States, October 29–31, 1962, persuaded me to get my thoughts on Hamilton into ordered form.

CLINTON ROSSITER
Ithaca
June, 1963

CONTENTS

Preface, vii

1. THE MANY HAMILTONS AND THE ONE, 3

2. HAMILTON AND THE CONSTITUTION: *1780–1788*, 34

3. HAMILTON AND THE CONSTITUTION: *1789–1804*, 71

4. HAMILTON'S POLITICAL SCIENCE: MAN AND SOCIETY, 113

5. HAMILTON'S POLITICAL SCIENCE: THE PATTERN AND PURPOSE OF GOVERNMENT, 153

6. HAMILTON'S CONSTITUTIONAL LAW AND THEORY, 185

7. THE RELEVANCE OF HAMILTON, 226

Short Titles and Abbreviations Used in the Notes, 255

Notes, 259

Index, 349

ALEXANDER HAMILTON AND THE CONSTITUTION

ONE

THE MANY HAMILTONS AND THE ONE

"Without numbers, he is an host within himself."
> Jefferson to Madison, on the subject of
> Hamilton, September 21, 1795

THE age in which we live is a great one for history, by which I mean both history in the making and history in the telling. One side of the American spirit reaches for the moon (and hopes to land on it in the 1970's); another side warms itself before the fires of national memory. The scientists are having a field day; so, too, are the historians.

The upsurge of traditionalism in the temper of this generation of Americans has brought new luster to the names of the famous men of our past. It is hard to think of a single notable American, from Roger Williams to Woodrow Wilson by way of Eli Whitney and Davy Crockett, who has not grown in stature in the last quarter-century, who does not command more attention from schoolchildren, more obeisance from politicians, and more respect from scholars than he did in the 1930's.

Despite our obsessive concentration of the moment—and what a long moment it is getting to be—on the leaders of the Civil War, this climate of nostalgia and piety has smiled most benignly on the choice band of heroes we venerate as the Founding Fathers, many of whom are twice

3

venerated as the Framers. At a time when scores of new nations are struggling to their feet, we are understandably proud of the men who not only put the American Republic on its feet but got it moving smartly in the right direction. Washington is as big and noble a figure as ever Parson Weems drew for our inspiration. Jefferson, secure at last in his own temple, has been sent forth with Lincoln on a two-man mission to convince mankind that we really are democrats. Franklin is saluted with ever increasing admiration as the patron saint of science, savings banks, volunteer fire companies, and a free press, John Marshall with ever increasing awe as a symbol of the rule of law. And John Adams and James Madison are at last emerging from the shadows cast by Washington and Jefferson to be recognized as giants without whose faithful services the founding of the Republic would very possibly have miscarried.

Still in the shadows—or at best half in and half out—is Alexander Hamilton, the comrade of Washington and the foe of Jefferson. Almost lost from view (except by a handful of spiritual and flesh-and-blood descendants) in the first half of the nineteenth century, taken up thereafter by historians and statesmen who were busy grinding right-handed axes, portrayed too conveniently in the mythology of democracy as the spoiler of the dreams of the faultless Jefferson,[1] Hamilton has never been given a full and fair shake by most of the men who write American history or most of those who teach it to our children. In these years of crisis, to be sure, we have all become tougher and braver, more open-eyed and less sentimental—in a word, more Hamiltonian—and he has been granted a new measure of respect.[2] Respect, however, is neither affection nor veneration, and he remains the one important Founding Father about whom it is considered bad form to be too enthusiastic. It is instructive to note that the revival of Hamilton's reputation has begun at the top among professors and publicists and is seeping down only slowly among the people, which is not at all the case with Washington, Franklin, Lincoln, and Jefferson, whose ever higher standing among historians seems to be buoyed up from below. Yet that, I imagine, would please rather than disturb a man who respected the power of public opinion always but its judgments and prejudices only seldom.

ONE reason for the growth of Hamilton's reputation in recent decades is that he strikes the eye as a host of men rolled into one. While he was never a match for either Jefferson or Franklin in the variety of his talents,

---

[1] Notes will be found on pages 255 to 348.

interests, and achievements, he did spread himself over many fields of public and private endeavor, and, forceful rhetorician that he was, he left messages of a compelling nature to many descriptions of men. Even those who are puzzled or repelled by the whole Hamilton can be enthralled by the special Hamilton who speaks to them. There are, it would seem, at least four Hamiltons who are firmly established as giants in the literature of the specialists, that is, who have won the respect of the men who teach the men who teach the men and women who teach our children.

The first of these Hamiltons, the financier, is a familiar figure who has never really been lost from sight, but whose claim to glory has been a conspicuous victim of the system of values embedded in the folklore of American democracy. We may very well be a race of capitalists, but our minstrels have small regard and often open contempt for the men who make capitalism go. While the inventor like Edison and even the producer like Ford are now generally accepted as folk heroes, the financier like Morgan remains outside the pale into which only the great, the worthy, and the fascinating are admitted. Even financiers who render their services exclusively to the public, and Hamilton was the archetype of the breed, can expect no more than an indifferent nod from history and a grudging vote of thanks from historians.

At least we can say that the first Secretary of the Treasury has been given that vote. It is a rare teacher of American history who is now disposed to withhold the accolade of eminence from this Hamilton. The acknowledgment of the Revolutionary debt, the assumption of the state debts, the funding of all these debts and the provision for their reduction,[3] the laying and collecting of those first painful federal taxes, the introduction of a viable currency and the establishment of bimetallism in law,[4] the creation and administration of the Treasury Department, the launching of the Bank of the United States,[5] and above all the establishment of the public credit of a virtually friendless government—these were the leading acts in a total performance to which even the most demure scholars are forced to attach such labels as "brilliant," "breathtaking," "cyclopean," and "masterful." [6] We may argue about the intellectual sources of Hamilton's financial measures, particularly about the lessons he learned from his acquaintance with the pioneering efforts of Robert Morris.[7] We may concede a point to those who insist that he realized the political implications of his financial measures much too well and the moral implications not at all. But we cannot harbor any lingering doubts, certainly not in this age of high finance on a global scale, of his brilliance as a practitioner in those days and usefulness as a model in these. We may be certain that C. Douglas Dillon, Secretary of the Treasury under John F. Kennedy, would be as ready as Richard Rush, Secretary of the Treasury under John Quincy Adams, to acknowledge gratefully that Hamilton directed the financial operations of the United States "with a forecast so luminous as still to throw a guiding light over the path of his successors." [8]

The story of Hamilton the financier is best told as one of those rare, earth-shaking meetings between a great national need and a great creative man, much of whose greatness arose out of the fact that he was one of the few men to recognize the need and perhaps the only man to assess it correctly. That he alone was ready—intellectually, politically, and temperamentally—to bring the new nation financially to its feet is the true measure of his brilliance. That he did his financial deeds, as the mature Lincoln played his politics, to serve the larger ends of national survival and progress is what makes him the model of the public financier, of the financier as statesman and not simply as technician.

If he was that kind of financier, he was also that kind of administrator. It is no wonder that, as the field of public administration has grown in scope and self-confidence, the first American public administrator should have grown with it in repute and influence, grown so large indeed that the historian of public administration in the United States, Leonard D. White, described him as "the greatest administrative genius of his generation in America, and one of the greatest administrators of all time," or that Lynton K. Caldwell went further to assess him as "our great teacher of the organization and administration of public power." [9] Hamilton had his defects as an administrator, as White also made clear: "He was impatient, he could not endure competition, he meddled in everything." [10] Yet these were in truth the defects of his virtues, which, in this special realm of administration, included energy, industry, order, discrimination, anticipation, originality, and the capacity to inspire confidence—all on a vast and, as it must often have seemed to the opposition, superhuman scale.

We shall dwell at some length in chapter 5 on Hamilton's theory of public administration, but it should be stated here that, alone among the statesmen and political thinkers of his generation (and indeed of several generations after his death), he understood the importance of administration to the success of popular government. He first made clear, in the musings of *The Federalist* as well as in the conduct of his office, that government is not all structure, authority, and decision-making, but day-to-day application to ledgers and minute books, week-to-week supervision of clerks and tax collectors, and month-to-month anticipation of the legitimate interests and grievances of a public that must be soothed as well as served. In an age when the art of managing the common affairs of men existed, if at all, at the most primitive level, Hamilton displayed the skills of a modern administrator in the service of the first broad experiment in popular government. In this, as in so many other matters, he had to wait more than a hundred years for men to arise who could grasp the full dimensions of his achievements.

THE third Hamilton, on whom we might paste the convenient if not quite accurate label of diplomat, had to wait even longer. Only since the end of World War II, in the years of painful retreat from Wilsonian idealism led by such men as Walter Lippmann, Reinhold Niebuhr, George Kennan, and Hans Morgenthau, has the Secretary of the Treasury who often imagined himself Secretary of State emerged from the mists of acrimony to be recognized as the champion of "realism" and "national interest" in the conduct of American foreign policy. Since the retreat of which I speak has been executed rather more neatly in the books of critics than in the activities of Secretaries of State, and since the critics themselves are not without their critics, Hamilton the diplomat by no means gets the unstinting acclaim that is the happy lot of Hamilton the financier and administrator. Morgenthau may assert that "the realistic position" was first put forth "with unsurpassed simplicity and penetration by Alexander Hamilton," but Adrienne Koch speaks of Hamilton's "failure to take account realistically of the international situation in his own time." [11] And there are many students of our diplomacy who feel that the new realists—with or without the support of Hamilton—have gone too far in their campaign against the ghost of Wilson. The result has been to cast Hamilton the diplomat as a rather controversial figure.

Even as such a figure he must be dealt with respectfully by anyone who takes part in the ongoing debate over the purposes, criteria, and style of American diplomacy. Thanks to his compulsive, life-long habit of writing public letters in support of his actions and policies, he left us what amounts to a "textbook for realists," and the book demands careful reading. It is not so much his restless activity in the crisis over neutrality in 1793 and the struggle over Jay's Treaty in 1795-1796 that makes him a man with a message to our generation; it is his logic and rhetoric as Pacificus in the first instance and as Camillus in the second. He was certainly the first American to speak with conviction to his fellow citizens of the primacy of "an enlightened view of her own interest" over "sympathy" or "sentiment" as the touchstone of this nation's foreign policies. As Pacificus he set out to meet the argument of the pro-French forces that a proclamation of neutrality by the President would be a show of "ingratitude" to our ally of the Revolution.

> Between individuals, occasion is not infrequently given for the exercise of gratitude. . . . But among nations they perhaps never occur. It may be affirmed as a general principle that the predominant motive of good offices from one nation to another is the interest or advantage of the nation which performs them.
> Indeed, the rule of morality in this respect is not precisely the same between nations as between individuals. The duty of making its own welfare the guide of its actions is much stronger upon the former than upon the latter, in proportion to the greater magnitude and importance of national compared with individual happiness, and to the greater permanency of the effects of national than of individual conduct.[12]

This passage is much loved by Professor Morgenthau and his fellow realists, as indeed it should be. So, too, are other passages in Hamilton's writings that advocate strict privacy in negotiations with other powers, insist that all such negotiations be carried on from a position of strength but also in a spirit of moderation, pay homage to the force of public opinion in the sphere of diplomacy, question the competence of the people at large to make sound judgments in this sphere, warn against the disposition to make permanent attachments and thus to suffer any reduction in the freedom to act in the national interest, and remind us not to expect favors and easy friendship from any other power on earth.[13] In private as in public, in the assembly as in the press, Hamilton's was the clearest voice of realism in those other days when realism in foreign policy was the price of survival.

> We ought to bear in mind that a nation is never to regulate its conduct by remote possibilities or mere contingencies, but by such probability as may reasonably be inferred from the existing state of things, and the usual course of human affairs.[14]

Yet for all his realism, for all his talk of "reasons of state" and the pursuit of self-interest, Hamilton was neither exponent nor practitioner of amorality in foreign affairs. To the contrary of what is fast becoming the myth of Hamiltonian realism, he was a sincere advocate of "good faith" and "justice" in dealings with other powers, a man almost obsessed with the necessity of maintaining a posture of "national honor" before the world.[15] As to the possibility of conflicts between interest and honor, he seems to have been convinced—and who, on any large view of the matter, can prove him wrong?—that "the interests of the nation, when well understood, will be found to coincide with their moral duties." [16]

I do not mean to give too high marks to Hamilton the diplomat. For one thing, he was not really a diplomat at all; he never knew what it was to hammer out a treaty with the likes of Talleyrand or Grenville. One wants to think that if Jay's Treaty had been Hamilton's Treaty, it would have been negotiated more shrewdly and successfully from our point of view,[17] but one cannot do more than think it. For another, even when we make allowances for the inner and outer pressures under which he acted, we must recognize that he overstepped the bounds of prudence and propriety in his efforts to direct the course of American diplomacy. Yet if he was not a model for future Secretaries of the Treasury who aspire to make foreign as well as financial policy, he was a mighty and largely benevolent influence in shaping the conduct of the young Republic, and he must remain forever the patron saint of our advocates of realism in foreign policy. It is a fact of much importance for an appreciation of Hamilton that some of the wisest heads of the age think of Pacificus and Camillus as reliable guides in a world of anxiety and envy.[18]

One reason why they may think this is the existence of still another giant Hamilton, the prophet of industrial America, a man who dwelled in the midst of a race of agrarians and dared to tell them that their future was bound up in ships, countinghouses, banks, highways, canals, and, above all, factories.[19] It would be stretching the truth to say that Hamilton ever had a clear vision of Pittsburgh and Detroit, yet the Report on Manufactures and the prospectus of the Society for establishing Useful Manufactures were the first conscious steps along the road from the America of Jefferson and Crèvecoeur to the America of Carnegie and Ford.[20] The commanding arguments of the Report, to be sure, fell on deaf ears, and the S.U.M. collapsed into the ruins one could have predicted—if one had the experience and hindsight of a twentieth-century economist—for an overdeveloped enterprise in an underdeveloped country.[21] When Hamilton spoke in 1794 of that "lively and profitable industry, which now spreads a smile over all of our cities and towns," [22] he spoke to and for only a handful of his fellow citizens, most of whom would have found nothing to smile about in the S.U.M.'s cotton mill on the banks of the Passaic. The failure of his general principles and specific plans in his own lifetime, however, testifies to a startling prevision of the America that was to come just as clearly as it does to an obstinate lack of understanding of the America in which he lived.

In this matter, as in so many others, Hamilton was far ahead of his time, which is exactly why he can appeal so powerfully to ours. Having put our faith in what he acclaimed with delight as "the spirit of manufacturing," we must admire his lonely insistence that out of this spirit would surely grow "the wealth, the strength, the independence, and the substantial prosperity" of the American people.[23] Having flourished so mightily with the aid of foreign capital in the nineteenth century, we must also admire his bold assertion that "every farthing" of such capital was "a precious acquisition." [24] And having learned the hard way that industrialism creates new problems even as it solves old ones, we may thank this first propagandist for industrial America for telling us at the outset that "great national prosperity" could lead to "insolence, an inordinate ambition, a vicious luxury, licentiousness of morals, and all those vices which corrupt government, enslave the people, and precipitate the ruin of a nation." [25] Knowing all this to be true, he nonetheless thought it essential, indeed a command of destiny, for his country to make the industrial gamble, and to make it under the guiding hand of government. And that is why we must agree with Richard B. Morris and say of Hamilton, as of no other man in his time, that "he anticipated America." [26]

THESE are by no means the only Hamiltons that invoke the attention of Americans who are anxious to learn from or simply to venerate the past. At the very least we should take note of these other Hamiltons: the politician, who showed us how to do it in the Poughkeepsie ratifying convention of 1788 and the Vermont settlement of 1789, and how not to do it in the miserable wrangles that tore the Federalists to pieces; * Hamilton the orator (or perhaps more accurately rhetorician), who was one of the half-dozen most effective persuaders in American history of the small and select kind of gatherings; [27] Hamilton the lawyer "without a rival," the gamecock of *Rutgers* v. *Waddington* and *People* v. *Croswell,* whom Chancellor Kent saluted as "indisputably pre-eminent" among the leaders of the New York bar; [28] and Hamilton "the very model of a modern major general" in the preparations for war (whether with France, Spain, or Virginia no one will ever quite know!) in 1798–1800, who set about raising, organizing, training, equipping, and deploying the United States Army with all the energy and self-confidence, if with little of the success, he had shown in the Department of the Treasury.[29] And surely if we are to understand him as man and myth, we should pay our respects

* When, as an exultant Jeffersonian wrote:

> "Fed pounc'd on Fed, and brother taunted brother,
> Spitting, like roasted apples, at each other." [30]

to the soldier of the Revolution. His labors for Washington as a staff officer won him a respectful footnote in all military histories of the Revolution; but, Romantic that he was in the inner world of emotion and aspiration, he would rather want us to remember that he shared in three of the supreme events of all American history: he crossed the Delaware; he froze at Valley Forge; he stormed the last redoubt at Yorktown. All these Hamiltons, however, are minor figures when contrasted with the four giants we have already looked upon.

Yet even these Hamiltons must make room for three others who are waiting to be brought forward out of the shadows of indifference or misunderstanding or hostility, three others who deserve to be recognized—and who, so far as I can judge, have not yet been recognized properly by either the professionals or the general public—as authentic giants.

The first of these is the Hamilton of this book: the constitutionalist. I speak here not only of the Hamilton of Annapolis, Philadelphia, and Poughkeepsie, the Hamilton of *The Federalist* and the Opinion on the Constitutionality of the Bank of the United States; but also of the Hamilton who, more than a year before Yorktown, proposed "a convention of all the states with full authority" to write a new constitution,[31] and who was on hand ten years later to make such imaginative use of this constitution that its alleged "father," James Madison, was shocked into loud protest. Without him in person the Constitution, despite all the efforts of men like Madison, Washington, Ellsworth, and Wilson, might never have got off the ground, or, even if the launching had been a success, would certainly have moved off in a different direction. Without him in spirit, without his vision of a charter out of which men yet unborn could summon up "all the possible abilities of the country,"[32] it must long ago have come down—and perhaps the nation with it—in a thunderous crash.

For these reasons, and for others that will emerge in the course of this book, I make bold to say that we live today under a Hamiltonian Constitution, a fundamental law of immense merit in the shaping of which his influence was supreme above that of any man of his time, and for the success of which in years to come his interpretation of its critical clauses will be more relevant than that of any American of any time. It is, I know, presumptuous to stamp the name of one man (and a man who was neither a Chief Justice nor a President) on the most successful of written constitutions, yet I am compelled to do this by the unsettling discovery that Hamilton is given far less than his due as maker, manipulator, and interpreter of the Constitution of his day and as prophet of the Constitution of ours. One searches largely in vain through histories of the Constitution, commentaries and casebooks on constitutional law, the *Reports* of the Supreme Court, and debates in Congress for instances of clear-cut recognition of Hamilton's unique role in shaping the Constitution. He is by no means ignored, and certainly not despised; but he is treated far too often in an offhand manner as a representative of the triumphant school of constitutional interpretation rather than the founder of it. A fellow named Publius has been getting ever more rapturous attention in the past few years, and we all know, or will admit under questioning, that Hamilton was at least one-half of Publius. Yet Publius was at best only one-fifth of Hamilton the constitutionalist, and it is time we went beyond *The Federalist* to trace the full, I would say colossal, dimensions of this Hamilton.

In the act of tracing those dimensions, we must take a close look at still another prominent yet largely unacknowledged Hamilton: the political thinker or, as he would have preferred, political scientist. The reasons for Hamilton's indifferent reputation as political thinker are fairly clear on the surface. He is thought to be too much the economist in his interests, too much the nationalist in purpose, too much the no-nonsense, no-doctrine operator in style; and once again he seems to get swallowed up in the vague bulk of Publius, a political thinker who, after all, reached his peak in two numbers of *The Federalist*—10 and 51—written by Madison. The result is that histories of American political thought pay him less attention than they should. If he is dealt with at all, he is presented simply as co-author of *The Federalist,* and is ranked well below Madison, Jefferson, Calhoun, Adams, and Lincoln in the hierarchy of American thinkers.[33]

This, surely, is to rank him too low. Like the other first-rate minds among the Founding Fathers, he was a shotgun political thinker who fired only under provocation and at scattered targets. The gulf between what he left us in the way of a formal political science and what he could have left us makes the historian of American thought, always a man with an apology on the end of his pen, almost weep with frustration. Hamilton was, for all that, a political thinker of the first order. If he was distressingly silent about some questions that no profound theorist is supposed to ignore, he was refreshingly insistent about some others that, except for him, would not even have been discussed in the intellectual climate of his generation. This Hamilton has to be dug out of his burrow of philosophical reticence; I hope to prove in chapters 4 and 5 that he is well worth digging for.

THE last of the larger-than-life Hamiltons to whom I would call attention is likely to appear as the most controversial, which is to say unacceptable to devoted Jeffersonians: the American. We are all well acquainted with Hamilton the nationalist or, as he would have put it, the "continentalist," who was second only to Franklin in time, second to no one in zeal, in shedding all vestiges of provincialism and in thinking entirely in terms of the nation. Indeed, it would appear that there were no vestiges to shed, that whatever attachments he had to the islands of his birth and boyhood were dissolved in the twinkling of the eye of fortune, and that he was a committed continentalist from the day he first set foot in America (in, of all places, Boston). So much a nationalist was he from beginning to end, so indifferent was he to state pride and to local prejudice, that he failed completely to understand the opposition to some of his most cherished schemes. Certainly he went too far in his hostility to both Virginia and Pennsylvania because he had almost no feeling, not even at second hand from his admirable father-in-law, for what it meant to be a New Yorker.

Yet, knowing all this, we have somehow passed him off as a cold-blooded nationalist, a man with a feeling for the Union as means rather than end, and we still cannot see him as an American patriot. Woodrow Wilson did severe damage to Hamilton's claim to have been a patriot in an age when patriotism was a high virtue with his celebrated observation—the observation, I venture to say, of an unpurged Virginian—that he was a "great man" but "not a great American." [34]

I am not sure that this damage can ever be undone, for Wilson played, and must have known he played, on an enduring streak of prejudice against men like Hamilton in the mind of democratic America. I am sure that a strong case can be made for exactly the opposite appraisal of Hamilton's standing as patriot, that he could be just as reasonably portrayed as the leading, because in an important sense the only, American of the 1790's. I do not mean to devalue the patriotism of Washington and Adams, whose devotion to the new Republic was more deeply rooted than Hamilton's in American soil. But in one case the soil was Virginia, in the other Massachusetts, and they went to their graves as men of dual loyalties. It may be said that one could not be a true American in the political and cultural circumstances of those days unless one were first of all a true Virginian or Pennsylvanian or New Englander. Let it be said, and thus let Washington and Adams take precedence over Hamilton as patriots in their time; but let it also be noted that another kind of patriotism, one demanding an overpowering commitment to the United

States, was bound to arise with the changing of circumstances, and thus let Hamilton be seen for what he was: once again a man born several generations too soon, the first (or, if we count Franklin, at worst the second) full-blooded American. It was no deceitful flight of oratory that he introduced into the Farewell Address, and it is no disrespect to Washington to guess that the captain, if he had been left to frame the thought for himself, would hardly have put it as strongly as did the lieutenant:

The name of American must always gratify and exalt the just pride of patriotism more than any denomination which can be derived from local discriminations.[35]

If, as F. S. Oliver once remarked, Hamilton loved his country more deeply than his countrymen,[36] that was because so few of them would rise with him above all petty allegiances and give their hearts unreservedly to the nation. To his last day he could not understand—and I repeat that it weakened him in his dealings with the present even as it strengthened him in his vision of the future—how Americans high and low could be so deaf to the call of nationhood. "Am I, then," he wrote in 1795 in a moment of despair to Rufus King, "more of an American than those who drew their first breath on American ground?" "Every day proves to me more and more," he wrote in an even more despairing mood to Gouverneur Morris in 1802, "that this American world was not made for me." [37]

These remarks were not simply flourishes on his part, for he was never allowed to forget, neither by the shouts of his detractors nor by the whispers of his memory, that he was an "alien," an "exotic," an illegitimate West Indian who sometimes seemed to know, as John Adams put the matter, "no more of the sentiments and feelings of the people of America than he did of those of the inhabitants of one of the planets." [38] Even more damaging to his reputation as an American in both his time and ours was the fact that he never made any secret, not even during the Revolution, of his admiration for British law and institutions, nor any apology, especially after 1792, for his preference for the Britain of George III to the France of the Directory.[39] Yet what man of fair mind in that age could deny the heritage of Britain, what man of feeling could ignore the confrontation of Britain and France? In the light of Hamilton's admittedly aristocratic tastes and of his poorly concealed admiration for constitutional monarchy, it is something of a wonder that he was not a less impassioned Revolutionist in 1776 and a less restrained "Angloman" in 1792.[40]

In the end, we can agree with the judgment of Senator Lodge that

Hamilton "cared for neither England nor France, except so far as he loathed the bloody anarchy of the one and respected the stability and order of the other. His thoughts were fixed on the United States, unbiased by a sentiment for or against any other nation." [41] "I know that you have not a wish," a friend wrote him in 1791, "but what is combined with the solid honor and interests of America." [42] If we may grant the patriotic Jefferson his preference for France, we may grant the patriotic Hamilton his for Britain. In neither case did this largely abstract sympathy for another country cripple the man in his role as maker of a pro-American foreign policy or render him any less an American patriot. It has been said of Hamilton that, had he been born in England, he could have lived there happily as the best of Englishmen, but that can be said of all manner of loyal Americans. Let him, therefore, have the last word in this discussion—another cry from the heart to his friend Rufus King:

We are laboring hard to establish in this country principles more and more *national* and free from all foreign ingredients, so that we may be neither "Greeks nor Trojans," but truly Americans.[43]

I HAVE thought it important to single out all these Hamiltons so that the reader may savor the astonishing variety of his talents, interests, and achievements as a public man. Yet we must not lose sight of the unity amid all this diversity. There was, after all, only one Hamilton, and he was just about as harmonious a human being as any of the major figures of his generation. He filled many roles, yet his career was all of a piece; his genius played over a multitude of issues and interests, yet he was remarkably single-minded. And this is because, above all, he was a man of purpose, and because the purpose, for all its grandeur and intensity, was a thing of unexpected simplicity.

If we are to understand the Hamilton of this book, we must first understand this purpose. And if we are to do that, we must recognize the peculiar quality of his commitment to public life. It can be said of him more confidently than of any other American of his generation, perhaps of all American generations, that the aims of his existence were social rather than personal, public rather than private. He was as easily moved as the men with whom he contended by all the drives of self-interest he found to be constants of human nature, yet he was also moved by a genuine concern for the public interest. As a young man of the Revolution he pronounced himself as "not interested more than as the felicity and prosperity of this vast continent are concerned," [44] and even his most severe detractors can admit that this is a fair description of the springs of his conduct throughout most of his life. While one can argue—most historians do—with his concept of the public interest, one cannot fail to see that his pursuit of this concept held sway over all other considerations in the critical stages, both the noblest and the meanest, of his career. He was pre-eminently a public man who shaped his conduct and decisions to what he saw and identified as the public interest. "It is in vain to kick against the pricks," Attorney General William Bradford wrote him during his first few months of retirement in 1795. "You were made for a Statesman." [45] "He lived, and as he lived he died," a Federalist editor wrote in eulogy in 1804, "a creature of the public, devoted to its service." [46]

As such a man he was moved powerfully by an image of the good society. Although he never took time off to study and record the details of this image, it was always there in his fancy to provide the independent standard of decision for which he felt a peculiar need. It was not the good society of either Adams or Jefferson. Like Adams he placed a high value on order and stability, yet he also wanted society to be progressive, animated, even adventurous; he wanted it to bubble and hustle. Like Jefferson he placed a high value on personal liberty and the pursuit of happiness, yet he assumed that the well-being of most individuals would arise out of the prosperity of the whole community; he sought for a real pattern of social logic in the apparent chaos of the bubbling and hustling. His image of the good society, it cannot be denied, had less room for the untrammeled individual than that of either Jefferson or Adams.

The point at which he clearly went beyond both these famous antagonists was in fixing upon glory as the distinguishing mark of the community. His image, in truth, was a grand one: the good society was a great society. It was a society of extent, riches, and might, for if the lives of its citizens were to be truly meaningful, it must of necessity be engaged in great undertakings. For this reason, if for no other, Hamilton could never make peace with public men whose horizons ended at the boundaries of a New England town or Middle Atlantic city or Southern state. The sentiments of loyalty that supported his ideal community could not be nourished on small tracts of land. They would need a continent in which to grow, and the people they would excite would be a mighty nation, a first-class power like Britain and France—in one word, always a favorite word of his, an "empire." Hamilton could never have been happy as a citizen of Denmark or Switzerland.

Although he had moments of doubt and even despair in the years of political disappointment at the end of his life,[47] Hamilton was gripped from beginning to end by a vision of the United States as just such a nation. In his first sally into the public arena he spoke confidently of "the future grandeur and glory of America," in his second of the "dawning splendor" of the nation struggling to be born.[48] In the hardest days of the Revolution he insisted publicly that each member of Congress should bear himself, and be looked upon by his fellow citizens, "as a founder of an empire." [49] In the hardest days of his own career he complained to Rufus King of "delay and feebleness" in high places, yet ended with a characteristic flourish:

I anticipate with you that this country will, erelong, assume an attitude correspondent with its great destinies—majestic, efficient, and operative of great things. A noble career lies before it.[50]

And in the last letter he wrote to a friend, to Theodore Sedgwick on the day before the "interview" with Aaron Burr, he begged his hotheaded comrades in New England not to indulge in activities that might lead to "dismemberment of our empire." [51] We cannot understand the motives or conduct of this astonishing man unless we recognize the power of this double image he carried in his fancy: the United States as "the embryo of a great empire," [52] himself as a founder of this empire. The one genuine Romantic among all the Puritans, children of the Enlightenment, and common-sense squires whom we call the Founding Fathers, Hamilton was led day in and day out by a vision which a few of his fellow countrymen saw only on July 4 and most of them saw not at all.

Whether America—a "Hercules in the cradle" [53]—attained glory or merely respectability, it could bring benefits to all mankind. Like the other leading men of his age, Hamilton was a true believer in the American Mission. "The world," he wrote as Phocion in 1784, "has its eye upon America," [54] for here in the most favorable of environments was to be carried out the decisive experiment in republican self-government. If the experiment was successful, America would become a bright testament to freedom, and from it would go out through all the world the good news of personal liberty and popular government. If it was a failure, the failure would press upon all men everywhere. In the privacy of the Philadelphia Convention Hamilton put the issue to the elite:

He concurred with Mr. Madison in thinking we were now to decide for ever the fate of republican government; and that if we did not give to that form due stability and wisdom, it would be disgraced and lost among ourselves, disgraced and lost to mankind forever.[55]

And in the open debate over ratification he put it to the public:

It has been frequently remarked that it seems to have been reserved to the people of this country, by their conduct and example, to decide the important question, whether societies of men are really capable or not of establishing good government from reflection and choice, or whether they are forever destined to depend for their political constitutions on accident and force. If there be any truth in the remark, the crisis at which we are arrived may with propriety be regarded as the era in which that decision is to be made; and a wrong election of the part we shall act may, in this view, deserve to be considered as the general misfortune of mankind.[56]

Although he could never bring himself to believe that the experiment had succeeded beyond a doubt, and that America was safely on the way to fulfilling its historic mission, Hamilton, like Washington, Jefferson, and Madison, was inspired at some of the critical points in his career by the assumption that his countrymen held "the most sacred deposit that was ever confided to human hands." It was for them to decide whether America was to endure as a "theme for the praise and admiration of mankind," an example for the world to "bless and imitate," or to be crushed by the knowledge that it had "betrayed the cause of human nature." [57] To understand Hamilton in his moments of both triumph and despair, we must pay tribute to this forceful sense of American destiny. Here was a man for whom the idea of "national purpose" was a living, enveloping presence.

To the upbuilding of this nation, glorious in itself and glorious in the eyes of the world, Hamilton devoted all his public energies. Some words he wrote in 1794 echo Washington's hope that the Convention of 1787 would "raise a standard to which the wise and the honest can repair": [58] the event, he insisted, was "in the hands of Providence." [59] Yet men of good will and high courage could help to realize the not entirely inscrutable purposes of a doubtless sensible God by laboring to give the Republic dignity, integrity, and authority, and thus a hold upon the confidence of its citizens and a place of honor among nations.

Such men had special reason to exert themselves in America, where fresh beginnings could be made and the most favorable circumstances, both natural and social, could be anticipated. Except in a few moments of despondency, Hamilton was what his spiritual descendants in Wall Street would have saluted as a "bull" on America. It is reported that his practice in interviews with Englishmen was to paint a bright-hued picture of the prospects of the United States, a nation launched on a voyage to grandeur and thus worth cultivating as a friend; [60] and he seems truly to have believed that in every circumstance out of which grandeur might be wrought—expanse of territory, richness of soil, abundance of resources, industry of men, fertility of women, isolation from the quarrels of Europe, attraction for its most talented and adventurous people, ascendancy of the spirit of enterprise—America had been accorded "the happiest lot that beneficent Heaven ever indulged to undeserving mortals." [61] As he wrote to Robert Morris in 1781:

Never did a nation unite more circumstances in its favor than we do; we have nothing against us but our own misconduct.[62]

By "misconduct" Hamilton meant all the private vices and public stupidities from which even men as hopeful as Jefferson did not think the American people safely exempt. He also had in mind the refusal of many of his fellow countrymen to admit the need of taking two giant steps that he had already come to see as the political prerequisites of national glory.

The first of these was the categorical imperative of his life and services: the creation and preservation of the Union. I have spoken of him already as a nationalist, a continentalist, an American, and it seems hardly necessary to add that, in all the struggles of the age over the distribution of power and prestige between nation and states, Hamilton fought tirelessly, cleverly, and if necessary even unscrupulously for the cause of Union. If ever he carried an article of secular faith in his bosom, an assumption about the world around him to which he came all the way on the first thought and never gave a second, it was a belief in the Union of states as "THE ROCK OF OUR POLITICAL SALVATION," as the "sacred and inviolable palladium of our happiness," and indeed as "the first wish of my heart." [63]

"There is something noble and magnificent," he declaimed in 1782,

in the perspective of a great Federal Republic, closely linked in the pursuit of a common interest, tranquil and prosperous at home, respectable abroad; but there is something proportionably diminutive and contemptible in the prospect of a number of petty states, with the appearance only of union, jarring, jealous, and perverse, without any determined direction, fluctuating and unhappy at home, weak and insignificant by their dissensions in the eyes of other nations.[64]

In his feeling for the Union he was perhaps less rapturous than Webster and less mystical than Lincoln, but he was a match for them in his refusal to permit "that sacred knot which binds the people of America together to be severed or dissolved by ambition or by avarice, by jealousy or by misrepresentation." [65] "The idea of disunion," an acquaintance testified long years after Hamilton's death, "he could not hear of without impatience, and expressed his reprobation of it, in very strong terms." [66] Indeed, in one important sense he was more committed a Unionist than either Webster or Lincoln, for he had, as we have already noted, no feeling at all for the states as a confederacy or even for his own state as an enduring community. If it is argued that this indifference to the states, to Virginia no less than to Delaware, made him a full nationalist but only half a Unionist, it can be argued in reply that the result rather than the inspiration of his activities counts in history. The result of his activities, as history records, was to give the Union unimagined strength to withstand the prodigious centrifugal forces that still threatened to tear it to pieces a full three generations after his own. He toiled throughout his mature life, not simply to keep the Union from breaking up into the "three confederacies" into which men of lesser vision predicted it would divide,[67] but to make it an object of interest and reverence, and his precedents and arguments were ready for the use of the men who followed him. It is said by his detractors, and even by some of his admirers, that he exacerbated state and sectional sentiment and helped set the stage for 1798, 1832, and at last 1861 by his measures in behalf of the Union. Is this not like saying that Earl Warren and Martin Luther King have exacerbated racial tensions by their measures in behalf of equality for all Americans? Try as they may, men who take giant steps can never tread softly; the step toward Union that Hamilton persuaded his countrymen to take was sure to leave bitterness and even some wreckage in its trail.

So, too, was the second of the radical changes in political circumstance in which he placed his hope for a glorious American future: the establishment of an energetic national government. This step was important for the sake of the Union, and it is characteristic of Hamilton's thinking that he always linked "Union" with "energy." In his famous apologia of 1792 to Colonel Edward Carrington of Virginia he laid down the essentials of his "political creed":

First, the necessity of Union to the respectability and happiness of this country, and second, the necessity of an efficient general government to maintain the Union.[68]

Without the Union there was no point in dreaming of the imperial glory that lay in the womb of the American continent; without a government that could reach out forcefully and benevolently to every person on this continent there was no prospect of preserving the shaky Union of 1789 and strengthening it for the future.

This step was important, too, because energy—that is, authority and the capacity to exploit it—was the mark of any good government, whether of a city or of a continent. We must put off to chapter 5 a full account of Hamilton's obsession with the idea of political energy (as well as a review of the functions he expected governments to perform), and simply record at this early stage that he attributed to political power a decisive role in the affairs of the community, that he feared weakness in government far more than he did strength, and that he derided the Jeffersonian hope of "emancipation from the burdens and restraints of government" as a "pernicious dream." [69] Addressing his fellow New Yorkers as the Continentalist in 1781, he set out a line that few men of his time had the courage, foresight, or gall to follow, and from which he himself, whether as actor or critic, insider or outsider, never deviated:

In a government framed for durable liberty, not less regard must be paid to giving the magistrate a proper degree of authority to make and execute the laws with rigor than to guarding against encroachments upon the rights of the community. As too much power leads to despotism, too little leads to anarchy, and both eventually to the ruin of the people.[70]

Other men spoke this truth in moments of crisis like Shays' Rebellion; Hamilton spoke it, because he believed it candidly, every day of his life.

THE chief problems of the age, as Hamilton saw them, were continental in scope, and it became his mission to invigorate the national government to meet them head-on. Since he could not imagine that the destiny of Alexander Hamilton and his posterity was tied up with the fortunes of his adopted city and state, he had few thoughts about two of the three governments under which he lived. State and local government was a subject for state and local minds. His mind was on the government of the Union.

The problems that it was to face for centuries to come were, in the final reckoning, only two in number: first, the problem of "growth," that is, the task of discovering and then applying the best means of exploiting the unique talents and resources of the American people, and thus of carrying this people all the way from underdevelopment to grandeur; and second, the problem of "peace," that is, the task of providing for the security of the nation in the face of a world of hate and envy. While he agreed with his fellow citizens (those who were even aware of it) that the solution to the first problem lay principally in the release of the energies of enterprising individuals, he was convinced that government, if it was astute, could give an enormous boost to the process of growth by creating favorable political and social circumstances, and that government, if it was brave, would give the process over-all direction. While he agreed with them that the solution to the second lay principally in exploiting the blessings of isolation and having "as little political connection as possible with foreign nations," [71] he was convinced that a simple resolve to stay aloof from the struggles for power in Europe was not enough, that a government unable to maintain a posture of strength would be dragged willy-nilly into the struggle.

And so he spent his public life pushing for programs that either made no sense or seemed wicked to most men of his time. Their idea of a national government was one that confined itself to a narrow range of mostly symbolic activities; his was of one that busied itself with the affairs of men, especially by stirring the economic pot forcefully and continuously. Having taken steps to secure the confidence of Amsterdam bankers and New York merchants in its solvency (chiefly by acknowledging its just debts and demonstrating its capacity to collect more than nominal taxes), his ideal government then went ahead to lure foreign capital, invite immigration, charter banks and corporations, lay protective tariffs, pay bounties and premiums, prohibit competitive imports, introduce machinery, reward inventors, elevate standards of production, build roads and canals, stimulate agriculture, establish a university, and generally spur the development of an enterprising, balanced, productive economy.[72] Few men in Hamilton's own time, indeed few in the century after his death, shared his faith in the power of the guiding hand of government. Men who thought at all about a guiding force in the process of economic and social development fell back upon the notion of the "hidden hand," and it was in fact this hand, which is to say a multitude of hands, that largely directed the course of the American economy in the first stages of its growth. Hamilton did rather more than he had any right to expect in persuading Congress to enact and his countrymen to accept—some of them rather grudgingly—the creative measures with which he established the public credit, that "palladium of public safety" on which "depends the character, security and prosperity of the nation." [73] If he was not permitted to give the directions, at least he helped set the stage for the development of the United States into the mightiest of industrial powers. And, all things historical and cultural considered, it may have been a blessing that the men of his generation could neither grasp nor act upon the message of the Report on Manufactures. The tools of stimulation and regulation he advocated for the national government might well have been used, by men with less stomach for enterprise, to slow down a process of economic growth in which, it must be admitted, the "hidden hand" worked with astounding efficiency.

In the area of national security Hamilton was almost as lonely (and prophetic) a figure, even if he did have Washington to keep him company in what he called "the Trade-Militant." [74] A soldier of the Revolution, a man with a "natural temper aspiring to military renown," [75] and a sharp-witted student of events in Europe, he never doubted for a moment—in contrast to a Jefferson full of doubts and fears—that the survival of the United States "depended to a great degree upon its warmaking potential." [76] Weak governments, not strong ones, got caught up in wars that were not of their own choosing; strong governments, not weak ones, could trust their fates to the processes of diplomatic negotiation.

Hamilton sought to increase this potential in at least three ways. In the first place, he argued forcibly, and in words that must have stunned many in his audience, for an expansive view of the power of the nation to make war. "The authorities essential to the common defense," he wrote in *The Federalist,* number 23, "ought to exist without limitation." [77] We shall return to consider his sweeping view of the war powers in chapter 6.

Second, he proposed that these powers be used openly in time of peace to provide the Republic with a trained force in being. He was aware of the deep-seated prejudice among all ranks in America against standing armies, and may even be said to have run a mild case of this prejudice himself. [78] Yet as a soldier of cruel experience he knew that the militia was simply not "equal to the national defense," that a reliance upon amateurs "had like to have lost us our independence." "War, like most other things," he wrote in *The Federalist,* "is a science to be acquired and perfected by diligence, by perseverance, by time, and by practice," [79] and he advised the Republic repeatedly to keep a modest supply of experts in this science on duty and a large supply in reserve. He wanted an army because he thought no country of consequence could be without one, because "a respectable military posture" was "the best method of securing our peace," and because, nationalist that he was, he guessed rightly that it would be "an essential cement of the union." [80] In 1783, which was hardly the time for an ex-soldier to be advocating such a step, he delivered a report to the Congress of the Confederation on the necessity of a "military peace establishment." [81] In 1788 he argued that "the steady operations of war against a regular and disciplined army"—the kind of operations that were sure to be the lot of the United States—could "only be successfully conducted by a force of the same kind." [82] And in the crisis of 1799 he gave up his private life to take on the impossible task of trying to hammer such an army into shape, thus earning for himself an unpleasant reputation as a man who was "loud for war." [83] It should be added that he was an early advocate of a national military academy. If his luck had been a little better in 1798 and 1799, he might be known today as the founder of West Point, and perhaps even of Annapolis.[84]

And third, he reminded his fellow citizens that a strong and diversified economy would permit us "to hold the scales of our destiny in our own hands." [85] Prosperity would make it possible for Americans to enjoy the arts of peace; it would also make it possible for them to practice the arts of war. It is interesting to note that Hamilton, sometimes thought of as the apostle of private enterprise, had little confidence in the desire or capacity of such enterprise to produce munitions. In his Report on Manufactures he came out quite strongly for government ownership and operation of "manufactories of all the necessary weapons of war." "There appears to be an improvidence," he wrote, "in leaving these essential implements of national defense to the casual speculations of individual adventure." [86]

In working for a government that could perform such mighty financial, commercial, social, diplomatic, and military tasks, Hamilton once again swept ahead of his generation along the course that America would finally travel. A few of his colleagues in greatness were almost as firm believers as he in the primacy of the Union; a few were almost as confident of the efficacy of political authority. But no one put these two faiths together— faith in the nation and faith in government—in quite so "high-toned" a formula for continental glory as did Hamilton. One may be irritated but not surprised by the extravagance of the language in which the Jeffersonians accused Hamilton of plotting to launch an American Leviathan. Even today this double image of "nation" and "energy"—or, as Senator Goldwater would put it, of "centralization" and "big government"—throws panic into the minds of many otherwise imperturbable Americans.

While Hamilton never doubted that the building of an energetic national government upon the solid confidence of the people was an event very much "in the hands of Providence," he was as willing in this matter as in all others to give Providence a prod. It was in this characteristic double role, as both oracle and spur of destiny, that he did his deeds in behalf of the Constitution. The first step toward a government worthy of an "empire" was to adopt a charter granting sovereign powers to the United States; and he had much to do, in circumstances not entirely favorable to the play of his peculiar talents, with the events that led to 1788 and the irrevocable adoption of the Constitution. The second step was to put the charter in train by making eager use of these powers; and he had a great deal to do with the events that led to 1801 and Jefferson's final declaration of peace with both the Constitution (as he, of course, proposed to interpret it) and most of the measures adopted under it (as he, of course, proposed to administer them). The point I am trying to make, and will make in detail in chapter 3, is that Hamilton, who was cast in only a supporting role in 1787 when the words of the Constitution were strung together, was cast in an epic role in 1791 and 1792 when the words had to be translated into actions. Surely we say nothing to demean the labors of Washington, or indeed of Madison, Ellsworth, Ames, and the other early leaders of Congress, when we grant to Hamilton the palm for having been the first to reach into the Constitution and pull out authority for acts of enduring consequence.

Not all these acts were politically wise; several, it can be argued, were socially mischievous. Yet if we consider them all together, we are bound to assess them as a remarkable beginning for this adventure in popular government. More than that, they gave a boost to the upward and outward course of the Constitution that even today has not spent its force. In giving sustenance, authority, dignity, stability, and security to the new government, Hamilton also gave momentum to the new Constitution. As we have all learned sorrowfully from the history of France, it is one order of achievement to write a constitution, quite another and far higher order to make it work. The most brilliant and enduring of Hamilton's achievements was to bring the Constitution of 1787 to robust life. In the field of constitutional development, as in those of finance, administration, and commerce, he earned himself—and must henceforth be granted—enduring fame as a builder of the nation.

THERE is, I confess, something abstract and almost bloodless about the many Hamiltons I have put up for inspection, even about the one Hamilton into which they all fit together with virtually no rough edges. We might therefore remind ourselves that he was also a man—a living, working, dreaming, fighting, loving, and occasionally sinning man who, even at this distance, can stir powerful feelings in those who observe him intently. His character commands attention in its own right, for he was one of the truly fascinating men in American history. It also commands attention because, as in the case of his patron Washington, the style of the man was the compelling force in shaping his policies and influence.

It would be foolish of me, by which I mean both redundant and presumptuous, to attempt a sketch of Hamilton's character. He has been painted in both loving and critical detail by a platoon of biographers (and a regiment of biographers of his friends and foes), and for the most part the portraits have been well done. What is more to the point, they all seem to be painted of the same man. It is agreed by even the most rapturous Jeffersonians that Hamilton gave fresh meaning to such over-worked adjectives as brave, brilliant, honest, dutiful, enthusiastic, indus-trious, strong-minded, and resourceful. It is conceded by even his most ardent admirers that he displayed a startling flair—not every day, to be sure, but on some of the most important days of his life—for pride, self-delusion, impulsiveness, officiousness, impatience, and immoderation in appraising both men and events. We know that he was intensely am-bitious, yet we defer to Washington's judgment that his ambition was "of that laudable kind which prompts a man to excel in whatever he takes in hand." [87] We know that, as "the darling of nature, and privileged beyond the rest of her favorites," he had trouble suffering even the most pleasant fool gladly, yet we accept Fisher Ames's observation that he was "trusted, admired, beloved, almost adored" by his intimates, so much so that "his power over their affections was entire." [88] Even the crustiest New Englanders and proudest Virginians could fall victims to "the charms of his conversation, the brilliance of his wit, his regard to decorum, his ineffable good humor." [89]

Lest some reader think that, were I to make my own sketch of Hamil-ton's character, I would be too kind to him, let me make clear that I would try to explain but certainly not write off the five or six bad shows of a generally honorable, sensible, and plain-dealing life: the uncivil break with a remarkably forbearing Washington at Newburgh in 1781; [90] the indifference to the outburst of jobbing and speculation that tainted the honor of his first measures in behalf of the public credit; [91] the unseemly newspaper squabble with Jefferson (or, rather, with Jefferson's friends) in 1792; [92] the sly and ultimately disastrous manipulation of members of Adams's Cabinet; the gratuitous attack on "the public conduct and character" of Adams in 1800; [93] the shabby attempt, born of a despera-tion that he ought to have conquered, to set aside the results of the New York election of 1800; [94] and the vulgar affair with Mrs. Reynolds, which found him grossly deficient in fidelity, taste, self-restraint, and common sense.* It helps only a little to recall that Hamilton was desperate to command troops in the field, that speculating came as naturally as

* A tale of lechery and treachery still best told by Hamilton himself, in a best seller entitled *Observations on Certain Documents* and published August 31, 1797.[95]

breathing to most men in those days, that Jefferson was as slippery as Hamilton was querulous in the in-fighting of 1792, that Adams was obstinate to the point of pigheadedness, that 1800 was a time of passion and despair, or that men close to Jefferson took the lead with delight in letting the world know of Hamilton's adulterous adventure. He was a man of abundant honor and sense whom an impetuous nature could carry—not often but, alas, at least thrice too often—over the line of self-control and into fields of shame and folly. All of this is to say that, like the other demigods who founded the Republic, he was not a demigod at all.

Yet he was, plainly, an extraordinary human being; and, although I persevere in my intention not to paint still another portrait of his character, I find it necessary to mention four or five qualities of spirit and intellect that had peculiar significance for the Hamilton of this book. Together they would go far, even if we knew nothing else about his preferences and prejudices, to explain his political and constitutional differences with Jefferson, Madison, George Clinton, and even Adams.

The first of these qualities we have already noted: the intensely public character of his aims and interests. He was, I repeat, pre-eminently a public man, one who rejoiced to deal in affairs of state, who was happy and vibrant in office and, despite an occasional hymn to the beauties of retirement,[96] rather doleful and ill at ease out of it. He dealt with such affairs, it must be added, on a level far above that of the politician whose first concern, whether explicitly avowed or implicitly controlling, is himself or his friends or his party. Hamilton wanted desperately to serve the public, which had, he was convinced, a set of enduring interests that dwarfed the interests of any group or class or section. He was certain that even his most controversial programs were designed to answer the needs of the whole community. He may have been naïve in his identification of the common needs and enduring interests of the new Republic, but he was not a hypocrite. Broadus Mitchell is essentially correct when he argues that Hamilton's "only client was the whole country." [97] "Regard to the public interest," Hamilton wrote to Washington in 1798, "is ever predominant with me. . . . It shall *never* be said, with any color of truth, that my ambition or interest has stood in the way of the public good." [98] "He gave his time," one of his closest associates wrote in retrospect to Lafayette, "and with that his gigantic talents exerted with untiring industry, in a word, he gave *his all* to his country." [99]

A corollary of this quality was Hamilton's feverish, sometimes even grotesque concern for his reputation.[100] Fame, not power or wealth, was the spur of this remarkable man. He wanted to be praised in his time and after his death for having done great deeds on the public stage, and doubly praised for having done them in an honorable manner. While he had a natural taste for power,[101] he thought of it almost exclusively in instrumental terms. It was always a means to some far grander end, never an end in itself. He could share power easily with men he trusted, and he proved on several memorable occasions that he could take it or leave it alone. While he preferred silk shirts to hair shirts and Madeira to rum, he was, as he said of another man, "more ambitious of leaving a good name than a good estate to his posterity." [102] Indeed, he seems to have been less concerned about money and the delights it can bring than almost any other person of his time and class. Surrounded by men who were bent on getting rich in the quickest way possible, Hamilton lived and died a comparatively poor man. Surrounded by temptations that men of ordinary appetite and honor could not have resisted, he let them pass him by with no second thoughts and no regrets.* Shortly after taking up his duties as Secretary of the Treasury, he wrote to a friend that "Caesar's wife" would be his model,[103] and even the most relentless efforts of his enemies in Congress could produce no evidence of misconduct in his five years in office. It is characteristic of the man that he invited them to be as relentless as they wished. As he wrote to the Speaker of the House in 1793:

It is known that in the last session certain questions were raised respecting my conduct in office, which, though decided in a manner the most satisfactory to me, were nevertheless unavoidably, from the lateness of the period when they were set on foot, so accelerated in the issue, as to have given occasion to a suggestion that there was not time for a due examination. Unwilling to leave the matter on such a footing, I have concluded to request of the House of Representatives, as I now do, that a new inquiry may without delay be instituted in some mode, the most effectual for an accurate and thorough investigation; and I will add, that the more comprehensive it is, the more agreeable will it be to me.[104]

Hamilton had, it would seem, a "character marked by indifference to the acquisition of property rather than avidity for it." [105] About his

---

* "I sincerely hope," his friend Robert Troup wrote him in 1795, "that you may by some fortunate and unexpected event acquire the means of perfect independence in spite of all your efforts to be poor. I have an interest . . . which perhaps you have forgotten—I have often said that your friends would be obliged to bury you at their own expense." Troup's letter was written in reply to one in which Hamilton made clear that he did not "want to be rich," but was interested only in "a moderate fortune moderately acquired" that would permit him to "live *in comfort* in the country." [106]

reputation, however, he could never be indifferent. He wanted badly to be reckoned a man of honor, and it was, characteristically, public rather than private honor to which he gave first consideration. He proved that point forever in the Reynolds affair when he chose to clear himself of an accusation of petty duplicity as Secretary of the Treasury by confessing himself an adulterer as man and husband.[107] "His honor rooted in dishonor stood"—and stands to this day as testimony to the power of his ruling passion.

Yet even if he had been impelled by neither of these desires, that is, to serve the people and to be thanked for his services, Hamilton would surely have become a mover-and-shaker of events. He had an intensity in his make-up, as all who knew him testified, that would have made it impossible for him to spend his life counting money, consoling clients, and delighting in bouts of ill health.[108] Every instinct drove him to find a wide stage on which to display his talents, and in the 1780's, in an underdeveloped and even unorganized America, that stage was public life. Once he found it, he was driven by the same instincts to dominate it. He was, above all, an activist, an "operator," a man of energy and audacity in whom we can recognize a familiar type: the fellow who stays perpetually in motion—in his case, creative motion—because it is unnatural for him to rest. He could not sit still; rarely could he let the dust settle; he had little faith in the healing powers of time. He meant always to control events, not to let them control him, and he kept his eye steadily on the road ahead. "I give you warning," he wrote publicly to Marinus Willett in March, 1789, "that I shall not be diverted from my main pursuit by cavils or trifles." [109] In the pay book of his artillery company, the blank pages of which he turned into a commonplace book, one may still read some words of Demosthenes that had been translated freely and then copied out in Hamilton's hand:

As a general marches at the head of his troops, so ought wise politicians, if I dare to use the expression, to march at the head of affairs; insomuch that they ought not to wait the *event,* to know what measures to take; but the measures which they have taken, ought to produce the *event.*[110]

Never, surely, did the orator of the Philippics speak to a more responsive young man than this self-styled "high-flyer." [111] Whatever he was in his politics and social preferences, Hamilton was in temperament one of the least conservative of men.

One of the more appealing aspects of this intensity, this surplus alike of energy and feeling, was Hamilton's insistence upon fighting his own battles. While Jefferson hid behind his "legion of scribblers," Hamilton did so much scribbling that he appeared to be a legion. Perhaps the nicest compliment Jefferson ever paid to his chief adversary was one of which Hamilton never learned, since it was in a letter to Madison. "He is really a colossus to the anti-republican party," Jefferson wrote in the midst of the struggle over Jay's Treaty. "Without numbers, he is an host within himself." [112]

One of the less appealing aspects was his insistence, if not upon fighting the battles of his friends, at least upon managing their affairs. When he was a young man on Washington's staff he drafted reports, memoranda, and letters for everybody around him, and as he gained in stature and self-confidence he moved beyond mere draftsmanship to indulge enthusiastically in advice, persuasion, manipulation, and, from time to time, plain meddling.[113] It was one thing for him, as a responsible official in a formless situation, to spill out of his own premises and share the duties of Secretary of State with Jefferson, Secretary of War with Knox, and Attorney General with Randolph, or to give Washington a helpful lecture on presidential etiquette.[114] It was quite another for him, as a man ostensibly withdrawn from public life, to pull the wires that jerked Adams's Cabinet into action.[115] Oliver Wolcott and James McHenry sought the advice of their *"Father confessor* in politicks" with pathetic confidence,[116] yet he would have given it to them, as he gave it even to Washington, quite unbidden. One can sympathize with Adams's tart complaint in 1815 that during his own four years in office Hamilton had been "'commander-in-chief' of the House of Representatives, of the Senate, of the heads of department, of General Washington, and last, and least, if you will, of the President of the United States." [117]

Hamilton was aware of this aspect of his character as a public man; again and again he wrote to intimates that he did "not wish to appear officious." [118] Yet his urge to give advice rarely failed to conquer his wish to seem discreet. He was more in character when he began a letter to Timothy Pickering in 1798 with the statement: "I make no apology for offering you my opinion on the present state of affairs." [119] A "leader of leaders," [120] a man of influence over the influential, Hamilton was too often lured by his zest and self-confidence to overstep the bounds of administrative and political propriety. Whatever confusion may have resulted, however, it was a reasonable price to pay for the kind of leadership he gave to colleagues, party, and nation. Jefferson, too, was compelled by circumstance and conviction to do his share of meddling and manipulating, and Hamilton might well have argued that he operated more openly than his antagonist—and under greater compulsion. If Madison could write in 1789 that "we are in a wilderness, without a single footstep to guide us," [121] can Hamilton, who was certain that he saw footsteps leading off in the right direction, be blamed for offering himself as a guide to his generation?

WE cannot leave this subject of Hamilton's influence over the men with whom he worked without saying a few words about the most important relationship to fill his public life, that with Washington the General, President, and Hero. This was from first to last, from his entry into Washington's service at Morristown in 1778 to the final exchange of confidences in 1799, an uncommon alliance, the subtleties of which I do not pretend to understand. While the biographers of both men have labored imaginatively and, for the most part, successfully to assess the consequences of this famous partnership, they have not carried us far into the realm of motives and sensibilities. The historian is never more conscious of the limits of his trade than when he reads the letters that passed between two famous men, and the Washington-Hamilton letters are especially notable for what they leave unspoken.

What we can say for certain—and it is all I would want to say in this study of the public Hamilton—is that a senior-junior relationship in the Revolution, which was helpful to Washington but vital to Hamilton,* grew into a historic partnership in the Federalist period. Whether either man could have managed without the other, and thus whether the Constitution could have been brought fully to life, is open to doubt. Washington's prestige and resolution gave Hamilton political room in which to maneuver; Hamilton's genius and vigor gave momentum to Washington's administration. Placed under any other man who might have been President in those first years—John Jay, John Rutledge, John Adams, John Hancock—Hamilton could hardly have expected to put more than half his controversial program in motion, and might have found it impossible to serve at all.[122] Saddled with any other man who might have been Secretary of the Treasury—Oliver Wolcott, Tench Coxe, John Pierce, William Duer, even Robert Morris (his first choice)—Washington could hardly have expected to get the new nation financially on its feet, and might have drifted into the role of a political Fabius. If Washington was "an Aegis very essential" to Hamilton,[123] Hamilton was the burr Washington needed under his saddle. If the example of Washington stiffened Hamilton's moral

* Looking back from 1798 to 1780, Washington himself described Hamilton as having served as "the principal and most confidential aid of the Commander in Chief." [124]

fiber, the teachings of Hamilton cleared Washington's political mind. No one can read through the correspondence between these two men in 1795 and 1796 without recognizing the almost touching dependence of Washington on Hamilton for information, advice, and opinion on a broad range of problems.[125] Hamilton's resignation as Secretary of the Treasury in January, 1795 took him out of Washington's official family but by no means out of service. And when both returned to the wars in 1798—or, rather, took charge of preparations for war—Washington made clear on a dozen occasions that he looked upon Hamilton as his principal "coadjutor" and "assistant" in the "turmoils I have consented to encounter." It was an entirely honest Washington who wrote of Hamilton that "his loss" would be "irrepairable," and that "his services ought to be secured at *almost* any price." [126]

Whatever their respective contributions to this partnership in the world of men and affairs, there is no doubt of Hamilton's primacy in the world of ideas. A student of Washington's political and constitutional principles is led inexorably, by way of documents drafted by Hamilton for Washington's consideration or signature, to read all the letters and papers Hamilton wrote for his own purposes.[127] A student of Hamilton's need look no further than the writings of the man himself. I do not mean to depreciate the tenacity of Washington's convictions, the degree of his influence over his younger colleague (notably in stiffening Hamilton's instinctive sense of nationalism and less instinctive respect for civil supremacy over the military arm), or, in more than one critical instance, the superiority of his judgment. Washington was no more the intellectual slave of the more clever Hamilton than Jackson was of Roger B. Taney, Roosevelt of R. G. Tugwell, or Truman of Dean Acheson. He came along his own stubborn route to the principles of Federalism; he was never stampeded or swindled by his effervescent partner. As Hamilton himself bore witness, Washington "consulted much, pondered much, resolved slowly, resolved surely." [128] No associate of Washington's, not even Hamilton in his most overbearing mood, could forget that he was dealing with the greatest man in the world—and a man whom it was hazardous to commit to a decision or policy he had not made all his own. Yet it cannot be denied that Washington's rough-hewn convictions about such questions as the purpose of government and the scope of the Constitution were given their final polish by Hamilton, and that, at several decisive moments, his mind was not only made up but changed by the persuasive arguments of the younger man. Hamilton's supreme effort as constitutional lawyer, the Opinion on the Constitutionality of the Bank of the United States,[129] was directed to a Washington who had been deeply impressed by the case for unconstitutionality as put by Jefferson, Madison, and Randolph. If ever the one man needed the other, and the Constitution needed both, this was the time.

IN the last reckoning, the dominating aspect of Hamilton's character as public man was, if one may put it this way, his spiritual and intellectual position on the spectrum of historical time. One after the other of the Hamiltons we have been examining has turned out to be a man born a generation or a century or perhaps even two centuries too soon, and that is perhaps the best way to think of the whole man. In style and vision, in comprehension and counsel, he was far out in front of the other men of his generation. The myth is that Hamilton was some kind of fabulous reactionary; the fact is that he dwelled by himself in a future that we are still in the act of securing—a future in which America was a nation rather than a collection of states or sections, the government of the nation was a forceful presence rather than a mere keeper of the peace, the armed forces were experts on guard rather than amateurs in hiding, the economy was dynamically industrial rather than quietly agrarian, and the Constitution was a document that said "yes" rather than "no" to determined men who went to it for support of their undertakings.

To say that Hamilton was out in front of his own generation is, of course, to say that he was, in more ways than one, out of touch with it. His uncanny ability to anticipate the America that lay over the horizon was, it must be conceded, the bright and saving side of an almost willful inability to understand the America in which he lived. He could take flight into the future because there was so much about the present toward which he displayed, in the words of a bitter foe, "a princely ignorance." [130] He could be a prophet of power and glory because he could not imagine how men of sense could rouse to the Jeffersonian dream of a stripped-down government and an agrarian economy. He was a utopian whose vision of the perfect society flourished quite independently of any dissatisfaction with the imperfect one in which he lived. If he did indeed, as he once or twice confessed in despair, feel himself an "alien" in America, his was a sense of alienation that could be cured only by a journey in time. Yet the fact that he could see clearly into the future only because he was half blind in the present cannot detract from the freshness of his appeal to modern minds. I hope to make clear in the course of this book why this appeal should be heard, pondered, and applauded by all Americans.

HAMILTON AND THE CONSTITUTION:

1780 – 1788

❦

"No man's ideas were more remote from the plan than his were known to be; but is it possible to deliberate between anarchy and convulsion on one side, and the chance of good to be expected from the plan on the other?"

Hamilton (as reported by Madison) to the Convention, September 17, 1787

W RITING to Gouverneur Morris in 1802—not one of the best years of his life—Alexander Hamilton let go a small burst of the frustration that had been building up inside him ever since the triumph of the Republicans under Thomas Jefferson:

Perhaps no man in the United States has sacrificed or done more for the present Constitution than myself; and contrary to all my anticipations of its fate, as you know from the very beginning, I am still laboring to prop the frail and worthless fabric.[1]

He was wrong, of course, to despair of the Constitution, for Jefferson was already well on his somewhat reluctant way to proving that this fabric, which had been stretched and strengthened by the Federalists during their twelve years at the loom, was neither frail nor worthless nor, for that matter, shrinkable. He was right to think that he had "sacrificed" and "done more" than any other man to bring the Constitution to life, for the evidence was overwhelming (although few men, including Hamilton, had eyes to see it) that the Constitution of 1801 was primarily his creation, that the United States had been launched on a constitutional course laid out largely under his direction, and that those who intended to reverse this course would have to go (as few of them really wanted to go) beyond mere politics to talk of resistance, nullification, and even of secession.

The next two chapters are a latter-day, hopefully objective review of that early, largely impassioned testimony, an attempt to fix the responsibility of Hamilton for both the Constitution as it was adopted in 1787–1789 and the Constitution as it had developed to the time of his death. I intend to say as little as possible about the details of his constitutional law and theory, a subject reserved for chapter 6, and nothing at all about his influence after death, a subject reserved for chapter 7, and to limit myself here to an account of what we might call his services to the Constitution. What did he do for and with this charter of government? What did he persuade other men to do for and with it? How different a charter did the nation have in 1801 from the one it might have had if he had not been alive and active in 1783 or 1787 or 1791? These are the questions I hope to answer in these chapters.

They will not be answered easily. For one thing, there is something a little strained about an attempt to examine a many-sided man like Hamilton in only one of his roles, especially when the role was played in conjunction with other, more familiar roles. Hamilton the constitutionalist is no Hamilton at all unless seen as a projection of Hamilton the financier, administrator, diplomat, soldier, lawyer, and politician. For another, any assessment of his influence upon the adoption and growth of the Constitution must be streaked with opinion. When one has read all the relevant documents (which are few and perplexing), when one has listened to all the judgments of the historians (which are many and conflicting), one is appalled to think how little he knows for certain about the motives and actions of men like Hamilton, Washington, Jefferson, Madison, Adams, Jay, Clinton, Gallatin, Marshall, the Morrises, and the rest, and one is sobered to recall that if he had been living in those days, he, too, would have chosen sides and joined with a will in the struggle. It is the historian-as-artist, not the historian-as-scientist, who tries to answer questions like those posed above.

Yet they are too important to ignore, and I shall try to answer them by describing the labors of Hamilton the constitutionalist in five stages of the early history of the Constitution: 1) the six or seven years of mingled frustration and hope that led to the Convention in Philadelphia in May, 1787,[2] 2) the four months of give and take that led to the signing of the Constitution September 17, 1787, 3) the sprawling battle over ratification in 1787 and 1788, 4) the first years of Washington's administration, and 5) the years of consolidation of the achievements of Washington and Hamilton, first under a hard-pressed Adams, then under an uneasy Jefferson. In the first of these stages Hamilton was a leading figure, in the second an uncomfortable one; in the third he was a man of influence, in the fourth a man of destiny. And in the fifth he was a discontented elder statesman, perhaps the youngest we have ever had, who should have shown more confidence in the system he had helped to build, in the people for whom he had built it, and in the charter under which this people was henceforth to be governed. The large events of these years will be familiar to most readers of this book, and I shall therefore focus attention almost entirely upon Hamilton's part in them.

THE story of Hamilton and the Constitution begins with a long, precocious letter written September 3, 1780 from Washington's camp at Liberty Pole (now Englewood), New Jersey, to James Duane, then a member of the New York delegation in the Continental Congress.[3] It may begin even earlier, for Duane and Hamilton seem to have already discussed "the defects of our present system" in a face-to-face meeting, and one may guess that Hamilton had turned his thoughts to the weaknesses of Congress as a law-giving, tax-collecting, and war-making body on his first cold and meatless night at Valley Forge.[4] In any case, the letter to Duane was a disquisition on government in which Hamilton went beyond any other Framer-to-be in indicting the Confederation as "neither fit for war nor peace," blaming Congress for a "diffidence" of its undoubted "power *to preserve the republic from harm,*" proposing to correct the "want of method and energy in the administration" by instituting departments with single heads, and giving Congress "complete sovereignty in all that relates to war, peace, trade, finance, and to the management of foreign affairs." Since Congress would doubtless persist in its diffidence, and thus prove itself unwilling to make use of the "discretionary powers . . . originally vested in them for the safety of the States," the only alternative was to call "immediately a Convention of all the States, with full authority to conclude finally upon a General Confederation." While the letter is full of other proposals we identify with Hamilton—ranging from the establishment of the army on a wholly national basis to the creation of an "American Bank" which could enlist the support of the "moneyed men of influence"—it is the straightforward call for a constitutional convention that makes this letter a notable document of early American constitutionalism. Lest it be thought that Hamilton was merely serving up a suggestion on which men could chew at their leisure, we might take note of the urgency of his call:

The Convention should assemble the first of November next. The sooner the better. Our disorders are too violent to admit of a common or lingering remedy. . . . I require them to be vested with plenipotentiary authority [so] that the business may suffer no delay in the execution, and may in reality come to effect.[5]

We do not know what use Duane made of the letter, although there is reason to believe that it was circulated respectfully among the nationalist-minded members of Congress.[6] We do know that Duane led the way to the limited constitutional revolution of 1781 that put single heads in place of committees or boards in charge of each of four principal areas of Congressional concern—diplomacy, naval affairs, war, and finance—and that Hamilton's prod encouraged him to make the attempt.[7] We also know that Hamilton's letter was the first clear-cut, responsible appeal for the kind of convention that met at last in 1787. Those other men who have been given credit for sounding the first trumpet—Tom Paine, Edward Rutledge, Philip Schuyler, Nathanael Greene, Henry Laurens, and John Sullivan are the most prominent—had made their proposals with none of the force, directness, and detail of Hamilton's letter.[8] It is doubtful that Hamilton deserves quite as much credit as he was given by the historian of the Continental Congress, E. C. Burnett, yet this judgment is certainly worth recording: "It was a long way from 1780 to 1787, but it would seem to have been directly, perhaps chiefly, from this implantation by Hamilton that the Federal Convention of 1787 eventually grew."[9]

Thus with a bang began a period of nearly seven years in which Hamilton argued and pushed—in private letters, public appeals, resolutions, speeches in assemblies, and maneuvers at conventions, indeed in every situation in which his powers of persuasion could be put to use—for a convention authorized to strengthen the powers of Congress or, better yet, to write a new constitution for the United States. He had other things to do in these years—get married, chase after Benedict Arnold, finish off soldiering, father three children, study law, manage a growing practice, play the game of New York politics, found a bank, and serve both New York and the nation in important posts—but this endeavor, above all others, gave purpose to his life. He was not, of course, alone in this great work. The long, stuttering movement toward Philadelphia and

1787 was one to which dozens of men—among them Washington, Schuyler, Jay, Duane, Greene, James Wilson, Henry Knox, Egbert Benson, the Morrises, and especially Madison—lent helping hands at one time or another. Yet his hand, from first to last, was put most firmly to the plow.

We must not grant Hamilton too much credit for knowing exactly what he wanted in a new constitution and exactly how to get it. His vision was strong but also crude; his methods were purposeful but also opportunistic. He knew that he would never rest easy, since the Revolution would never be secure, until three nationalizing instruments—a bank, an army, and an energetic government with "general funds" at its command [10]—had been set up to serve the larger interests of the nation and thus to "attach" the people to the idea of real and perpetual Union. Yet until at least 1783 he was content to focus his energies on strengthening the Confederation Congress. Even when he had committed himself to the bold course of replacing the Articles of Confederation with an entirely new charter, he did not slam the door on the possibility that the Congress could be kept going for a long time with the addition of a new power here and a new organ there. Even as he shot off private letters and introduced public resolutions calling for a "general convention of the States," he labored to keep the Congress from foundering in a sea of impotence and indecision. For a man who came in time to an almost physical loathing for the Articles of Confederation, he showed much practical devotion to this frail if not entirely worthless fabric.[11]

Hamilton had a useful opportunity to play this dual role of scout for a new government and solicitous physician to an old one during a one-year term as delegate from New York to the Confederation Congress in 1782–1783.[12] He did his duty as physician with his customary energy and devotion. He spoke often, and with none of the diffidence expected of the freshman legislator, on every subject with which he was at all familiar;[13] served busily on dozens of committees, especially if they had anything to do with the army or finance;[14] wrote dozens of reports for the consideration of his colleagues;[15] and generally matched his pleas for more energy in the government by putting on a dazzling display of the energy he carried in his slight frame. If Washington needed praise, if Robert Morris needed defending, if Rhode Island needed persuading, if the army needed calming, if no one else would call for the "yeas and nays," if the states had to be prodded to send their delegates or Congress itself prodded to open its debates to the public, "Mr. Hamilton of New York" would be on the spot with a report or speech or motion or recommendation;[16] and more often than not he would be working hand in hand with another eager young nationalist, "Mr. Madison of Virginia."[17] The fact that Madison was a nationalist because he took the large-state point of view and Hamilton a nationalist because he cared neither for large states nor small did nothing to embarrass a fruitful partnership that extended over the next seven years. Whatever Hamilton may have thought of the Articles of Confederation, he did his best to make this first American constitution work, not merely with speeches and maneuvers in behalf of a larger view of the powers of Congress and pleas to the states for support and understanding, but also with plans for propping up the Articles of Confederation with liberating amendments.[18] If Congress would not honor the doctrine of "implied powers" and seize what already belonged to it on any "reasonable" construction of the Articles of Confederation, then Congress must have these powers thrust explicitly upon it—so ran Hamilton's line of argument before, during, and after his year as delegate.

In the meantime, he did his duty as scout with increasing enthusiasm and deftness. Having anticipated the famous letter to Duane with a letter (possibly to Robert Morris, possibly to his future father-in-law, General Schuyler) proposing a Bank of the United States,[19] he followed it with yet another letter, this time to Robert Morris, making the same proposal.[20] Having taken the name of The Continentalist in July, 1781 to persuade the citizens of New York to set their sights upon "a great Federal Republic, closely linked in the pursuit of a common interest,"[21] he then, in July, 1782, extracted a resolution (which he probably wrote) from the New York legislature (of which he was not even a member) calling for a constitutional convention. In the resolution, the first official step toward 1787, he was all politeness:

Resolved, That it is the opinion of this Legislature, that the present system of these States exposes the common cause to a precarious issue, and leaves us at the mercy of events over which we have no influence. . . .

Resolved, That in the opinion of this Legislature the radical source of most of our embarrassments is the want of sufficient power in Congress. . . .

Resolved, That . . . there should be as soon as possible a conference . . . on the subject, and that it would be advisable for this purpose to propose to Congress to recommend, and to each State to adopt, the measure of assembling a general Convention of the States, specially authorized to revise and amend the Confederation, reserving a right to the respective Legislatures to ratify their determinations.*

---

* Hamilton had some right of access to the legislature in his position as Receiver of Continental Taxes in New York, a post to which he had been appointed by Robert Morris a few weeks before. In this small coup he worked closely with his father-in-law.[22]

In the letter to Morris he was not quite so polite:

It has ever been my opinion that Congress ought to have complete sovereignty in all but the mere municipal law of each state; and I wish to see a convention of all the States, with full power to alter and amend finally and irrevocably the present futile and senseless confederation.[23]

Feeling as he did, and being Hamilton in the best of health and spirits, he could have been expected to thrust his views upon his colleagues in Congress. This he did a number of times in private and public, most notably April 1, 1783, near the end of his year in Congress. In the midst of a debate over the propriety of special regional conventions "for regulating matters of common concern," Hamilton spoke his mind. Madison records the event in these words:

Mr. Madison and Mr. Hamilton disapproved of these partial conventions, not as absolute violations of the Confederacy, but as ultimately leading to them and in the meantime exciting pernicious jealousies; the latter observing that he wished instead of them to see a General Convention take place and that he should soon in pursuance of instructions from his constituents propose to Congress a plan for that purpose; the object would be to strengthen the federal Constitution.[24]

The press of events, especially the mutiny of the troops in Lancaster and Philadelphia that eventually sent Congress packing to Princeton, seems to have thwarted Hamilton's intention to put the matter squarely before Congress. Two things, however, he was able to do before withdrawing in despair from that mortally wounded body: first, to bring the resolution of the New York legislature officially to the floor, whence it was referred to a committee and, after an inconclusive report, allowed to die quietly;[25] second, to write out a powerful and thoroughly "whereased" resolution of his own, probably in July, calling for a "convention" with "full powers to revise the confederation." Harried and discouraged, indeed now well started on the long slide to its death, the Congress of 1783 was no place to debate such a resolution, and this forceful document, a twelve-count indictment of the Confederation that left almost nothing unsaid, was circulated among Hamilton's friends and then stuffed back in his desk—with the bitter endorsement in his own hand, "Resolution intended to be submitted to Congress at Princeton in 1783; but abandoned for want of support."[26]

FOR the next three years Hamilton tended to his private affairs in New York. Since his private affairs always seemed to have public implications or consequences, he remained a man to be reckoned with by those who, like him, thought ever more "continentally" and those who, like Governor Clinton, thought ever more parochially. In his conversations and correspondence, even in his law practice—as in the notable case of *Rutgers* v. *Waddington* (1784)—he tried to keep the prospect of a firm Union under an energetic government before the eyes of the men who would sooner or later have to bring it about.[27] While he had reason to feel that his term in Congress had been an irksome experience, he must also have known that it was time not entirely wasted. It was, after all, a splendid apprenticeship in the arts of educating, persuading, and governing men, a critical year in his development as politician, financier, administrator, and constitutionalist, and I feel that biographers have never given the Hamilton of 1782–1783 his full due. In any case, he had used his term in Congress, as best he could under sticky circumstances, to lay the question of a second constitution flatly before the people, and he had impressed more than one colleague as a man to whom the future opened a dazzling prospect.[28] So rapidly had he risen in the high councils of the nation that he seemed like "a planet, the dawn of which was not perceived." [29]

His next direct service to the cause was rendered in the Annapolis Convention of September, 1786, a meeting of twelve "commissioners" from five states who refused to be put off from a historic task by the casual or hostile attitude of the other states. Convoked at the call of the Virginia Assembly to discuss the economic difficulties of the states and to "consider how far a uniform system in their commercial regulations may be necessary to their common interest and their permanent harmony," [30] the commissioners adopted a report calling upon their own states, and thus openly if obliquely upon Congress, to appoint delegates "to meet at Philadelphia on the second Monday in May next,"

to take into consideration the situation of the United States, to devise such further provisions as shall appear to them necessary to render the constitution of the Federal Government adequate to the exigencies of the Union; and to report such an act for that purpose to the United States in Congress assembled as, when agreed to by them and afterwards confirmed by the Legislatures of every State, will effectually provide for the same.[31]

The Annapolis Convention, the next-to-last and crucial step toward Philadelphia, was a joint triumph for Hamilton and Madison. It was the former who, acting his favorite part of the audacious man of destiny, persuaded his colleagues to exceed their limited mandates and to strike for a constitutional solution to all their problems, and who probably wrote out the resolutions adopted September 14. It was the latter who, acting his favorite part of the creative politician, had brought about this meeting in the first place, and who seems to have persuaded Hamilton (with the aid of Edmund Randolph) to pitch his proposal in the blandest language of which he was capable.

The Confederation Congress, as history records, was finally persuaded on February 21, 1787, to do its part and call for a convention to meet "on the second Monday in May next,"

for the sole and express purpose of revising the Articles of Confederation and reporting to Congress and the several legislatures such alterations and provisions therein as shall when agreed to in Congress and confirmed by the states render the federal constitution adequate to the exigencies of government and the preservation of the Union.[32]

Hamilton had already taken his own steps toward "May next" by being elected to the New York Assembly in 1786,[33] persuading the legislature to prod Congress and also to send a delegation, and getting himself chosen as one of the delegates.[34] The delegation from New York had neither the size nor the composition he had advocated. Instead of a five-man team that included nationalists like Duane and R. R. Livingston, it was a three-man team in which he was outnumbered, if not outgunned, by two confirmed antinationalists, Robert Yates and John Lansing, Jr. Yet he was safely aboard; he would be there in Philadelphia to call out "present" when the event he had foreseen in 1780 at last came to pass. And no man, surely, would have a better right to be there. It is a tricky chore to apportion responsibility for the calling of the Convention of 1787, and one who tries to give each of the eight or ten obvious candidates for praise his exact due gets lost soon enough in a swamp of too many opinions and too few documents. Yet most historians now seem disposed to grant Hamilton the chief credit for 1787. Only Madison did as much at the right moments to bring this event to fruition, and he must have been stiffened more than once in his own nationalism, and encouraged to fight on against the parochialists in Virginia, by the example of his gallant friend from New York. I find it hard to disagree with John A. Krout's assertion that it "was Hamilton, neither Washington nor Madison nor Jay nor Franklin, who had made the Constitutional Convention possible," [35] or with Robert Troup's remembrance of Hamilton in 1828 as "the principal instrument, used by Providence" to save "our country from incalculable mischiefs, if not from total ruin." [36]

In the end, of course, obstinate events rather than purposeful men made

Philadelphia possible. Much has been made by historians, as it should be made, of the shock visited upon the sensibilities of the leading men of the time by the Shays Rebellion in Massachusetts, yet almost as much could be made of the refusal of Rhode Island to ratify the Congressional Impost of 1781, the withdrawal of Virginia's own ratification at the exact moment when pressure was about to be put on recalcitrant Rhode Island,[37] the real and apparent discriminations in British orders-in-council against American shipping, the arrogance of the British in refusing to surrender the northwest posts,* the refusal of several states to give Congress power to retaliate against British commerce, the depredations upon the rights of creditors in the more "mutable" states, and the almost pig-headed refusal of the New York legislature in early 1787 (despite a virtuoso performance by Hamilton on the floor of the Assembly) to ratify the Impost of 1783.[38] All of these frustrations served, as John Jay said, "to raise a *national* spirit in our country." [39] All of them added up, as Gouverneur Morris testified, to "political good" for the men who were getting ready to abandon Congress and strike for a new government.[40] They set the stage of aspiration and desperation for the amazing event of 1787.

HAMILTON had a far less creative hand in that event than one would have expected of the eager young nationalist of Liberty Pole, Annapolis, and Poughkeepsie, or of the delegate whom William Pierce of Georgia described in one of his famous character sketches as "deservedly celebrated for his talents." [41] For reasons both personal and political, more than one of which remains indecipherable, he was a strangely uneasy, unhelpful, silent witness to the proceedings that took place between May 25 and September 17 in the State House (the once and future Independence Hall) in Philadelphia.[42] His claim to membership in the inner circle of the Founding Fathers gains only small support from this disappointing performance.

Most of his troubles seem to have arisen out of the ironic fact that he, the most continental-minded of all delegates at the Convention, was a member of the most state-minded of all delegations. To tell the truth, Hamilton must have been half surprised to find himself in Philadelphia at all. If Governor Clinton had been more sure of his own mind or his

---

* It was probably the urge to take economic reprisals against Britain that persuaded Clinton's party to send Hamilton and Egbert Benson, another nationalist, to the Annapolis Convention under a limited mandate. They do not seem to have known their Hamilton quite as well in 1786 as they were to come to know him in later years.

antinationalist comrades more obstinate,[43] New York might have followed
the lead of Rhode Island and refused to send a delegation to the Convention. If Hamilton had been less tactful and his father-in-law less powerful
and solicitous, he would hardly have been included in the delegation of
three that was finally sent, after much jockeying, to look out for New
York's interests. Hamilton got to Philadelphia, and got there for opening
day, but his spirit must have been sobered by the weight of the two
albatrosses who hung from his neck and who, since the vote of each
state delegation was to count as one, were sure to render him impotent at
every moment of decision.[44] Whatever Hamilton may have thought of the
command of the New York legislature, which sent him forth for "the sole
and express purpose" of reporting amendments to the Articles of Confederation for adoption by Congress and the "several states," [45] Yates and Lansing meant to honor it meticulously. If it would be somewhat less than
fair to say that they went to Philadelphia simply in order to spy on
Hamilton and the other nationalists and to report back to Clinton, it
would be somewhat more than fair to say that they went as men of good
faith, by which I mean men determined to work out a scheme, however
limited, that would "render" Congress "adequate to the exigencies of government and the preservation of the Union." By their staunch support of
Governor Clinton they had consistently demonstrated their own lack of
interest in a stronger national government.

Hamilton was not merely too continental-minded for all but the most
nationalist tastes on display at the Convention; he was also, it would
seem, too "high-toned" for even the most antidemocratic and backward-
looking. As his fellow New Yorker Lansing noted, he was "for tuning
the Government high," [46] as high as public opinion would permit it to go.
Alone among the delegates he expressed a wholehearted admiration for the
British government—"in my private opinion . . . the best in the world"—
and alone among them he wondered if a "good" executive could ever "be
established on republican principles." [47] If even he could admit that the
principles he voiced on the floor of the Convention were unacceptable to
American opinion and inconsistent with American tradition, his colleagues
could hardly be expected to take him entirely seriously as a source of
useful ideas or a broker in compromise. Yates and Lansing saw to it that
his vote would never count on a crucial issue; he saw to it himself that
his voice would be listened to more respectfully than attentively. This
may not be the whole explanation of Hamilton's failure to exert creative
influence at Philadelphia, but it is all that has been recorded in the documents and must be enough for our purposes.

The tale of Hamilton in the Convention is quickly told. Having opened May 25 with a typical burst of energy by nominating William Jackson for Secretary and getting named (with George Wythe and Charles Pinckney) to the Committee on Rules,[48] he then drifted along on the current of debate for three weeks, making only an occasional remark or motion or point of order.[49] The Virginia Plan (largely the work of Madison) was laid before the Convention May 29, and then countered June 15 with the New Jersey Plan (probably the work of Roger Sherman, Luther Martin, and William Paterson), but the best that Hamilton could do was announce that he was not "in sentiment with either plan,"[50] thus placing himself not between but outside the two forces that had formed up for the struggle over the nature of the American Union.

Just how far removed in purpose and prescription he was from either Madison the nationalist or Paterson the confederationist became plain on June 18,[51] at once the most glorious and most fruitless day of all those he spent at the Convention. On this day the delegates paused, whether out of respect for Hamilton or simply because they were themselves out of breath, and gave over an entire session (five hours or more, so we are told)[52] to a lecture in political science by their uncomfortable colleague from New York. In it he came as close as he ever did to a candid exposition of the political principles he would have espoused if he had been born and bred in England, and in it he presented—not as a "proposition" but as a "model"—a plan of government that was based squarely on these principles. We shall take careful note of the principles—a hard-grained amalgam of Hume, Locke, and Hobbes—in chapters 4–6. It is the plan of government to which we must pay attention here.

That plan, which Hamilton sketched in eleven short paragraphs,[53] was in its turn a heady blend of continentalism and high tone that must have startled men like Sherman and Martin and discomfited men like Madison and Washington. Its continentalism, that is to say, its urge to consolidate the political authority of the American people in one central government and to reduce the states to a subordinate position is evident in provisions for a two-chambered legislature with "power to pass *all laws whatsoever*" and a "Governor" or "President" in each state who, having been "appointed by the *General Government*," would have a *"negative upon the laws about to be passed"* in his state. Its high tone, that is to say, its resolve to place this authority in the hands of the "wise and good" and to put restraints on "the amazing violence and turbulence of the democratic spirit" is evident in provisions for a "Governor" elected for life by *"electors* chosen by *electors* chosen by the people,"* a Senate also chosen indirectly and for life, and an absolute power of veto in the executive. Although Hamilton knew that circumstances made it impossible to place "complete sovereignty in the General Government," he meant to go as far as public opinion would approve to give the Union a system that would indeed "render" it "perpetual." Although he knew that American tradition made it "unwise to propose . . . any other form" of government than the "republican" to the people, he meant "to go as far . . . as republican principles" would "admit" to attain "stability and permanency." Since the American people could not listen in on the proceedings, because of the rule of secrecy adopted at the outset,[54] Hamilton had seized the opportunity to speak his mind, or, rather, one forceful side of it, in full candor. We shall never know just how strongly he felt about each particular in the plan of June 18, but we cannot doubt that it was something more than a trial balloon,[55] an effort to shock, an angry slap at Yates and Lansing, or an erratic flight of fancy. Any man can expound any political philosophy either tentatively or firmly or extravagantly, and all the political and personal circumstances of June, 1787 moved Hamilton to expound his own philosophy in extravagant terms.

Hamilton's prodigious effort of June 18 provoked almost no response, unfavorable or favorable, among the men who listened to him all through that hot day. William Samuel Johnson of Connecticut mentioned it June 21 as one that "boldly and decisively contended for an abolition of the State Governments," but he had noted the lack of response himself and was quite unworried. Hamilton, he was happy to say, had been "praised by every gentleman, but supported by no gentleman." [56] Only George Read of Delaware, a small-state man with big-nation views, made any effort to fix attention upon it. On June 29, according to Madison, he "repeated his approbation of the plan of Mr. Hamilton, and wished it to be substituted in place of that on the table." [57] Since no one else seemed to wish it to be substituted, the plan died a quick death.* In later years it was exhumed from the memories of men to serve as "clear proof" of Hamilton's "predilections for monarchy," [58] but the Convention itself never again gave it the slightest direct consideration.

NOW that Hamilton's usefulness as a member had been compromised by his own audacity as well as by the obstinacy of his fellow delegates from New York, he dropped out of sight if not out of touch. He followed up

---

* That there was at least a flurry of reaction off the floor is evident in Hamilton's complaint of June 19 that "he had not been understood yesterday," that he "did not intend . . . a total extinguishment of state governments." [59]

Read on that same June 29 with a few sharp words in behalf of "individual" rights as against the rights of artificial beings called "states," [60] and then went home to attend to his private affairs. Lansing recorded on June 30, doubtless with delight: "Mr. Hamilton left Town this morning." [61] Hamilton's lack of success in Philadelphia did not prevent him from doing what he could in New York, and at all points in between, to persuade the "minds of the people" that this was "the critical opportunity for establishing the prosperity of this country on a solid foundation." To Washington in Philadelphia he sent words of encouragement and warning on July 3:

> The prevailing apprehension among thinking men is that the Convention, from a fear of shocking the popular opinion, will not go far enough. . . .
>
> These appearances, though they will not warrant a conclusion that the people are yet ripe for such a plan as I advocate, yet serve to prove that there is no reason to despair of their adopting one equally energetic, if the Convention should think proper to propose it. . . .
>
> I own to you, Sir, that I am seriously and deeply distressed at the aspect of the councils which prevailed when I left Philadelphia. I fear that we shall let slip the golden opportunity of rescuing the American empire from disunion, anarchy, and misery. No motley or feeble measure can answer the end or will finally receive the public support. Decision is true wisdom and will be not less reputable to the Convention than salutary to the community.

And then he added, as if to invite a call to return to the scene of battle:

> I shall of necessity remain here ten or twelve days; if I have reason to believe that my attendance at Philadelphia will not be mere waste of time, I shall after that period rejoin the Convention.[62]

Washington, who understood better than any other delegate how hard a trial this had been for Hamilton, responded with words that must have gladdened his young aide's heart (and made him chastise himself a little more sharply than usual for his conduct at Newburgh six years before):

> I am sorry you went away. I wish you were back. The crisis is equally important and alarming, and no opposition under such circumstances should discourage exertions till the signature is fixed.[63]

Despite this plea Hamilton confined his own "exertions" for most of the next two months to working on men of influence in private and to chastising Clinton in public for having "without reserve, reprobated the appointment of the Convention." [64] Yates and Lansing, convinced that "further attendance" at a convention intent upon creating the tyranny of a "consolidated government" would be "fruitless and unavailing," had withdrawn July 10 with no intention ever to return.[65] This made it almost impossible for Hamilton, a delegate without a delegation, to pick up again in Philadelphia. Still, the urge to be on the spot when history was about to be made was stronger than his doubts and scruples, and, after an unexplained one-day appearance August 13 and an unsuccessful plea to Yates and Lansing to "accompany him to Philadelphia . . . for the sake of propriety and public opinion," [66] he came back September 5 or 6 and stayed to the end.[67] He spoke a number of times on such controversial subjects as the method of electing the President and the number of seats in the House, handed to Madison a second plan of government (at once more elaborate and moderate than the plan of June 18),[68] made a stout plea to the doubters on the other side to sign the finished document, and then signed it himself on September 17 with an apparently clear conscience.[69] That he was, despite all discouragements, the same Hamilton is attested by Madison's comment of September 8 that "Col. Hamilton expressed himself with great earnestness and anxiety." * That he was, despite his long absence, a man trusted by his colleagues is attested by his election the same day (with those four stalwarts Madison, Gouverneur Morris, King, and Johnson) to the Committee on Style.[70] And that he was, despite the strength of all his convictions, a statesman-in-the-making is evident in Madison's austere report of his final speech:

Mr. Hamilton expressed his anxiety that every member should sign. A few characters of consequence, by opposing, or even refusing to sign the Constitution, might do infinite mischief by kindling the latent sparks that lurk under an enthusiasm in favor of the convention, which may soon subside. No man's ideas were more remote from the plan than his were known to be; but is it possible to deliberate between anarchy and convulsion on one side, and the chance of good to be expected from the plan on the other? [71]

Thus ended one of the few disappointing episodes in the years of Hamilton's service to the Constitution. The wide gap between the possible and the actual in his performance at Philadelphia comes as an unpleasant shock to the historian who admires Hamilton. He had so much to give, and yet he gave so little. Even when we take his anomalous position on the New York delegation into account, then add his apparently eccentric hopes for a strong and splendid government, we are left with the suspicion that he could have done a lot better if he had known what 1787

---

* And by the amusing fact, first noted by the editors of *The Papers of Alexander Hamilton,* that the names of the states under which the Framers signed their own names on the original document are in Hamilton's hand.[72] He was, I repeat, a man who could not sit still, even in the company of Washington and Franklin.

would come to mean to generations of Americans yet unborn. There must have been, as I suggested above, other reasons for his lackluster performance. He was not all that dogmatically committed to continentalism and high tone, and thus unable to work closely with men who had less "advanced" views, as he had proved in Congress in 1782–1783 and was to prove again in Washington's service in 1789–1795. He was not all that paralyzed by the obstinacy of Yates and Lansing, as he proved with his signature on September 17 and with his eloquence on a number of occasions.

This last point seems to me especially important, for one may read for himself in the notes of Madison and King, and even in those of his hostile fellow delegates from New York, that Hamilton could make reasonable, useful, and more often than not acceptable suggestions to the Convention. His motion of May 30 in support of representation in Congress "proportioned to the number of free inhabitants"; his suggestion of June 5 that the Senate be given the "right of rejecting or approving" all nominations to the judiciary; his plea of June 21 that the lower house "be directly elected by the people" and for a three-year term; his searching and good-tempered speech of June 22 in behalf of the proposal in the Virginia Plan that members of the legislature be ineligible to any other state or national office; his random observations on the uses of a second house, the advantages of a large lower house, the proper way to elect the President,[73] the importance of an amending procedure neither too loose nor too rigid, and the experiences of Great Britain and New York with the executive power of veto; his scrupulous concern for the right of the Confederation Congress to pass judgment on the new Constitution; even his gracious seconding of Franklin's motion of June 2 for an unsalaried executive and his perhaps less gracious refusal to support Franklin's motion of June 28 in behalf of a daily prayer "imploring the assistance of Heaven" [74]—these were the contributions of a man who seemed no less adept than Madison at the game of give-and-take (or, as some would have it, blindman's buff) that produced the Constitution.[75] But they were too few and occasional, one must admit, to give him a place with Madison, or indeed with Wilson, Morris, Sherman, Rutledge, Ellsworth, King, Franklin, and Washington, as one of the truly useful men of the Convention. If he had "done as much and perhaps more than any other individual to engineer the Federal Convention," [76] he had done almost nothing to steer it toward the best of all possible conclusions. "General Hamilton," said his friend and colleague Gouverneur Morris in later years, "had little share in forming the Constitution." [77] Hamilton's reputation as constitutionalist might be higher today if he, like Adams, Jefferson, and Jay, had been prevented by destiny from being in Philadelphia at all.

HAMILTON set out for home as determined as any man who had sat in the Convention to see the Constitution safely through the trials of ratification, and then to help launch it well and truly toward the splendid goals announced in the Preamble. He never looked back to Philadelphia, whether in anger or scorn or sorrow, never again let the extravagances of June 18, 1787 get the upper hand in his political temper. He was no John Adams, a lover of constitutions in general; he was no James Madison, a lover of this constitution in particular. But he had made up his mind September 17 that the choice was between this plan and no plan, between the "chance of good" and the certainty of "anarchy and convulsion," and from that moment forward he was a zealous advocate of both the beauties and the necessity of the Constitution.

His resolve to go all out for the Constitution, a resolve that called for a compromise with abstract desire but not with concrete principle, now combined with his natural audacity and energy to carry him through one of his most creative years. From September 17, 1787, when he put his name to the work of the Convention, to July 28, 1788, when he rode into New York City from Poughkeepsie bringing official notice of his state's ratification for presentation to Congress,[78] Hamilton labored without rest to carry New York fully and contentedly into the new Union. As usual he was caught up in making a living for himself and his growing family, and the days must have been especially wearing when the courts were sitting and clients were begging for his undivided attention.[79] Yet he never flagged—never missed a chance to instruct the public or smoke out the opposition or rally his own forces or exhort his friends in other states—and he rarely allowed himself the luxury of negative thoughts.

The stage upon which he strode was, for the last time in his career, a narrow one. His thoughts soared outward to embrace the Union, but it was one recalcitrant part of the Union, the state of New York, on which Hamilton now concentrated all his hopes and talents. The campaign for ratification of the Constitution was, in the nature of things political and geographic in the young Republic, really twelve separate campaigns—or, counting alienated Rhode Island, thirteen. Each one had to go its own way in its own time; no man or committee could sit in New York or Philadelphia or Richmond and co-ordinate, much less direct, the efforts of the friends of the Constitution in all the states; only by sending on news of ratification or rejection could men in one state influence the course of events (and then only indirectly) in any other state. Hamilton the continentalist had to play, and play in good faith, the role of a New Yorker among New Yorkers in this critical year.

New York was clearly a more consequential state to win for the new Constitution than, say, Delaware or New Hampshire or South Carolina, and the man who could win it would produce something more than another vote for a more perfect Union. Four facts gave the struggle over ratification in New York marked importance: first, the position of this rich and growing state on the Atlantic seaboard, which made it, perhaps even more than Pennsylvania, the keystone of the Union; second, the power of the political forces centered around the sturdy person of Governor Clinton and opposed to the Constitution; [80] third, the way in which these forces were concentrated in the upstate counties and the forces favoring ratification in and around New York City; and fourth, the way in which chance, purpose, and cross-purpose conspired to place the moment of decision in New York at the end of the timetable of ratification. When the New York Convention met at Poughkeepsie June 17, 1788, eight states had already agreed to the Constitution; when the Convention rose on July 26, two more had decided to make the gamble.

It is a measure of Hamilton's brilliance as a politician in this year that he saw these four facts while standing in the midst of them just as clearly as we see them with the gift of hindsight, and that he seized upon them to win an astounding victory. He knew from the beginning that there would be no Union without New York, and he turned this truth around to persuade a number of influential men that there might be no New York without the Union. He knew almost from the beginning, after an early bout of optimism, that the opposition would muster a majority of the delegates, and he laid his plans to lure enough of these delegates away from Governor Clinton's camp to build a majority of his own. Most important of all, he fell in with the oddly assorted forces that put off the decisive trial of strength to a late moment. Whether he himself could have speeded up or retarded the course of events in New York is extremely doubtful. What is not the least bit doubtful is that the course, as it finally ran, was well suited to his purposes, for it permitted him to render two services to the Constitution for which later generations of Americans must always be grateful.

The first of these was the conception and execution of that series of occasional papers on the Constitution we have come to know, study, and cherish as *The Federalist*. These papers are, by common consent of both scholarly and popular opinion, the most important work in political science that has ever been written, or is likely ever to be written, in the United States. *The Federalist* is, indeed, despite all its blemishes, the one product of the American mind that is rightly counted among the classics of political thought, and as such it deserves our careful attention.

This work has always invited widespread respect as the first and most authoritative commentary on the Constitution of the United States. It has been searched minutely by lawyers for its analysis of the powers of Congress, quoted confidently by historians for its revelations of the hopes and fears of the Framers, and cited magisterially by the Supreme Court for its arguments in behalf of executive independence, judicial review, and national supremacy. It would not be stretching the truth more than a few inches to say that *The Federalist* stands third only to the Declaration of Independence and the Constitution itself among the sacred writings of American political history. It has a quality of legitimacy, of authority and authenticity, that gives it the status of a public document, one to which, as Thomas Jefferson wrote in his old age, "appeal is habitually made by all, and rarely declined or denied by any as evidence of the general opinion of those who framed, and of those who accepted the Constitution of the United States, on questions as to its genuine meaning." [81] The "appeal" to *The Federalist* was indulged in by gentlemen of the first session of Congress and continues unabated to the present day. [82]

In recent years respect for *The Federalist* has blossomed into admiration. It is now valued not merely as a clever defense of a particular charter, but as an exposition of timeless truths about constitutional government. It has caught the fancy of political scientists throughout the world, has been translated into a dozen languages, [83] and—surely the most convincing evidence of its lofty status—has become one of the three or four staples of the American college curriculum in political science. George Washington, who had a high opinion of *The Federalist,* wrote some prophetic words to Hamilton in the summer of 1788:

When the transient circumstances and fugitive performances which attended this crisis shall have disappeared, that work will merit the notice of posterity; because in it are candidly and ably discussed the principles of freedom and the topics of government which will be always interesting to mankind so long as they shall be connected in civil society. [84]

The immense prestige of *The Federalist* seems especially remarkable when viewed in the light of its origins. It is essentially a collection of eighty-five letters to the public over the pseudonym of Publius that appeared at short intervals in the newspapers of New York City beginning October 27, 1787.* These letters were still appearing in late March, 1788, when the first thirty-six were issued in a collected edition by J. and A. McLean. Continuous publication was halted with number 77 on April 4, then resumed June 14 and concluded August 16. In the meantime, a second volume containing numbers 37–85 was published May 28.

Conceived in the pressure of a crisis in human events, written with a haste that often bordered on the frantic,[85] printed and published as if it were the most perishable kind of daily news, *The Federalist* bore no marks of immortality at birth. It was, in fact, only one of several hundred salvos in the war of words that accompanied the struggle over ratification.[86] The difference is that this salvo was fired by Alexander Hamilton and James Madison (with a useful assist from John Jay), political scientists of the first rank and men who ended up on the winning side. I mean no disrespect to Madison, who was at his most brilliant in *The Federalist,* when I say that Hamilton was the key figure in the operation that produced these papers. Without his foresight, energy, and organizing skill there would have been no Publius to stiffen the friends of the Constitution and to instruct the minds of posterity. He hit upon the idea of a series of thoughtful communications that would explain the proposed Constitution; he scrambled for worthy contributors and finally found them in Madison and Jay; [87] he wrote almost two-thirds of the total of 175,000 words; he carried on the project to its scheduled end long after the other two men had been forced to leave the field. While the Publius we read today is a composite of three men, one of these men, Alexander Hamilton, was the political magician who brought him to life.

THROUGHOUT the long months during which *The Federalist* ran in the New York newspapers, and indeed until several years after publication of the collected essays, the identity of Publius was a secret known for certain only to a few intimates of Hamilton, Madison, or Jay.[88] (The *Freeman's Journal* in Philadelphia guessed as early as January, 1788 that "lawyers *Hamilton* and *Madison*" were the authors, but since it also had Madison proposing "a king" to "the great conclave" of 1787, it was concocting its guesses out of fairly thin air.) [89] By donning the mask of

---

* These included, at one stage or another, the (New York) *Independent Journal* (Nos. 1–85), *New York Packet* (Nos. 1–76), (New York) *Daily Advertiser* (Nos. 1–50), and *New-York Journal* (Nos. 23–38). In addition, the (New York) *American Magazine* of Noah Webster published a synopsis and review of all numbers of *The Federalist* in its issues of March, April, May, June, 1788.[90]

anonymity for sound political purposes, the authors of *The Federalist* unwittingly kindled a tortuous dispute among their political heirs over the exact responsibility for the various papers, especially numbers 49–58 and 62–63. Hamilton, in particular, contributed to the confusion of later generations by writing a note just before his death—perhaps designed to be discovered just after—in which he laid claim to a full sixty-three numbers of *The Federalist,* some of which plainly belonged to Madison. Just why this man of honor and sound memory should have engaged in this extraordinary action is impossible to explain, except in terms of a careless transcription of numbers from Roman to Arabic or two slips of a nervous pen.* In any case, the damage was done, and it has taken much scholarly effort to undo it—to the extent that it ever can be undone. Thanks chiefly to the labors of Edward G. Bourne and Douglass Adair, we can now say with some confidence that Hamilton wrote fifty-one numbers (1, 6–9, 11–13, 15–17, 21–36, 59–61, 65–85), Madison twenty-six (10, 14, 37–58, and probably 62–63), and Jay five (2–5, 64), while three (18–20) were the product of a joint effort by Madison and Hamilton in which the former used some notes put together by the latter. The skimpiness of Jay's contribution is explained by an illness that overtook him in the fall of 1787,[91] the impressive bulk of Hamilton's by the intensity of his commitment to the cause of ratification in New York. Madison's contribution, which is far more important for the reputation of Publius than its modest size would indicate, was made possible in the first place only because the Virginian was in New York in the fall of 1787 as a delegate to Congress. His participation ended abruptly upon his departure for home March 4, 1788. His last article had appeared three days before.[92]

* Hamilton is said to have slipped this note rather ostentatiously into a copy of Pliny's letters in the office of his friend Egbert Benson the day before his duel with Burr. Although the original copy has been lost, we can be fairly sure, thanks to the faithful William Coleman, that it read:

> "Nos. 2, 3, 4, 5, 54, Mr. Jay;
> Nos. 10, 14, 37 to 48 inclusive, Mr. Madison;
> Nos. 18, 19, 20, Mr. Hamilton and Mr. Madison jointly;
> all the rest by Mr. Hamilton."

It seems reasonably clear that 54 should have read 64 and 48 should have read 58, which would then leave Hamilton claiming only two numbers now generally attributed to Madison.[93]

In point of fact, neither Hamilton nor Madison, each of whom naturally changed his mind on a number of issues and interpretations as the years passed and the Constitution evolved, was overly anxious to establish precise responsibility for each paper. There had been, moreover, "a sort of understanding" between the two that "there should be no disclosure but by mutual consent," and the understanding was honored scrupulously even when they had become uncompromising political enemies.[94]

Despite all claims that have been made for the influence of *The Feder-alist* at the time it ran in the newspapers,* it seems to have altered the course of events at most one or two degrees during the struggle over ratification.[95] Promises, threats, fears, bargains, and face-to-face debates, not eloquent words in even the most widely circulated newspapers,† won

* Including the claim of the acidulous William Maclay, who, although he considered buying *The Federalist* in 1789 and then decided to "get" it "without buying it" because it was "not worth it," believed that "it certainly was instrumental in pro-curing the adoption of the Constitution." [96]

† A survey of the American press in the period between October 27, 1787 and August 31, 1788 has produced the following facts about the republication of *The Federalist* in newspapers and magazines outside New York City:

Out of a total of 82 such newspapers, 16 reprinted at least one number of *The Federalist*. The list of reprintings by states (with dates of ratification) is:

MASSACHUSETTS (February 6, 1788).

1) (Boston) *American Herald*, Nos. 1, 2, 3, 5, 14, 15, 23, running sporadically from November 12, 1787 to January 7, 1788.

2) (Boston) *Massachusetts Centinel*, No. 13, December 8, 1787.

3) (Boston) *Massachusetts Gazette*, an extract from No. 14, December 11, 1787.

4) *Salem Mercury*, an extract from No. 14, January 15, 1788.

NEW HAMPSHIRE (June 21, 1788).

5) (Exeter) *Freeman's Oracle*, No. 37 (now 38), February 15, 1788.

NEW YORK (July 26, 1788).

6) *Albany Gazette*, Nos. 1–6, 8–10, 12, 13, 17, running from November 15, 1787 to March 13, 1788. (It seems almost certain that other numbers of *The Federalist* appeared in issues of this newspaper that have not been preserved.)

7) *Hudson Weekly Gazette*, Nos. 1–11, November 22, 1787 to January 17, 1788.

8) (Lansingburgh) *Northern Centinel*, Nos. 1–10, running from November 13, 1787 to January 15, 1788, which moved to Albany in February, 1788 and became the (Albany) *Federal Herald*, printing No. 68 (now 69), March 31, 1788.

9) (Poughkeepsie) *Country Journal*, Nos. 15–21, January 16 to February 5, 1788.

PENNSYLVANIA (December 12, 1787).

10) (Philadelphia) *Pennsylvania Gazette*, Nos. 2–19, November 14, 1787 to March 19, 1788.

11) (Philadelphia) *Pennsylvania Journal*, Nos. 1, 2, 3, 5, November 7–28, 1787.

RHODE ISLAND (May 29, 1790).

12) (Providence) *United States Chronicle*, Nos. 1–3, November 22, December 27, 1787.

VIRGINIA (June 26, 1788).

13) *Norfolk and Portsmouth Journal*, No. 6, January 9, 1788.

14) (Richmond) *Virginia Gazette*, Nos. 4, 5, December 22, 29, 1787.

15) (Richmond) *Virginia Independent Chronicle*, Nos. 1–3, December 12, 19, 26, 1787.

16) (Winchester) *Virginia Gazette*, No. 16, April 9, 1788.

Out of a total of two such magazines, one, the (Philadelphia) *American Museum*, reprinted Nos. 1–6, November, December, 1787.

It should be plain to see that the letters of Publius were not snapped up eagerly by editors in other parts of the country, that those who set out to reprint the series grew weary and wary in fairly short order, and that *The Federalist* therefore reached its audience in other states largely through the circulation of the New York news-papers and the two volumes issued by McLean March 22 and May 28.[97]

hard-earned victories for the Constitution in the crucial states of Massachusetts, Virginia, and New York. Publius, by his own admission, spoke to a select audience of established men, and most such men had already been convinced of the need for a change in the system of government. The chief usefulness of *The Federalist* in 1787–1788 was as a kind of debater's handbook in Virginia and New York. Fifty-two copies of the collected edition were rushed to Richmond at Hamilton's direction and used by advocates of the Constitution in the climactic debate over ratification, and, thanks to the efforts of James Kent, Egbert Benson, and doubtless Hamilton himself, probably even more copies could have been found lying about in the courthouse and taverns at Poughkeepsie.[98]

The fame of *The Federalist* derives, therefore, not from the events of one decisive year but from the whole course of American history. It is a sign, as it were, of the success of the Constitution, which, as it has endured over the generations, has called attention ever more insistently to the men who, having helped to write it, first tried to explain it. Viewed from this perspective, which is the one we are privileged to take, *The Federalist* appears as four books in one: an explanation of the blessings of federal government; an indictment of the Articles of Confederation for their failure to provide such government or indeed to provide much in the way of government at all; an analysis and defense of the new Constitution as an instrument of federalism and constitutionalism; and, lighting up these practical subjects with bursts of brilliance, an exposition of enduring truths about both the dangers and the delights of free government.

As an explanation of the federal form of government *The Federalist* comes closest to being an original piece of work. Other men, to be sure— most notably Althusius and "the celebrated Montesquieu"—had discoursed intelligently on some of the problems of unity and disunity among states with close emotional and commercial ties; it remained for Publius, in the person of Madison (with some help from Hamilton), to make the first real stab at expounding the merits of genuine federalism, which is a full and tricky step beyond federation in the direction of consolidation. *The Federalist* deserves praise for the clarity with which it insists that both levels of government in a federal system must exercise authority over individuals, that the central government must enjoy supremacy in its assigned fields, and that federalism is to be cherished not alone for its contributions to peace within the land and security without, but for the firm foundation it provides for the enjoyment of individual freedom over a wide expanse of territory. *The Federalist,* it could be said, converted federalism from an expedient into an article of faith, from an occasional

accident of history into an enduring expression of the principles of constitutionalism. It did all this rather reluctantly, to tell the truth, and at more
than one point lamely, but it did the job as well as it could possibly have
been done by men who were feeling their way toward an untried pattern
of government.

The pages of *The Federalist* that catalogue the weaknesses of the
Articles of Confederation make much the least interesting reading today.
In 1787–1788, however, they made interesting reading indeed, and many
friends of the new Constitution valued *The Federalist* principally for its
merciless indictment of the "palpable defects of the subsisting Confederation." Since the indictment had to be made with force and in detail, one
cannot begrudge Publius (in this instance largely Hamilton) the joys he
must have experienced in beating a horse that looks dead to us but was
very much alive to him. And even in the muddiest parts of numbers 15 to
22 there are solid observations on a major theme of *The Federalist*: the
dreadful circumstance of a weak government in a disordered society.

Up to now, at least, *The Federalist* has worked its chief influence on
events as the most authoritative commentary on the Constitution. Today,
as all through the history of American constitutional development, an
interpretation of some clause in that document can be given a flavor of
authenticity by a quotation from Publius. If he was understandably wrong
in his interpretation of some details in the Constitution—for example, in
assigning the Senate a share in the power of removal—he was remarkably right about many more. Publius the constitutional lawyer, in the bold
person of Hamilton, reached the peak of intellectual power and of historical influence in the assertion of judicial review in number 78.

Publius the political scientist, in the perceptive persons of both Hamilton
and Madison, is the man who has brought both fame and influence to
The Federalist in recent years—despite the fact that the speculative musings of *The Federalist* make up at best a fragment on government. What
Hamilton and Madison could have produced as political thinkers in the
closet of leisurely detachment and what they managed to produce as
political strategists in the arena of zestful engagement were, alas, two
different matters. *The Federalist* is a contribution to political thought only
by accident—by the happy accident that neither of its chief authors could
ever make a point in the most earth-bound debate without pausing, if
only for a moment, to put it in a larger perspective. Yet this, after all, is
the way in which some of the most notable contributions to political
science were brought into being. We should not spend too much time
regretting the startling omissions and uneven quality of *The Federalist*

lest we fail to pay the homage of painstaking study to Madison's reflections on the plural society in numbers 10 and 51, Hamilton's appraisal of executive power as an agency of free government in number 70, and the musings of both authors—so remarkably in tune on this particular point—about the passions, weaknesses, self-interest, and irrationality of political man.

In recent years it has been popular to describe Publius as a "split personality" who spoke through Madison as a federalist and an exponent of limited government, through Hamilton as a nationalist and an admirer of energetic government.[99] One critic has gone further to accuse each author of blatant inconsistencies, some of them intentional, in the course of his contribution.[100] Neither the diagnosis of tension between Hamilton and Madison nor the indictment of each man for self-contradiction strikes me as a useful or perhaps even fair-minded exercise. Publius was, on any large view—the only correct view to take of an effort so sprawling in size and concentrated in time—a remarkably "whole personality," and I am far more impressed by the large area of agreement between Hamilton and Madison than by the differences in emphasis that have been read *into* rather than *in* their papers. Hamilton was, on the same view, as consistent as we should expect a sophisticated man to be when he has to deal with such paradoxes as two sovereign authorities within one community or three equal and independent organs sharing the whole power of government—and so, too, was Madison. The intellectual tensions of *The Federalist* and its creators are in fact an honest reflection of those built into the Constitution it expounds and the polity it celebrates. The wonder must always be, not that Publius spoke some of the persistent truths of politics in an offhand manner and with a hoarse voice, but that, in the circumstances of the case, he spoke as coherently as he did. He managed to do this principally because the thoughts of his creators, while hastily written down, had not been lightly conceived. They were, indeed, the product of years of learned study and hard experience. Many of Hamilton's main points in *The Federalist* had already been made again and again in the writings and speeches of the seven or eight years that led to October 27, 1787.

I do not mean to ignore the faults and falterings that make *The Federalist* a less satisfactory work in political thought than *Leviathan* or *The Social Contract*. It was, of course, a piece of special pleading for a plan of government that had been portrayed as an engine of despotism, and it had to meet the opponents of this plan at least partly on their own grounds. Publius, we must admit, says the same thing over and over in a half-dozen ways, tiptoes around some of the reasonable criticisms directed against the Constitution and slogs through some of the silliest, and makes a few arguments and appeals which his creators must have had trouble framing. *The Federalist,* I repeat, is a work written at high speed and under high pressure by two men who were trying to explain a bundle of compromises,[101] indeed of novelties, that had been framed in frugal language, who were asked to elaborate upon a string of words—general welfare, commerce, advice and consent, executive power, appellate jurisdiction, full faith and credit, supreme law of the land—out of which history alone would be able to make sense. The wonder is that there are not more weak spots and wrong turns in these hundreds of pages. To spin out the inconsistencies indulged in unknowingly by Hamilton or Madison is an exercise in scholastic hindsight; to accuse either one of these men of deliberate inconsistencies and deceptions is an exercise in spiteful abuse.

It has also been popular to describe Hamilton as a man who believed almost nothing that he wrote in the name of Publius, as a clever lawyer who took on a case he knew to be weak and won it with arguments he knew to be false. To a large extent, this is all a matter of subjective opinion that could be noted and passed over except for one large implication: that the searcher for the "true principles" of Hamilton's politics must not look into *The Federalist* lest he find too reasonable, too republican, and too constitutional a man. This, it seems to me, is one of the worst of the many bad judgments that have been passed on the mind and character of this admittedly perplexing man. A reading of all his other papers, both public and private, in the broad field of political science has convinced me that Hamilton as Publius was neither a devious nor an eccentric nor a dishonest Hamilton. While he argued the case for a plan of government he would not have written himself, it was a plan under which he was fully prepared to live and to hazard his fortunes. While he sang the praises of arrangements tuned about one-half as high as he would have tuned them himself, he did it with the aid of insights and maxims, of principles and prejudices, indeed of a psychology and sociology of politics, which were the core of his science of government. Hamilton as Publius was the real Hamilton, a political thinker who drew on a supply of basic principles that he had been drawing on for years—even on June 18, 1787—and would draw on to his death. The irrationality of political man, the blessings of political energy, the curse of anarchy, the need for order, the limited reach of popular judgment—all these and a dozen other underlying themes of his contribution to *The Federalist* are forthright restatements of his basic principles. Even the gap between the speech of June 18, 1787 and the most republican of his musings as Publius is not one-quarter as large as some critics would have it. I think it important to say this clearly before we get to chapters 4–6: Except for a few rhetorical flourishes—and every advocate is entitled to a few—the tough yet not despairing political theory that runs through Hamilton's fifty-odd contributions to *The Federalist* is the same political theory that carried him through his mature life.

HAMILTON's second service to the Constitution in this year was his resourceful command of the forces favoring ratification in New York, forces strong in influence but weak in numbers which he led from the likelihood of defeat through the near-certainty of stalemate to the actuality of victory. His total performance in the course of this struggle is grist for the mill of scholars who insist that there is such a thing as "the hero in history," that a determined and lucky man can occasionally bend events to his own purposes.

The likelihood of defeat for the Constitution lay embedded in the pattern of New York politics. The recalcitrance of Yates and Lansing at Philadelphia was no display of eccentricity; it was, rather, the consequence of a powerful parochialism that had gripped most of the politicians of New York, especially those in the upstate counties, ever since the war had begun to draw to a close and men like Hamilton had begun to talk of a more perfect Union. Hamilton must have known long before September 17, 1787 that the fight for ratification in his own state would be hard and chancy. While he may have been cautiously optimistic about the cause of the Constitution in the United States generally,[102] he must have been thinking only of his friends and followers in the city, or perhaps just whistling in the dark, when he wrote Washington in October, 1787 that "the prospect thus far is favorable to it." [103] A few days later he had to admit that "the event cannot yet be foreseen."

> The constitution proposed has in this state warm friends and warm enemies. The first impressions everywhere are in its favor; but the artillery of its opponents makes some impression.[104]

The artillery of its chief foe, the doughty Governor Clinton, had gone into action only ten days after the adjournment when the first of a series of letters by Cato appeared in the strongly anti-Federalist *New-York Journal*. Hamilton got off his first shot as Publius in reply one month later; lesser gunners from each side—including Detector, Baptist, Roderick Razor, One of the Nobility, Brutus, Sidney, Constant Reader, and Rough Hewer—began to fire at will; and by early November the war of words was at its peak. Words, however, were not votes, and the real war was already being fought with promises, pleas, and threats in courthouses, law offices, taverns, and private homes. Hamilton and his friends had to persuade the legislature to call for a convention, to persuade the voters to elect delegates favorable (or at least not angrily opposed) to the new Constitution, and to persuade the convention itself to take the right action. This, in George Clinton's state, would add up to a lot of persuading.

The key figure in the opening stages was Clinton himself. To this day no one can say for certain what he had in mind to do about the difficult question put to the states by the Convention September 17, 1787 and put again by Congress September 28.[105] While he was a states'-righter who wished that the Convention had never been held at all, he was not a disunionist who would reject its work so recklessly as to hazard a dissolution of the Republic or, more to the point, either an isolation of New York from the other states or a secession of Federalist New York City from the upstate counties. What one can say is that he dragged his feet as long as he could, hoping in vain that five other states would reject the Constitution and thus relieve New York of the burden of acting one way or another; sat by while the regular session of the legislature wrangled, writhed, and finally resolved on February 1, 1788 to hold a special election of delegates to a convention;[106] went into this election, which was set for late April (and was open to "all free male citizens of the age of twenty-one years upwards"), with every nerve strained to produce a majority opposed to the Constitution; and came out of it in early June with a majority so overwhelming (46–19)[107] that even Hamilton was stunned for the moment into expressing to Madison his "fear" of an "eventual disunion and civil war."[108] Only for the moment, however: a few days later he wrote from the prospective field of battle at Poughkeepsie that, despite all the blows the cause of Union had suffered, "the thing is not despaired of."[109]

The thing was not despaired of for two good reasons: first, because Hamilton was Hamilton and did not despair easily at this stage of his life; and second, because the group rallied around Clinton was something less than monolithic in its distaste for the Constitution and something less than cocksure about the best way to reject it without damaging the status and interests of New York. Clinton himself would probably have disagreed with his friend James M. Hughes, who wrote gleefully from Poughkeepsie that "the number of antis astonish the Federalists and they look on their case as desperate."[110] By now he had come to know Hamilton well enough to realize that the "little Great Man," however "slender" his "chance of success" might appear, had not come to Poughkeepsie simply to be annihilated.[111]

The Convention that met in the courthouse at Poughkeepsie June 17, 1788 was an assembly of most of the talents that New York had to offer in those days.[112] The minority of Federalists, as the friends of the Constitution had come to be known (to the disgust of Clinton and his colleagues), included Hamilton, John Jay, John Sloss Hobart, James Duane, Richard Harison, Richard Morris, and, as nominal leader, R. R. Livingston. The nineteen men who made up this minority were all from the area in and around New York City. The majority of anti-Federalists included Clinton, Yates, Lansing, Gilbert Livingston, John Williams, Samuel Jones, and, as one of the delegates from Dutchess County (since he had no hope of being elected in his county of residence, New York), that lawyer, merchant, and politician of no mean parts, Melancton Smith. The forty-six men of this majority were from the upstate counties, Queens, and Suffolk. The line between Federalism and anti-Federalism was sharply drawn on the map of New York. Despite Clinton's division of the delegates into the "Friends to the Rights of Mankind" and the "Advocates of Despotism," [113] the line was not at all sharply drawn in the minds of many New Yorkers. Even Clinton professed himself to be "open to conviction." [114]

In the end, three men came to dominate the proceedings. One was Hamilton, who from first to last was recognized as the real leader of the Federalists, not least because he was the only New Yorker who had signed the Constitution. The second was Clinton, who chose to have himself elected presiding officer, and thus took himself at least halfway out of the open fight. The third was Smith, on whom much of the responsibility for the anti-Federalist cause devolved as a result of Clinton's desire to play the role of a Washington (but without Washington's majestic style and inflexible purpose). The story of the Poughkeepsie Convention is, in essence, one in which the first of these men hammers incessantly upon the third to change his mind while the second refuses to give the lead to his own followers that will mean outright rejection of the Constitution. If Hamilton had been more cautious and less tactful, if Smith had been more vain and less reasonable, or if Clinton had been more obstinate in his dislike of the Constitution and less concerned about the possible consequences of a quick and adverse decision, the Convention must surely have followed its real desires and voted New York at least temporarily out of the "more perfect Union."

Let us summarize the position as it must have appeared to Hamilton as he sat in his rooms in Poughkeepsie and made ready for the struggle. Working in favor of eventual ratification of the Constitution were the following facts: a hard core of Federalist delegates who were men of status and influence, and who, though in a minority, could be counted on to hold firm for the cause; a concrete proposal of obvious merit, to which Washington and Franklin had put their names; the signed and sealed ratifications of eight states, including the crucial states of Pennsylvania and Massachusetts and the neighboring states of New Jersey and Connecticut; the hoped-for ratifications of two more, Virginia and New Hampshire; the shadings of opinion among the opponents of the Constitution, some of whom were open to persuasion; and Hamilton's own iron determination to win approval for the Constitution, if not now then in Governor Clinton's good time. Working against ratification was, as I have said, the long-term political situation in New York, a state more powerfully affected by local sentiments than any other, even Rhode Island, in all the shaky Union. The forty-six "antis" may not have been entirely of one mind, as were the nineteen Federalists, but they formed a barrier that must have seemed imposing to Hamilton even in his most sanguine mood.

These being the forces working for and against the fondest public hope Hamilton had ever entertained, six courses of action (or inaction) must have presented themselves as possibilities: 1) immediate adjournment (with little debate and no decision), 2) adjournment after several weeks (with much debate and still no decision), 3) outright rejection, 4) ratification with conditions (that is, with amendments that would have to be accepted by the other states before New York's vote could be counted), 5) ratification with recommendations (the practice adopted in several other states), and 6) outright ratification. The first and second of these prospects Hamilton found displeasing but at least endurable, if only as something better and less final than rejection. The third and fourth (which would now, because of the unconditional ratification of the other states, amount to the same thing) he saw as an invitation to disaster both for the Union and New York. The sixth was a delightful but altogether utopian prospect. The fifth was, in the end, the one course on which he could concentrate all his energies.

TO achieve this second best of all possible endings one tactic had to be successfully pursued and one small miracle duly passed. The tactic was to keep the Convention in session as long as necessary or possible, which meant persuading Clinton and his friends that the becoming thing to do was to examine the Constitution clause by clause. The miracle was to win over twelve or so of the most reasonable, pliable, or merely uncertain anti-Federalists.

The success of the tactic was assured in the beginning when Clinton, for all his stubborn hostility a man with doubts, worries, and regard for the Union, failed to sound the call for retreat, and the delegates in both camps agreed to R. R. Livingston's motion that the Constitution, as well as all proposed amendments, be "considered clause by clause." [115] The miracle, small but gratifying, was passed in the end when Smith himself was persuaded to step gingerly across the line into the camp of ratification—and with him came such prominent anti-Federalists as Gilbert Livingston, Samuel Jones, and Zephaniah Platt. The conversion of Smith was the most notable success of Hamilton's checkered career as politician, for at the beginning of the Convention no one would have predicted—unless it were Smith himself in a moment of piercing self-analysis—that the floor leader of the anti-Federalists would be counted with the Federalists in each of three key votes at the end. Yet converted and counted he was, and it is hard to see what agency other than the persuasive talents of Hamilton brought about this astounding result.

This is, to be sure, a matter of some conjecture, for the documents in the case are, once again, distressingly few. We can read in the records of the Convention the rough outline of the intellectual conversion of Smith and his friends.[116] What we cannot read, because few men in those days saved scraps of paper or published their memoirs, are the details of the personal conversion. This assembly of distinguished New Yorkers was noted, by and large, for its courtesy across the sharp line that ran between Hamilton and Clinton. Smith was, as James Kent (an eyewitness to the proceedings) * testified in later years, a man "of the most gentle, liberal, and amiable disposition"; [117] Hamilton was never more tactful and gallant than he was at this critical moment of his life; [118] and the opportunities for exercising the arts of private persuasion were many and easily taken. That he took them is evident in a letter of Charles Tillinghast to his father-in-law John Lamb of June 21, 1788, in which Hamilton, Livingston, and Jay were said to be "continually singling out the Members in opposition (when out of convention) and conversing with them on the subject." [119] There were plenty of obdurate anti-Federalists ("a set of ignorant Dutchmen," one admirer of Hamilton called them in private) [120] who never opened their mouths and never failed to vote "no," but Smith, as he demonstrated in his first speech, was not one of them. The wonder is that

* Unlike the Convention of 1787, this meeting was open at all times to the public.[121]

Clinton and his cohorts handed over the burden of debate to a man with whom Hamilton could talk so easily, whether in public or private,* and who never wandered from the standard of reasonableness he raised at the outset. In the words of the recorder:

Mr. SMITH again rose. He most heartily concurred in sentiment with the honorable gentleman who opened the debate yesterday that the discussion of the important question now before them ought to be entered on with a spirit of patriotism, with minds open to conviction, with a determination to form opinions only on the merits of the question, from those evidences which should appear in the course of the investigation.[122]

This point of courtesy deserves elaboration, for it is worth pondering the implications of the fact that Hamilton scored his sweetest victory as a political leader in a well-mannered climate—amazingly well-mannered when we recall the size of the bets on the table. So far as the records show, there were only three occasions in the course of these six weeks when tempers got a little out of control. The first, in which Hamilton had a hand, took place June 28, and was touched off by what Stephen Potter would admire as an anti-Clinton "ploy," a decision to read into the record a number of speeches, resolutions, and messages of 1780–1782 in which the Governor and his faithful followers had lamented "the want of powers in Congress" and pointed out "the defects of the Confederation."[123] If it did nothing else, this action forced Clinton to declare openly and "solemnly" that he was "a friend to strong and efficient government," and was anxious only lest this particular plan "destroy the liberties of the people."

The second, in which Hamilton was involved through no choice of his own, came at the end of the same day—obviously a long, hot Saturday in Poughkeepsie—and spilled over into Monday. It was the first of many occasions in which the speech of June 18, 1787 was to be used against him as the years passed and he rose to power. Let the record of the Convention, too contracted and entertaining to be paraphrased, speak for itself:

The Hon. Mr. LANSING. . . . It has been admitted by an honorable gentleman from New York, (Mr. Hamilton) that the state governments are necessary to secure the liberties of the people. He has urged several forcible reasons why they ought to be preserved under the new system; and he has treated the idea of the general and state governments being hostile to each other as

---

* Tillinghast seems to have said something more than he intended to say when he told Lamb in his letter of June 21: "I can assure you that Mr. Smith and Mr. Lansing keeps close to Hamilton." Much too close, so it turned out, for a man a good deal more reasonable than the obdurate Lansing.

chimerical. I am, however, firmly persuaded that an hostility between them will exist. This was a received opinion in the late Convention at Philadelphia. That honorable gentleman was then fully convinced that it would exist, and argued, with much decision and great plausibility, that the state governments ought to be subverted, at least so far as to leave them only corporate rights, and that, even in that situation, they would endanger the existence of the general government. But the honorable gentleman's reflections have probably induced him to correct that sentiment.

[Mr. Hamilton here interrupted Mr. Lansing, and contradicted, in the most positive terms, the charge of inconsistency included in the preceding observations. This produced a warm personal altercation between those gentlemen, which engrossed the remainder of the day.]

Monday, *June* 30, 1788.—The personal dispute between Mr. Hamilton and Mr. Lansing was again brought forward, and occupied the attention of the committee for a considerable part of this day.[124]

One wonders how much more about Hamilton's manner, character, and views we would know if this whole proceeding—described in the *Maryland Gazette* as a "warm turn" in the convention [125]—had been recorded, not to mention taped or televised. This was not the only occasion in this year of give-and-take over ratification on which Hamilton had to defend himself against personal attack. The quarrel with Washington came back to plague him in October, 1787, and he was moved to ask his old commander for a denial of the "insinuation that I *palmed* myself off on you, and that you *dismissed* me from your family." [126] This Washington gave him explicitly and graciously,[127] and meanwhile kept locked in his discreet bosom the true story of Hamilton's behavior of February, 1781.

The third descent from the plateau of good manners at Poughkeepsie took place July 2, when Chancellor Livingston was called to task by a battery of anti-Federalists for "haranguing the committee" with a "torrent of illiberality." Livingston himself managed to dampen the fires of partisan zeal with another torrent in which friendly apologies and stout reaffirmations of principle were cleverly mixed together. All in all, however, it was a meeting marked by good will as well as good manners, and Hamilton, who knew how to be as charming as any man alive, could not have asked for a more suitable climate in which to exploit his talents. It is recorded that the Federalists and their opponents dined at different taverns the night of July 4, and that there was much friendly visiting between the two groups.[128] It can be imagined that Hamilton seized this occasion of "delicacy and politeness" to turn his charm, and also his powers of persuasion, upon Smith and the other wavering Clintonians.

However he may have carried himself off the floor, he was at his parliamentary best on it. His longest recorded speeches [129]—one on the defects of the Confederation, one on representation in the proposed House, two (on successive days) on the proposed Senate, and two on taxation—were masterpieces of the art of persuading small groups of reasonable men. They were aimed right over the heads of the stubborn, silent Clintonians at the sensible minds of men like Smith and Gilbert Livingston, and they were full of arguments from experience and reason that were hard to parry. Smith, to his credit, was not afraid to acknowledge openly the force of many of Hamilton's arguments. One witness to the opening debate described the give-and-take of these two men in this way:

The first objections were stated by Mr. Smith, with a long and labored introduction. The American Cicero then rose, the force of whose *eloquence* and reasoning were irresistable. The objections that were made vanished before him; he remained an hour and twenty minutes on the floor;—after which Mr. Smith with great candor, got up, and after some explanations, confessed that Mr. Hamilton had, by his reasoning, removed the objections he had made, respecting the apportioning, the representation and direct taxes. Several of the anti-federal members are not so prejudiced as we feared. Much depends on the conduct of a few GREAT MEN.[130]

Hamilton's speeches were also full of the persistent themes of his political and constitutional thought: the frailty and perversity of human nature, the difficulties and yet also the joys of popular government, the necessity of guarding against abuses of power and yet also of using power for great ends, the fatal weakness of confederate governments forced to depend upon constituent states for money and the use of force, the importance of order to society and of energy to government, the curse of faction and the omnipresence of private interests, the inevitability that a constitution created by compromise would be imperfect and the necessity that any constitution designed to last "should consist only of general provisions," and above all the insistence that liberty and authority could be brought into a tolerable balance in an extended republic.[131] The Hamilton of Poughkeepsie was the best of all possible Hamiltons, not alone as politician and rhetorician but also as political scientist.* Smith might comment,

* During his lifetime, and especially at the end of it, Hamilton was given a full measure of credit for the triumph at Poughkeepsie. In the golden words of the Reverend John M. Mason, who pronounced the funeral oration to his brethren in the Society of the Cincinnati: "He argued, he remonstrated, he entreated, he warned, he painted till apathy itself was moved, and the most relentless of human things, a preconcerted majority, was staggered and broken. Truth was again victorious, and New-York enrolled herself under the Federal standard." [132]

politely as usual, that "few observations" had "fallen from the gentleman which appear to be new,"[133] and Clinton might complain to a confidant that "the most that has been said by the new Government Men, has been only a second Edition of Publius, well delivered";[134] but this is only to say that Hamilton was the most penetrating of political scientists at Poughkeepsie, that the words he spoke were those he had already given to posterity in *The Federalist,* and that *The Federalist* itself was the chief ammunition dump of the forces favoring ratification. The thoughts of Publius were there for any of his comrades to use, and if they needed any new thoughts or any new ways of putting old ones—as Chancellor Livingston apparently did for the declamation that opened the Convention—Hamilton's pen was free for the asking.

The hero makes history occasionally, but history makes the hero always. However casually the anti-Federalists could pass off New Hampshire's ratification (which was learned of in Poughkeepsie June 24),[135] they were jammed down hard on the horns of their dilemma by word of Virginia's favorable action. Thanks to Hamilton's foresight and willingness to dig into his own only half-filled pocket,[136] the good news from Richmond reached Poughkeepsie July 2.[137] At once he must have pressed home with the argument that New York could not afford to be isolated politically from a full ten other states, and also raised the specter of the secession of New York City and some of the southern counties in order to join the nearly perfected Union.[138] The anti-Federalists were now forced to take some action on the Constitution; adjournment was no longer a way out of their troubles.[139]

From here to the happy end of the Convention July 26 Hamilton threaded his way with nimble feet through a maze of amendments, motions, and resolutions.[140] He was neither arrogant nor obstinate; in fact, on several occasions he seemed almost too willing to compromise.[141] In particular, he was not as certain as he should have been that conditional ratification was now, after the ninth state had been recorded in favor of the Constitution, simply a backhanded vote for rejection. Perhaps at the bidding of his cohorts, he asked Madison's opinion July 19 on the legality of the kind of ratification that now seemed the best way out to the anti-Federalists—"*conditions subsequent,* or the proposition of amendments upon condition, that if they are not adopted within a limited time, the state shall be at liberty to *withdraw* from the Union"[142]—and back it came by the next post from New York, to which Madison had now returned:

I am sorry that your situation obliges you to listen to propositions of the nature you describe. My opinion is that a reservation of a right to withdraw if amendments be not decided on under the form of the Constitution within a certain time, is a *conditional* ratification; that it does not make New York a member of the new Union, and consequently that she could not be received on that plan. . . . The Constitution requires an adoption *in toto* and *for ever*.[143]

Thus braced by his friend (or gently chastised?), Hamilton now threw all his energies into squeezing out a majority favorable to "ratification with recommendations." In a burst of "argumentative and impassioned" eloquence on July 12 he had already made his case for this manner of ratification, and had begged his fellow delegates "to make a solemn pause . . . before they decided on a subject so infinitely important."[144] Following up with an audacious gamble on July 16—a motion to adjourn in order to take a new reading of sentiment for and against the Union, which the Clintonians were obliged to vote down 40–22[145]—he pressed home the attack in public and private. Sometime in these few days Smith, Platt, and the other open-minded anti-Federalists began to crack,[146] and in two crucial votes July 23 and 25 the victory was secured.

The question put July 23 was on the motion of Samuel Jones, himself elected as an anti-Federalist, that the words "in full confidence" be substituted for "on condition" in the form of ratification. The vote of 31–29 found Smith, Platt, Gilbert Livingston, Jones, and eight other pliable anti-Federalists voting with Hamilton and his eighteen loyal colleagues.[147] (It is revealing that five anti-Federalists had dropped out of the proceedings—but not one Federalist.) The question put July 25 was on a last-ditch motion of Lansing's "that there should be reserved to the state of New York a right to withdraw herself *from the Union* after a certain number of years, unless the amendments proposed should previously be submitted to a general convention." It was defeated 31–28 by roughly the same combination of sure Federalists and unsure anti-Federalists.[148] The final vote of July 26, which was a formality and yet too close a thing for Hamilton to take lightly, was 30–27 in favor of unconditional ratification. Clinton himself abstained from this vote,* but Yates and Lansing, and with them all the delegates from the counties north and west of Poughkeepsie, went down to defeat with the flag of a sovereign New York still flying.[149]

The form of ratification was "unconditional" only in a technical sense, for Hamilton and his colleagues had agreed to a declaration of rights,

* But not from the key votes of July 23 and 25, on which he voted against the Federalists.

a list of thirty-two amendments, and a circular letter to the governors of all the states calling for a general convention to revise the Constitution—this last concession doubtless proving decisive in the attempt to persuade Smith.[150] Several of his friends, including Washington and Madison, wondered if he had not himself been too pliable, and thus had opened the way to the one event no Federalist could bear to think about, a second convention.[151] But Hamilton was the man in the frying pan, and his judgment of the extent to which compromise was necessary to produce a paper-thin majority was probably as accurate as any man's could be in such fickle circumstances.* History, in any case, proved him right and his friends wrong; the move for a second convention never got off the ground.[152]

The close of this splendid period in Hamilton's life found him, of all places, back in Congress, which was now sitting quietly, and with no premonition of immortality, in New York. Having been elected by the legislature January 22, 1788, and having taken his seat February 25,[153] he put in few appearances until the great work had been accomplished at Poughkeepsie. From then until mid-October, when Congress lay down and died, he was a surprisingly faithful participant in the business before it, especially the business of making ready for the new government under the new Constitution.† What part he hoped to play in that government we cannot say, although we certainly can guess. No one who knew how hard he had worked to make it a reality could doubt that he would be in it—and not too far from the top. The editor of the *New Hampshire Spy* predicted that he would be New York's next governor, but those who knew him more intimately saw him entering in full panoply onto the "noble field" of "the new Constitution." The sight, one friend of Hamilton's confessed to another, "would almost persuade me to be in love with a Republick against my better judgment." [154]

---

* That Hamilton was alert to opinion outside as well as inside the Convention is demonstrated by his vote with the minority against Jay's easily-passed motion of July 25 providing that the President, Vice-President, and members of Congress be freeholders.

That opinion outside the Convention judged him to be its leader was demonstrated in a parade in honor of the impending ratification on July 23 in New York City. The highlight of the parade was a miniature ship—with spotless sails and thundering guns—named the *Alexander Hamilton*.[155]

† A good deal of his time seems to have been spent voting "no" to proposals to shift the seat of the new government away from New York.[156]

THREE

HAMILTON AND THE CONSTITUTION:

1789 – 1804

> *"The powers contained in a constitution of government . . . ought to be construed liberally in advancement of the public good."*
> Hamilton to Washington, in the Opinion on the Constitutionality of the Bank of the United States, February 23, 1791

HAMILTON knew that the encounters at Philadelphia, Poughkeepsie, and Richmond were only probing skirmishes in a struggle over the power of the central government that would be fought, often with passion and occasionally even with intent to kill, so long as the United States remained a federal Union. He also knew that the next phase of this struggle, the first few years under the Constitution, would set the stage for all other phases to come. The Constitution was a spider's web of words about whose meaning no two men, not even Hamilton and the faithful Rufus King, had agreed exactly. The words would have to be given content by men ready to use them in concrete situations,[1] and thus the whole Constitution be launched on a course from which men of contrary mind would find it hard to turn back. We do not know whether Hamilton had ever read *Don Quixote;* if he had, he might well have pinned to his study wall the advice of Sancho Panza that "the main point in this point of government is to make a good beginning." His hopes for an American empire rode upon a government of energy and tone, his hopes for such a government on a spacious view of the

71

Constitution, and his hopes for everything—glorious nation, splendid government, indulgent Constitution—on the kind of beginning the friends of the Union would now make. He therefore pressed Washington almost brazenly to do his duty and accept the Presidency, rejoiced to hear of his friend Madison's election to the House of Representatives, and made clear to all stalwart Federalists that their labors for a united America had only begun in Philadelphia and in the state conventions.[2]

Hamilton had to wait for what, in his nation-building mood of 1788 and 1789, must have seemed an eternity before he could begin his own labors for the Union in a public capacity. The Confederation Congress signed its death warrant September 13, 1788 by setting a timetable for the election of the President and both a date ("the first Wednesday in March next," that is, March 4, 1789) and a place ("the present seat of Congress," that is, New York) for "commencing proceedings" under the new Constitution.[3] Roads being what they were in the new Republic, and weather being what it still is in February and March, a quorum of both the House and Senate was not gathered until April 6. It was April 23 before Washington, who had to wait at Mount Vernon to be notified officially of his election, could get to New York, April 30 before he could be sworn in as first President of the United States.[4] Congress had already gone to work under Madison's prodding on measures to produce revenue,[5] and Washington was soon at work, too, sifting out the names of the Federalists—some stalwart and others merely hopeful—who were being pressed upon him for the executive and judicial positions which, it was anticipated cheerfully by one and all, would be created in the course of the year.

It would be pleasant to have unimpeachable evidence that Hamilton, who lived within easy walking distance of both the President and the Congressman from Virginia,* worked closely with them throughout these first months when they were in office and he waited in the wings for his office to be set up, but such evidence as we have is scanty and circumstantial, for example, Washington's request of Adams, Madison, Hamilton, and Jay that they favor him with advice on presidential etiquette.[6] As the cherished colleague of both Washington and Madison, and also of Sen-

---

* For the amusement of those who frequent the lower reaches of Manhattan, it may be noted that Hamilton lived at 57 Wall Street (and probably worked at 58), Madison boarded at 19 Maiden Lane, and Washington was assigned the former residence of the President of Congress at 3 Cherry Street (a spot obliterated in the building of the Brooklyn Bridge). The seat of the new government was Federal Hall, long since demolished and replaced by the old Sub-Treasury building on the northeast corner of Wall and Nassau Streets. Washington moved to 39–41 Broadway, just south of Trinity Church, on Washington's Birthday, 1790.[7]

ators like Read and Ellsworth and Representatives like Theodore Sedgwick and Egbert Benson, Hamilton must surely have been granted "the
right to be consulted, the right to encourage, the right to warn." It was
not at all his fault, merely a by-product of the frugality of the Constitution, that the positions to which he could reasonably aspire had to be established by statute. One can easily imagine—to imagine the contrary is
preposterous—that he had a useful hand in many of the activities of the
first four months under the Constitution, especially in the creation of
machinery to handle the fiscal affairs of the new government.[8] One can,
however, give Hamilton no firm credit—and must give Madison credit in
abundance [9]—for the fruits of this historic first session of Congress: the
Excise and Tonnage Acts; the acts creating the Departments of State,
Treasury, and War; the Judiciary Act; and, of course, the resolutions proposing those amendments to the Constitution we cherish as the Bill of
Rights.[10] With neither this neat package of organic legislation, nor with
the techniques through which Madison took the lead in putting most
of it together, could Hamilton find much fault. Madison's broad interpretation of the President's power of removal, which was made in the
debate over the tenure of the Secretary of State, and his insistence upon
putting one man rather than a board over the operations of the Treasury
must have been especially gratifying to Hamilton,[11] who doubtless did
a good deal in private to persuade wavering friends to cast their votes with
Madison. The most telling arguments against setting up a three-man board
to conduct the financial business of the new government were presented
by Hamilton's close friend Elias Boudinot, who followed faithfully the
line laid down in the letter to Duane of September 3, 1780.[12]

The only sharp point of difference between Hamilton and Madison in
these first months was over the question whether provisions to discriminate against ships and merchandise of countries having no commercial treaties with the United States (in other words, Great Britain)
should be placed in the Tonnage Act. Madison did his best to win assent
to such provisions; Hamilton made clear that he considered such a step
a mistake. Madison finally lost out on this issue, but whether Hamilton
had a hidden hand in the defeat no one can say.[13] We can say for certain
that Madison advised Washington to take Hamilton into his official family
as head of the proposed Department of the Treasury.[14] Since Robert
Morris was also in the corner of this "damned sharp" young man whose
"reputation" was already "the boast of America," [15] and was apparently
not interested in the job himself,[16] Hamilton must have known in the
middle of the summer that he had been singled out for the Treasury.[17]

For Hamilton the happiest days of this session of Congress, which were a long time coming, were September 2, when the Department of the Treasury was established in law, and September 11, when his nomination as first head of this Department was confirmed with rare dispatch by the Senate.[18] The second of these days found him, as might be expected, sitting at his desk,[19] and when Congress adjourned September 29 it left him hard at work on a request of the House of Representatives to report a "plan" at the "next meeting" for the "support of public credit as a matter of high importance to the national honor and prosperity." [20] For a man who had studied the intricacies of public finance in the field and mastered them in the old Congress, who might have been a Senator or even the first Chief Justice and yet held out for the hottest spot in the new government,[21] such a request was pure joy to honor.

When Congress met again in January, 1790, the Secretary of the Treasury, who seems to have done his first creative stint of work without consulting Washington,[22] was ready for action. On January 9, according to the Journal of the House:

A letter from Alexander Hamilton, Secretary of the Treasury, was read, informing the House that, agreeably to their resolution of the 21st of September, he had prepared a Plan for the support of the Public Credit, and that he was ready to report the same to this House, when they should be pleased to receive it.

It was proposed that Thursday next be assigned for this purpose.[23]

Hamilton asked for the privilege of making an oral report in full knowledge that the House, over Madison's protest, had already rejected this "indelicate" and "dictatorial" technique in the discussion that led to the act of September 2, 1789.[24] So anxious was he to make use of the parliamentary talents he had displayed at Poughkeepsie that he now hazarded a rebuff; and, despite the efforts of his loyal friends Boudinot and Benson, he got it.

On the question, the resolution for receiving the report of the Secretary of the Treasury in writing, was carried in the affirmative.[25]

Thus passed away the opportunity, which at best was fleeting, for Hamilton to exercise the arts of legislative leadership under the public eye and perhaps bend the Constitution toward some form of parliamentary government. The Report on the Public Credit was delivered "Thursday next" in writing.[26] Hamilton had spoken for the last time in a popular assembly; the principle of the separation of powers had been given an early and somewhat unexpected stiffening.

This famous Report brought an abrupt end to the spirit of good will that had reigned in the first session of Congress [27] and to the partnership of Hamilton and Madison that had endured through more than seven historic years.[28] Only after the hardest kind of legislative struggle, indeed after seven months of mounting anger, four adverse votes in the House, and one memorable deal among Hamilton, Madison, and Jefferson,[29] were Hamilton's proposals for funding the national debt and assuming state debts enacted into law. He had exerted every political skill he owned to produce this favorable result, and both his friends and enemies had been made aware of his commitment to the Union—and of his commitment to those "descriptions" of men he found best suited to conduct its affairs. William Maclay, the model of all unreconstructed Senators, observed tartly a few months later: "Congress may go home. Mr. Hamilton is all-powerful, and fails in nothing he attempts." [30] While this was the exaggerated comment of a bitter enemy, it does give some idea of the impact Hamilton had on Congress, even when it chose to rebuff or harass him, throughout his more than five years in office. If his measures and methods, in John Marshall's words, "seemed to unchain all those fierce passions which a high respect for the government and for those who administered it, had in great measure restrained," [31] this was a price he was willing to pay for a more perfect Union.

IT is not necessary to our purpose to trace Hamilton's footsteps as he moved along the highroad of power, sometimes like a ballet dancer and other times like a fullback, in these five heady years. The political, financial, diplomatic, and personal battles he fought as Secretary of the Treasury with the leaders of the opposition, notably Jefferson and Madison, have been drawn in detail by a host of able historians; so, too, has every last shading of the fascinating relationship between him and Washington. We need only take note that many of these battles were also constitutional in nature, that they added up to a decisive five-year war over the meaning of the Constitution of 1787, and that out of it Hamilton emerged the undoubted victor. In one sense, every falling-out he had with the Jeffersonians, no matter how petty the issue, was a conflict of constitutional principle. The habit of beating one's enemies over the head with the Constitution—or, rather, with the "un-Constitution"—had become entrenched in American minds during the Revolutionary period, and the habit had become so compulsive by 1792, especially among men who were on the defensive against Hamilton's assaults, that Fisher Ames could write with both feeling and accuracy: "The practice of crying out this is unconstitutional, is a vice that has grown inveterate by indulgence." * Hamilton could ignore much of the crying-out of "unconstitutional" against his measures because he knew that the men who cried it really meant to say "wrongheaded" or "wicked."

On at least five occasions when he locked horns with the opposition, however, the Constitution itself was at issue, and on every occasion in which the battle was fought to a decision—whether it had to be made finally by Congress, the President, or the Supreme Court—Hamilton's enlarged view of the purposes of the Constitution prevailed over the restrictive views of Jefferson and Madison.

The first of these occasions took on the character of a constitutional struggle only in retrospect, yet it was an important one for Hamilton to have won. While his proposal that the national government assume the unpaid Revolutionary debts of the states was attacked in Congress as immoral and impolitic, it drew only desultory fire on the issue of its conformity with the Constitution. Hamilton himself had found it unnecessary in his Report to point to the constitutional sources of the power of Congress both to fund the national debt and to assume the state debts.†

James Madison, after all, had virtually invented the policy of federal assumption of state debts in 1783,[32] and if it was considered constitutionally possible for Congress to take such a step under the Articles of Confederation, certainly no reasonable man would argue—and Madison never did argue—that it had become impossible under the Constitution of 1787. The legislature of Virginia, however, was in no mood to be reasonable. Outraged by Hamilton's success in putting through his schemes for securing the public credit, it jumped right over Madison's head and adopted a resolution of protest in which assumption was stigmatized as "repugnant" to the Constitution.[33]

Hamilton did not even wait for this protest to be acted upon finally and sent on to Congress before fashioning his reply. Writing to John Jay, who was now Chief Justice, November 13, 1790, he said of the reaction in Virginia:

* To which he added, with more feeling and less accuracy: "And those cry out most frequently who were opposed to its adoption." [34]

† His only direct appeal to the Constitution in the First Report on the Public Credit was to brand any discrimination between original and current holders of securities as a violation of Article VI, section 1, thus proving that he, too, had learned to brandish the stick of unconstitutionality.[35]

This is the first symptom of a spirit which must either be killed, or it will kill the Constitution of the United States. I send the resolutions to you, that it may be considered what ought to be done. Ought not the collective weight of the different parts of the government to be employed in exploding the principles they contain? This question arises out of sudden and undigested thought.[36]

So "sudden and undigested" had his thinking been that he did not even pause, as he would have done later in his career as expounder of the Constitution, to think about the impropriety of dragging the Court into an affair of a nonjudicial nature—or, indeed, about the loss of dignity the national government might suffer in tilting aimlessly with a state legislature. Life for Jay on a court with no business was much easier than was life for Hamilton in an executive position with no boundaries, and the Chief Justice was able to cool off his impetuous friend by advising him not to treat Virginia's words "as very important" lest he "render them more so than I think they are." "The assumption will do its own work," he added. "It will justify itself and not want advocates." [37] The assumption, as history records, did its own work, and did it perhaps more effectively and less cruelly than the funding system. In persisting doggedly all through 1790 in his demand for this particular plank in his platform of public credit, Hamilton had struck almost casually a stout blow for the broad, nationalistic, consolidating view of the Constitution.

On the second occasion the Constitution was so directly at issue that one can cock an alert ear and hear the distant thunder of the struggle still reverberating in our constitutional system. I speak, of course, of the conflict over the meaning of the Constitution touched off December 13, 1790 by Hamilton's response to a command of the House dated August 9 "to prepare and report . . . such further provision as may . . . be necessary for establishing the public credit." [38] The response was a proposal that Congress incorporate a national bank to serve as fiscal agent for the Treasury, to facilitate payment of taxes, to control the operations of state banks, to provide a secure depository for government funds, to issue bank notes that would serve as the principal currency of the United States, and generally to stimulate the flow of capital into and around the country.[39] Some of these services were explicitly described in his message, some were left for friends and enemies of a national bank to conjure up out of the wide spaces between the lines. No one who read this message could deny that, in the Secretary's own words, "a political machine of the greatest importance to the State" was to be built on his careful specifications; no one who read it could guess that a constitutional issue was involved. Once again, and this time it would seem deliberately, Hamilton chose to leave the Constitution out of the discussion.* The issue, he knew, was bound to be raised, but he was not going to be the one to raise it.

The Bank Act of 1791 encountered somewhat less opposition in Congress than the funding-assumption measures of 1790. It was passed in a form completely acceptable to Hamilton by a nearly 3-1 majority in the Senate January 20 and by a nearly 2-1 majority in the House February 8.† The unconstitutionality of this incorporation had been argued strenuously by Madison and others, but Hamilton's friends Ames, Boudinot, Sedgwick, and William Smith, who knew where to go for their arguments, were able to parry "the Father of the Constitution" with little trouble.[40] To show how far Madison and Hamilton had drifted apart on this issue, and indeed how far Madison had retreated from his nationalistic days (including the day he wrote expansively on the "necessary and proper" clause in *The Federalist,* number 44),[41] let us hear the peroration of the first of the Virginian's two major speeches against the proposed bank:

In fine, if the power were in the Constitution, the immediate exercise of it cannot be essential; if not there, the exercise of it involves the guilt of usurpation, and establishes a precedent of interpretation, levelling all the barriers which limit the power of the General Government, and protect those of the State Governments. . . .

It appeared on the whole, he concluded, that the power exercised by the bill was condemned by the silence of the Constitution; was condemned by the rule of interpretation arising out of the Constitution; was condemned by its tendency to destroy the main characteristic of the Constitution; was condemned by the expositions of the friends of the Constitution, whilst depending before the public; was condemned by the apparent intention of the parties which ratified the Constitution; was condemned by the explanatory amendments proposed by Congress themselves to the Constitution; and he hoped it would receive its final condemnation, by the vote of this House.[42]

The field of battle now shifted from the floor of Congress to the mind of George Washington. The President, it is safe to say, was disposed to give his approval to this legislation. He was punctilious in his respect

---

* The only mention of the Constitution is a word of praise for the "additional security to property" that it "happily gives." [43]

† The exact vote was 16–6 in the Senate (all six dissenters from the deep South), 39–20 in the House (fifteen of the twenty dissenters also from the deep South). Most leaders of the South distrusted a strong national government principally because of the fear that such a government would interfere with slavery.[44]

for the judgments of Congress, especially when a judgment had been given by a large majority in both houses; he knew how much this proposal meant to his valued helper in the Treasury Department; and, although his thoughts about the Constitution were neither subtle nor precise, he had always taken the large view of the powers of Congress, whether the old or the new. Yet Madison had also taken this view, and when he could assert so positively that this proposal was "condemned" under any sensible view of the Constitution, Washington, to whom Madison was nearly as cherished a colleague as was Hamilton in 1790 and 1791, hesitated before putting his name to it.

If Madison's orations in Congress made him hesitate, the advice of his Secretary of State and his Attorney General, which was first rendered in at least "two conversations" and then in writing,[45] stopped him dead in his tracks. Jefferson and Randolph both told the President that the United States had no power to incorporate a bank, and that to concede it such a power would "stretch the arm of Congress into the whole circle of state legislation."[46] It must have been a troubled Washington who turned to Hamilton February 16 for his opinion on the "validity and propriety" of this bill. Anxious to play entirely fair with Hamilton, he sent along the objections of Jefferson and Randolph (which he forbade Hamilton to copy); anxious to rebuff Congress in the most courteous manner (if rebuff it he must), he then asked Madison to draft a proper form for returning the bill without his approval.[47] Madison, to his credit as politician, sent back a short draft February 21 that would make it possible for Washington to kill the bank on grounds of either unconstitutionality or unsuitability.[48]

Hamilton, to his renown as constitutionalist, sent back a long opinion— 15,000 of his best words, written at top speed [49]—that made it impossible for Washington to do anything but sign the bill and let the building of the Union proceed. I must put off the details of Hamilton's argument to chapter 6, and confine myself here to the simple assertion, which no constitutional historian now seems disposed to contradict, that the argument was the most forceful ever made for the view that the frugal words of the Constitution of 1787 "ought to be construed liberally in advancement of the public good." [50] The words most heatedly in dispute in this instance were "to lay and collect taxes," "to borrow money," "to regulate commerce," and "to make all laws which shall be necessary and proper for carrying into execution the foregoing powers," and Hamilton spun a web of "implied powers" out of these words that has proved more indestructible with each passing year.

The Opinion on the Constitutionality of the Bank of February 23, 1791 was perhaps the most brilliant and influential one-man effort in the long history of American constitutional law. No man of that time, not even Madison at his most persuasive, could have bested Hamilton in this battle of wits and wills; no man who thought continentally, except Washington at his most obstinate, could have denied the logic of his arguments. It is pleasant to think that Washington, who thought continentally and therefore had no need to prove his obstinacy, breathed a large sigh of relief as he read through the clearheaded yet impassioned opinion of his Secretary of the Treasury, alarming to imagine what the Secretary would have done if his view of the Constitution had not been accepted. For him, but even more surely for the Constitution, this was the moment of truth—a hackneyed phrase and yet a wonderfully exact one—and it was the truth as Hamilton conceived it that became the constitutional policy of the United States. We must honor Washington, in the words of a contemporary newspaper, for the "judgment and prudence" he devoted to this critical decision which he sealed with his signature February 25.[51] Although "every attempt" had been made, according to Hamilton's friend William Smith, "to intercept the Presidential Sanction," the "energetic mind of the great Washington burst from the trammels which had been prepared for him" by the "triumvirate" of Madison, Jefferson, and Randolph.[52] We must honor Hamilton for answering Washington's question about the meaning of the Constitution with an unanswerable question of his own: "Why may not the United States, *constitutionally,* employ the *means,* usual in other countries, for attaining the *ends* intrusted to them?"[53] A man who had only the largest ends in view, he first made of the Constitution a supple means for achieving these or any other reasonable ends that made sense to a "persistent and undoubted" majority of the American people.

ANOTHER of Hamilton's measures was pushed successfully through Congress in these weeks. No strenuous objection on constitutional grounds was raised to the Excise Act of March 3, 1791,[54] which, in laying substantial "duties on spirits distilled within the United States" (that is, a "whisky tax"), made the first domestic use of that clause in the Constitution giving Congress its powers of taxation. It was branded by the opposition—a surprisingly small opposition in this instance, and one in which Madison did not join—as "odious," "oppressive," and "unfriendly to the liberties of the people," but only one or two obstructionists, who had apparently run out of all other arguments, appealed to the Constitution in their efforts to untrack the Secretary of the Treasury.[55] Only in retrospect—partic-

ularly in the form of a backward look by Thomas Jefferson in his draft
of the Kentucky Resolutions [56]—was the hue and cry of unconstitutionality
raised, and once again it would seem that Hamilton had settled a poten-
tially explosive argument over the Constitution even before it could get
started. When Hamilton next asserted the power of Congress to collect
internal revenue, in 1794, some of his own friends, the makers of snuff
and refined sugar, sounded this cry,[57] but he had long since learned to
distinguish real controversies over the meaning of the Constitution from
false ones.

The second time Hamilton went to Congress with a proposal to use
the delegated powers in Article I, section 8 for a large end—once again
at the bidding of Congress [58]—he went with arguments in support of
the constitutionality of his scheme. The Report on Manufactures of
December 5, 1791 was a breath-taking, even visionary set of recommendations for encouraging the growth of commerce and industry
under the benevolent leadership of the national government. Some of
the techniques with which he hoped to stimulate this growth—duties
and prohibitions on imported articles—presented, in his opinion, no
serious question of constitutionality; others—bounties, premiums, aids to
transportation—were sure to be challenged by the strict-constructionists
in the opposition. As far as Hamilton was concerned, "the Legislature
of the Union" had a "constitutional right" to do "all the good that might
be wished," but he was not going to spoil his case, which he knew to be a
tricky one on both political and constitutional grounds, by advertising
his full-blown continental sentiments of June 18, 1787. He therefore
confined himself to wishing "that there was no doubt of the power of the
National Government to lend its direct aid on a comprehensive plan," [59]
and got down to specific words in the Constitution in the one controversial instance of his proposal to pay "pecuniary bounties" to producers
of materials and articles that would stimulate economic growth. The
essence of his argument was that the opening words of Article I,
section 8 gave Congress an almost unfettered power to tax and spend in
pursuit of "objects which concern the general welfare," [60] and thus gave
it the specific power to pay such bounties.

Neither Congress nor the country at large was ready for the advanced political, economic, and constitutional views expressed in the
Report on Manufactures. Hamilton had to be content with modest
tariffs on a variety of articles (everything from "clogs and golo-shoes" to
glass and perfumes), prohibitive tariffs on cotton, hemp, and iron, and
a bounty only for the fishermen of New England.[61] It would be many

years before the struggle over this part of the Constitution would be fully joined, but he had driven the entering wedge for the expansive assumption that the words about "the general welfare of the United States" in the opening paragraph of Article I, section 8 were, in effect, a grant of power to Congress and not merely a gratuitous prologue to the enumerated powers. That he had driven such a wedge, and driven it deeply, is plain in the reactions of both Jefferson and Madison to the constitutional arguments of the Report on Manufactures. To the former, who spoke his mind in private to Washington, Hamilton's proposition seemed to go "far beyond every one ever yet advanced" toward making the Constitution "a very different thing from what the people thought they had submitted to," and had indeed forced men to decide "whether we live under a limited or an unlimited government." [62] From the latter, who had his say on the floor of the House, it evoked a straightforward assertion of the view that the words "general welfare" were simply a "sort of caption or general description of the specific powers" that followed, and had "no further meaning" and gave "no further power" than what could be "found in that specification." "In short, sir," Madison concluded,

I venture to declare it as my opinion, that were the power of Congress to be established in the latitude contended for, it would subvert the very foundation, and transmute the very nature of the limited Government established by the people of America; and what inferences might be drawn, or what consequences ensue from such a step, it is incumbent on us all well to consider.*

Hamilton had already considered these things, had decided that the broad view of the powers of Congress was creative rather than subversive in character, and thus had parted constitutional as well as political company from his old friend forever.

FINALLY, Hamilton never missed an opportunity in his term as Secretary of the Treasury to give a permissive interpretation to the words of Article II in which the powers and status of the President are described. "Energy" stood first, in his opinion, among all the qualities of good government, and energy was to be looked for principally in the executive branch. With-

---

* In the end, Madison was able to vote "aye" on this bill (in opposition to many of his new political friends) by persuading the House to substitute the word "allowance" for "bounty," and by persuading himself that this payment was a "drawback" and thus simply a "regulation of trade" under the commerce power. William Branch Giles and John Page of Virginia were even more positive than Madison in branding Hamilton's interpretation in general and bounties in particular as subversive of the Constitution. [63]

out a strong and dignified Presidency there could be no hope for the new national government; without a permissive Article II there could be no such Presidency.

While opportunities to give substance to the shadows of Article II did not come as often in the first years under the Constitution as Hamilton might have wished, he stood always ready with advice to his chief to take the highroad of strength and dignity. As examples of such advice, he persuaded Washington to extract as much time as reason would permit out of the phrase "ten days" in the clause granting the power of veto; [64] argued in flat contradiction to the opinions of Jefferson, Madison, and Randolph that the President could, on an "extraordinary occasion" (in this instance, the presence of the plague in Philadelphia), specify another city for an anticipated meeting of Congress; [65] asserted the right of the President to deny a Senate request for copies of diplomatic correspondence; [66] asserted his authority to send a special envoy to negotiate a treaty with a foreign country; [67] interpreted statutory grants of the power to borrow money almost too flexibly; [68] and read in the broadest possible light his constitutional and statutory powers to keep the peace and enforce the laws. [69]

Hamilton did not go beyond the bounds of common sense in his efforts to assert the prerogatives of the President. On one occasion, mindful of political considerations, he advised Washington to be certain that the "occasion" was in fact "extraordinary" before exercising his constitutional power to convene Congress in special session; [70] on another, recognizing the distinction between executive and legislative authority, he asked that Congress vest the President with the power to lay an embargo, partial or general. [71] Most of the time, however, he went to Article II as a well of power, and his broad interpretation of its directions to the President aroused cries of "unconstitutional" among the followers of Jefferson. While some of these cries were petty or gratuitous, some were unquestionably sincere expressions of a constitutional philosophy far more limited in reach than the philosophy of Alexander Hamilton.

Washington usually read the Constitution with the same magnifying glass as did Hamilton. On one occasion, however—one in which he demurred from Hamilton's attempt to equate the President's *opinion* on a matter (in his instructions to Jay) with the *policy* of the United States—Washington took the opportunity to lecture his audacious lieutenant, first, on the differences between his authority and that of executives in other systems then flourishing in the world, and, second, on his intention to acknowledge the difference in all his actions:

The powers of the Executive of the United States are more definite, and better understood perhaps than those of almost any other Country; and my aim has been, and will continue to be, neither to stretch, nor relax from them in any instance whatever, unless imperious circumstances should render the measure indispensable.[72]

While Hamilton, we may be sure, nodded assent to Washington's balanced view of his obligations under the Constitution, his regard for the President's delicate position rarely stopped him from pressing Washington to "stretch" the words of Article II.

One opportunity to strike a blow for the Presidency stands out above all others that came to Hamilton in these years. To his lasting credit as constitutionalist, he seized it every bit as boldly as he had seized the opportunity presented by the clash of opinions over the Bank. I speak of the decisions forced upon Washington in late March, 1793 by the arrival of news of an outbreak of war between France and Great Britain. The situation was one of exorbitant complexity for a President anxious to honor his obligations to Congress, the Constitution, and the world; and the way in which Washington handled the problems of the recognition of the French Republic, the reception and eventual dismissal of its envoy, the incredible Genêt, the interpretation of the French Alliance of 1778, and the statement of America's intentions in this crisis is a tribute to the prudence and sense of duty of the best of all imaginable first Presidents.[73] Thanks to Washington and the men around him, the Presidency emerged from this ordeal by fire as a tempered instrument of popular government, the Republic as a political community that could take care of itself amidst the clash of mighty powers.

On several of the hottest issues about which Washington had to make up his reluctant mind, Jefferson rather than Hamilton seems to have been the more persuasive pleader, for example, the decision to recognize the new French government and to receive its envoy. But on the issue that held most consequence for the future of the Constitution—the President's power (or, as many insisted, lack of power) to proclaim American neutrality—Hamilton was clearly the victor. He pursued his own solution to this issue so forcefully that he gave a lasting boost to the principle of presidential leadership in the making of American foreign policy.

The constitutional question of the hour in April, 1793 was very simply: Which branch of the national government, President or Congress, has the power to make a declaration of American neutrality in a foreign war? While men of all shades of opinion, including Hamilton and

Jefferson, were agreed that such a declaration ought to be made, they were not agreed, because of a silent Constitution, political animosities, and different attitudes toward executive power, about the way to make it.

To Jefferson there was only one possible answer: a resolution of Congress. Since Congress alone had the power to declare that the Republic was at war, it alone must have the power to declare that the Republic was not.[74] Hamilton, to the contrary, was certain that the President could issue a proclamation of neutrality on his own constitutional authority. Washington, who was faced with the two-edged situation of a war that had just blazed forth and a Congress that had just departed for home, behaved in characteristic fashion by "consulting much, pondering much, resolving slowly, resolving surely;" and out of a series of intense sessions with his Cabinet, in one of which his principal ministers argued the constitutional issue face to face,[75] came the famous Proclamation of April 22, 1793,[76] in which he managed to declare our intention to be rigorously neutral in the war of the European powers without actually using the word "neutrality" in the text.

If many Federalists were disappointed that this proclamation had not been worded more strongly, many Republicans were shocked that it had been issued at all. Madison, for example, considered it a "most unfortunate error," since it seemed "to violate . . . the Constitution by making the Executive Magistrate the organ of the disposition, the duty and the interest of the nation in relation to war and peace";[77] and some of the more ardent spirits behind him branded it a "royal edict."[78] The political storms that followed, most of them touched off by the brash behavior of Genêt, were the worst the young Republic had experienced, and no one was allowed to forget that the fate of the Constitution was at stake. As one week of passion followed another, the political temperature rose too high for Hamilton to maintain his self-control, and on June 29 he exploded into print in the *Gazette of the United States.* In a series of seven articles as Pacificus, which were widely reprinted,[79] he defended the policy of neutrality against the men of "acrimony and invective" who had assaulted the administration.[80] The first of these articles was given over entirely to the constitutional question. On the basis of a sweeping interpretation of the opening words of Article II as a grant of power, Hamilton argued forcefully that the President was the "proper" organ of government to "make a declaration of neutrality." We will examine the details of this first letter of Pacificus in chapter 6, for it was as momentous an intellectual source of the strong Presidency as the Opinion on the Constitutionality of the Bank was of the strong Congress.

In pressing Washington to issue the Proclamation of April 22, 1793, and then bringing the eloquence of Pacificus to his support, Hamilton placed the President in a position of clear superiority in the field of foreign relations.

Jefferson was so disturbed by the direction of Hamilton's articles that he implored Madison: "For God's sake, my dear Sir, take up your pen, select the most striking heresies and cut him to pieces in the face of the public." [81] Madison, who had little stomach for the fight,* replied with five articles as Helvidius,[82] four of which dealt with the constitutional question and branded Hamilton's doctrine "as no less vicious in theory than it would be dangerous in practice." Having won the battle of practice, Hamilton left the battle of theory to other men, and Madison's painful arguments went unanswered.[83] That Publius had his share of inner tensions, if not a fully split personality, was proved by Madison's extensive use of numbers 69 and 75 of *The Federalist*.[84] It was not the first time, nor would it be the last, that Hamilton's ruminations as Publius were used against him in his lifetime.

HARRIED by the assaults of the Republicans and convinced that frustration would henceforth be his lot in public office, Hamilton hardened his impetuous heart against the wishes of Washington (and the pleas of his friends) and resigned his post as Secretary of the Treasury January 31, 1795.[85] As he rode back from Philadelphia to New York and to private life (or to a life as private as he could ever hope to lead),† he could congratulate himself on a series of startling successes in his labors for the Union. He had known some bad days; he had several times tasted the bitter fruits of failure; he was aware that some of his most consequential achievements had alienated men whose good will was essential to the

---

* "One thing that particularly vexes me," Madison complained to Jefferson, "is that I foreknow, from the prolixity and pertinacity of the writer, that the business will not be terminated by a single fire." [86]

† Of the several real or alleged chances he had to return to full-time public office in this last period of his life, Hamilton accepted only one—the one that promised him the maximum of psychological satisfaction as well as of glory. The position he took with delight was, of course, as Inspector General of the Army in 1798; among those he declined were as Chief Justice in 1795 (or at least as the Attorney General's candidate for the opening left by Jay) and as Senator from New York in 1798.[87]

The notion of Hamilton as Chief Justice is an exciting one with which to play. Having played with it on many occasions, I must state my own opinion that, even had he managed to stay alive and irremovable as long as did Marshall, he would never have achieved the successes of that superb judicial politician. His reach would have been longer than Marshall's; his grasp, under the political circumstances of the Jeffersonian era, would therefore have been shorter.

American cause. For the most part, however, he had a right to think in terms of success, whether political, financial, commercial, diplomatic, or constitutional. "In this new sphere of action," a knowledgeable colleague was to say some years later in eulogy, he had "displayed a ductility and extent of genius, a fertility in expedients, a faculty of arrangement." His "arduous duty" had been "not to improve upon precedent, but to invent a model," and no one could deny, least of all the shocked Jeffersonians, that he had come close to "inventing" a new Constitution.[88]

His position had been an ideal one in which to pursue lofty ends. Only the Presidency itself was a more powerful and strategically located office than the Secretaryship of the Treasury. "Most of the important measures of every government," he wrote in 1792, "are connected with the treasury," [89] and certainly this was true of the fledgling government in which he served, as it had also been true of the embryonic government of 1782 into which Robert Morris had tried to breathe life. Hamilton was uniquely situated to make policies for the administration, and thus was uniquely entitled to give content to the words of the Constitution. He presided over much the largest department, and thus had control over the way in which many of these policies were to be administered. He had access to Washington because his advice was badly needed, and because he was rarely timid about giving it; he had access to Congress because Congress went out of the way to invite leadership in the broad area of financial and commercial affairs. If it would be going too far to repeat the tired observation that Hamilton played the prime minister to Washington's king (or chancellor to Washington's emperor),[90] it is no exaggeration to say that this assiduous administrator—if he were alive today we would tag him as a "first-class operator"—was the most dynamic figure in Washington's administration. And Hamilton "operated," be it remembered, in every area—in diplomatic, military, and Indian affairs as well as in his own preserve of finance and commerce. Small wonder that the British Minister, who had reason to be grateful to Hamilton, described him as "the most influential member" of the new government, or that Harvard asked to testify its "esteem" to the man "whose wisdom and unremitted exertions" were responsible for the "tranquility and prosperity, and the national respectability" of "these United States." [91]

His timing, too, had been excellent. The fact that he was on the spot months before Jefferson gave him an advantage that he never lost, and his promptness in responding to the calls of Congress kept the opposition constantly off balance. He had, moreover, the qualities of mind and heart—professional knowledge, industry, pride, integrity, and audacity—

that were needed in abundance for the struggle with the opposition in Congress and in the press. Even those who take sides with Jefferson and Madison must admire his triumphant defense against the climactic attack of these enemies, the censorious resolutions of 1793 introduced into the House (certainly with the approval and probably at the urging of Madison and Jefferson) by William Branch Giles.[92] Finally, he had a clear-cut program where other leading men had only vague intentions or obstinate prejudices. One may doubt that, in his single-minded pursuit of this program, he gave daily thought to the Constitution, which was a vague abstraction when contrasted with the concrete reality of the Bank of the United States. Still, he must have realized that the success of the Bank, and indeed of all future instruments of American prosperity and power, depended upon a large view of the Constitution, and he may even have suspected that his success in getting other men to take this view was as consequential for the future as was his success in securing the public credit.

He had not, to be sure, been uniformly successful in getting the most important of all other men, President Washington, to read the Constitution exactly as he read it. On at least two occasions the President had indulged himself in the unusual luxury of refusing to accept Hamilton's line of argument on what could be construed as constitutional questions. In May, 1790 Hamilton advised him to veto a joint resolution of Congress ordering the Secretary of the Treasury to pay arrears to certain veterans of the Virginia and North Carolina lines who had assigned their claims to other persons.[93] Despite the Secretary's insistence that this was a "law impairing the obligation of contracts," and therefore an insult to the spirit if not to the exact letter of the Constitution, Washington followed Jefferson's reasoning in the matter (which refused even to acknowledge that an interpretation of the Constitution was at issue) and signed the resolution.[94]

In April, 1792 Hamilton advised him not to veto a bill in which Congress, after a bitter wrangle between North and South, had apportioned seats in the House of Representatives on the basis of the census of 1790. The method used was to fix the number of Representatives at 120—which was roughly one to each 30,000 persons (the minimum established in the Constitution)—and then, each state having been rendered its due, to give the surplus seats (eight in this instance) to those states with the largest fractions left unrepresented.[95] Unfortunately for Washington, who took no delight either in political squabbles or numerical exercises, the South was shortchanged by this method, and both Jefferson and Randolph urged him to veto the bill on grounds of unconstitutionality because it had not applied the same ratio to each state separately.[96] Hamilton recognized that Congress could have gone about this business in a different way simply by fixing the ratio of representation and letting the seats (and, if it chose, the remainders) fall where they might; and since it appeared to him that neither way bent the Constitution out of shape, he advised Washington to sign the bill. In the last paragraph of a short but well-ordered review of the problem, he stated the principle on which he asked Washington to take a stand:

There appears, therefore, no room to say that the bill is unconstitutional, though there may be another construction of which the Constitution is capable. In cases where two constructions may reasonably be adopted, and neither can be pronounced inconsistent with the public good, it seems proper that the legislative sense should prevail. The present appears to the Secretary clearly to be such a case.[97]

Washington, who had listened to Hamilton rather than Jefferson on the important constitutional issues to arise in his first term, now listened to Jefferson rather than Hamilton on this fairly unimportant one, and thus was recorded the first of all presidential vetoes.[98] Although Washington gave this small victory to Jefferson in 1792, the growth of the nation gave it back to the shade of Hamilton in 1850 when the present general method of first fixing the number of seats and then distributing them among the states as fairly as possible was established in law. History made inevitable, and therefore constitutional, the scheme of apportionment on which Congress had first acted and Hamilton had bestowed his modest blessing.[99]

Another instance in which Washington may have disregarded the constitutional advice of his Secretary of the Treasury was one of the lesser scenes in the drama of 1793. Anxious to have the most learned and commanding of opinions on the many problems of international and municipal law that had been raised by his adoption of the policy of neutrality, Washington put a full twenty-nine questions to the Supreme Court in a message of July 18.[100] In doing this he is said to have overridden a mild objection of Hamilton that it was not the business of an independent Supreme Court to give advisory opinions to anyone, not even to the President, on points of law.[101] While Hamilton never felt any qualms about asking his friend the Chief Justice for private advice on issues of moment for the Constitution,[102] he may well have realized that a formal application by the President to the Court would set a precedent full of unpleasant consequences for the principle of the separation of powers. Washington knew that he was treading on swampy ground,[103] and he could not have been very surprised when Jay and his associates, after some backing and filling in the vicinity of the great man they wanted to oblige, declined the invitation to serve as constitutional advisers in a deferential but conclusive letter of August 8.[104] If the President wanted opinions on the laws of war and peace, and especially on the powers he enjoyed under the Constitution, he would have to turn, the Justices agreed, to the "heads of departments." Thus was established, not at all to Hamilton's regret (and, for that matter, probably not to Washington's), a leading principle of the independent judiciary under the Constitution.[105] As a loyal aide to Washington he had suppressed any doubts he may have entertained, and had helped to frame the questions to be put to the Court,[106] but as a thoughtful expounder of the Constitution he must have agreed with the logic of Jay's denial of aid to their harried friend in the Presidency.

None of these issues presented a challenge either to Hamilton's financial and diplomatic program or to his hopes for a high-toned Constitution on which to mount it; none raised him to the level of passion on which he dwelled in his arguments for the constitutional rightness of the Bank Act and of the Proclamation of 1793. They were issues on which he was prepared to be argued down, and it is hard to believe that he lost any standing in Washington's eyes as a result of these mild rebukes. He was willing to let others, even Jefferson, make up Washington's mind on the small problems of the Constitution so long as he could have his way on the large ones.

HAMILTON continued to render services to the Constitution throughout the remaining years of his life, and thus continued to steer it, as best he could from his private station, along the course of energy and flexibility. He had resigned as Secretary of the Treasury but not as "King of the Feds" or as intimate adviser to Washington,* and the hot political battles of these years gave him several opportunities to play the role of constitutional lawyer. Two events in particular are worth recalling.

The first was the storm over Jay's Treaty that convulsed American politics in 1795–1796. Although he was no longer in office, Hamilton found

---

* "I beg, Sir," he wrote to Washington September 4, 1795, "that you will at no time have any scruples about commanding me. I shall always with pleasure comply with your commands." The scrupulous Washington rarely missed a chance in the last years of his incumbency to command—or, rather, to "beg"—Hamilton's opinion on matters of importance. As he wrote in a heated moment in 1796, "Your sentiments in this interesting crisis will always be thankfully received." [107]

himself at the center of the storm, and he fought the good fight for this maligned bargain relentlessly and skillfully. Twice in the course of the battle—and he had at least one large lump on his head to prove that it really was a battle *—he had occasion to deliver lectures in constitutional law; both lectures, needless to say, were designed to expose the constitutional "sophistries" of the opposition, which once again was led by Jefferson and Madison. In a long series of public letters over the pseudonym Camillus he defended the wisdom and legality of the treaty article by article,[108] and then at the end, in an attempt to silence some of the loudest cries of the Republicans, he turned to the question of its constitutionality.[109] Much of what he had to say was a laboring of the obvious, but the attacks of the Republicans had left him little choice.[110] As he noted with scorn at the beginning of the crucial number on the constitutionality of the treaty, it had become the "fashion with some politicians, when hard pressed on the expediency of a measure, to intrench themselves behind objections to its constitutionality," [111] and he was forced to prove that the fashion was, at least in this instance, absurd. This he did by pointing generally to the "comprehensive" and "plenipotentiary" nature of the treaty-making power, and by refuting specifically the restricting argument of the Republicans that for the President to negotiate (and the Senate to confirm) a commercial treaty was to usurp the power of Congress to regulate foreign commerce.[112] Since I shall have more to say in chapter 6 on Hamilton's interpretation of the treaty-making power, I shall confine myself here to two quotations from Camillus, the first of which proves that he was once again the expounder of the permissive Constitution, the second that he was once again the advocate of the strong Presidency. It was the intent of the Framers, he asserted bluntly (and "from the *best opportunity of knowing the fact*"),

to give to that power the most ample latitude—to render it competent to all the stipulations which the exigencies of national affairs might require; competent to the making of treaties of alliance, treaties of commerce, treaties of peace, and every other species of convention usual among nations; and competent, in the course of its exercise for these purposes, to control and bind the legislative power of Congress.

"Let it be remembered," he said to the partisans of legislative supremacy,

that the nation is the *constituent*, and that the executive, within its sphere, is no less the organ of its will than the Legislature.[113]

---

* It is said that he was stoned at a public meeting in Wall Street July 18, 1795, an event that moved his friend George Cabot to observe that the Republicans had tried "to knock out Hamilton's brains to reduce him to an equality with themselves." [114]

Once again he had thumped the Republicans so mercilessly that Jefferson let go with another "For God's sake" to Madison, and begged him to "take up" his pen and "give a fundamental reply." [115] This time, however, Madison decided to leave the literary struggle against the "colossus" to lesser men.

His other lecture was designed for delivery in the first instance to Washington, who had invited it, and in the second to the House of Representatives, which most certainly had not.[116] The occasion was a show of double-barreled recalcitrance by the House in March, 1796, first, in requesting the President to "lay before this House" the instructions to Jay and all other papers "relative" to the treaty, and second, in asserting a constitutional right to refuse to appropriate the money needed to execute the treaty.[117] Having managed to push the treaty safely through the Senate, the Federalists were startled by the appearance of this new roadblock, and now it was their turn to raise the cry of unconstitutionality. Hamilton made his most important contribution to the cause in a proposed draft of a message from Washington to the House which denied both of these contentions in the most explicit language. Although this draft, which left Hamilton's hand March 29, reached Washington too late to be used (and was, in any case, probably too long to be used),* it was recognized as the most forceful statement of the Federalist view of the relations between the President and the House in this muddy area. Most of its ideas had already been conveyed to Washington directly by letter or indirectly through King and Wolcott, and the Republicans in opposition had few doubts about Hamilton's part in persuading the President. To the editor of the *Independent Chronicle* up in Boston the "artful, well-informed, intriguing and indefatigable" Hamilton appeared to have "seized the reins" of the "executive branch of the Government." [118] To Madison down on the floor of the House it was evident that "the advice and even the message itself were contrived in New York." [119]

In the end, the tactical situation rather than rational argument decided what the sense of the Constitution would be on these two issues, and on one of them Hamilton and his friends were right, on the other wrong. They were right in asserting the power of the President to withhold confidential papers from Congress "in the public interest" because there is still no practical way to get at papers he holds in his obstinate grasp. They were wrong in denying the power of the House to make an independent judgment on whether to appropriate money called for in a ratified

---

* Washington's own message, which was largely the work of Timothy Pickering, was forwarded to a disbelieving House March 30.[120]

treaty because there is still no practical way to force obstinate legislators to act against their will. Let us end discussion of a difficult problem in constitutional interpretation, on which Hamilton as usual took up the cudgels for "energy," with the observation that both sides marched off with flags flying. Washington spoke earnestly of his desire to "harmonize" with the House, at the same time denying as a "dangerous precedent" its right to "demand, and to have as a matter of course, all the papers respecting a negotiation with a foreign power." The House, after a series of debates and maneuvers that left it exhausted, voted 51–48 to give the President his funds on this occasion, 57–35 to let him know that it retained the right both to pass on the merits of a treaty and to have all papers pertaining to the negotiation thereof.[121] All in all, it was a grand constitutional battle, and those who are still fighting it may thank Hamilton and Madison for having given them all the ammunition they could possibly need.

A second opportunity presented itself to Hamilton a year after his resignation, and found him engaged for the first and last time in his life as counsel before the Supreme Court of the United States.* The case was *Hylton* v. *United States,* like many another famous case a controversy fictitious in form if real in consequence.[122] The question before the Court was the validity of a tax on carriages levied by Congress in 1794 at the suggestion, of course, of the Secretary of the Treasury.[123] This apparently sensible tax, which fell almost entirely on men who could afford to pay it, aroused violent opposition among the planters of Virginia, for whom richly appointed carriages were the Cadillacs and Continentals of the age; and behind the brilliant, acrimonious figure of John Taylor of Caroline, who loathed Hamilton and all his works, they formed up for the attack upon this "despotic" and "odious" levy. When suit was brought against Daniel Hylton, a Virginian, for evading the tax, Taylor argued before the Circuit Court that, as a direct tax and not an excise, it was a gross violation of the requirement in the Constitution that such a tax be apportioned among the states according to population.[124] He argued, moreover, in words borrowed unabashedly from Publius, that "the law of the Constitution is superior to the law of any legislative majority," that amid the clash of laws it behooves "every good citizen to cling to the superior law," and that a law which "violates the Constitution" must be considered "void." [125]

---

* He was asked in July, 1796 to appear as counsel in *Hunter* v. *Fairfax's Devisee* (on what he certainly would have considered the wrong side), but declined with the observation that it was not his "general plan to practice in Supreme Court of US." [126]

The Circuit Court having divided on the question of constitutionality, the government decided to take the case to the Supreme Court. Attorney General William Bradford begged Hamilton to "have a little parental concern" and join in the defense of a measure of his "own begetting." [127] Hamilton chose, doubtless with reason, to interpret the resistance to the carriage tax as an assault upon the whole system he had toiled to build, and he responded with a will to Bradford's call to lead the forces of truth in the "greatest" issue "that ever came before that Court." He worked closely with Henry Lee, Bradford's successor (and himself a Virginian), on the government's brief, and then on February 24, 1796, in one of the grand efforts of his career as advocate, appeared before the Court to argue that this was an excise rather than a direct tax and therefore a valid use of the power of Congress. "Mr. Hamilton spoke in our Court," Justice James Iredell wrote only two days after the event,

attended by the most crowded audience I ever saw there, both Houses of Congress being almost deserted on the occasion. Though he was in very ill health, he spoke with astonishing ability, and in a most pleasing manner, and was listened to with the profoundest attention. His speech lasted about three hours.[128]

His manner seems to have been persuasive as well as pleasing. The Court accepted his argument that the carriage tax was not "direct"—on the theory that, since the Constitution required that direct taxes be apportioned, only those taxes that could be apportioned were direct! [129]—and went further to accept his latitudinarian method of construing the Constitution. In his argument he had said with feeling, as he had said many times before:

No construction ought to prevail calculated to defeat the express and necessary authority of the government.

It would be contrary to reason, and to every rule of sound construction, to adopt a principle for regulating the exercise of a clear constitutional power which would defeat the exercise of the power.[130]

Every one of the three Justices who delivered an opinion in this case— Samuel Chase (whom Hamilton had branded a scoundrel in 1778 for his profiteering activities as a delegate to Congress),[131] William Paterson (whose New Jersey Plan had excited his contempt in 1787), and James Iredell (whom he had never given occasion for displeasure)—bestowed approval, however obliquely and cautiously, on this notion of the Constitution as an "accommodating system" that ought to set free rather than to paralyze the authority of the national government.[132] For the first time in its short history the Supreme Court had sat in judgment upon the constitutionality of an act of Congress, and it had been led to a favorable judgment by the eloquence of Alexander Hamilton.

IT might be argued that Hamilton's career as constitutionalist reached its zenith, paradoxically, in two other events of these years of retirement in which he played no active part. The willing protagonist of one of these events, the memorable case of *Marbury* v. *Madison* (February 24, 1803), was a respected colleague, Chief Justice John Marshall. The reluctant protagonist of the other, the purchase of Louisiana (announced officially July 4, 1803), was his bitter political enemy, President Thomas Jefferson. Each of these two men was in an office that fate had denied forever to Hamilton; each was handed a rare opportunity to give substance to some of the shadows in the Constitution; each took the opportunity and, in his own way, gave a lasting Hamiltonian twist to the Constitution.

The story of *Marbury* v. *Madison* needs no retelling in this book. It should be enough to pay homage to the vital role of Hamilton in paving the way for Marshall's assertion of the doctrine of judicial review of acts of Congress. The antecedents of this doctrine are, of course, extremely murky. Even today, with all the extant records of the colonial, Constitutional, and Federal periods laid open for our inspection, we cannot say for certain just when and where the doctrine was born or how and why it came to maturity in the minds of men.[133] All we can say is that Marshall deserves immense credit for seizing upon a weak case to strike a strong blow for an independent Supreme Court, and that Hamilton deserves no less credit for having been the most outspoken of the early advocates of this most dramatic of judicial weapons. It was he who, in the heated case of *Rutgers* v. *Waddington* (1784), made the first clear-cut, well-reported assertion of the power of a court to set aside an act of a legislature on grounds of conflict with a higher law under which both court and legislature were supposed to function. It was he who, in *The Federalist,* number 78, first broke the news to the American people (or at least to those patient friends who were still following the arguments of Publius) that they were instituting a system of government in which it would be the "duty" of the courts to exercise the almost unprecedented power to censor unconstitutional acts of Congress.[134]

The fact that *Rutgers* v. *Waddington* is considered to be a leading precedent for judicial review in the years before 1789 should be proof enough that the power asserted by Hamilton was indeed "almost unprecedented." The court in this instance was the Mayor's Court in New York City; the act was a New York statute of 1783 (the so-called Trespass Act) under which patriots were encouraged to sue Tories who had used their property during the British occupation of New York; the higher law to which this law ran counter was a compendium of the law of nations, the treaty of peace with Great Britain, and, by logical extension, the Articles of Confederation.[135] When Elizabeth Rutgers, a widow and patriot, sued Joshua Waddington, a merchant and Tory, for four and a half years' rent on a brewery that she had owned but he had used during the occupation, Hamilton took up the defense of the unpopular Waddington. In the course of this litigation he made himself even more unpopular than Waddington, yet he did bring to the attention of bench and bar—and, because of a vocal press, to the public at large *—the notion that a court had no business enforcing a law that was in clear conflict (as this statute certainly was) with a higher law.[136]

The exact identity of the higher law was a matter of much dispute, the court (presided over by James Duane) was unsure of its powers, and the political situation was heated; it is therefore not surprising that the decision was somewhat disappointing to Hamilton. The court was willing to construe the Trespass Act in such a way as to give Mrs. Rutgers only part of the rent she had demanded, but not to accept the power thrust upon it by the audacious counsel for the defense—for "this," the voiding of an act of the legislature, "were to set the *judicial* above the legislature, which would be subversive of all government." [137] Hamilton, in any case, had made one of the first attempts to convert the vague notion of "unconstitutionality" into a technique of popular government, and the attempt must have sharpened his own thinking on the subject. From the crude assertions of *Rutgers* v. *Waddington* it was not more than two or three steps to the subtle reasoning of *The Federalist,* number 78, which presented judicial review as a power not "subversive" but sustaining "of all government." We shall give a full hearing to this reasoning in chapter 6.

From *The Federalist,* number 78 to *Marbury* v. *Madison* it was perhaps a few more steps—some tentative assertions in several of the ratifying conventions,[138] the wording of section 25 of the Judiciary Act of 1789,† the

---

* This is a point of considerable importance, for most of the real or alleged instances of judicial review in the state courts of the 1780's went unreported and unnoticed until many years after the event.[139]

† Which plainly assumed the existence of the power of judicial review over acts of Congress—in state as well as federal courts—in the following passage: *"And be it further enacted,* That a final judgment or decree in any suit, in the highest court of law or equity of a State in which a decision in the suit could be had, where is drawn in question the validity of a treaty or statute of, or an authority exercised

implied voiding of an act of Congress by the Circuit Court for Pennsylvania in the so-called Hayburn Case,[140] the lectures of James Wilson in 1790–1792 to students of the University of Pennsylvania,[141] the repeated exercise of the power of judicial review by state courts over state legislation,[142] the arguments of the opposition in the courts against the carriage tax (and indeed in the newspapers against the Bank),[143] the retorts of Northern state legislatures to the Virginia and Kentucky Resolutions,[144] the obiter dicta of Paterson, Iredell, Chase, and other Justices in such cases as *Van Horne's Lessee* v. *Dorrance, Hylton* v. *U.S., Ware* v. *Hylton,* and *Calder* v. *Bull,*[145] a case (*Ogden* v. *Witherspoon*) decided in 1802 by Marshall himself on circuit duty in North Carolina [146]—yet the line of march was so direct, and so quickly covered in the Federalist mind of John Marshall, that we must consider the decision of 1803 a stunning triumph for Alexander Hamilton. One seeks in vain in his private letters or even in the columns of the *Evening Post** for comment on the statement of the power of judicial review in *Marbury* v. *Madison,*[147] but then one seeks

---

under the United States, and the decision is against their validity; or where is drawn in question the validity of a statute of, or an authority exercised under any State, on the ground of their being repugnant to the Constitution, treaties or laws of the United States, and the decision is in favor of such their validity, or where is drawn in question the construction of any clause of the Constitution, or of a treaty, or statute of, or commission held under the United States, and the decision is against the title, right, privilege, or exemption specially set up or claimed by either party, under such clause of the said Constitution, treaty, statute, or commission, may be re-examined and reversed or affirmed in the Supreme Court of the United States upon a writ of error." [148]

* Convinced of the need for a stoutly Federalist newspaper in New York City, Hamilton took the lead in 1801 in founding the *New York Evening Post* and also in choosing William Coleman as first editor. Although he had time to contribute only a few pieces directly, notably a series of strictures on Jefferson's policies under the pseudonym of Lucius Crassus,[149] there is much substance in J. C. Miller's judgment that this newspaper, "under Coleman's direction, became a mirror of Hamilton's mind." [150] If the testimony of Senator Jeremiah Mason can be believed, Coleman himself held up the mirror gladly for all the world to see. "His acquaintances," Mason wrote of Coleman, "were often surprised by the ability of some of his editorial articles, which were supposed to be beyond his depth. Having a convenient opportunity, I asked him who wrote, or aided in writing those articles. He frankly answered that he made no secret of it; that his paper was set up under the auspices of General Hamilton, and that he assisted him. I then asked, 'Does he write in your paper?' 'Never a word.'—'How then does he assist?' His answer was, 'Whenever anything occurs on which I feel the want of information, I state the matter to him, sometimes in a note. He appoints a time when I may see him, usually a late hour of the evening. He always keeps himself minutely informed on all political matters. As soon as I see him, he begins in a deliberate manner to dictate, and I to note down in short-hand' (he was a good stenographer); 'when he stops my article is completed.' " [151]

The files of the *Evening Post* for the few years before Hamilton's death show

almost in vain for such comment in any private letter or public writing during the weeks following Marshall's decision. Although the parties fell out sharply over this case, the Federalists concentrated their fire on Jefferson's "arrogance" in refusing to deliver up the commissions to Marbury and his friends,* the Republicans on Marshall's "presumption" in going out of his way to lecture Jefferson about the rights of Marbury and the duty to honor them.[152] Almost no one expressed an opinion on the Court's exercise of the hitherto formless power of judicial review, which may have been exactly what was anticipated by the foxy Chief Justice. Had the first assertion of this power been directed against a law dear to the Jeffersonians, the first assertion might have been the last.

It was, to tell the historical truth, a lucky thing that Marshall rather than Hamilton was Chief Justice in those critical years, for the latter could not have resisted the temptation to make a trial of strength with Jefferson over the Repeal Act of 1802.[153] In a public letter of March, 1802 he did everything but invite Marshall by name to declare this act unconstitutional,† and he must have been sorely disappointed by the outcome, which I shall discuss shortly, of *Stuart* v. *Laird* (1803). Still, on reflection he should have been well satisfied with the results of *Marbury* v. *Madison*. A shrewder politician than he—yet no less staunch a Federalist—had seized upon the best of all possible opportunities to write the creative doctrine of *The Federalist*, number 78 into the living Constitution.

THE story of the Louisiana Purchase needs even less retelling.[154] Thanks to a whimsical turn of the wheel of history, it was given to the most adamant of strict-constructionists, Thomas Jefferson, to stretch both the letter and spirit of the Constitution almost to the breaking point in order to complete this fateful transaction. Napoleon had dumped his surplus real estate on Jefferson's envoys Monroe and R. R. Livingston; they, in their turn, had dumped it on Jefferson; and he, in his turn, decided reluctantly

the constant touch of his guiding hand. The *Post* is therefore, if used with care, an important source of ideas and opinions for the searcher into Hamilton's mind.

* An editorial on the case was run in the *Evening Post* March 23 under the heading "Constitution violated by the President." Neither at this time nor in the days that followed did the *Evening Post* comment upon the fact that Marshall had pronounced a law (or at least part of a law) unconstitutional.[155]

† Quoting *The Federalist*, number 78 at length, and embellishing it with additional passages from Madison (numbers 47 and 51), he asserted solemnly that one of "the means contemplated by the Constitution" to preserve the principle of the separation of powers was "the right of the judges, as interpreters of the laws, to pronounce unconstitutional acts void." [156]

that even a badly damaged Constitution was not too high a price to pay for an "empire of liberty."

Jefferson's constitutional scruples, which were not shared by all Republicans, led him first to consider the possibility of an ex post facto amendment to the Constitution that gave effective sanction to what he had already done [157] (or what had been done for him in Paris) illegally, improperly, and unconstitutionally, indeed in contradiction to every principle of interpretation in which he had ever believed. In the end, after an almost comic debate in Congress and the country, in which many Republicans and Federalists exchanged their positions of the previous decade with no apparent concern for consistency, Jefferson presented the terms of the Purchase to the Senate on the assumption that he and they had some inherent, extraconstitutional power to do what simply had to be done by and for the nation. To his own constitutional past he bowed deeply:

> I had rather ask an enlargement of power from the nation, where it is found necessary, than to assume it by a construction which would make our powers boundless. Our peculiar security is in possession of a written Constitution. Let us not make it a blank paper by construction.

And then to reality he bowed even more deeply:

> If, however, our friends shall think differently, certainly I shall acquiesce with satisfaction; confiding, that the good sense of our country will correct the evil of construction when it shall produce evil effects.[158]

One of "our friends" in the Senate, John Taylor, salved his own conscience in words that must have been borrowed straight from Jefferson:

> I have no doubt our envoys had no authority to make such a treaty, and that it is a violation of the Constitution; but I will, like an attorney who exceeds the authority delegated to him by his client, vote to ratify it, and then throw myself on the people for pardon.[159]

For obvious political and personal reasons Hamilton was discomfited by the purchase of Louisiana, and he found it hard to rejoice in the sudden expansion of the "empire" to which he had given his unreserved allegiance. Yet on constitutional grounds he, unlike many of his old Federalist comrades, voiced no complaint.[160] The only complaint he could have made—and one wishes that he had made it—was that Jefferson, in assuming his action to be unconstitutional and in appealing for support to the nation, had done a far greater disservice to the cause of limited government than Hamilton had ever done. There can be no doubt that, if Hamilton had been President when the news of the Purchase arrived in Washington, he would have discovered a half-dozen phrases in the Constitution that authorized the government of the United States to accept the offer without qualms. Since Jefferson was President and Hamilton an outsider, he had to content himself with a grim satisfaction in the thought that, while his foe had given a "Hamiltonian twist" to the Constitution, he had done it, naturally, in a most un-Hamiltonian style. Hamilton's own friends, it might be added, were never loathe to point out that it was their man's interpretation of the Constitution which had met the test of history. As Story wrote in his *Commentaries* of this and another memorable action of Jefferson under the pressure of reality:

> The most remarkable powers, which have been exercised by the government, as auxiliary and implied powers, and which, if any, go to the utmost verge of liberal construction, are the laying of an unlimited embargo in 1807, and the purchase of Louisiana in 1803. . . . These measures were brought forward, and supported, and carried, by the known and avowed friends of a strict construction of the constitution; and they were justified, only upon the doctrines of those, who support a liberal construction of the constitution.[161]

The struggle with Jefferson over the scope and purpose of the Constitution continued to the last day of Hamilton's life. Almost every political controversy during his five and a half years in power and nine and a half in retirement raised a question of constitutional interpretation on which he and the Republicans proceeded to divide. Let me top off this discussion by taking note of two other controversies of the years of retirement.

The first was the fierce contest over the passage and enforcement of the Alien and Sedition Acts, which Jefferson considered, in the words of his draft of the Kentucky Resolutions, as "palpably against the Constitution." [162] Hamilton and the Federalists, to the contrary, never doubted that these acts were well within the competence of Congress,[163] first, because it had all reasonable powers to defend the Republic against foreign and domestic enemies, and second, because seditious libel was a crime at common law. It seems always to have been Hamilton's view, although he was far from dogmatic or insistent in expressing it, that the federal courts had been endowed by the Constitution with cognizance over all cases arising under the common law.[164] To Jefferson, who was understandably dogmatic and insistent in his view, this was an "audacious, barefaced and sweeping" interpretation, a "wholesale doctrine" of "encroachment" on the states that could lead only to the closing down of the state courts and the abolition of the federal system. History seems to have vindicated Hamilton's opinion of the power of Congress to provide for prosecution of seditious libelers and Jefferson's opinion of the limited nature of the common-law jurisdiction of the federal courts.[165]

The other was the related struggle over the structure and personnel of the federal courts which burst into flames with the passage of the Judiciary Act of February 13, 1801,[166] grew more violent with Adams's appointment of the "midnight judges" to fill the new positions created in the act,[167] raged almost out of control with the repeal of the act by the victorious Republicans March 8, 1802 (with no provision for the displaced judges),[168] and then died out slowly after the Supreme Court's prudent refusal in *Stuart* v. *Laird* (1803) to go out of its way and declare the Repeal Act unconstitutional.[169] The case against this act was stated most forcefully by Hamilton as Lucius Crassus in a series of articles that tore Jefferson's message to Congress of December 7, 1801 into small and, as he thought, ridiculous pieces.[170] The essence of the case was simply that Congress had a "right to change or abolish inferior courts, but not to abolish the actual judges." [171] There was a good deal of sound constitutional logic beneath the frothy surface of Hamilton's rhetoric, but since none of the midnight judges who had lost his job seemed willing to contest the matter in the courts,[172] the question whether Congress can effect the removal of a judge by abolishing his post remains unanswered to this day.[173] It should be noted in passing that, if Hamilton had had his way, the act of 1801 would have created a judicial system so elaborate and self-sustaining as virtually to abolish the courts of the states. More and more irritated by the tactics of the Republicans in 1798–1799, he is said to have drafted a bill, which was introduced into the House of Representatives March 11, 1800, dividing the United States into twenty-nine judicial districts without much regard for state boundaries.[174] This product of a resurgence of the extreme continentalism of June 18, 1787 had no chance of passage, and Hamilton had to be content, as he had learned to be content in 1787, with a less satisfactory measure that was still too much for his enemies.

ONE last event out of Hamilton's public life should be recorded before we close the book on his career as maker and manipulator of the Constitution of the United States. While it was not an incident in which an interpretation of the Constitution was directly at issue, it did give him an opportunity, which he exploited brilliantly, to refine the law of libel as understood and applied in the courts of the states, and thus to give new substance to the law of freedom of the press. Since the Supreme Court has emerged in recent years as overseer of the states in defense of this critical freedom, it seems entirely proper to say that here, too, Hamilton left an indelible mark on the living Constitution.

The event was the memorable case of *People* v. *Croswell*,[175] which he argued in Albany before the Supreme Court of New York only five months before his death. This case arose, as many memorable cases in legal history have arisen, because an obscure man engaged in a trivial act, because one group of powerful men decided to set an example by punishing him for this act, and because another group of powerful men, fearing the political consequences of this example, came running to his defense.

The obscure man was Harry Croswell, an editor of *The Balance,* a Federalist newspaper in Hudson, New York. His trivial act was the republication and embellishment, in a peppery newsheet called *The Wasp* (September 9, 1802),[176] of an already widely published report that Thomas Jefferson had paid the wretched James T. Callender for writing *The Prospect Before Us,* a tract in which Washington had been branded "a traitor, a perjurer, and a robber" and Adams saluted as a "hoary-headed incendiary." The men who set out to punish Croswell were the Republicans of New York, led in this instance by Attorney General Ambrose Spencer. They had matched Jefferson's victory with a sweeping victory of their own in the state elections of 1801, and were thus in a position and a mood to exact a little vengeance.* Having fought tooth and nail against the Sedition Act of 1798 and the prosecution of men like Thomas Cooper, William Duane, and, of course, James T. Callender under it, and thereby having earned a high place in all histories of freedom of speech and press in the United States, they celebrated the happy results of 1801 by prosecuting Federalist editors for printing the same sort of thing about their hero that they had been printing about the heroes of Federalism. Being Republicans, and thus devoted states'-righters, Spencer and his cohorts launched their own assault upon "licentious scribblers" in the courts of the state. Rather than go after a really big fish (or should it be bumblebee?) like Coleman of the *Evening Post,* they chose a small one like

---

* Jefferson, understandably but unfortunately, did little to dispel this mood. To the contrary, in a letter of February 19, 1803 to Governor Thomas McKean of Pennsylvania he gave his "confidential" advice that "a few prosecutions" of the worst of the Federalist editors "would have a wholesome effect in restoring the integrity of the presses." "Not a general prosecution, for that would look like persecution: but a selected one . . . If the same thing be done in some other of the states it will place the whole band more on their guard." [177]

It is not hard to imagine that similar advice went forth to the Republicans of New York—or would have gone forth if they had been dilatory in prosecuting men like Croswell.

Harry Croswell of *The Wasp,* who thus found himself arraigned, first at the "general sessions of the peace," then in the circuit court in Claverack, New York on an indictment for libel.

The Republicans may have expected to take easy revenge on the Federalists by prosecuting a small-town editor in a small-town court, but they found out soon enough that the enemy was just as ready to fight it out in Hudson or Claverack as in Albany or New York City. The "persecution" of Croswell roused the Federalists of the state from the despair of the long months since Jefferson's victory. The defense of the country editor was taken up as an affair of honor, and a battery of Federalist lawyers was enlisted to serve as counsel. Although Hamilton was implored to lend his talents to the cause,* the press of business made it impossible for him to take part in the defense of Croswell in July, 1803. It is altogether likely that he was saving himself for the third and final round, for it was clear from the outset that Croswell would be convicted in the circuit court. The judge in his case was Chief Justice Morgan Lewis, who came down from Albany as trial justice, and he was known to be an enthusiastic Republican. Hewing to the law of libel as it was then interpreted, Lewis refused to let counsel for Croswell prove the truth of the offensive remarks in *The Wasp.* More than that, he instructed the jury, in accordance with Lord Mansfield's famous decision in the case of the Dean of St. Asaph (1784),[178] that they were "judges only of the fact, and not of the truth or intent of the publication." Since no one disputed the fact that Croswell had published the offending remarks, he was convicted of libel. His counsel immediately entered a motion for a new trial, and the case went on appeal to the full Supreme Court in Albany.

When the case came up for hearing in February, 1804, Hamilton was ready to do his duty as "King of the Feds" and made "a mighty effort in the cause of liberty." [179] Taking over the defense of Croswell in team with Richard Harison and William W. Van Ness, he put on a display of scholarship and rhetoric that left James Kent, one of the four judges sitting in the case, limp with wonder. "This argument and speech of General Hamilton's," he wrote in his notes of the case, "was a masterpiece of

---

* The venerable Schuyler wrote to his daughter June 23, 1803: "I have had about a dozen Federalists with me intreating me to write to your General if possible to attend on the 7th of next month at Claverack as Counsel to the Federal printer there who is to be tried on an Indictment for a libel against that Jefferson, who disgraces not only the place he fills, but produces Immorality by his pernicious examples." [180]

The father-in-law of the Federalist leader had plainly lost none of his own zest for battle.

pathetic, impassioned and sublime eloquence. It was probably never *surpassed* and made the deepest impression. I never heard him so great." [181] And many years later Kent wrote to Mrs. Hamilton:

I have always considered General Hamilton's argument in that cause the greatest forensic effort that he ever made. He had bestowed unusual attention to the case, and he came prepared to discuss the points of law with a perfect mastery of the subject. . . .

There was an unusual solemnity and earnestness on the part of General Hamilton in this discussion. He was at times highly impassioned and pathetic. His whole soul was enlisted in the cause. . . . He never before, in my hearing, made any effort in which he commanded higher reverence for his principles, or equal admiration of his eloquence.[182]

In the course of his argument, which lasted the better part of two days, Hamilton built up the case for Croswell on four main points.[183] While no one of them was original with him, each was put so freshly and forcefully that he must be given much credit for having impressed them upon the American legal and political mind.

The first was a definition of libel for which he drew alike on the observations of some of the celebrated English lawyers and on his own talent for proclaiming the obvious to men who had not been willing to see it:

My definition of a libel . . . is this: I would call it a slanderous or ridiculous writing, picture, or sign, with a malicious or mischievous design or intent, towards government, magistrates, or individuals.[184]

Since the law of libel had never been "settled," he added, "it was a *floating and litigious question,* and we are at liberty to examine it on principle." [185]

The second was a definition of "the liberty of the press," which consisted, so he contended, "in the right to publish with impunity truth, with good motives, for justifiable ends, though reflecting on government, magistracy, or individuals." [186] This liberty was, in truth, "essential to the preservation of free government." If it were driven underground or even allowed to decay, "then in vain will the voice of the people be raised against the inroads of tyranny." As a man dedicated to ordered liberty, indeed as a Federalist who had cut short the life of a Republican newspaper by encouraging a prosecution for libel against it,[187] he made clear that there were limits upon freedom of the press:

In speaking thus for the freedom of the press, I do not say there ought to be an unbridled license; or that the characters of men who are good will naturally tend eternally to support themselves. I do not stand here to say that no shackles are to be laid on this license.[188]

In placing the responsibility in the "tribunals of justice" for laying these shackles upon "calumniators," Hamilton made his third main point,[189] which was that the jury must be regarded as a principal agent of the judicial process in any action for libel. "For reasons of a political and peculiar nature, for the security of life and liberty," it must in all "criminal cases," and most certainly in a case such as this, be "intrusted with the power of deciding both law and fact." Never noted as a man who would expect to find more virtue and intelligence in a jury ("a changeable body of men chosen . . . by lot") than in a court ("a permanent body of men, appointed by the executive"), Hamilton was forced by the circumstances of this case—in which his one hope of victory was a new trial and an impressionable jury—to contend that it was not for judges alone to decide on the "intent" and "tendency" of an allegedly libelous writing.

His fourth and final point, which he hoped would prove decisive, was that truth was a defense, although by no means an unassailable defense, in an action for libel. As his own notes for argument put it:

That in determining the character of a libel, the truth or falsehood is in the nature of things a material ingredient, though the truth may not always be decisive, but being abused, may still admit of a malicious and mischievous intent which may constitute a libel.[190]

Aware that Chief Justice Lewis had ruled, in the trial at Claverack, against the admission of evidence proving the truth of the libel, and aware, too, that Lewis was following the law of libel as it had been transported to America, Hamilton took pains to point out:

That the doctrine of excluding truth as immaterial originated in a tyrannical and polluted source, the court of Star Chamber, and that though it prevailed a considerable length of time, yet there are leading precedents down to the Revolution, and even since, in which a contrary practice prevailed.*

Since the Sedition Act of 1798 (in which Hamilton may have had more of a hand—both restraining and encouraging—than the documents suggest) [191] affirmed the right of the defendant in a prosecution for seditious libel to "give evidence" of the "truth," [192] as well as the right of the jury to "determine the law and the fact, under the direction of the court," he stood upon tested ground in insisting upon this interpretation of the

---

* As a consistent if never dogmatic Whig he also attacked "this doctrine" as contrary to "reason and natural justice." [193]

law of libel. He was not a man who had thought about these matters for the first time when his friends had called for help in defending Croswell. Nor was he a man to miss a splendid chance to summon his friends rhetorically to arms or to belabor the absent Jefferson. "We ought to *resist—resist—resist,*" he declaimed in the course of his salute to truth, "til we hurl the demagogues and tyrants from their imagined thrones"— and a few moments later he added, "It ought to be distinctly known whether Mr. Jefferson be guilty or not of so foul an act as the one charged. It is in every view interesting." [194]

Unfortunately for Croswell's peace of mind, if not for Hamilton's reputation, not all the learning and eloquence in the world could have persuaded the court to grant the motion for a new trial. Two of the judges were Republicans, Lewis and Brockholst Livingston;* two were Federalists, Kent and Smith Thompson. The vote on the motion was 2–2, and the conviction in the lower court was thereby left to stand, although the prosecution made no move, for good political reasons, to have sentence passed on Croswell. Hamilton went back to New York and, as it proved, to his death. Croswell went back to Hudson and, as it proved, to a career of contentious journalism that ended unexpectedly in 1815 with his migration to the softer climate of the Episcopal ministry.[195]

Hamilton, however, had not pleaded in vain,† for this well-reported case was one of the longest steps taken in this country toward the acceptance of a revised and, as it were, democratized law of libel. Thanks in no small part to the labors of his friends Van Ness and Kent, an act emerged from the New York legislature April 6, 1805 that declared his assertions about libels and juries to be the law of the state. So complete was this posthumous victory for Hamilton, so faithful to his language was the phrasing of the act, that the declaratory passages ought to be quoted:

Whereas doubts exist whether on the trial of an indictment or information for a libel, the jury have a right to give their verdict on the whole matter in issue:

I. *Be it therefore declared and enacted by the People of the State of New York, represented in Senate and Assembly,* That on every such indictment or information, the jury, who shall try the same, shall have a right to de-

---

* Both of whom had been, interestingly enough, Hamilton's associates in the defense of Joshua Waddington.

† This was not the only instance in which Hamilton went to the defense of a Federalist editor under attack from outraged Republicans. Samuel Freer of the (Kingston) *Ulster Gazette* was given the benefit of his advocacy in a contempt-of-court case growing out of some bold comments on the trial of Croswell in the lower court.[196]

termine the law and the fact, under the direction of the court, in like manner as in other criminal cases, and shall not be directed or required by the court or judge, before whom such indictment or information shall be tried, to find the defendant guilty, merely on the proof of the publication by the defendant of the matter charged to be libellous, and of the sense ascribed thereto, in such indictment or information. . . .

II. And be it further declared and enacted, That in every prosecution for writing or publishing any libel, it shall be lawful for the defendant upon the trial of the cause, to give in evidence in his defense, the truth of the matter contained in the publication charged as libellous: *Provided always,* That such evidence shall not be a justification, unless on the trial it shall be further made satisfactorily to appear, that the matter charged as libellous, was published with good motives and for justifiable ends.[197]

Sixteen years later, when New York turned to write its second Constitution, the principles for which Hamilton had contended were given the character of fundamental law in Article VII, section 1, clause 8:

Every citizen may freely speak, write, and publish his sentiments, on all subjects, being responsible for the abuse of that right; and no law shall be passed, to restrain, or abridge the liberty of speech, or of the press. In all prosecutions or indictments for libels, the truth may be given in evidence, to the jury; and if it shall appear to the jury, that the matter charged as libellous, is true, and was published with good motives, and for justifiable ends, the party shall be acquitted; and the jury shall have the right to determine the law and the fact.[198]

Kent was a distinguished if mournful member of the Convention of 1821, and in the debate over this clause he lectured the men of a new generation about Hamilton's "able and eloquent argument" and the influence it had worked, if not upon the two Republicans sitting in judgment on Harry Croswell, then upon all the Republicans and Federalists in the New York legislature of 1805.[199] It might be noted that Kent objected in vain to the insertion of the peremptory words "the party shall be acquitted," as well as to the elimination of the qualification "under the direction of the court." One wonders how Hamilton would have reacted to this further democratization of the freedom of the press.

This monument to Hamilton's common sense and eloquence as advocate remains today—with only a few of its commas eroded by the passing of the years—in the Constitution of New York. Since something very much like it is to be found in the laws, precedents, or constitution of every state, it could be said that monuments to Hamilton are spread all through the Union. From New Jersey to California, from Mississippi to North

Dakota, men indicted for libel can take refuge in constitutional clauses that speak of "good motives" and "justifiable ends" and that award juries the "right to determine the law and the fact." [200]

We must not give him too much credit for leading the way to the generally satisfactory balance we maintain today between the rights of some men to publish the truth and the rights of other men not to be hounded and defamed.[201] By 1804 lawyers, politicians, and judges all over America were in the process of working out a law of libel more suitable to the genius and political practices of a free people than was the suffocating law of libel that had been proclaimed in Star Chamber and then carried to the colonies.[202] Yet Hamilton's advocacy, it would appear, was the catalyst that touched off the final and decisive steps in the process. A child of fortune whose luck was about to run out in one sickening burst, he was given a last chance to be in the right place at the right time, and he seized the chance with all the skill and bravado he had displayed in 1775, 1781, 1788, and 1790. In a lifetime of fine hours there was none finer, and few more productive of beneficial consequences, than the defense of Harry Croswell in 1804.

THE death of Alexander Hamilton under the malice-directed fire of Aaron Burr sent a shock of horror all through the United States.[203] The response of press, pulpit, and public meeting—the mass media of those simpler days—was overwhelming, and Hamilton found in the grave the kind of unstinting esteem that he had always hoped to find in the field and assembly. Those who had loved him were "agonized beyond description," and plunged violently into an orgy of apotheosis; [204] those who had hated and feared him expressed (with a few notable exceptions) the charitable sentiments of ordinary men who are proud to have fought with a giant; those who had merely stood and watched felt a wave of awe surge through their memories. In the words of the *Charleston Courier*, "whose political sentiments," its editor confessed proudly, "were so nearly allied to those of that great man":

Perhaps no illustrious personage, ancient or modern, has ever had a more glorious monument heaped upon his ashes, than General Hamilton has received from the concurrent testimony of all parties, and all characters and descriptions of men in America.[205]

A good deal of the testimony was shrill or simply maudlin,* but here and there in the purple torrent one stumbles upon a sober attempt to take the

* Or designed to serve Federalist ends, as men like Paine and Gallatin were forced to point out. An anonymous author expressed the opinion of many Republicans

measure of the man with the yardstick of history. While the most prominent consideration was given to his financial and administrative triumphs as Secretary of the Treasury, a respectable number of tributes were bestowed upon his labors as constitutionalist.[206] And while most of these fixed attention on the Convention at Philadelphia and on *The Federalist,* for both of which Hamilton was given perhaps more credit than he deserved, a few observed that a "peculiar greatness" had been demonstrated in his career as "constitutional counsellor of the executive." [207] Yet even they seemed unable to recognize how decisive this career had proved in the development of the Constitution.*

Today, surely, we cannot fail to grant this recognition, and thus to acclaim Hamilton as the most influential constitutionalist of his age. No one, not even the most patriotic Briton, would deny that the fate of constitutions everywhere hung for at least a generation upon the success of the American experiment, and no one, not even the most dedicated Jeffersonian, would deny that the Constitution inherited by the Republicans in 1801 was an instrument of nationalism that had been tested repeatedly and had been strengthened with each testing. It was, as several of them were later to admit ruefully, not at all the restrictive, decentralizing, Whiggish Constitution they had hoped to inherit. In planting their financial, administrative, commercial, and diplomatic institutions and ideas in the soil of an only half-willing America, the Federalists had also planted a series of expansive interpretations in the Constitution that no men of power and destiny—neither Jefferson in 1801 nor Madison in 1816 nor Calhoun in 1832, neither the secessionists of 1861 nor the corporation lawyers of 1935, neither the critics of the strong Presidency nor the

---

when, in a jibe at the New-England Federalists, he wrote:

> "Our General's gone, the sobbing varlets cry:
> Our General's gone, the echoing hills reply:"

As for himself, a hard-core Republican:

> "Nay, though you whet your daggers, foam and lie,
> I cannot swear your Chief was—*six feet high!*" [208]

* One of the toasts at a July 4 celebration in 1803 in Schoharie County, New York was: "Alexander Hamilton, and the Constitution." Another, which reveals the politics of the celebrants, was: "The President of the United States. Reverence and respect for the *office,* tho' it be holden even by—Thomas Jefferson." These and other toasts were drunk under the approving discharge of the "musquetry" of a "company of volunteers commanded by Gen. Daniel Shays." This, amusing to note, was *the* Daniel Shays, who removed to Schoharie County several years after his pardon in 1788, embraced the respectability of the Federalist creed, and was promoted informally from captain to "general" by the enthusiastic editor of the (Hudson) *Balance,* Harry Croswell.

opponents of a strong Union in any generation—could ever quite manage to uproot. Most Federalists, it is true, took what Hamilton had called "an enlarged view" of the powers granted in the Constitution only because it served their immediate political ends. Those men of the old breed who gathered at Hartford in 1814 with every intention of dismembering the Union proved beyond a doubt that in the 1790's they had been "consolidationists" and even "broad-constructionists" only by chance, and one can certainly imagine them adopting a severely limitationist (that is to say, Jeffersonian) interpretation of the Constitution in 1896 or 1912 or 1935.

For Hamilton, however, the enlarged view of the Constitution was an article of faith for seasons of exile as well as for seasons of power, and one can never imagine him, neither at Hartford in 1814 nor before the Supreme Court in 1935,[209] abandoning the principles of constitutional law he had thrust into public debate in *The Federalist,* number 23, the Opinion on the Constitutionality of the Bank, and the first letter of Pacificus. He, too, carried an order of priorities in his mind that attached more importance to political goals than to constitutional interpretations. Yet so essential to national glory was the more perfect Union, so essential to national energy an indulgent Constitution—and so direct therefore the connection between the dream of American empire and the expansive view of its charter of government—that his brand of constitutional interpretation must be regarded as an expression of the most tenacious convictions.[210] While the social circumstances and political accidents of the early years of the Republic helped mightily to make Hamilton a consolidationist and broad-constructionist, they worked on highly congenial materials in the form of his mind, spirit, and, as we shall shortly see, political philosophy.

It is informed conjecture rather than exact measurement that gives Hamilton clear title to first place among the men who shaped the Constitution of 1801. One cannot deny that the aspirations of the Federalists under Washington pointed the way from the beginning toward an enlargement of those clauses in the Constitution having to do with the supremacy of the Union, the powers of Congress, the energy of the Presidency, and the independence of the Supreme Court; one cannot say that Hamilton's presence in the Cabinet was decisive all by itself in this process of enlargement. Yet the evidence amassed in these two chapters should have made clear that, to the extent that any one man could or did shape the course of the Constitution, that man was the strong-willed and imaginative Hamilton. One may talk with propriety about the collective urge of the Federalists to mount a strong national government, and show how Washington, Adams, Jay, Wilson, King, Ellsworth, Boudinot, Ames, and, let us not forget, the Madison of 1789 all helped to focus this urge on concrete problems, but one cannot escape the judgment that it was Hamilton's requests of a purposeless (if never leaderless) Congress and Hamilton's advice to a confused (if never befuddled) President that gave form to largely formless aspirations, and that forced men to stand up and be counted on the constitutional as well as financial and political issues of the age. While some men wondered what unimagined powers lay hidden in the Constitution and others denied that any not already listed lay hidden in it at all, Hamilton approached it audaciously and pried it open with his Reports. While some men moved cautiously toward the goal of an energetic national government and others sat down in the road in protest against the "rapid strides toward a corrupt despotism," Hamilton forced a pace that swept up the whole lot, the vague well-wishers along with the prickly doubters, in the onward rush of constitutional history.

In the end, I would take a stand on the modest position that, while we must be careful not to give Hamilton too much praise for a development—the evolution of the Constitution of 1787 into the Constitution of 1801—that lay in "the womb of history," we must also not underestimate the influence of his words and deeds upon a train of events that moved even Jefferson to speak of "a republic in the full tide of successful experiment" in his Inaugural Address. This influence was persuasive when the Constitution was anticipated, prominent when it was written and ratified, commanding when it was first put to work, and decisive when it was first put on trial. Despite the patent fact of multiple paternity, we still like to call Madison the "Father of the Constitution," and certainly Hamilton, in the light of his eccentricities and obstinacies in 1787, has no claim to this splendid title. Yet if he was not the father, he filled at least four other roles—marriage broker, midwife, guardian *in loco parentis,* and teacher—that added up to the most useful service rendered to the Constitution by any man of the first generation of free Americans.

It is one of the nicer and more humbling touches of American history that the service was rendered by a man whose own idea of an enduring constitution was, as he confessed, "remote from the plan" of 1787. More than a quarter-century after Hamilton's death, Madison looked back through the haze of memory to salute his old enemy (and older friend) for the "merit of cooperating faithfully in maturing and supporting a system which was not his choice." * More than a century and a half after, we can look back through the crisp air of scholarship and do somewhat better than that. The acknowledgment that Hamilton co-operated faithfully is only half the story of his life with the Constitution. The other half, surely, is that he led boldly and creatively, that he gave far more to the maturity of the system inherited by the Jeffersonians than he, his best friends, and his worst enemies were ever able to recognize. In a moment of political and personal despair he may have judged the Constitution of his last years to be a "frail and worthless fabric," but we who have inherited the fruits of his labors know that the fabric was to prove tough and resilient beyond his imagining. We know, too, that Hamilton's insistent demands upon it had been the single most important force in rendering it worthy of a rising empire of free men.

* To which he could not refrain from adding: "The criticism to which his share in the administration of it, was most liable was, that it had the aspect of an effort to give to the instrument a constructive and practical bearing not warranted by its true and intended character." [211]

FOUR

HAMILTON'S POLITICAL SCIENCE:

MAN AND SOCIETY

*"The science of policy is the knowledge of
human nature."*
Hamilton (*as reported by Yates*) *to
the Convention, June 22, 1787*

A MAN of action who roused to the challenges of assembly, courtroom, and field of battle, Hamilton was also a man of thought who found comfort and inspiration among the books in his study. In a letter to his friend James A. Bayard of Delaware, in whose hands chance had placed the power to decide the disputed election of 1800, he explained why, much as he hated Jefferson, he simply could not prefer Burr as President of the United States:

The truth is, that Burr is a man of very subtle imagination, and a mind of this make is rarely free from ingenious whimsies. Yet I admit that he has no fixed theory, and that his peculiar notions will easily give way to his interest. But is it a recommendation to have *no theory?* Can that man be a systematic or able statesman who has none? I believe not. *No general principles* will hardly work much better than erroneous ones.[1]

This letter, one of the most fascinating from Hamilton's pen, is an admirable introduction to the political thought of an eminently "systematic" and "able" statesman. He had a strong preference for men of intellect in public life because he was himself a man of intellect, and because he did not see how he could have achieved even the first of his goals if he had not valued learning, logic, wit, and judgment.

He was not, to be sure, a closet thinker, and distrusted men who were—especially if they preached the Jacobin heresy. For intellect divorced from tradition and experience, as for intellect divorced from conviction and morality, he had all the horror of Burke or Adams. The "ideologue" or "empiric" was, in his judgment, almost as dangerous a man as the obscurantist,[2] and he never tired of berating "those political doctors whose sagacity disdains the admonitions of experimental instruction," whose minds had fallen prey to "too great abstraction and refinement," and "who, enveloped all their lives in the midst of theory, are constantly seeking for an ideal perfection."[3] As he wrote to his comrade Lafayette at the beginning of the French Revolution:

I dread the reveries of your Philosophic politicians who appear in the moment to have great influence, and who, being mere speculatists, may aim at more refinement than suits either with human nature or the composition of your Nation.[4]

Whatever else he was, Hamilton was neither an ideologue nor an obscurantist. He was, in company with most of the Founding Fathers, a thinking man who read the Great Books, reflected upon his rich experience, and tried his best to arrive at conclusions that were reasonable as well as verifiable, that drew support alike from the speculations of Aristotle, Locke, and Hume and from the behavior of, say, Madison, Washington, Clinton, Burr, and Samuel Chase. He was motivated throughout his mature years by a political philosophy that was never fully articulated but always strongly held. This philosophy was his servant, yet he was also its ward. He could put it to flexible use in political combat, and even, on occasion, put it aside. As he warned one of his followers who insisted upon standing flatly on a "general principle . . . of political economy" (which Hamilton had doubtless taught him), it is often "very important to relax in theory, so as to accomplish as much as may be practicable."[5] Yet he knew perfectly well when, as man of action and passion, he ignored or stretched or overstepped a fundamental of his philosophy. I think it entirely fair to say that Hamilton was as much governed by general principles as was Adams, Madison, or Jefferson. No doctrinaire, he was nonetheless a man of doctrine.

While I have called Hamilton a political thinker or political philosopher,

I suspect that he would have preferred the label of political scientist. As we shall learn in the course of the next two chapters, he was distinctly more concerned with the "how" than with the "why" of government. He was more interested, for example, in the ways men can be persuaded to obey the commands of sovereign authority cheerfully than in the reasons why they should have to obey them at all, in discovering rules of effective operation for governments in general than in proving the superiority of any specific form, in teaching rulers how to respond to public opinion than in fixing eternal standards to which such opinion ought to conform.

More than that, he was a sanguine man who looked upon politics as something of a science. In this, as in many things, he was a disciple of David Hume, who had taught him that "those who employ their pens on political subjects, free from party rage and party prejudices, cultivate a science," and who had offered the bewitching proposition "that politics may be reduced to a science." [6] Although the science of politics was very much in its infancy, Hamilton insisted that it had "received great improvement" in his own time.[7] The boundaries of ignorance were slowly being rolled back, and one by one the enduring truths of politics were revealing themselves to discerning men. While Hamilton found those instances "rare" in which "a political truth can be brought to the test of a mathematical demonstration," and denied that "the mensuration of the faculties of the mind" had any "place in the known arts," [8] he never doubted that men of reason owned a respectable and growing stock of generalizations about politics. If they were not applicable to all men everywhere, they were at least descriptive of the conduct of men and working of institutions in civilized societies. He called these generalizations "maxims" or "axioms," [9] and he seems to have been entirely honest in giving them the status of scientific truths. We shall become acquainted with some of his favorite maxims as we go exploring in his political mind. We may leave this subject for the moment with the observation that he classed himself confidently among "the ablest adepts in political science" because he had labored to divine "those wise, just and temperate maxims, which will forever constitute the true security and felicity of a state." [10]

THE quest for the steady principles of Hamilton's political mind is not endless, as is the quest for those of Jefferson and Adams (and as it might have been in his case if Burr had not been both a scoundrel and a sharp-shooter), but it is full of difficulties. Hamilton rarely paused in one of his flights of fact or fancy to elaborate upon the maxims from which he drew support, and even when one comes upon a short essay in political science, one must be careful to establish the context in which it was written—by which I mean everything from the identity of the man or audience he was addressing to his mood of the moment. Still, if one moves discreetly through his writings, one can find, and be certain to have found, the principles for which we are searching. The most important of these writings are:

1) the great Reports, and also the occasional public messages and exhortations of the five years in the Treasury Department;

2) the drafts of public documents—resolutions of the New York legislature, reports of committees of the Confederation Congress, proclamations of the President—which he, like Adams, was always willing to frame for the consideration or use or even glory of other men;

3) the precious notes and jottings, his own and those of his listeners, of the notable speeches in the Philadelphia Convention of 1787 and Poughkeepsie Convention of 1788;

4) several volumes of letters to his friends, in many of which he appeared in his most self-revealing guise;

5) several volumes of "letters to the editor," not all of which, alas, will ever be discovered and identified positively;

6) a series of pamphlets on occasional subjects, some of which began as letters to the editor and were put together for wider consumption; and

7) most important of all, the fifty-odd numbers that he contributed to *The Federalist.* I repeat what I said in chapter 2 about that splendid effort: Hamilton as Publius was the real Hamilton. While he was arguing the case for a plan of government he would not have written himself, he did it with the aid of insights and maxims, of principles and prejudices, which were the core of his political science.

James Kent told Mrs. Hamilton in 1832 that her husband had intended to make "a full investigation of the history and science of civil government, and the practical results of the various modifications of it upon the freedom and happiness of mankind"; [11] and it is certainly conceivable that, in the dull winter of his retirement, Hamilton would have turned to writing a "great work" on political science. If he had kept his balance—admittedly a substantial "if"—and had put himself relentlessly to the task, he might have produced one of the treasures of Western political thought. There is little doubt in my mind that he could have done it.* While he

---

* And no doubt at all in the mind of Kent, who comforted Mrs. Hamilton with the thought that her husband, had he "lived twenty years longer, would have rivalled Socrates, or Bacon, or any other of the sages of ancient or modern times, in researches after truth and in benevolence to mankind." [12]

lacked the philosophical touch of Adams, Madison, and Jefferson, he had the cold eye—the eye, let us suggest, of a Machiavelli—that was needed to sort out the realities and appearances of the American gamble with popular government. While he lacked their learning, he did not lack their ability to learn. No one who has observed Hamilton in the role of forced-draft student of law and finance will doubt that he could have mastered the corpus of political science in a few months. His mind did not range, as did the enlightened mind of Jefferson, over the whole sweep of human endeavor and aspiration, yet it found questions to ask about the political community that had not even occurred to most thinkers of the age. One has the feeling that the great work on politics never written by Alexander Hamilton would have contained many more chapters than the great works never written by James Madison and Thomas Jefferson. The chapters, moreover, would have fitted together tightly. Hamilton once described his own mind obliquely but accurately as "naturally attached to order and system," [13] and we can imagine him working overtime with all his skill as a lawyer to tuck in the loose ends. Whatever inconsistencies might have emerged in his exposition would have been reflections of the inconsistencies of the human condition, not consequences of slovenly thinking.

But all this is to speculate about what Hamilton might have achieved as political thinker, and we must confine ourselves to the ideas he actually touched upon, too many of them simply in passing, in the course of a public life of unexampled intensity. If we are to discover the consistent and enveloping pattern of his political thought, we must dig a little here and pan a little there in letters and documents that were almost ripped from his mind. "I have not even time to correct and copy," he writes at the end of his impressive letter on "the defects of our present system" to James Duane in 1780.[14] "They . . . have been copied just as they flowed from my heart and pen, without revision or correction," he warns Washington in 1792 about some points he has made in defense of his financial system.[15] "I give you my ideas full *gallop* and without management of expression," he tells Oliver Wolcott, as if Wolcott needed telling, in an untidy but forceful letter of 1797.[16] Only rarely did he manage to take his own advice that writings of public importance "should be done with great care, and much at leisure touched and retouched," [17] and the product of such pains was certain to be an ornament of eloquence and logic.* The image we must hold of Hamilton the political thinker is not of a man of leisurely habits sitting quietly in his study, but of a harried man standing in a printer's

* The product in this instance was his final draft of Washington's Farewell Address.

office and scribbling a last few sentences over the signature Publius—while the printer stands by with a deadline written on his face.

The thoughts of Publius, while hastily written down, had not been lightly conceived. In the crisis of 1787–1788 Hamilton, like Madison, was able to draw on years of study and experience. His reading, to be sure, had a quality of voracity about it—large bites at long intervals—yet we have evidence that he had made a firm acquaintance with such as Demosthenes, Cicero, Plutarch, Bacon, Hobbes, Montaigne, and Rousseau.[18] Hamilton went to these and other famous thinkers for instruction, was seriously in debt to a handful, was the prisoner of none. He took his political ideas wherever he found them, and made each one fit into a philosophy that he arrived at early, perhaps more intuitively than rationally or empirically, and held on to ever more tightly to the end.* Four large categories of learned men he came to know as the closest of friends.

The first, naturally enough, was the English lawyers—Blackstone, Coke, Camden, Mansfield, and the rest—who educated him in the law and Constitution of Great Britain, and thus provided him with a standard, not perfect but highly serviceable, for judging the progress of law and constitutionalism in his own country.[19] Hamilton, who never despised England even in his most zealous moments as soldier of the Revolution, was not afraid to study, copy, and cite the English lawyers. A rough measure of his deep-seated differences with Jefferson, another lawyer trained in the English texts and cases,[20] may be found in their contrasting salutes

---

* I cannot agree with John C. Miller's judgment that Hamilton "changed his political philosophy" between, say, 1778 and 1787. In his one allegedly "radical" expression of political ideas—the letter to Gouverneur Morris, May 19, 1777—he labored several of the themes for which he was to become famous, for example, the need of "vigor in the executive" and the inability of "the people at large" to make a wise choice of a chief executive. And even in the zealous year of 1775 he seems to have held a jaundiced view of human nature in the aggregate. As he wrote to John Jay in November of that year:

"In times of such commotion as the present, while the passions of men are worked up to an uncommon pitch there is great danger of fatal extremes. The same state of the passions which fits the multitude, who have not a sufficient stock of reason and knowledge to guide them, for opposition to tyranny and oppression, very naturally leads them to a contempt and disregard of all authority. The due medium is hardly to be found among the more intelligent, it is almost impossible among the unthinking populace. When the minds of these are loosened from their attachment to ancient establishments and courses, they seem to grow giddy and are apt more or less to run into anarchy. These principles, too true in themselves, and confirmed to me both by reading and my own experience, deserve extremely the attention of those, who have the direction of public affairs. In such tempestuous times, it requires the greatest skill in the political pilots to keep men steady and within proper bounds."[21]

to that archetype of Tory judges, Lord Mansfield. While Jefferson talked of the "poison" in Mansfield's decisions, and thus held it "essential in America to forbid that any English decision" of his tenure "should ever be cited in a court," [22] Hamilton paid public tribute to "that truly great man—for great he was," and added: "No one more fully estimates him than I do, yet he might have some biases on his mind not extremely favorable to liberty." [23] At no time in his intellectual progress does he seem to have been afraid to borrow an idea from a writer simply because the writer had a reputation for bad politics or worse behavior.

Hamilton studied the international lawyers every bit as carefully, and he stood first among all his colleagues at the bar of the new Republic in his working knowledge of the law of nations, which he always regarded as "a part of the law of the land." [24] His public writings on foreign policy as Pacificus and Camillus, as well as his private memoranda to Washington on the rights and obligations of the United States, are studded with adroit references to Vattel, Grotius, Burlamaqui, Domat, Barbeyrac, Heineccius, Pufendorf, Valin, and Bynkershoek, not to mention Cicero and Justinian's *Institutes*.[25] It was not simply as "approved writers" on the law of nations that these men helped to shape Hamilton's mind. Most of them, we should recall, were honored spokesmen of the ancient school of natural law and natural rights.

Some of Hamilton's most consequential beliefs as political scientist were picked up in the writings of the leading British economists of his time. It is characteristic of his intellectual style, as self-confident as it was eclectic, that he was indebted in almost equal amounts to the lexicographer of mercantilism, Malachy Postlethwayt (and through his good offices to "the great COLBERT"),[26] and to the oracle of *laissez faire*, Adam Smith. We shall return in due course to worry the disputed question of Hamilton's allegiance to the principles of mercantilism. It should be enough to point out here that he found a rich source for his expansive notions of political authority in the writings of men like Postlethwayt, and that all the mercantilists and neo-mercantilists in England and France could not have spoiled his taste for the common-sense views of Adam Smith.

Finally, as a young man Hamilton did the reading required of prospective Founding Fathers in such heroes of all true Whigs as Locke, Aristotle, Cicero, Coke, and Montesquieu, and he also ran, with an eye out for useful insights as well as wicked doctrines, through such anti-heroes as Hobbes and Machiavelli and such "sophists" as Spinoza and Rousseau.[27] To no one of these famous philosophers, not even to Locke,[28] did he pay much homage by way of quotation or salutation in his public or private writings. He was not a man, except when cast as lawyer, to appeal to authority for support of his eloquence and logic. Like Hobbes he seems to have chosen to be remembered as a wise man who used his brains rather than his bookshelves.

There can be no other reason, save perhaps that of wholly untypical carelessness or ingratitude or cowardice, for his failure ever to acknowledge properly his single largest debt of an intellectual nature, which was owed to that misunderstood and misrepresented exemplar of Scottish genius, David Hume. In all Hamilton's writings one comes across not more than a half-dozen references to Hume. To his credit, he did salute Hume graciously, when he remembered to mention him at all, as "a celebrated author," a "profound" thinker, and "a writer equally solid and ingenious." [29] Yet he could have done much better than that—and much more often. One has only to lay his speculative musings as Publius side by side with Hume's essays of a political nature to conclude that the debt may have been larger than Hamilton realized even in his most humble moments.

Hume was not, of course, a man much quoted by Americans. He was thought by some to be an unpleasant atheist because of his skeptical approach to the postulates of rational religion, by many more to be an unspeakable Tory because of his well-documented exposure of the dogmas of Whig politicians; and his ruthless demolition of the claims of natural law to scientific validity could hardly have pleased men, even the most sophisticated, who were bent on proving that this law authorized armed resistance to tyrants. Americans were too deeply committed, emotionally as well as legally, to the doctrine of the original contract to applaud a man who insisted that it was "in vain to say that all governments are or should be at first founded on popular consent."

This largely undeserved reputation as a philosopher to be read with suspicion and cited with circumspection does not seem to have lessened Hume's appeal to Hamilton, not even in the latter's most headstrong moments as pamphleteer of the Revolution. In Hume's *Essays, Moral and Political* (1741–1742), *An Enquiry Concerning Human Understanding* (1748, 1750), and *Political Discourses* (1752),[30] the young American in search of sound political judgments and principles found a no-nonsense approach to the blessings and trials of ordered liberty that caught his fancy and never let it go. It is always hard to measure one man's intellectual debt to another man he has never seen, especially hard if the first man is as apparently self-reliant as Hamilton and the second as wide-ranging as Hume; yet it seems almost certain that Hume introduced Hamilton to a half-dozen or more of his fundamental assumptions about

man and politics. Even if he did not introduce them, he certainly reinforced them and sharpened them for Hamilton's use. I am reluctant to
get ahead of the story by listing these assumptions at this preliminary
stage, and will content myself with the observation that, if Hamilton
had ever produced that "full investigation," it would surely have read a
good deal like the *Political Discourses*. While he wrote, like most culti-
vated pleaders of his time, in a style compounded of Gibbon, Johnson,
Addison, and Steele, his political vocabulary comes straight from Hume.
Neither man seems ever to have been able to discourse for more than one
page on politics without calling on such favorite words as "passions,"
"anarchy," "order," "public good," and "factions."

IN the final reckoning of the sources of Hamilton's political philosophy,
we would still have to give first place to the air he breathed in the New
York of 1774 and the Philadelphia of 1787. He, too, for all his leanings
toward Toryism, was an American Whig,[31] and thus a willing prisoner of
that venerable line of natural-law thinkers stretching from Cicero to Locke.
Once he had committed himself to the American cause, of course, he
could have been nothing else. It is amusing to read, in *The Farmer Refuted,*
how well the young adventurer from the West Indies had learned his
lessons in "the spirit of Whigism" from William Livingston and Elias
Boudinot,[32] as well as from the sharp-tongued men masquerading as
Cato, Sydney, Americanus, Ploughjogger, and A Friend to Liberty and
Property who filled the colonial newspapers with their appeals to heaven.
No American apologist could have been a more submissive votary of
those "excellent writers . . . Grotius, Puffendorf, Locke, Montesquieu,
and Burlemaqui." Having already done so himself, he could say in good
conscience to his eminent opponent, the Westchester Farmer: "If you will
follow my advice, there still may be hopes of your reformation. Apply
yourself, without delay, to the study of the law of nature." [33]

In later years Hamilton, in company with most of the ardent spirits of
1776, was somewhat less full of emotion and more full of guile in his
apostrophes to the principles of the Revolution, and in all his years he
ranged far beyond Locke to search for answers to questions that no
natural-law thinker had even thought to ask. Yet lukewarm though the
Hamilton of 1801 may have been when contrasted with the Hamilton of
1776, or, for that matter, the Hamilton of 1776 with the Jefferson of 1776,
he was never moved, as was his mentor Hume, to challenge the hegemony
of the school of natural law and natural rights. Through all his writings
run the familiar threads of this noblest, if not necessarily most "scientific,"

of political philosophies. He invoked the pleasant and useful image of the state of nature,[34] and, doubtful though he must have been—especially after reading Hume—of the historical validity of the idea of contract, he found it impossible to break away from the first article of Whig faith: that "the origin of all civil government justly established must be a voluntary compact, between the rulers and the ruled." [35] In later years he may have smiled at the youthful exuberance of his request to the Westchester Farmer for information—"What original title can any man or set of men have, to govern others, except their own consent?" [36]—yet he clung to the belief that, for all its logical and historical difficulties, the Whig answer to the riddle of political obedience was essentially sound. No more disposed was he to question such Whig tenets as the existence of an "eternal and immutable law" of nature; [37] the capacity of "natural reason, unwarped by particular dogmas," to discover the commands and sanctions of this law; [38] the existence of certain natural and inalienable rights, including the right to property and to a free conscience, which carry with them the "natural duties of humanity"; [39] the fact of equality among all men in the enjoyment of these natural rights; [40] the notion of public office as a public trust, and of each officer as servant of the people; [41] and the persistence in the body of the people of an ultimate power to choose their own political destiny, whether peacefully by "abrogating the old compact and establishing a new one" or bloodily by offering armed resistance to manifest tyranny.[42]

Hamilton's refusal to break loose from the benevolent despotism of the school of natural law and natural rights may be explained partly in terms of intellectual habit, of which even he was a prisoner, partly in terms of the limited range of his curiosity, which would never have led him to a logical or sociological investigation of the origin and nature of the political community. The real explanation of his failure to ask the unanswerable questions that men like Hume had already put to the heirs of Locke, however, was simply the pressure of his own spiritual and political needs. For reasons that cannot be deciphered from this distance and yet appear to have been altogether commanding, he found it impossible to challenge the famous preachers of a universal moral order. Contrary to the myth of Hamilton as a latter-day Thrasymachus, a cold-blooded realist who drew a positivist and essentially amoral political theory out of the crudest teachings of *The Prince* and *Leviathan,* he was first and last a stout believer in morality, both public and private, as the foundation of free government. Like all the leading men of his time, he had read in Montesquieu and the English moralists that "virtue" was the "principle" or "spring" of a republic,[43] and he echoed this sentiment in all his writings and most of his doings. Of all the thousands of sentences he drafted for Washington, none came more naturally from his pen than this observation in the Farewell Address: " 'Tis essentially true that virtue or morality is a main and necessary spring of popular or republican governments." [44] And it was true not just because the experience of men had proved it to be true, but because it was "a dictate of natural justice, and a fundamental principle of law and liberty." [45]

The fact is, and it is of the highest importance for an understanding of Hamilton's political science, that he believed in the law of nature as a living presence. He may have been fuzzy about definitions and details, especially about the sanctions and sources of the higher law; [46] he may have called too piously upon this law to bless his own endeavors; the "clear voice of natural justice" that spoke to him did not speak quite as clearly to his opponents of the moment, whether Tory apologists or Republican stalwarts or Federalist mavericks. [47] Yet this is only to say that he was a child of his time and place, a man driven by nature and nurture, as was his every friend and every enemy (probably even Burr!), to seek amid the turmoil of events for an ordered pattern of values, to identify this pattern with the notion of a timeless and universal justice, and then to relate himself and his aspirations to it. He was certain that men of good will could listen thoughtfully to the "dictates of reason and equity," and thus learn a little more in each generation of the "great principles of social right, justice and honor." [48] He was certain, too, that free and popular government could not exist for long in contempt of these principles, that a broad commitment to pursue them in a spirit of fundamental decency marked "the essential distinction between free and arbitrary governments." [49] It was no vulgar Machiavellian in search of power but a candid Lockean in search of moral certainty—a man well deserving of Dartmouth's honorary degree of *"Doctor* of the *Laws* of Nature* and *Nations"* [50]—who warned his fellow citizens against repudiation in these words:

Governments like individuals have burthens which ought to be deemed sacred, else they become mere engines of violence, oppression, extortion, and misery. Adieu to the security of property, adieu to the security of liberty! Nothing is then safe.

All our favorite notions of natural and constitutional right vanish. Every thing is brought to a question of power. Right is anathematized, excommunicated, and banished. [51]

As further evidence of Hamilton's moral approach to the problem of power, it should be noted that he often used "political science" and "moral science"—even "ethics" and "politics"—as interchangeable terms.[52] The "great improvement" in the science of politics that had taken place in the seventeenth and eighteenth centuries was essentially the result of an advance in men's capacity to discriminate between right and wrong.

Hamilton's dedication to both morality and the moral law had strong if hardly imperious religious overtones. Once again in company with most men of his generation, he thought it inconceivable that "national morality" could be "maintained in exclusion of religious principles"—"morality," he wrote, *"must* fall with religion"[53]—and he found the ultimate source of the commands of natural justice in a "supreme intelligence, who rules the world, and has established laws to regulate the actions of his creatures."[54] He was not a man of deep religious conviction. He was, as far as we can tell, a believing Christian who felt no urge to probe beneath the surface of polite belief. Neither an enthusiast nor a deist, neither a fountain of piety nor a torrent of skepticism, he left questions of religious belief to other men more anxious or qualified to discuss them. While he seems to have been confident in the existence of a God who would sit in benevolent judgment upon him, he was not much more certain than was Jefferson of any other reliable truth about Him. In any case, he seems to have anticipated tens of thousands of later American politicians by being more interested in the social than in the spiritual implications of organized religion. If he was horrified, as Jefferson was not, by the assault upon religion in Jacobin France, his horror was more sociological than theological in character. Atheism was wicked because it denied the existence of God, but even more wicked because it bred anarchy and disorder, and threatened "the subversion of civilized society."[55] Religion was good because it was true, but even better because it was the rock of ordered freedom and, to be quite honest, the custodian of morality among the less educated classes. Hamilton's late (and unfortunate) proposal of a "Christian constitutional Society" would have put Christ to work for the Constitution rather than the Constitution for Christ.[56]

As a final touch to this quick portrait of Hamilton as Whig, we should note that he put abundant trust in "reason" and "experience" as the chief guides to personal conduct, social decision, and moral progress. Like the English masters of the school of natural law, Hamilton would have denied the existence of any sharp conflict between these two ways of knowing and deciding. When he appealed to reason, as he did from time to time, he had in mind what we would call Aristotelian reason— reason applied within the limits of history, facts, and human nature.[57] When he appealed to experience, "the least fallible guide of human opinions," as he did all the time, he had in mind what we would call digested experience—experience appraised with the aid of critical intelligence.[58] And when he appealed to both in the same breath,[59] as he did when he was feeling especially sure of his position, he had in mind nothing less than the great law of nature. The commands of this law could be understood by men who used their powers of reason; its truth was revealed in the "common sense and common practice of mankind." [60] For Hamilton, as for all the men of his generation, experience was the test of reason and reason the interpreter of experience, and both together were the highest source of political wisdom. His constant search was for "solid conclusions, drawn from the natural and necessary progress of human affairs," [61] and it is testimony of the lasting power of the Lockean dispensation that he thought of his own major conclusions as at least crude approximations of the dictates of the law of nature.

Yet again I must insist that Hamilton was a Whig of a somewhat different order from most of his associates in the noble experiment. If he did not break with the orthodox school of natural law and natural rights, neither did he remain its docile prisoner. If Locke and Pufendorf were at the center of his political philosophy, there was plenty of room around them for Hume and Postlethwayt, and even a toe hold on the periphery for Hobbes and Machiavelli. Unconcerned about conflicts that might exist between, say, the whole Locke and the whole Hume, willing to listen to any philosopher with an insight to spare, careful to reject any teaching that could not be squared with his ultimate commitment to the moral order, Hamilton ended with a political philosophy quite unlike that of any other man of the early Republic. His interest in such matters as banking and administration and defense carried him beyond the boundaries of Whiggery into fields of political speculation where he worked almost alone, and some of the ideas with which he chose to work are unique contributions to the development of American political thought. Upon these contributions must finally rest his claim to consideration as a notable political thinker.

ALMOST every political philosopher worth his salt is first of all a psychologist, a man who shapes his descriptions of social reality and prescriptions for political sanity to a core of assumptions about the urges, needs, habits, and capacities of men. Generalizations about something called "human nature" flow impulsively from his pen, and he seeks everywhere—in history, personal experience, tables of statistics, medical lore, even in the writings of poets and theologians—for evidence to support them.

Hamilton was no exception to this rule. Indeed, it would be hard to find a working and thinking politician in his generation, except perhaps John Adams, who talked more about principles of human behavior, or was more certain that these principles fixed the limits within which the arts of governing could be practiced. All his writings, from the most sober and public to the most passionate and private, are shot through with references to human nature—or, more exactly, with appeals to it for support of his schemes and arguments. "The science of policy," he told the members of the Philadelphia Convention, "is the knowledge of human nature." "All political speculation, to be just," he warned the citizens of New York, "must be founded" on a clear understanding of a "principle of human nature." No ruler of men, certainly no builder of a new political system, could be "ignorant of the most useful of all sciences—the science of human nature." [62]

It may seem absurd to us, evidence of both his overconfidence as a politician and naïveté as a political thinker, that he should have described his own fund of knowledge and prejudice about human behavior and capacities as a "science." Yet, as a disciple of Hume, he seems to have believed sincerely that some "principles of human nature" were as "infallible as any mathematical calculations," [63] and that some of his opponents were either weakly or willfully in contempt of the commands of these principles. In a paper written sometime after 1795 in defense of his financial measures, he put the question of human nature and politics in words so revealing of his style and convictions as political psychologist that we may well quote them as an introduction to this discussion:

In all questions about the advantages or disadvantages of national credit, or in similar questions with respect to all the sources of social happiness and national prosperity, the difference between the true politician and the political empyric is this: the latter will either attempt to travel out of human nature and introduce institutions and projects for which man is not fitted and which perish in the imbecility of their own conception and structure or with puzzling and embarrassing every practicable scheme of administration which is adopted. The last indeed is the most usual because the easiest course, and it embraces in its practice all those hunters after popularity who, knowing better, make a traffic of the weak sides of the human understanding and passions.

The true politician, on the contrary, takes human nature (and human society its aggregate) as he finds it, a compound of good and ill qualities, of good and ill tendencies, endued with powers and actuated by passions and propensities which blend enjoyment with suffering and make the causes of welfare the causes of misfortune.

With this view of human nature he will not attempt to warp or disturb its natural direction, he will not attempt to promote its happiness by means to which it is not suited, he will favor all those institutions and plans which tend to make men happy according to their natural bent, which multiply the sources of individual enjoyment and increase national resources and strength, taking care to infuse in each case all the ingredients which can be devised as preventives or correctives of the evil which is the eternal concomitant of temporal blessing.[64]

If human nature was a science, Hamilton the tutor in human nature was hardly a scientist.* His observations are scattered at random through his political and economic writings; never did he pause for long, not even in *The Federalist,* to elaborate on the earnest judgments about the motives and conduct of men that he tossed into the most severely practical arguments. He was not, so far as we can tell, a serious student of the psychological treatises of Locke, Rousseau, Hobbes, or even Hume; he was not a careful cataloguer of the range of emotions and traits he professed to have found at work in men; he did not even try to be precise in his definitions, often using quite different words to describe the same quality and the same word to describe quite different qualities. His convictions about human nature were, in truth, instruments of his political purposes, and the instruments were, even by the loose standards of those days, rather rudimentary in design.

Despite an occasional reference to the universality of the rules of human behavior, Hamilton was not interested in working out a set of abstract standards that applied to all men everywhere regardless of circumstance. When he talked of human nature, he seems to have meant the observed behavior of all men—or perhaps all but a few secular saints—in all situations of which he was cognizant. Natural man, man untouched by the influences of society, was a phenomenon, real or hypothetical, he could not imagine. His generalizations in psychology did not even range beyond the boundaries of Western society. Yet, despite the manifest inadequacies of Hamilton's psychology of politics, it is important for us to study his convictions for two reasons: first, because they were in fact convictions, articles of a faith strongly held, which did much to shape his approach to the practical business of making and manipulating constitutions; and, second, because many of them, however summarily arrived at and casually

---

* Certainly not in the eyes of the opposition, which spoke through the *New-York Journal* in the midst of the financial panic of 1792. "This great minister," it was observed with sorrow, "seems not to be so skilful in the science of human nature as his genius and philosophy deserve." [65]

expressed, were among the first crude American models of more sophisticated and tested hypotheses about man that we use today in our political calculations. At the risk of bringing too much order to the most disordered area of Hamilton's political science, let me reduce the many convictions he held about human nature to five major themes.

The first is well known to all readers of *The Federalist:* the universal, enduring depravity and frailty of men. Even in the most sanguine days of his life, as an undergraduate enlisted in the glorious cause of the Revolution, he refused to be softheaded about his fellow men, and thus doused his audience with the cold water of Hume:

"Political writers (says a celebrated author) have established it as a maxim, that, in contriving any system of government, and fixing the several checks and controls of the constitution, *every man* ought to be supposed a *knave.* . . . It is therefore a just *political* maxim, that *every man must be supposed a knave.*" [66]

Never in all his writings, never in all his doings, did Hamilton indulge in the Pelagian dream of the perfectibility of men, nor even in the Jeffersonian dream of amelioration. "The depravity of mankind, in all countries and at all times," was his relentless theme,[67] and he did not even imagine that the improvement of social conditions might give a lasting boost upward to the general level of human conduct. Not "till the millenium comes," and perhaps not even then, would men break loose from the bonds of wickedness and weakness that nature had laid upon them in common.

Among the specific varieties of "natural depravity" that might occasionally take command of even the best of men, including presumably Alexander Hamilton and George Washington, were hatred, cruelty, envy, dishonesty, hypocrisy, treachery, avarice, and bellicosity.[68] He was particularly insistent upon the power of the last of these unfortunate traits. As he demonstrated in *The Federalist,* he had a rather sophisticated grasp of the causes of war,[69] but he always found the first cause to be the rapacious and vindictive nature of men. "The seeds of war are sown thickly in the human breast," he warned those of his countrymen who looked forward to enduring peace.

To judge from the history of mankind, we shall be compelled to conclude that the fiery and destructive passions of war reign in the human breast with much more powerful sway than the mild and beneficent sentiments of peace; and that to model our political system upon speculations of lasting tranquillity is to calculate on the weaker springs of the human character.[70]

Among the varieties of "natural frailty" were fear, pride, vanity, ingratitude, fickleness, laziness, fallibility, intemperance, irresolution, narrow-mindedness, obstinacy, and the capacity for self-delusion.[71] While these evidences of human weakness did not disturb him as much as did cruelty or hatred or avarice, he thought of them as equally menacing hazards to social stability and political sanity.

Hamilton did not always paint his impressionistic pictures of human nature in dark and forbidding colors. "The supposition of universal venality in human nature," he wrote with feeling in *The Federalist,* "is little less an error in political reasoning than the supposition of universal rectitude."[72] Depravity was a powerful but not omnipotent presence in the community. As he said in 1788 in defending the character of the future Congress of the United States against charges of easy corruptibility, "Human nature must be a much more weak and despicable thing than I apprehend it to be if two hundred of our fellow-citizens can be corrupted in two years."[73] If this is not the most handsome compliment ever paid to the human race, it does show him in his usual frame of mind—"a man disposed to view human nature as it is, without either flattering its virtues or exaggerating its vices."[74]

Like the implicitly loyal Whig he was, Hamilton found man a mixture of degrading vices, discouraging imperfections, and ennobling virtues. "Human conduct," he wrote, "reconciles the most glaring opposites."[75] While the last of these categories was the weakest by far in the characters of all but a few extraordinary men, virtue did exist in most breasts, and it had a way of bursting forth at the most unexpected moments. At one point or another in his writings Hamilton spoke hopefully of honor, generosity, bravery, humaneness, love of liberty, desire for learning, and the sense of justice;[76] and he knew from experience that there were situations in which "human nature" could be made to "rise above itself."[77]

In those great revolutions which occasionally convulse society, human nature never fails to be brought forward in its brightest as well as in its blackest colors.[78]

Yet if Hamilton had a Whiggish belief in the mixed nature of man, he was one of those Whigs like John Adams who found the mixture to be overloaded with vice and folly. Not only was wickedness more deeply planted than goodness in the human breast; it had a way of asserting itself with unusual vigor. "It is a common observation," Hamilton wrote as Phocion in 1784, "that men, bent upon mischief, are more active in the pursuit of their object than those who aim at doing good."[79]

Unlike some of the men with whom he contested, Hamilton denied that Americans had any reason to think themselves "wiser, or better, than other men."[80] In one of the most famous passages in *The Federalist,* he made clear his belief that Americans would bear the common burden of depravity and frailty.

What reason can we have to confide in those reveries which would seduce us into an expectation of peace and cordiality between the members of the present confederacy, in a state of separation? Have we not already seen enough of the fallacy and extravagance of those idle theories which have amused us with promises of an exemption from the imperfections, the weaknesses, and evils incident to society in every shape? Is it not time to awake from the deceitful dream of a golden age and to adopt as a practical maxim for the direction of our political conduct that we, as well as the other inhabitants of the globe, are yet remote from the happy empire of perfect wisdom and perfect virtue?[81]

ALTHOUGH he attached great importance to the everlasting tension between well-armed vice and frail virtue in the character of men, Hamilton seems to have believed that three other traits or drives—of an essentially neutral moral nature—were dominant in directing social behavior. Borrowing alike from Hume's *Treatise of Human Nature* and Adam Smith's *Theory of Moral Sentiments,* and relying as always on the lessons he could draw from his own experience, he made much in his own writings of three consuming "loves"—of esteem, of gain, and of power.

The first of these Smith had called "emulation," a drive which ran the gamut of intensity from a simple need for respect to a prodigious thirst for glory. This was, of course, an urge whose power Hamilton could hardly have depreciated. As I wrote in chapter 1, fame was the spur that goaded him to his best efforts, and he had no reason to believe that he was an eccentric in this matter. If he was prompted by "the love of fame, the ruling passion of the noblest minds," to "plan and undertake extensive and arduous enterprises for the public benefit," men of every stripe could be roused to unaccustomed effort by the lure of "places, pensions, and honors."[82] Hamilton agreed unreservedly with Hume that "a noble emulation is the source of every excellence," and with Smith that such a feeling of emulation was an "anxious desire."[83]

Hamilton used the word "ambition" to describe a number of related drives,[84] the most forceful of which was the desire of material gain. While he never spun out any elaborate theories of the universality and utility of the profit motive, he did recognize that in most men, if not in himself, it was at least as strong a drive as emulation, and that the operations of this motive in a well-ordered society could lead to happiness and prosperity on a broad scale. "Is not the love of wealth as domineering and enterprising a passion as that of power and glory?," [85] he asked in a rhetorical passage in *The Federalist* that covered all three of the mightiest spurs to human endeavor. The behavior of his friend William Duer was proof enough of the force of this spring of human conduct.

The love of power was, of course, a favorite theme of the "approved writers" from whom Hamilton learned his lessons in political realism, and he never found anything in his own experience that gave him reason to dispute them. His comments on this tendency in the human spirit had force and feeling. "The love of power" was a major theme in his speech of June 18, 1787 to the Philadelphia Convention; it was restated with eloquent variations all through *The Federalist;* and he even managed to slip a sentence into the Farewell Address about the "love of power which predominates in . . . the human heart." [86]

I have said that he seems to have looked upon these powerful drives as neither virtuous nor vicious in nature.[87] They were facts of life that simply could not be placed into moral categories. Yet if they were neither good nor bad in essence, they could produce good or bad results. In a man held to paths of right behavior by the inner checks of reason and self-discipline and the outer checks of law and order these three "loves" could quite possibly work wonders of self-advancement and self-realization, and all society would be the gainer. Upon a man holding a license to behave as freely and arrogantly as he wished they would almost certainly bring down the sins of lust and corruption, and all society would be the loser.

Hamilton pointed clearly to the degenerate form of each of these mighty human urges. An overdose of emulation resulted in vanity,[88] of ambition in avarice,[89] of the love of power in the "lust of domination"—and, worse than that, in the abuse of power.[90] Vanity, avarice, even the desire to play the tyrant were evidences of corruptibility which did not trouble Hamilton too deeply. The abuse of power, however, presented a stiff problem to a political scientist who put power at the center of his system, and it is important for us to know that, even in the midst of his campaigns for an energetic government, he held no illusions about the ultimately corrosive effects of power on all but the most saintly men, and perhaps even on them. One can imagine him as a young man nodding assent to Hobbes's awesome words about the "perpetual and restless desire of power after power, that ceaseth only in death." [91] In 1775 he stated a belief from which he never wandered, and which lay at the core of his commitment to constitutionalism:

A fondness for power is implanted in most men, and it is natural to abuse it when acquired. This maxim drawn from the experience of all ages makes it the height of folly to entrust any set of men with power which is not under every possible control; perpetual strides are made after more as long as there is any part withheld.[92]

And ten years later he stated the problem in terms that ought to have special meaning for this generation of Americans. "How easy it is for men," he wrote as Phocion,

to change their principles with their situations—to be zealous advocates for the rights of the citizens when they are invaded by others, and as soon as they have it in their power, to become the invaders themselves—to resist the encroachments of power, when it is in the hands of others, and the moment they get it into their own to make bolder strides than those they have resisted.[93]

THE third of Hamilton's major convictions about human nature centered upon the idea of "interest." He never tired of pointing out that every man was, in one important sense, a self-contained unit in the social structure whose first obligation was to himself. He described "self-preservation" respectfully as the "first principle of our nature," "self-love" ironically as an "indispensable duty," "self-interest" coldly as the "most powerful incentive of human actions." [94] Every man had his "interests," whether in gain, esteem, power, pleasure, or simply survival, and there was not much point in telling him that he ought to pursue them in a spirit of moderation and with an eye out for the interests of others. "We may preach," he wrote, "till we are tired of the theme, the necessity of disinterestedness in republics, without making a single proselyte." [95] Having noted already the young Hamilton's approving use of Hume's warning that *every man* ought to be supposed a *knave*," we may now observe that Hume went on, still with Hamilton's approval, to describe his "everyman" as having "no other end in all his actions, but private interest." [96] While Hamilton, contrary to his own advice, did a fair share of preaching "the necessity of disinterestedness," he based almost all his political calculations on the assumption that he had not made a "single proselyte."

I say "almost" because Hamilton occasionally relaxed the rigidity of his stance as political psychologist and acknowledged the existence of a handful of men to whom the laws of human nature seemed to apply imperfectly or not at all. Having admitted to his colleagues at Philadelphia that "there may be in every government a few choice spirits" who could rise above interest and passion and "act from more worthy motives," [97] he went on some months later in *The Federalist* to rest his case for a strong executive at least partly on the assumption that men of "stern virtue," "men who could neither be distressed nor won into a sacrifice of their duty," would be available for service.[98] While such men were, to be sure, "the growth of few soils," they did exist in sufficient numbers in the United States for the friends of ordered liberty to count upon their presence in the new government. They were evidence of the existence of a "portion of virtue and honor among mankind"; they provided "a reasonable foundation of confidence" in the outcome of the American gamble in freedom. Hamilton did not pause to explain just how the voters, men laden with the average burden of fallibility and envy, could be persuaded to elect men of stern virtue to office. Yet he seemed to have confidence, not as strong as Jefferson's but strong enough to raise his hopes for liberty, that the machinery of election and appointment would throw up enough such men to give a tone of virtue and wisdom to the whole enterprise. As he wrote in an earlier number of *The Federalist*:

There are strong minds in every walk of life that will rise superior to the disadvantages of situation and will command the tribute due to their merit, not only from the classes to which they particularly belong, but from the society in general.[99]

And how could he have believed otherwise than in the existence of a "few choice spirits," and in the possibility of their recognition by the community, when he had been a friend and servant of George Washington?

Another theme of Hamilton's political psychology was the unending war in the minds and hearts of men between "reason" and "passion." This is one of those points at which Hamilton's meaning is especially hard to pin down because he was so casual in his use of words. We can excuse him for having made "reason" serve a half-dozen important purposes, for this is a word that all political thinkers call upon too easily and often. He could, however, have been more precise about "passion," a word he called upon so easily and often that it gives a special flavor to all his writings on human nature. A favorite of many of the Founding Fathers, who would have come across it in Hobbes or Hume,[100] or for that matter in Shakespeare or Pope or Adam Smith, it was used by Hamilton, often in the plural, as a shorthand term for each of the neutral drives or "loves," and for all of them together;[101] for each of the categories of wicked behavior, and for all of them together; for "interests" and "prejudices"; for "vanity," "anger," "pride," "ambition," and "caprice";[102] and, in company with most other men who found it useful, for what I can only describe as "unreason."[103] In any case, Hamilton thought of every man, including himself, as a kind of grand prize in a perpetual "conflict between Reason and Passion"—reason being the faculty of thinking coolly, objectively, and broadly about problems of political allegiance and decision, passion being any trait or impulse from obstinacy to "rage and frenzy" (by way of ignorance and fear and prejudice) that corrupted reason and often drove it from the field. As he wrote to Bayard in 1802 in exasperation over the trend of events:

Nothing is more fallacious than to expect to produce any valuable or permanent results in political projects by relying merely on the reason of men. Men are rather reasoning than reasonable animals, for the most part governed by the impulse of passion.[104]

Since reason is largely a product of nurture and passion a product of nature, the latter generally holds the upper hand—"Passion wrests the helm from reason"—and even "wise and good men" are led to the "wrong side of questions of the first magnitude to society" by the "numerous . . . and powerful causes which serve to give a false bias to the judgment." [105] Like most men, including most famous political thinkers, Hamilton found himself to be a man of reason and his critics men of passion, yet this evidence of his own frailty should not obscure the essential candor of one of the constant themes of his declamations on mankind.

Finally, Hamilton insisted that the bad side of human nature, always in a position of natural superiority in its contests with the good, was put in an even more commanding position by the fact of human association. Men in groups, especially groups unrestrained by law or custom, behaved worse than men on their own. "There is a contagion in example," he noted sorrowfully in *The Federalist*, "which few men have sufficient force of mind to resist," [106] and in the nature of things most examples of human behavior were sure to be degrading rather than uplifting.* In a critical passage of *The Federalist* he put the matter bluntly:

Has it been found that bodies of men act with more rectitude or greater disinterestedness than individuals? The contrary of this has been inferred by all accurate observers of the conduct of mankind; and the inference is founded upon obvious reasons. Regard to reputation has a less active influence when the infamy of a bad action is to be divided among a number than when it is to fall singly upon one. A spirit of faction, which is apt to mingle its poison in the deliberations of all bodies of men, will often hurry the persons of whom they are composed into improprieties and excesses for which they would blush in a private capacity.[107]

* He also seems to have thought that a passion such as pride took on an added intensity when transmuted from an isolated into a shared sentiment.[108]

In due course we shall note some of the implications of this insight into human nature, in particular Hamilton's lack of confidence in the virtue and reason of men who come together in that most influential of political groups, the popular assembly. We shall also note the political implications of his whole theory of human nature, in particular his need to go searching for constitutional restraints, a need he felt in common with all the Founding Fathers.

We may conclude this survey of Hamilton's psychology by noting that he listed a sound knowledge of human nature among the qualifications for lawgivers, especially those who set themselves the task of writing a fundamental law for free men. Somehow the vices of these free men must be brought under control, somehow their virtues must be encouraged, somehow their "loves" must be directed toward healthy ends, somehow their powers of reason must be fortified for the endless duel with prejudice and passion. Most important of all—and here we come close to the core of Hamilton's "science of policy"—their interests must be looked after, secured, if possible gratified, and thus enlisted in the service of the whole community. Again and again in the crucial debates of his public career Hamilton fell back upon this "axiom of political science," which taught him, even if it apparently did not teach men like Jefferson, that the interests of governors and governed alike could be made to "coincide with their duty." [109] Writing in 1775 as A Sincere Friend to America, and also as a man unafraid to quote Hume, he said of "private interest":

By this interest, we must govern him, and by means of it, *make him co-operate to public good,* notwithstanding his insatiable avarice and ambition. Without this, we shall in vain boast of the advantages of *any constitution,* and shall find in the end, that we have no security for our liberties and possessions, except the *good will* of our rulers; that is, we should have *no security at all.*[110]

Writing in 1784 as Phocion, this time as a man unafraid to argue the cause of the New York Tories, he applied this axiom to a concrete situation:

But, say some, to suffer these wealthy disaffected men to remain among us will be dangerous to our liberties; enemies to our government, they will be always endeavoring to undermine it and bring us back to the subjection of Great Britain. The safest reliance of every government is on men's interests. This is a principle of human nature, on which all political speculation, to be just, must be founded. Make it the interest of those citizens who, during the revolution, were opposed to us, to be friends to the new government, by affording them not only protection, but a participation in its privileges, and they will undoubtedly become its friends.[111]

And speaking in 1787 as the delegate from New York he insisted:

Our prevailing passions are ambition and interest; and it will ever be the duty of a wise government to avail itself of the passions, in order to make them subservient to the public good.[112]

Perhaps the most pointed statement he ever made of this working principle of his political science is to be found in his letter of 1779–1780 on a national bank. Speaking boldly to the problem of inflation, he set his own course as public financier:

The only plan that can preserve the currency is one that will make it the *immediate* interest of the moneyed men to cooperate with government in its support.[113]

It must be acknowledged that Hamilton fell too easily into the assumption that the interests of "the moneyed men" were the most important to enlist in the service of the community. While he was by no means indifferent to the fact that the poor, too, have interests, and that these interests must be recognized and secured,[114] he always showed special concern for the aspirations of the rich and would-be-rich, whether in his defense of the New York Tories, his plans for funding the debt, or his advocacy of the Bank of the United States. This concern, it has been argued, was altogether natural for a man who liked rich men better than poor men; his theory of interests was in fact nothing more than a cloak of verbiage to drape around his desire to give handouts to friends and neighbors. But this, I think, is unfair to Hamilton, a political realist who believed quite sincerely that some men had a great deal more power than others over the fortunes of the community, and that it was idle to make plans for the general welfare unless such men could be persuaded to support them. He also believed, as he told the Poughkeepsie Convention in a burst of candor, that the "vices" of "the wealthy" were "probably more favorable to the prosperity of the state than those of the indigent," and partook "less of moral depravity." [115]

No accusation we can level against Hamilton for being a Samaritan toward the rich and a Levite toward the poor can detract from the authority of his message to all makers and manipulators of constitutions: men have interests; these interests govern their comings and goings; government must look to these interests and enlist them in the cause of order, prosperity, and progress. One may argue with Hamilton's identification of the principal interests of the community, or fault him for having enlisted them too lavishly, but one must admit that he put his finger on a fact of political life to which all successful American politicians have paid implicit homage. It is his peculiar merit as political thinker to have been refreshingly explicit in his many references to this first principle of his political science. It was his peculiar merit as political actor to have exploited this principle to build up the Union. One consideration which, so he acknowledged, convinced him of "the expediency of assuming the State debts" was "its tendency to strengthen our infant government by increasing the number of ligaments between the government and the interests of individuals." [116] Rarely has it been given to an American statesman to act so directly upon a fundamental of his political philosophy.

HAMILTON's opinions about society had the same style as his opinions about men: dispersed and yet consistent, intuitive and yet thoughtful, offhand and yet highly serviceable. His thinking was always oriented toward society rather than individuals, toward the public welfare rather than the private pursuit of happiness. The community as something more than the men who made it up was an inarticulate major premise of his political creed, and we may acclaim him as one of the first and most conspicuous *social* thinkers on the American scene. If he was not a full-blooded collectivist in his analysis of society, he was most certainly a man who had the higher purposes and claims of the community in full view. He had, moreover, a feeling for the community as an aggregate of men who had a "common national sentiment" and a "uniformity of principles and habits." A "heterogeneous compound" was not his idea of a healthy society.* While variety was essential to a healthy social order, it needed a consensus on which to focus.

Like most men with a bias toward society and away from the individual, Hamilton seems to have thought of the community, perhaps more wishfully than analytically, as a working equilibrium of groups, interests, classes, even estates, each of which drew strength and support from all the others. He was, for example, almost pathetic in his insistence that "the aggregate prosperity of manufactures and the aggregate prosperity of agriculture are intimately connected." "Suggestions of an opposite complexion

---

* These remarks were made in 1802 during the debate whether to eliminate the fourteen year clause in the Naturalization Act of 1798. Hamilton, writing as Lucius Crassus, made shrewd use of Jefferson's warning against a sudden influx of "foreigners" in the *Notes on Virginia*. His own preference was for a five-year period of residence before naturalization.[117]

are ever to be deplored," he said with at least as much sincerity as design, "as unfriendly to the steady pursuit of one great common cause, and to the perfect harmony of all the parts." [118] As for manufacturing (and presumably agriculture) alone, "There is a certain proportion or level in all the departments of industry. It is folly to think to raise any of them, and keep them long above their natural height." [119] If Hamilton, like the men with whom he contested, seemed more solicitous about the place of some "parts" than of others in the "perfect harmony of all," he, unlike many of them, had an apparently guileless belief in the existence, real or potential, of "proportion" and "balance" among all groups and interests in society. For him the beauty of "the design of civil society" was that "the united strength of the several members might give stability and security to the whole body, and each respective member." It was, moreover, "in a civil society . . . the duty of each particular branch to promote, not only the good of the whole community, but the good of every other particular branch." [120]

He was not, alas, precise about the terms he used to describe the component parts of the community. His favorite seems to have been "class," and the temptation to catalogue him as a "class thinker" is very strong until one notices that he used it as a label for all manner of social and economic divisions within the community: social strata, yes, but also levels of wealth, occupations, economic interests, sections, "factions," and even groups different from one another in tastes, opinions, manners, or morals.[121] If society was, or was supposed to be, a "perfect harmony of all parts," the parts were many, various, and overlapping, especially under conditions of liberty.

One wishes that Hamilton had been a little more candid, or simply concerned, about the social strata of the young Republic. It may be noted that he acknowledged, without regret, the existence of social classes, and assumed, also without regret, that they would go on forever; that he, like most men of his generation (and of every American generation before and since), made economic achievement and possession the chief criterion of status; that he thought of society as a whole series of layers, yet could not resist the urge to reduce all these layers to two, "the *few* and the *many*," the "rich and wellborn" and "the mass of the people"; [122] and that he betrayed, so far as one can tell, not the slightest interest in the middle class.[123] He might have agreed with Adams, for whom this was a major theme, that the middle class was "that great and excellent portion of society upon whom so much of the liberty and prosperity of nations so greatly depends." [124] He might have been persuaded by his mentor Hume to acknowledge that the "middling rank of men . . . are the best and firmest basis of public liberty." [125] But he never did, and one is left with the feeling that he was essentially a prisoner, and a willing one at that, of the ancient habit of dividing all men simply into the few and the many.

For these few, of course, he had a deep-seated concern. While he was once again casual about a point that Adams, and even Jefferson on occasion, labored forcefully and in detail, Hamilton was as certain as they were that every healthy community nourished a "natural aristocracy" of virtue and talent, and he was a good deal more willing than either of them to identify it with the visible aristocracy of wealth and birth.[126] I have spoken already of his confidence in the existence of "a few choice spirits," and will add only that he expected these spirits somehow to be propelled to the top of the political structure, there to exercise benevolent rule by command, persuasion, and example. I agree unreservedly with Professor Miller that Hamilton "held the 'great man' view of history," that he "tended to glorify the hero, the great state builders, the daring and farsighted who had brought order out of chaos and raised nations to the pinnacle of power," [127] and will add only that he also held, with few reservations, the "great man" theory of politics. For a nation-builder who knew himself rather well, and who had worked in harness with George Washington, it was not unnatural to believe in "the agency of personal considerations in the production of great national events." [128] In his view, the success of popular government depended largely on the commitment of affairs to the "management of disinterested, discreet, and temperate rulers." [129] The rulers, in turn, would find the support they needed in "the generality of considerate men," in "those whom I call," as he put it to Washington, "the sober-minded men of the country." [130] These men made up the audience to whom Hamilton as Publius appealed for support in the crisis of 1787–1788, and it seems plain that he counted their support essential in easy times as well as in hard. When he appealed, as he so often did in his public and private writings, to "the candid and judicious part of the community," to "honest men of whatsoever class and conviction," [131] he was identifying not only his favorite audience but the "saving remnant" of the good society.

The notable marks of this society, we have learned already, were order, stability, and prosperity, and, at the same time, progress, adventure, and a solid measure of glory. He wanted his society to be good, but he also wanted it to be great, and he was not sure that it could ever be the one without being the other. In this as in all his hopes for America he wanted the best of both worlds, by which I mean the best features of both the traditional, organic, structured, prescriptive society and the progressive, open, fluid, self-directing society. He had great respect for custom and usage, and condemned "the spirit of innovation" and "the rage for change," [132] yet he was better prepared psychologically than any other man of his time to hazard the fortunes of the Republic in political and social experiment. He put "substantial and permanent order in the affairs of a country" at the top of his list of social goods,[133] yet he seemed to think that such order would be strengthened rather than sapped by the spirit of enterprise.

Whether he looked at the United States through the eyes of tradition or of imagination, he saw a community in which even a rough sort of equality of status and possession among its citizens was an idle dream. Lacking the admirable talent for self-delusion about the fact of social equality displayed by men like John Taylor of Caroline, Hamilton acknowledged both the existence and the staying power of social and economic distinctions. Even if all the unequal privileges inherited from a less rational past were to be wiped away at one stroke, a new inequality would assert itself sooner or later—in a free society, sooner rather than later. He insisted that one of the certain fruits of liberty was inequality—in the first instance inequality of property and thus, in the second instance, inequality of power, consideration, and privilege. Madison records Hamilton as having reminded the Convention that "nothing like an equality of property existed; that an inequality would exist as long as liberty existed, and that it would unavoidably result from that very liberty itself." And Yates records him as having added that "commerce and industry" would "increase the disparity" of property "already great among us." [134]

Since Hamilton was a true believer in the benefits of commerce and industry and at least a modest advocate of the uses of liberty, one must describe him as a man unwilling to sacrifice the prosperity and glory of the nation on the altar of a specious dedication to equality. He never went out of his way, as did Adams in his own generation and Calhoun in the next, to applaud the distribution of "unequal portions" of virtue and talent among men,[135] but he would doubtless have agreed with them that inequality was a major spur of progress in all the affairs of mankind. While he professed a Whiggish belief in "the sublime idea of a perfect equality of rights among citizens," [136] he was not prepared to give the operative word "rights" an expansive definition. While he took pains to tell Jefferson in 1791 (who took pains to commit it to writing "in the moment of A.H.'s leaving the room") that a "mind must be really depraved which would not prefer the equality of political rights which is the foundation of pure republicanism," he added at once the critical qualification—"if it can be obtained consistent with order." [137] Equity, not equality, was the last notable mark of Hamilton's good society. Each man deserved his due, but what was due to any two men was, in the total view of their rights, not exactly the same. When he said to the Convention "that every individual of the community at large has an equal right to the protection of government," [138] he meant only to say that the laws must not discriminate willfully among classes or interests or sections. That these differences among men would and should exist, that they were differences of status and influence as well as of vocation and property, and that they should be protected against the rage for leveling were all fundamentals of Hamilton's social thought.

If he was less committed than Jefferson to the idea of natural or social equality, he was more committed to the ideal of racial equality. One learns with surprise in an excursion through Hamilton's writings that this child of the West Indies (in many ways a harsher mentor in racial matters than Virginia) was singularly free of cruel or careless notions about the "natural" inferiority of the Negro. In a letter dated March 14, 1779 to John Jay, who was then President of the Continental Congress, he supported the quixotic proposal of his friend John Laurens to raise several battalions of Negroes in his native South Carolina. "I have not the least doubt, that the negroes will make very excellent soldiers," he wrote, "for their natural faculties are probably as good as ours." [139] As to their supposed lack of talent and sensibility, "the contempt we have been taught to entertain for the blacks, makes us fancy many things that are founded neither in reason nor experience." One of these things, it is clear from other public and private musings on the plight of the Negro, was the alleged conformity of the institution of slavery to the dictates of social expediency or natural justice. While Hamilton was too much a man of his age and social milieu and too zealous an advocate of Union to push for emancipation through political action, he was moved deeply "by the dictates of humanity and of true policy" to hope for steady improvement in the fortunes of "this unfortunate class of men." The laws of slavery were "the laws of degraded humanity"; the surrender of escaped Negroes to slavery was as *"odious* and *immoral* a thing as can be conceived." [140]

As an enthusiastic member of the New York Society for Promoting the Manumission of Slaves, Hamilton is said to have once brought in a motion that the members of the society begin by freeing their own slaves. The motion, unfortunately, was defeated, and Hamilton, unfortunately, may have had a slave or two around his own house.[141] Yet prisoner that he may have been of the mood and customs of his age, and perhaps of his own lack of imagination about how to give a slave both the appearance and substance of freedom, he seems to have been entirely sincere in his belief that Negroes were "men" and "human beings" in every sense of these words.[142] Out of such beliefs, vague but essentially decent, was to come in time a national conscience that had to be done with human slavery. It is pleasant to record that Hamilton's political philosophy, as well as his social conscience, had no place in it for the concept of racial inferiority. It would be pleasant—but it is, alas, impossible—to say as much for some of his more "democratic" opponents.

HAMILTON the social thinker was an interesting blend of the "pluralist," the "dualist," and the "unitarian."[143] The last of these approaches to the study of society was, I think, ascendant in his philosophy. Sometimes he seems to have been most impressed with the diversity of groups and classes in the community, and concerned to discover and adjust the delicate balance of forces among them; other times he was more impressed with the way in which all men could divide, at least for political purposes, into "the few" and "the many," and concerned to give each of these mighty forces the most suitable weapons for the struggle. But almost always he was most impressed with the community itself, and concerned to discover the terms of the higher unity into which, he was certain, all men and groups and classes must finally merge. Throughout his life, in every medium and on every occasion, he stated his belief in the existence of "the public interest." So strong was this belief, so often did he fall back upon it for inspiration, that one historian of American political thought has labeled him the "Rousseau of the Right."[144] Although the equation of Hamilton's belief in an overriding public interest with Rousseau's theory of the General Will raises more questions than it answers, it does point up the streak of political Romanticism that ran all through this area of his thought.

Hamilton's favorite label for the common interest that transcends all private interests was "the public good," a phrase much loved by the leading men of his generation and easily discovered in the treasure house of political thought, notably in Hume's political essays.[145] Of the hundreds of examples of his use of this phrase that we might quote, let this handful serve to give the flavor of his thought:

To James Duane in 1780 on the subject of Congress's putative authority:

The manner in which Congress was appointed would warrant, and the public good required, that they should have considered themselves as vested with full power *to preserve the republic from harm.*

To his colleagues at Philadelphia in 1787 on the subject of unchecked democracy:

Can a democratic assembly, who annually resolve in the mass of the people, be supposed steadily to pursue the public good?

To his colleagues at Poughkeepsie in 1788 on the nature of representation:

The entire and immediate dependence the representative feels on his constituent . . . will generally incline him to prefer the particular before the public good.

And a few days later on the same problem:

What we apprehend is, that some sinister prejudice, or some prevailing passion, may assume the form of a genuine interest. The influence of these is as powerful as the most permanent conviction of the public good, and against this influence we ought to provide.

To the readers of *The Federalist* on the necessity of sure sources of revenue for the new national government:

How is it possible that a government half supplied and always necessitous can . . . undertake or execute any liberal or enlarged plans of the public good?

To the same audience in defense of the President's power of veto:

It establishes a salutary check upon the legislative body, calculated to guard the community against the effects of faction, precipitancy, or of any impulse unfriendly to the public good.

To the citizens of New York in 1789 on the ever fresh subject of Governor Clinton:

In all struggles for liberty, the leaders of the people have fallen under two principal discriminations; those who, to a conviction of the real usefulness of civil liberty, join a sincere attachment to the public good, and those who are of restless and turbulent spirit, impatient of constraint, averse to all power or superiority which they do not themselves enjoy.

To Washington in 1789 on the subject of presidential etiquette:

The public good requires as a primary object, that the dignity of the office should be supported.

To no one in particular in 1791 in defense of the sovereign right of the community to dispense with an established rule of sound government in moments of national crisis:

There are certain great cases which operate as exceptions to the rule, and in which the public good may demand and justify a departure from it.

To Washington in 1792 on the rules of constitutional interpretation:

In cases where two constructions may reasonably be adopted, and neither can be pronounced inconsistent with the public good, it seems proper that the legislative sense should prevail.

To his Federalist colleagues in 1800 (and, thanks to Aaron Burr, to the whole reading public) on the manner in which John Adams had ignored his Cabinet in making a critical decision:

A President is not bound to conform to the advice of his ministers. He is even under no positive injunction to ask or require it. But the Constitution presumes that he will consult them; and the genius of our government and the public good recommend the practice.[146]

This is, I repeat, only a sampling of Hamilton's uses of this famous phrase—and of the major premises to which it tried to give expression. When he appealed to Washington to run (and run again), when he warned the Federalists not to support Burr, when he felt more than the usual pressure to justify his own conduct, it was "the public good" to which he repaired for support. Nor was this the only phrase he called on to express this consuming belief. For the record, and for the guidance of other explorers into Hamilton's mind, it might be useful to note a score of other labels that he used interchangeably with "the public good": "the public interest," "the public weal," "the public safety," "the public welfare," "the public safety and welfare," "the public felicity," "the public happiness," "the general good," "the general good of society," "the general interest," "the general happiness," "the common interest," "the national interest," "the national happiness," "the welfare of the community," "the true interests of the community," "the permanent welfare of society," "the permanent happiness of society," "the good of the whole community," "the peace and happiness of the community as a whole," and, in an unaccustomed burst of supra-nationalism, "the common interests of humanity."[147] He even spoke in one instance of "the general will" as the vehicle of the people's commitment to the public good.[148]

Plainly this was one of the three or four leading principles of Hamilton's political philosophy, and plainly it raises interesting questions about the quality of this philosophy. It was a leading principle because, as this string of quotations must have proved, he needed it desperately, not simply as a refuge to which he could execute a self-righteous retreat from political warfare, but as a kind of base camp, a majestic point of reference, from which he could set forth confidently on his forays into the wilds of political speculation. It was what he would have called an "enlarged" and "liberal" way of thinking about the nature and purpose of politics, and it encouraged him to think primarily in terms of energy, efficiency, power, and authority. The public good was a deep-seated major premise that drove Hamilton inexorably to take the broad view of the powers needed by the national government and thus granted or to be discovered in the Constitution.

This principle raises questions about the quality of Hamilton's philosophy because he never paused for more than a sentence or two to define his terms or to give them content and application. We can say a few things with confidence about his idea of the public good or public interest:

1) It encompassed and yet rose above all private interests, and indeed had a life of its own.

2) It was neither the sum nor the lowest common denominator of the many private goods or interests in the community.

3) It provided the great context of liberty, law, order, stability, and progress within which private interests could be pursued with hope of gain and esteem, yet it also provided limits beyond which the pursuit of these interests would corrupt and subvert the community.

4) All men in the community, not just the rich and well-placed, shared in its blessings.

5) All men in the community were aware of its existence, and all men of average intelligence could understand its commands.

6) Because of the nature of man and the nature of society, however, only a few men of exceptional virtue would respond to these commands willingly, that is, without wasting much thought about carrots and sticks.

7) The nature of man was such that he almost always preferred special, local, private interests (which he could see and touch) to general, national, public interests (which he could only imagine).

8) The nature of society, especially free society, was such that private interests flourished in abundance, that most men prospered by pursuing them hotly, and that inevitably this pursuit carried them beyond the limits within which the public interest and private interests were at peace with one another.

This is another of those instances in which one wishes mightily that Hamilton had been spared to write his great work on politics, for his pages on the conflict and reconciliation of the public good and private interests must surely have made his reputation once and for all as a front-rank American political thinker. As matters stand, however, we again know only a few things for certain, the most important of which is that this reconciliation was the essence of successful politics. By directing the pursuit of private interests into channels of service to the whole community, by encouraging compromises among the claims of competing interests,[149] by clamping down on any form of pursuit that was palpably in defiance of the welfare and sense of the community, and by giving easy access to the seats of power to the "few choice spirits" who were moved largely by public considerations, the community could at least attempt the reconciliation. While Hamilton was concerned to discover constitutional solutions to this problem, he also had some faith in the "hidden hand" of a free political process. In a letter to Governor Clinton in 1783 he expressed his confidence in "the constant operation of a general interest which, by the very collision of particular interests, must in the main prevail in a Continental deliberative." [150]

The most serious question one is forced to ask is whether Hamilton was not in fact caught up in a fundamental inconsistency that a more penetrating or simply more patient mind could have recognized and then resolved: the inconsistency between a view of politics, which he held in moments of idealism, that focused upon something great and noble called "the public good," and a view of politics, upon which he fell back in moments of realism, that focused upon something tenacious and seminal called "private interests." Now there is no doubt that this inconsistency lay deep in his political consciousness, and that he never made a final choice of one view or the other as the core around which to group all his other insights and assumptions about society. There is also no doubt that his mind was caught in the middle of an undeclared (and thus unacknowledged) war between the consequences of these views, and that as a result he is a something less than satisfactory exponent of the theory of social interests. Yet it is probable that his attempt to have it both ways—to celebrate the splendors of the public good and exhort men to honor it, to acknowledge the primacy of private interests and expect men to pursue them—was the mark not of a mind too confused to see that a choice must be made or too weak to make it, but of a mind honest enough to reflect the tension in the community itself between the needs that each man shares with all other men and the needs he shares with only a few men or even with none at all.

One cannot help but think that Hamilton did the right thing intellectually—by which I mean that he kept his thoughts in touch with reality—when he paid equal respect, if never equal homage, to the public good and, as a social force not exactly identical with it, to the sum of all the private goods. If he was confused and contradictory, so, too, was the reality of the society for which he was hoping to lay down a few effective rules of decision. Is there not, he would have a right to ask his critics, a public good that envelops the common and long-range interests of the community and of every man in it? Is there not also a vast array of groups and personal interests that poses a constant threat to the public good? And are there not ways—prizes, penalties, examples, threats, incantations, customs—to make each man conscious of the public good, to persuade him of his own stake in it, to teach him the limits of pursuit of his private interests, and, most important, to create a situation in which even a selfish attention to these interests will perhaps strengthen the public good?

Hamilton always insisted that there were such ways, and one must admire his tenacity in refusing to give up the search for a workable pattern of popular government in which, as he told his friends in Philadelphia, laws and rulers "availed" themselves of the passions and interests of men "in order to make them subservient to the public good." [151] It must always be his distinction that he, more pointedly than any other political thinker of his time, introduced the concept of the public good into American thought. Because of the inherent complexity of the concept and the shotgun methods of the conceiver, the introduction was certain to be confusing. Yet if a Romantic named Rousseau is celebrated for having confused us with his vague idea of a General Will, a Romantic named Hamilton can be admired for having confused us with his vague idea of a Public Good. There are those who argue that the first duty of the political scientist is to throw thinking men into studied confusion, and both Rousseau and Hamilton did this duty with a vengeance.

HAMILTON's simultaneous celebration of the public good and deference to private interests goes far to explain his ambivalent yet basically censorious attitude toward political parties, which is most clearly revealed in his draft of the Farewell Address.[152] On one hand, he knew that associations of like-minded men for political purposes were bound to arise in a free society, and he admitted that parties, when they were doing their best, might provide "salutary checks upon the administration of the government" and "invigorate the spirit of liberty." [153] On the other, he had a low opinion of their "best," and no opinion at all of their will to do it, and would gladly have looked forward to a future without them. Like most men of his time, he had given no real thought to these still formless phenomena. He never made room in his political science for a theory of political parties because he never imagined them as fully developed, essential, both dynamic and stabilizing adjuncts of the political process. To the end of his life he refused to believe that the party he led was a party at all. It was, rather, a kind of *ad hoc* committee of correspondence of men with a large view of America's destiny, a rudimentary instrument of the public good that had been reluctantly created by him and his friends to meet the wrongheaded challenge of men like Clinton and Jefferson.

The truth is that he identified "party" with "faction," and defined "faction" simply as a "small number" of men "inimical to the common voice" of the country.[154] Hobbes had told him that a faction was "as it were a city in a city," and such an image was deeply disturbing to this advocate of the public good.[155] Hume had told him that "factions subvert government, render laws impotent, and beget the fiercest animosities among men of the same nation, who ought to give mutual assistance and protection to each other," and this self-conscious builder of a nation agreed that "founders of factions" ought therefore to be "detested and hated." [156] Faction was simply private interest writ large; it was the passions and ambitions of a self-regarding group of men in hostile array against "the good of the whole community." Factions, by definition, were vehicles of particular interests, and the clash of faction with faction would too often do damage to the public interest. All in all, he was forced to conclude, the "spirit of faction" was the "bane of free government" and the "mortal poison of our land," faction itself a "demon" of "pestilential breath," [157] not least because it represented the challenge of a selfish minority to the large majority. The notion of faction as majority seems never to have occurred to him. As he put the matter rhetorically but honestly at the time of the Whiskey Rebellion:

Shall the majority govern or be governed? shall the nation rule or be ruled? shall the general will prevail, or the will of a faction? shall there be government or no government? [158]

In Hamilton's political science, "faction" and "party" were two labels for the same political phenomenon, and it was a phenomenon to strike fear into the hearts of all friends of orderly self-government. "Sedition and party rage," "petulance of party," "rage of party spirit," "unaccommodating spirit of party," "delirium of party spirit," "rage of party," "baneful spirit of party," "cant phrases of party," "heats of party," "that intolerant spirit which has at all times characterized political parties" [159]—these were plainly the words of a man who did not imagine that parties, as he knew them or perhaps even as we know them, could be useful instruments in the political process, who meant what he said when, in a typical burst of political Romanticism, he told the Poughkeepsie Convention that "we are attempting by this Constitution to abolish factions and to unite all parties for the general welfare." [160] Even if we discount his natural propensity to call any group of men who opposed his plans for the nation a "faction," we must conclude that his belief in the essentially malevolent influence of self-willed minorities extended to almost all political groupings in the community. For a man who was one of the first and most explicit to direct attention to the tenacious power of private interests, he was strangely reluctant to make a full place in his political science for the concerted pursuit of these interests by groups of like-minded men. He should have been persuaded by his own wisdom in such matters that this pursuit was a natural agency of free government; he could never rid himself of the assumption that it was a "natural disease." [161]

ONE reason why Hamilton was concerned to discover ways in which government could serve the private interests of influential men—without prejudice, of course, to the public interest of all men—was his refreshingly modern grasp of the political significance of "confidence." The first of the "great and essential principles for the support of government" was "an active and constant interest" among the people "in supporting it"; the "greatest misfortune that can befall a nation" was conduct that served "to destroy confidence in the government." [162] No popular government could expect to endure for long unless it performed "all those acts" which would "familiarize and endear" it to the people.[163] While the confidence of the men of property, the "sober-minded and virtuous men" with a special interest in "order" and "constancy," was essential to secure,[164] so, too, was the confidence of the people at large. Unless men of every class felt some measure of "affection, esteem, and reverence towards the government," [165] and looked upon that government as the guardian and promoter of their interests, even the best constitution in the world would not save the United States. To *"render odious"* the wise laws adopted under the Constitution of 1787 was, he thought, to "subvert" them, "for in a popular government these are convertible terms." [166] Hamilton's constant purpose as a politician was to "attach" the people to the new national government. Not until they were persuaded to rise above their natural preference for the state governments would they give this government the confidence it needed in order to endure.[167] As he argued in 1787 in support of a government with "the power of extending its operations to individuals":

> The government of the Union, like that of each State, must be able to address itself immediately to the hopes and fears of individuals; and to attract to its support those passions which have the strongest influence upon the human heart.[168]

Hamilton's salutes to "confidence" are honest witnesses of the respect he always paid to public opinion. Sometimes he praised it, other times damned it; once in a self-righteous letter to Washington he sneered at it as of "no value." [169] Yet not even the most radical democrat in his time was more alert to its power or more anxious to persuade it.[170] Again and again, even in the most active moments of his career, he took up his pen to appeal to his fellow citizens—to the "leaders" from whom "in popular governments, the sentiments of the people generally take their tone," to the "prudent and honest men of whatever party" who were alert spectators of the political struggle, even to "the illiterate and uninformed part of the community" whose whims, after all, could play hob with orderly government.[171] The man who helped to found the *New York Evening Post,* like the man who dressed himself in carefully chosen pseudonyms, acted always on the firm belief, which he shared with Edmund Burke, that "all governments, even the most despotic, depend, in a great degree, on opinion," and that "in free republics it is most peculiarly the case." [172] A Sincere Friend to America, An American, Publius, the Continentalist, H. G., Civis, Fact, Observer, Phocion, Americus, Americanus, Camillus, Horatius, Pacificus, No Jacobin, Lucius Crassus, Pericles, Detector, Tully, Titus Manlius, Amicus, Metellus, and A Plain Honest Man all knew that the "habits," "dispositions," "feelings," "sentiments," and "prejudices" of the people—"however these may be regretted"—could not "be excluded from political calculations." [173] Public opinion, in Hamilton's view, was the parent of credit, the arbiter of taxes, the spirit of the laws, the sovereign of civil liberty, the key to war and peace, the shaping hand of justice, the censor of executives, the dictator to legislators, all in all, "the governing principle of human affairs." [174] In a letter written during the crisis of the Virginia Resolutions he showed how seriously he valued such opinion. "What, my dear sir," he asked of Theodore Sedgwick, "are you going to do in Virginia?"

> This is a very serious business, which will call for all the wisdom and firmness of the government. The following are the ideas which occur to me on the

occasion. The first thing in all great operations of such a government as ours is to secure the opinion of the people.[175]

While Hamilton had little faith in the discernment or discretion of the people at large, he recognized clearly that their opinions of men and measures would be the decisive force in the political process of freedom. He recognized, too, however grudgingly, that this was right and just. He was concerned only that the impact of these opinions upon governors and legislators be softened by techniques of delay and indirection. It was the second or even third thoughts of the people that he wanted to introduce into the decision-making process. And it was "the progress of public opinion" in which he put his hopes for the success of popular government.[176]

Hamilton had no unusual views on the best way for the leaders of such a government to inform public opinion and win it to their side. For the most part, it was the same old problem of educating men in the public interest while protecting and encouraging their private interests. He did, however, put particular emphasis on the importance of "appearances." Four bits of professional advice from his hand should suffice to make the point.

To Congress in the First Report on the Public Credit:

The Secretary thinks it advisable to . . . bring the expenditure of the nation to a level with its income. Till this shall be accomplished, the finances of the United States will never wear a proper countenance. . . . In nothing are appearances of greater moment than in whatever regards credit. Opinion is the soul of it, and this is affected by appearances as well as realities.[177]

To an unknown correspondent on the causes of inflation:

A degree of illusion mixes itself in all the affairs of society. The opinion of objects has more influence than their real nature. The quantity of money in circulation is certainly a chief cause of its decline; but we find it is depreciated more than five times as much as it ought to be by this rule. The excess is derived from opinion, a want of confidence.[178]

To the House of Representatives on a proposed coinage for the United States:

A still greater depreciation, in the public opinion, would be to be apprehended from the *apparent* debasement of the coin. The effects of imagination and prejudice cannot safely be disregarded in any thing that relates to money. If the beauty of the coin be impaired, it may be found difficult to satisfy the generality of the community, that what appears worse is not really less valuable;

and it is not altogether certain, that an impression of its being so, may not occasion an unnatural augmentation of prices. . . .

The devices of the coins are far from being matters of indifference, as they may be made the vehicles of useful impressions. They ought, therefore, to be emblematical, but without losing sight of simplicity.[179]

To the Secretary of War from Major General Hamilton:

Pursuant to an instruction some time since received from you, I have now the honor to offer to your consideration a new plan for the uniform of the army.

You are too sensible of the influence of good appearance in point of dress and equipment upon the spirit and temper of an army, to make it necessary to illustrate its importance.[180]

Hamilton would surely have echoed Winston Churchill's acclaim of the "enormous and unquestionably helpful part that humbug plays in the social life of great peoples dwelling in a state of democratic freedom." [181] "Mankind," he knew from his own experience, "are much led by sounds and appearances." [182] It was, in truth, this kind of deduction from experience that makes him one of the most exciting and original of American political scientists.

HAMILTON'S POLITICAL SCIENCE:

THE PATTERN AND PURPOSE OF

GOVERNMENT

"You must place confidence, you must give power."

> Hamilton to the New York
> Convention, June 27, 1788

W E HAVE now been brought along a convenient line of approach to the crucial and much agitated question of Hamilton's commitment to republican government. In his own lifetime he was forced to spend a good deal of breath and ink protesting that he was "affectionately attached to the republican theory" and had never once advocated a monarchy for America,[1] and ever since his death his reputation has been smudged, if not tarnished, by the suspicion that he was a monarchist first,* an aristocrat second, and a republican not at all. Such was the early and late opinion of

---

* At least some of Hamilton's critics used the word "monarchy," whether carelessly or maliciously or stupidly, as an easy way to stigmatize (and thus, presumably, to be done with) the ideas of a man a few degrees to their right—exactly as some careless, malicious, or stupid people today use the word "communism" to describe the ideas of those a few degrees to their left.

Perhaps the best of all examples is the communication of "Franklin," (Philadelphia) *National Gazette,* Feb. 19, 1793, in which it is stated that "the direction of public money, concentered in one person, constitutes the essence of monarchy." Whether the monarch was "called emperor, king, pope, or secretary of the treasury" was of no importance to "Franklin," for it all "amounts to the same thing."

Thomas Jefferson, and such is the opinion of many of Jefferson's spiritual descendants. There is no argument with Hamilton's "essential criteria" of a government "purely republican": that "the principal organs of the executive and legislative departments be elected by the people, and hold their offices by a *responsible* and temporary or *defeasible* tenure." [2] There is argument about his own devotion to such government, and in many minds the argument has gone overwhelmingly against Hamilton. He has been judged and found wanting as a true friend of the Republic by those partisans of Thomas Jefferson who agree with their hero that "Hamilton was not only a monarchist, but for a monarchy bottomed on corruption." [3]

This is, in my opinion, quite unfair to Hamilton—malicious in its perversion of the motives of the politician, careless in its ignorance of the persuasions of the thinker. The politician, thanks to his labors for the Republic, has long since been cleared of the charge of heresy. The thinker, however, still troubles the consciences of many historians. This is, to tell the truth, a situation weighted with irony, for it was precisely as political thinker that Hamilton made his choice for republicanism. In particular, two principles of his political science—one positive in influence, the other negative—forbade him to be anything other than a republican.

The positive principle arose out of his conviction that the spirit and forms of each government on earth had to be shaped to the "temper, habits, and genius of the people." [4] As he put the matter in a letter to Lafayette (in which he acknowledged the chief source of this conviction):

'Tis needless to detail to you my political tenets. I shall only say that I hold with *Montesquieu,* that a government must be fitted to a nation, as much as a coat to the individual; and, consequently, that what may be good at Philadelphia may be bad at Paris, and ridiculous at Petersburgh.[5]

Hamilton was fully and, so far as I can tell, not at all sadly aware that American opinion, which by 1787 had a century and a half of memory and aspiration behind it (not to forget a revolution against a famous monarch),[6] would simply not put up with any form of government except the visibly republican. He was, I again insist, genuinely committed to America, and since America was genuinely committed to republican government, so, too, was he. It was all as simple as that. Having paid tribute in the Convention of 1787 to the British government as "the best in the world," Hamilton turned his back without much regret on that eminent model. Having acknowledged that he did not always "think favorably of republican government," he then helped as best he could in the search for an American constitution that would also unite "public strength with individual security." [7]

"I trust that the proposed Constitution affords a genuine specimen of representative and republican government," he said to the delegates at Poughkeepsie, "and that it will answer, in an eminent degree, all the beneficial purposes of society." And a few days later, as if eager to settle the issue in his own conscience once and for all, he added:

We all, with equal sincerity, profess to be anxious for the establishment of a republican government on a safe and solid basis. It is the object of the wishes of every honest man in the United States; and I presume I shall not be disbelieved when I declare, that it is an object, of all others, the nearest and most dear to my own heart.*

The negative principle arose out of his lack of speculative interest in forms of government.[8] If he did not, like many of his opponents, look upon republican government as an institutional rendering of the principles of natural law, neither did he bend his knee to monarchy. If he was not, like them, a republican by do-or-die conviction, he had no convictions that prevented him from becoming a republican by amiable necessity. From first to last, as we shall note in due course, his concern was results and not forms, energy and not structure, effectiveness and not abstract principle. In making his decision that republican government had a chance to succeed in the United States, he was not acting the traitor to any other faith. He may have been unorthodox in his approach to republicanism, but he was no heretic in his abandonment of monarchy. In point of fact, the image that the magic slogan "British Constitution" raised in his mind was the aristocracy gathered for business in the House of Lords rather than the monarch killing time at Kew.

The manner in which these two principles joined to make Hamilton an essentially republican political thinker is best illustrated in a letter written to Timothy Pickering near the end of his life. "This plan," he said in defense of the draft constitution he had handed to Madison toward the end of the Convention of 1787, "was predicated upon these bases":

1. That the political principles of the people of this country would endure nothing but republican government. 2. That in the actual situation of the country, it was in itself right and proper that the republican theory should have a fair and full trial. 3. That to such a trial it was essential that the government should be so constructed as to give all the energy and stability reconcilable with the principles of that theory.

* That Hamilton was "disbelieved" by many of the anti-Federalist delegates is plain in a letter of June 21, 1788 from Charles Tillinghast to John Lamb: "You would be surprised, did you not know the Man, what an *amazing Republican* Hamilton wishes to make himself be considered—*But he is known.*" [9]

These were the genuine sentiments of my heart, and upon them I acted. I sincerely hope that it may not hereafter be discovered that, through want of sufficient attention to the last idea, the experiment of republican government, even in this country, has not been as complete, as satisfactory, and as decisive as could be wished.[10]

"For forms of government let fools contest," he would have said with Pope, and might have added, with feeling if not with grace: that which acts energetically to promote stability and to protect liberty is "best." Such a government he had toiled to build, and he took much delight in quoting Jefferson's testimony of March 4, 1801—after twelve years of Federalist rule—that the United States had a "republican" government "in the *full tide* of successful *experiment.*" If that were not enough, he had the word of Governor Clinton that to accuse Alexander Hamilton of wanting to introduce a monarchy was an act both "odious and disreputable." [11]

It is characteristic of Hamilton's pragmatic republicanism that, while he had enough confidence in this novel form of government to give it a "fair and full trial," he voiced enough doubts to make clear that the trial would not necessarily end in a favorable verdict. "I said that I was affectionately attached to the republican theory," he wrote to Colonel Carrington in 1792.

This is the real language of my heart, which I open to you in the sincerity of friendship; and I add that I have strong hopes of the success of that theory; but, in candor, I ought also to add that I am far from being without doubts. I consider its success as yet a problem. It is yet to be determined by experience whether it be consistent with that stability and order in government which are essential to public strength and private security and happiness.[12]

Hamilton's doubts were standard items in the theory of eighteenth-century republicanism, and he gets credit only for having expressed them more vigorously than most of his friends. Montesquieu had taught him that a republican government would not easily be established over "so great an extent" of land as that claimed by the United States.[13] Plutarch and Thucydides had taught him that "foreign influence" was the "natural disease of popular government," "truly the Grecian horse to a republic." [14] And he had taught himself, probably in the hard school of Valley Forge, that a "good executive" on "republican principles" was next to impossible to invent.[15]

His chief worry, of course, was the instability that, as he thought, must plague the operations of even the most carefully constructed republics. The "passions," especially those "not very worthy," acted "with peculiar force in republics," he informed a kinsman in Scotland. "Vibrations of

power," he reminded Rufus King, "are of the genius of our government." [16]
It was not the forcible elimination of all traces of heredity and nonaccounta-
bility that troubled Hamilton when he contemplated republican government, but the forcible introduction of the element of populism—the play
of popular will and whim, the sway of passion and faction, in one word,
democracy.

IF Hamilton was, in his best moments, a fair-to-middling republican, he
was never, in any of his moments, even a lukewarm democrat: so runs the
joint verdict of the makers of our myths and the writers of our texts (not
always the same men). With this verdict I am bound to agree, although
I think it important to state my views in a concurring opinion. The
subject of Hamilton on democracy, which embraces the subject of Hamilton on the people, is not easy to handle. This is one of those areas of Hamilton's thought in which we must be especially on guard against the blan-
dishments of words, whether bright words tossed out to cajole the public or
gloomy words written to a friend in a moment of defeat or defamation.
It is the judicious Hamilton, the man of Philadelphia and Poughkeepsie,
the creator of Publius and Pacificus, to whom we must listen in this
matter. If we listen to him carefully, we will soon enough learn that
he used the word "democracy" in four senses, and that he had revealing
things to say about each.

In the first place, like all men of his time he used it to denote a particular
form of government, one that we would call "direct democracy," the immediate, untrammeled rule of the majority of the citizenry. The pure form
of democracy was the assembly of "the collective body of the people"; the
form most common in his time was "the assembly, who annually resolve
in the mass of the people." Both forms he found "tumultuous," "turbulent,"
and "changing." [17] "It has been observed," he told the Poughkeepsie Convention in a vein reminiscent of John Adams,

that a pure democracy, if it were practicable, would be the most perfect government. Experience has proved that no position in politics is more false than
this. The ancient democracies, in which the people themselves deliberated, never
possessed one feature of good government. Their very character was tyranny;
their figure deformity. When they assembled, the field of debate presented an
ungovernable mob, not only incapable of deliberation, but prepared for every
enormity. [18]

As to the unchecked popular assembly grounded immediately on the
popular will, he knew where to find the worst possible example:

Is not the State of Rhode Island, at this moment, struggling under difficulties and distresses, for having been led blindly by the spirit of the multitude? What is her legislature but the picture of a *mob?* [19]

These two passages are, in truth, vintage Hamilton, honest expressions of the honest convictions of a man who had never seen a New England town meeting, and who, if he had seen them all, would have drawn his conclusions from Boston at its worst rather than from Ipswich at its best. The popular assembly was suspect on several counts: because it was a reflection of all the "prejudices and passions" of the people, because it bred factions like flies in the summer, because faction clashed with faction amid scenes of anarchy, and because out of anarchy must sooner or later emerge the tyrant-as-demagogue to bend the so-called agents of the people to his own will. As a "mere *mob,* exposed to every irregular impulse, and subject to every breeze of faction," [20] how could the assembly ever take the unhurried, unfogged view of the issues before it and thus catch at least distant sight of the public interest?

Hamilton also seems to have used "democracy" as a short handle for the concept of the sovereignty of the people, and for the related concept of the welfare of all the people as the principal object of government.[21] Both concepts were, of course, staples of Whiggery, and Hamilton contributed nothing original to American political thought in his scattered references to the legal and logical basis of government. He did, in any case, think of the Union and the state of New York as governments grounded on the consent of the people and designed to protect, through the commands and persuasions of equal laws, the rights of all citizens regardless of status or merit. Democracy, in this view, was the notion of a government whose existence everybody wills and in whose blessings everybody shares.

Democracy was also, it would seem, the notion of a government in whose deliberations everybody takes some part. While Hamilton was far less eager than either Franklin or Jefferson to provide for popular participation in the government of city, state, and nation, he recognized that it was both just and expedient to give "the *many*" as well as "the *few*" a "distinct, permanent share in the government," [22] to provide for the controlled yet powerful play of popular opinion in at least one branch of the constitutional system. He was therefore concerned, in two of his few words of advice to the Constitutional Convention, to stress the importance of a House of Representatives based on a "broad foundation," indeed "directly elected by the people" to stand guard over "the democratic rights of the community." [23] Article II, section 1 of his draft constitution placed the vote for members of the House in "the free male citizens and inhabitants of the several States comprehended in the Union, all of whom, of the age of twenty-one years and upwards, shall be entitled to an equal vote." [24] Other articles set a modest property qualification for voters in senatorial and presidential elections, and this may be an accurate measure of how far Hamilton was prepared to go in making popular government truly popular. While he welcomed some political democracy in his ideal polity, he certainly did not want it to take command.

Finally, in moments of bitterness Hamilton used "democracy" as a blanket term for all the "excesses" that had stained the history of republican government—disorder, mob rule, anarchy, knavery, the "demon of faction"—thus revealing his distrust of unchecked popular rule and announcing his diagnosis of the diseases to which it was most susceptible. "Amidst the triumphant reign of democracy," he asked C. C. Pinckney in Jefferson's second year in the Presidency, "do you retain sufficient interest in public affairs to feel any curiosity about what is going on?" [25] One has a feeling in reading this letter that Hamilton was not being especially ironical. Democracy had become his generic label for what we would call demagoguery.

Distaste for demagogues runs all through Hamilton's writings and marks him off clearly from Jefferson, whose distaste was for kings—or king-makers. "No popular government was ever without its Catilines and its Caesars," he warned Washington. "These are its true enemies." "A people so enlightened and so diversified as the people of this country" would be brought to tyranny, if brought at all, "from convulsions and disorders, in consequence of the arts of popular demagogues." [26] It was Clinton, Giles, and Jefferson himself—that is to say, his political enemies—whom Hamilton branded the "Catilines and Caesars" of the American Republic, and one must certainly take care to discount much of the crabbed subjectivity of his comments on the problem of demagoguery. Still, he seems to have intended even the most subjective to have general application, and no one who knows him would deny that the authentic Hamilton, the political scientist as well as the politician, is speaking in the following passages:

First, as Catullus, of the leaders of the opposition to his financial program:

These comprise the advocates for separate confederacies; the jealous partisans of unlimited sovereignty, in the State governments—the never to be satiated lovers of innovation and change—the tribe of pretended philosophers, but real fabricators of chimeras and paradoxes, the Catilines and the Caesars of the community (a description of men to be found in every republic), who, leading the dance to the tune of liberty without law, endeavor to intoxicate the people with delicious but poisonous draughts to render them the easier victims of their rapacious ambition.[27]

Then as Camillus, of the leaders of the opposition to Jay's Treaty:

It is only to consult the history of nations to perceive that every country, at all times, is cursed by the existence of men who, actuated by an irregular ambition, scruple nothing which they imagine will contribute to their own advancement and importance: in monarchies, supple courtiers; in republics, fawning or turbulent demagogues, worshipping still the idol—power—wherever placed, whether in the hands of a prince or of the people, and trafficking in the weaknesses, vices, frailties, or prejudices of the one or the other.[28]

Despite all this talk of demagoguery, and despite the unfortunate twist he occasionally gave to the word "democracy," Hamilton never gave up on either popular government or the people. Through indirect and staggered elections, constitutional restraints, checks and balances, education and exhortation, the leadership of the "wise and good," and the example of the "few choice spirits," popular government could somehow be made to work in America. I must reserve for chapter 6 a discussion of Hamilton's faith in constitutionalism as the guardian of ordered liberty, and merely note at this point that, if he did not search as enthusiastically as Adams or Madison for ways to parcel out the total power of the state among a number of independent organs, he was quite sincere in his Whiggish allegiance to "the most approved and well-founded maxims of free government, which require that the legislative, executive, and judicial authorities should be deposited in distinct and separate hands." [29] In particular, he was anxious to fit the "democratic" organ, the assembly elected directly to represent the people, into a scheme that would cool off the "heats of faction," control the ambitions of demagogues, and give reason a voice amid the din of passion. In his notes for the speech of June 18, 1787 he warned that "there ought to be a principle in government capable of resisting the popular current"; [30] and, like most sober-minded men of his time, he thought it wise to put his faith in two "principles": an independent executive and a high-toned second chamber. He was speaking of the Senate, but he could also have been speaking of the President (and, for that matter, of the Supreme Court), when he told his fellow delegates at Poughkeepsie:

There are few positions more demonstrable than that there should be in every republic some permanent body to correct the prejudices, check the intemperate passions, and regulate the fluctuations of a popular assembly.[31]

Although the "popular current" was to be resisted, it was not to be turned aside. Like law, custom, tradition, and the opinions of the wise and good, it had a part to play in the process of free government, and Hamilton never doubted that, in the long run, the people would and must have their way. As the covenanters and "natural guardians of the Constitution," as electors of the lower house, as electors of the electors of the upper house and of the executive, as "vigilant and careful" overseers of all their rulers, as keepers of the federal balance, as supporters of the judiciary in its exercise of the power of judicial review, even as reluctant exploiters of the untarnished rights of resistance and revolt, the citizens of the United States, he was certain, would have all the controls they might need over their own destinies.[32] The controls were to be employed in a restrained and orderly manner, but there could be no doubt that they rested finally in the hands of the American people.

As to the character and wisdom of the people, Hamilton saw society as human nature writ large, which is to say that he always had misgivings but only rarely feelings of despair. Men are "turbulent and changing; they seldom judge or determine right." "Temporary caprice" leads them "to make choice of men, whom they neither love nor respect" nor ought to trust; "ignorance," "misinformation," and "passion" lead them "into the grossest errors." They are especially susceptible to the flattery of "seducing and treacherous leaders," and more than usually "incompetent" in making judgments in the area of diplomacy.[33] As to the commonplace that they are always for peace and their ambitious leaders for war:

> There have been, if I may so express it, almost as many popular as royal wars. The cries of the nation and the importunities of their representatives have, upon various occasions, dragged their monarchs into war, or continued them in it, contrary to their inclinations, and sometimes contrary to the real interests of the state.[34]

These are, I think, forthright expressions of Hamilton's settled opinion of the political capacity of the people, yet one must remember to take them with three grains of salt. First, the context of most of his comments was one in which he was forced to give rhetorical emphasis to the dark side of human nature, for example, a debate over the necessity of a second chamber or a public plea for professionalism in diplomacy. Second, he was speaking of the behavior, real or potential, of the people in the absence of any restraints in law or tradition, and he was confident that provision for such restraints would improve this behavior immensely. And third, he also had a number of things to say on the bright side. Again and again, in private as well as in public, he spoke of the "good sense" of the people, even going so far as to tell the delegates at Poughkeepsie: "It is the fortunate situation of our country, that the minds of the people are exceedingly enlightened and refined." [35] Hamilton certainly had no mystic feeling of kinship with the people at large. As I pointed out with the aid of his biographers in chapter 1, he doubtless loved his country better than he loved his country-men, and the malice and ignorance of much of the opposition to his plans sometimes led him to indulge in rhetoric about "the worthlessness of the human race." [36] Yet no one can spend much time in his writings and fail to recognize a man with tenacious hopes for the glory of the American people and the success of their government. Those who go about quoting Hamilton to the effect that "your people, sir—your people is a great *beast*" ought to realize that they are really quoting Theophilus Parsons, Jr., who said in 1859 that a friend had told him some years before that a friend of his had heard Hamilton make this remark at a dinner in 1788 or 1789.* And while they are about it, they might remember that Jefferson, too, had his moments when he described people—at least people in cities—as *"ca-naille"* and "mobs." [37] Or would it be more appropriate to conclude this discussion with the observation that it was Madison, not Hamilton, who painted the really harrowing portraits of "the mob," of men "sunk below the level of men," in *The Federalist?* [38]

UNLIKE Adams, Hamilton was not much interested in forms of govern-ment; unlike Jefferson, he was a republican only by chance, the chance that had set him down in the midst of a republican people. In point of fact, he had room in his undogmatic political science for all the recognized forms of government—monarchy, aristocracy, republicanism, the mixed polity, sometimes even democracy. While he had preferences among these forms, he was reluctant to proclaim that, for example, aristocracy was "naturally" better than monarchy or monarchy than democracy. Whether any form was to prosper in any society depended, he insisted, on the opinions and prejudices of the people, the state of morality and enlighten-ment, and the presence of men of wisdom and virtue. Most of all it de-pended on whether the government had a sufficient measure of what he liked to call "tone." Tone was legitimacy, confidence, dignity, authority, in one word, *energy;* the absence of tone was caprice, contumacy, mis-trust, atrophy, in one word, *weakness.* His concern, therefore, was not to

---

* Henry Adams, who tossed this phrase into the first volume of his famous *History* (1889), had much to do with fixing it in the popular (and even scholarly) mind.[39]

convince his fellow countrymen of the glories of republican government, but to lecture them on the importance of injecting enough energy into their own model so that it could perform its appointed tasks in an approved manner. His dislike of the demagogue was not a moral judgment on a man who dispensed wickedness, but a political judgment on a man who exploited weakness. Energy was the essence of good government, impotence the sign of bad: here was one obsessive principle of his political science that set him off sharply from the progressives of his time.

Hamilton praised energy and despised impotence because he had perhaps the highest respect for government of any important American political thinker who ever lived. Even from this distance, from a staging point in the progress of human affairs in which government is a mighty and ubiquitous presence, he strikes the eye as a man of immense faith in the uses of political authority. Government, he asserted, was the arbiter of the destiny of the community; the services that it alone could render were essential to liberty, order, and progress. Men who wished for "as little government as possible" were indulging in "pernicious dreams"; men who promised "emancipation from the burdens and restraints of government" were talking rubbish, "perfect Godwinism." [40] Not one bit wiser than those who affirmed "that religious opinion of any sort is unnecessary to society" were those, often members of the same "visionary sect," who insisted

that but a small portion of power is requisite to government; that even this portion is only temporarily necessary, in consequence of the bad habits which have been produced by the errors of ancient systems; and that as human nature shall refine and ameliorate by the operation of a more enlightened plan, government itself will become useless, and society will subsist and flourish free from shackles. [41]

Even if human nature were to improve out of all recognition, government would still have critical tasks to perform. Hamilton agreed with most of the other Founding Fathers that it was instituted primarily to bring peace, order, and security to the community, and to protect men in the enjoyment of their natural and social rights, including the right to private property. [42] He went beyond them to insist that these tasks be given the broadest possible definition, and that they be pursued with relentless energy. He went beyond even that point to bestow the role of promoter on government, recognizing it clearly as the most powerful stimulus to economic growth and social progress. His great Reports were based squarely on the assumption that "the fostering care of government" could carry the American economy from infancy to maturity in the least possible time and with the best possible results.[43] It was not just Hamilton the point-scoring politician but Hamilton the objective political thinker who, looking back in the aftermath of Jefferson's victory, insisted that "the most operative causes" of the "prosperity" of the country had been centered in the Federalist use of the powers in the Constitution.

Fellow-citizens . . . in vain are you told that you owe your prosperity to your own industry, and to the blessings of Providence. To the latter, doubtless, you are primarily indebted. . . . You are likewise indebted to your own industry. But has not your industry found aliment and incitement in the salutary operation of your government—in the preservation of order at home—in the cultivation of peace abroad—in the invigoration of confidence in pecuniary dealings—in the increased energies of credit and commerce—in the extension of enterprise, ever incident to a good government well administered? Remember what your situation was immediately before the establishment of the present Constitution? Were you then deficient in industry more than now? If not, why were you not equally prosperous? Plainly, because your industry had not at that time the vivifying influences of an efficient and well-conducted government.[44]

If Hamilton had had his way, by 1801 the government of the United States would have launched a program for stimulating commerce and industry, supported a small but highly professional (and easily expansible) army and navy, made "the cultivation of the soil more and more an object of public patronage and care," established a national university and a military academy, provided "nutriment" to the "higher branches of science," gone into the munitions and shipbuilding business on a sizable scale, built a network of roads and canals, given "care and attention" to the extraction of precious metals (and even made them "absolutely the property" of the nation), and fostered the progress of "the arts" and "enterprise" throughout the land.[45] Whether as a practical politician and administrator or a political thinker, Hamilton harbored the most amazing expectations of the government of the United States. Few other men of his time called upon government to "form manners"; few others were anxious lest timid men "destroy its capacity of blessing the people." [46]

It should be plain to see that Hamilton took a mixed view, both collectivistic and individualistic, of the purpose and reach of government. As to purpose, he once summed it up in a phrase that, as in so many other matters, let him have things both ways: "This government has for its object public strength and individual security." [47] As to reach, he expected much of the ambitions and passions of individuals, but assumed that these ambitions and passions would need a stern and persuasive guide. The open hand of purposeful government, not the hidden hand of profit and chance, was the guide that Hamilton recommended to the American people. He agreed with Adam Smith on the primacy of self-interest; he disagreed with him on the need to "let it be and do." Roused in 1801 by criticisms of his plans for promoting commerce, agriculture, industry, and the arts, he answered with an observation that sums up almost perfectly his view of the relative importance of private initiative and public leadership:

To suggestions of the last kind, the adepts of the new school have a ready answer: *Industry will succeed and prosper in proportion as it is left to the exertions of individual enterprise.* This favorite dogma, when taken as a general rule, is true; but as an exclusive one, it is false, and leads to error in the administration of public affairs. In matters of industry, human enterprise ought doubtless to be left free in the main; not fettered by too much regulation; but practical politicians know that it may be beneficially stimulated by prudent aids and encouragements on the part of the government. This is proved by numerous examples too tedious to be cited; examples which will be neglected only by indolent and temporizing rulers, who love to loll in the lap of epicurean ease, and seem to imagine that to govern well, is to amuse the wondering multitude with sagacious aphorisms and oracular sayings.[48]

To govern well, he insisted all his life, was to govern strongly. The government of the United States in particular must be "strong and nervous." [49]

JUST why Hamilton should have been so zealous an advocate of high-toned, energetic government is a question impossible to answer. The search for the many forces that shaped his uncommon views would invite us into areas of psychology and personal experience that are barred forever to even the most subtle biographers. One can go far toward an intellectual and thus partly psychological answer, however, by taking note of a "passion" that held him firmly in its grasp. If we can explain Hobbes largely in terms of his fear of death, we can explain Hamilton largely in terms of his hatred of "tumult and disorder," of instability, irregularity, and unpredictability, of what he described as "the hydra Anarchy." [50] He hated anarchy for its own sins against the lives and hopes of decent men; he hated it because, like all readers of the Greek historians and philosophers, he knew it to be the open road to tyranny. His plea for "a firm Union" in *The Federalist,* number 9 was based squarely on the lesson he first learned in the experience of men long dead.

It is impossible to read the history of the petty republics of Greece and Italy without feeling sensations of horror and disgust at the distractions with which they were continually agitated, and at the rapid succession of revolutions by which they were kept in a state of perpetual vibration between the extremes of tyranny and anarchy.[51]

Striking hard in 1792 at those who described his financial program as a long stride toward "monarchy," Hamilton made clear how he, were he a would-be despot, would go about subverting the Republic:

On the whole, the only enemy which Republicanism has to fear in this country is in the spirit of faction and anarchy. If this will not permit the ends of government to be attained under it, if it engenders disorders in the community, all regular and orderly minds will wish for a change, and the demagogues who have produced the disorder will make it for their own aggrandizement. This is the old story. If I were disposed to promote monarchy and overthrow State governments, I would mount the hobby-horse of popularity; I would cry out "usurpation," "danger to liberty," etc., etc.; I would endeavor to prostrate the national government, raise a ferment, and then "ride in the whirlwind, and direct the storm." [52]

Those "who resist a confirmation of public order," he told Washington (who was hardly inclined to disagree), "are the true artificers of monarchy." Men who let their community slide into anarchy would surely go "from thence to despotism and a master." [53]

Although in the abstract Hamilton despised anarchy and tyranny in roughly equal measure, his own nature and the political circumstances of the Federalist era caused the possibility of anarchy to weigh more heavily on his political mind, and led him to dwell almost obsessively on the sources of anarchy: passion, faction, atheism, immorality, an "excess of popularity," and, most immediate source of all, weakness in government. Again and again in his writings he bracketed "disorder" or "convulsion" with "weakness." Again and again he made clear his belief that weak government was a greater danger to liberty than was strong government, that a vacuum of power was to be feared perhaps even more than an overdose of it. As a young man still caught up in the pursuit of revolution he stated a general point of view from which he never wandered, and which he was quite prepared to apply in specific situations:

In a government framed for durable liberty, not less regard must be paid to giving the magistrate a proper degree of authority to make and execute the laws with rigor than to guarding against encroachments upon the rights of the community. As too much power leads to despotism, too little leads to anarchy, and both eventually to the ruin of the people.[54]

He sounded the same theme in a report to the Confederation Congress in 1782:

There is a happy mean between too much confidence and excessive jealousy in which the health and prosperity of a state consist. Either extreme is a dangerous vice; the first is a temptation to men in power to arrogate more than they have a right to—the latter enervates government, prevents system in the administration, defeats the most salutary measures, breeds confusion in the state, disgusts and discontents among the people, and may eventually prove as fatal to liberty as the opposite temper.

It is certainly pernicious to leave any government in a situation of responsibility disproportioned to its power.[55]

A few years later he told the Convention at Philadelphia of the most likely consequence of an overindulgence in constitutional restraints:

Establish a weak government and you must at times overleap the bounds. Rome was obliged to create dictators.[56]

He persuaded Madison to go along with him in *The Federalist,* number 20 in a variation on this theme:

Tyranny has perhaps oftener grown out of the assumptions of power called for, on pressing exigencies, by a defective constitution, than out of the full exercise of the largest constitutional authorities.[57]

And he even planted this idea in the Farewell Address:

And remember also, that for the efficacious management of your common interests, in a country so extensive as ours, a government of as much force and strength as is consistent with the perfect security of liberty is indispensable. Liberty itself will find in such a government, with powers properly distributed and arranged, its surest guardian and protector. In my opinion, the real danger in our system is, that the general government, organized as at present, will prove too weak rather than too powerful.[58]

And so he pushed, in 1801 no less ingenuously than in 1792, in 1792 no more relentlessly than in 1780, for power in the government of the United States, for spacious authority and for the will to use it, for "sufficient means . . . to answer the public exigencies" and for "vigor to draw forth those means."[59] Rising in the Convention at Poughkeepsie on June 27 to allay the fears of opponents that too much power was concentrated in the proposed national government, he began his reply with a characteristic reference to human nature:

It is more easy for the human mind to calculate the evils than the advantages of a measure; and vastly more natural to apprehend the danger than to see the necessity of giving powers to our rulers.[60]

Then, having pointed to the safety measures in the Constitution—division of powers, "free representation," "mutual checks"—he went to the root of the matter in a forthright, revealing statement:

This organization is so complex, so skillfully contrived, that it is next to impossible that an impolitic or wicked measure should pass the great scrutiny with success. Now, what do gentlemen mean by coming forward and declaiming against this government? Why do they say we ought to limit its powers, to disable it, and to destroy its capacity of blessing the people? Has philosophy suggested—has experience taught—that such a government ought not to be trusted with everything necessary for the good of society? When you have divided and nicely balanced the departments of government, when you have strongly connected the virtue of your rulers with their interest, when, in short, you have rendered your system as perfect as human forms can be, you must place confidence, you must give power.[61]

"You must place confidence, you must give power"—this was Hamilton's earnest message to the men of his time, his prescription for a sound polity in any time. Others might wish to make "the spirit of government a spirit of compromise and expedient"; his choice was for a spirit of "system and energy." [62] With those who feared that public energy was a threat to private liberty he took issue in the opening number of *The Federalist*. Let it not be forgotten, he pointed out,

that the vigor of government is essential to the security of liberty; that, in the contemplation of a sound and well-informed judgment, their interests can never be separated; and that a dangerous ambition more often lurks behind the specious mask of zeal for the rights of the people than under the forbidding appearance of zeal for the firmness and efficiency of government. History will teach us that the former has been found a much more certain road to the introduction of despotism than the latter, and that of those men who have overturned the liberties of republics, the greatest number have begun their career by paying an obsequious court to the people, commencing demagogues and ending tyrants.[63]

And to those who conjured up the specter of the "abuse of power" he made answer in the New York Assembly:

Upon every occasion, however foreign such observations may be, we hear a loud cry raised about the danger of intrusting power to Congress. We are told it is dangerous to trust power anywhere, that *power* is liable to *abuse,* with a variety of trite maxims of the same kind. General propositions of this nature are easily framed, the truth of which cannot be denied, but they rarely convey any precise idea. To these we might oppose other propositions, equally true and equally indefinite. It might be said that too little power is as dangerous as too much; that it leads to anarchy, and from anarchy to despotism. But the question still recurs, what is this *too much or too little?* Where is the measure or standard to ascertain the happy mean?

Power must be granted, or civil society cannot exist; the possibility of abuse is no argument against the *thing;* this possibility is incident to every species of power, however placed or modified.[64]

No practical application of Hamilton's principle of energy seems more persuasively modern than his derision of those opponents who thought they could have both peace and low taxes. To the Convention of 1787 he gave fair warning:

Unless your government is respectable, foreigners will invade your rights, and to maintain tranquillity it must be respectable—even to observe neutrality you must have a strong government.[65]

And in *The Federalist,* number 11 he added epigrammatically:

A nation, despicable by its weakness, forfeits even the privilege of being neutral.[66]

While I do not wish to anticipate in too much detail a subject to be discussed in chapter 6, it might be useful to point out that Hamilton looked to the executive branch as the chief source of political energy. His musings on the Presidency in *The Federalist* make up a highly original statement of the proposition, so shocking to the popular consensus of his time, that "energy in the executive is a leading character in the definition of good government" and entirely consistent with "the genius of republican government." [67]

Yet the legislature, too, had its part to play. No power was more important to energetic government than the power to lay taxes, and Hamilton was enough of a Whig to recognize that, even in the most benevolent monarchies, it must be lodged in the legislative branch. "Power without revenue, in political society, is a name," he wrote publicly in 1781. "Power without revenue is a bubble," he wrote privately in the same year.[68] And in *The Federalist* he made the point persuasively:

Money is, with propriety, considered as the vital principle of the body politic; as that which sustains its life and motion and enables it to perform its most essential functions. A complete power, therefore, to procure a regular and adequate supply of revenue, as far as the resources of the community will permit, may be regarded as an indispensable ingredient in every constitution. From a deficiency in this particular, one of two evils must ensue: either the people must be subjected to continual plunder, as a substitute for a more eligible mode of supplying the public wants, or the government must sink into a fatal atrophy, and, in a short course of time, perish.[69]

This, I need hardly declare, is the essential Hamilton speaking. He was as fascinated by public finance as Jefferson was by public education. Unfortunately for his reputation as both statesman and political thinker, the way a community instructs its youth has always seemed more important to the makers of taste and myth than the way it gets and spends its common wealth. Perhaps it is, both politically and morally, yet one must be grateful that occasionally a hardheaded man comes along to remind us of this "vital principle of the body politic."

DESPITE his lifelong attachment to the idea of energy in government, Hamilton never fell into the easy assumption that it was the only solution to the problem of the well-ordered polity. He recognized clearly that the application of political energy, like the pursuit of personal freedom, could be overdone. As liberty was not at all the same thing as license, so energy, he told Oliver Wolcott in 1798 in a letter of warning on the proposed Sedition Act, was "a very different thing from violence." [70] The acknowledged authority of government must be used with sense and moderation. Taxes, for example, should be neither "arbitrary nor discretionary." "The great art," he said in a lecture to the tax collectors of posterity,

is to distribute the public burthens well, and not suffer them, either first or last, to fall too heavily upon parts of the community, else distress and disorder must ensue. A shock given to any part of the political machine vibrates through the whole.[71]

Authority must also be exercised, except in moments of social dissolution, in a context of constitutional restraint. While Hamilton was never so eager a constitutionalist as Adams or Madison, he did subscribe heartily to the Whig dogmas of divided and balanced government. In recommending the bicameral principle to the Poughkeepsie Convention, he stated a hope common to all the architects of the new Constitution:

There are two objects in forming systems of government—safety for the people, and energy in the administration. When these objects are united, the certain tendency of the system will be to the public welfare. If the latter object be neglected, the people's security will be as certainly sacrificed as by disregarding the former. Good constitutions are formed upon a comparison of the liberty of the individual with the strength of government. If the tone of either be too high, the other will be weakened too much. It is the happiest possible mode of conciliating these objects, to institute one branch peculiarly endowed with sensibility, another with knowledge and firmness. Through the opposition and mutual control of these bodies, the government will reach, in its operations, the perfect balance between liberty and power.[72]

Authority should also, of course, be exercised under the benevolent guidance of the rule of law. Hamilton had the good lawyer's respect, even reverence, for law. Government must be strong, he insisted, with the strength of legality.

And strong, too, with the strength of morality. Hamilton was much concerned, as I have already pointed out, with national "reputation," with the idea that a government must earn—mostly through solid deeds, but also through imaginative show—the confidence of the people to be governed at home and the respect of the powers to be dealt with abroad. He talked incessantly of the "honor" of the United States; he worried incessantly lest "humiliation," "disgrace," or "scorn" be visited upon it. "Whatever refined politicians may think," he wrote to Governor Clinton in 1778 in protest against American violations of the Saratoga Convention, "it is of great consequence to preserve a national character." [73] Driven as few Americans have ever been driven by a powerful sense of personal identification with the national community, he drew a rule for all men out of the experience of his own uncommon "passion": it is glorious to live in a great society, meaningless to live in an obscure one, demoralizing to live in a despised one. "Either as a *man* or *citizen,*" he told Pickering in the crisis of 1797, "I, for one, had rather perish than submit to disgrace." [74] And to the public he described what can happen to a nation that submits to the blackmail of an aggressive power:

The humiliation of the American mind would be a lasting and a mortal disease in our social habit. Mental debasement is the greatest misfortune that can befall a people. The most pernicious of conquests which a state can experience is a conquest over that just and elevated sense of its own rights which inspires a due sensibility to insult and injury, over that virtuous and generous pride of character, which prefers any peril or sacrifice to a final submission to oppression, and which regards national ignominy as the greatest of national calamities. . . .

Moderation in every nation is a virtue . . . but to *capitulate* with oppression, or rather to surrender to it at discretion, is, in any nation that has any power of resistance, at all times as foolish as it is contemptible. The honor of a nation is its life. Deliberately to abandon it, is to commit an act of political suicide. . . .

The nation which can prefer disgrace to danger is prepared for a *Master,* and deserves one.[75]

Never, perhaps, in all his writings did Hamilton express more unequivocally his commitment to the idea of community. Men were citizens, he believed, or they were at most half-men; as citizens they should feel in their own bones the ebb and flow of the reputation of the community. He wanted to be, and thought every man of sense would want to be, a citizen of a great community, a nation raised to power and glory. That is why he insisted that "unqualified humiliation" by another power "is in almost every situation a greater evil than war." [76] He believed this as a sober principle of applied political science, and he put it in a memorandum to Washington long before he put it in a polemic to the public.

One does not have to search far to learn Hamilton's prescription for the government of such a community. The first ingredient, we have learned, was strength—in fact and in appearance. As to the fact of strength:

A weak and embarrassed government never fails to be unpopular. It attaches to itself the disrespect incident to weakness, and, unable to promote the public happiness, its impotencies are its crimes.[77]

As to the appearance:

Whenever the government appears in arms, it ought to appear like a *Hercules,* and inspire respect by the display of strength. The consideration of expense is of no moment compared with the advantages of energy.[78]

One wonders how Hamilton would have applied this general "principle and caution" to the specific instance of Little Rock in 1957. Would he, too, have had Hercules carry a rifle with fixed bayonet, or would he have thought a night stick and side arms sufficient to command respect? The precedent of the Whiskey Rebellion suggests that he, like President Eisenhower, would have taken no chances.

The second ingredient was good faith, the will to honor obligations. He was, I repeat, no vulgar Machiavellian. He had an almost physical loathing for repudiation as a course of action—to be condemned on grounds of both "right" and "policy." As he put it to Congress in the First Report on the Public Credit:

States, like individuals, who observe their engagements are respected and trusted: while the reverse is the fate of those who pursue an opposite conduct.[79]

"The principle which shall be assumed here," he wrote of his funding system, "is this":

that the established *rules of morality and justice are applicable to nations as well as to individuals; that the former as well as the latter are bound to keep their promises; to fulfil their engagements to respect the rights of property* which others have acquired under contracts with them. Without this there is an end of all distinct ideas of right or wrong, justice or injustice, in relation to society or government. There can be no such thing as rights, no such thing as property or liberty; all the boasted advantages of a constitution of government vanish into air. Every thing must float on the variable and vague opinions of the governing party, of whomsoever composed.

A relaxation of this kind would tend to dissolve all social obligations— to render all rights precarious, and to introduce a general dissoluteness and corruption of morals.[80]

Honest dealing abroad was as important as honest dealing at home. Hamilton wanted his country to be known for the way it kept its word. He did not expect it to be fatuously punctilious at the expense of the national interest, yet he insisted that it would almost always be to the the interest of the United States to act with "upright intention"—and not to go around appealing to "mighty and dazzling reasons of state." [81]

In the wise order of Providence, nations, in a temporal sense, may safely trust the maxim that the observance of justice carries with it its own and a full reward.[82]

Yet another necessity was dignity, which Hamilton seems to have identified with a measured exercise of public authority and, at the same time, with a measured regard for the rules of public etiquette. "*Real firmness* is good for everything," he counseled Wolcott in the crisis of 1797. "*Strut* is good for nothing." [83] And he wrote to William Smith in the same crisis:

In such a state of things law and dispassionate views are indispensable. Neither the suggestions of pride nor timidity ought to guide. There ought to be much cool calculation, much *calm* fortitude. The Government ought to be all intellect while the people ought to be all feeling.[84]

No nation could be counted great, in his opinion, if its agents behaved like boors, clowns, cads, or fops. Occasionally given to some rather fancy strutting himself, he knew it to be a venial sin for a man in a position of trust. He wanted his public men to be gentlemen; he wanted the government they served to be firm and, whenever possible, magnanimous.[85]

Hamilton added a fourth ingredient that would have occurred to few men in his time: efficiency. He was, indeed, the first American political thinker to insist upon the importance of sound administration to the success of popular government. At a time when other first-rate minds were concerned almost entirely with the problem of how much power should be granted and where it should be located and how it should be checked, his first-rate mind had gone on to wonder how power could be most effectively and systematically wielded. Hume had been moved by Pope's famous couplet to raise the question "whether there be any essential difference between one form of government and another, and whether every form may not become good or bad, according as it is well or ill administered?" [86] Hamilton was moved by Hume, and by his dealings with Congress in the Revolution, to raise it again; and although his answer, like Hume's, was to "condemn" Pope's "sentiment," he gave it with obvious misgivings. In *The Federalist,* number 68 he wrote:

Though we cannot acquiesce in the political heresy of the poet who says:

> "For forms of government let fools contest—
> That which is best administered is best,"—

yet we may safely pronounce that the true test of a good government is its aptitude and tendency to produce a good administration.[87]

In other words, a "bad" form of government—for instance, an oligarchy of priests—could not be made "good" by the simple fact of a "respectable and prosperous administration of affairs," but a "good" form of government—for instance, a constitutional monarchy—could be made "bad" by a "want of method and energy in the administration." [88] While Hamilton took an instrumentalist view of "vigor," "consistency," and "expedition" in the "administration of affairs," [89] he had no doubt that efficiency was a quality as essential for a government to display as was dignity or honor. No matter how carefully power was divided and restrained, no matter how well-behaved the people and well-meaning their leaders, the American political system would crash in ruins, he warned, if a science of administration did not come in time to replace the "very vague and confined notions of the practical business of government" with which his countrymen had begun the Revolution.[90]

Hamilton's administrative theory, which Leonard D. White acclaimed as "the first systematic exposition of public administration, a contribution which stood alone for generations," [91] must be dug out piece by piece from his public and private writings. Nowhere did he halt for more than a page or two to expand on such favorite topics as the administrative incompetence of legislatures, the superiority of single-headed departments to boards with two or more heads, the irritations of mutable government, the costliness of inefficient government, the relative simplicity of private business as contrasted with public administration, the need for executive leadership in preparing plans for taxing and spending, the need for special knowledge and skills in public administrators, the importance of a decent compensation and status for civil servants, and the hardheaded notion that the success or failure of the American Republic might depend on the handling of such seemingly trivial problems as the regulation of coinage or the purchase of stores or the flow of diplomatic correspondence.[92] Yet, even in default of the chapters on administration he would have written for his "full investigation," he left behind an imposing and original contribution to the development of an American theory of public administration. Whether one contents himself with the flashes of insight in *The Federalist,* or labors through the accounts and reports of his stewardship as Secretary of the Treasury, one is bound to agree with Professor White that "it was Alexander Hamilton who . . . first worked out a philosophy of public administration" for Americans.[93]

STRENGTH, good faith, dignity, efficiency, in one encompassing word, *energy*—to this catalogue of qualities of the model government for the great society Hamilton added a final imperative: devotion to liberty. We must not be blinded by his uncommon admiration for power to the fact that he intended this power to be used in behalf of free men. His ideal society was not, as F. S. Oliver once suggested, a "hive" of "self-sacrificing men" who were "filled with the joy of life" and yet "humbly and piously subordinate" to the state.[94] It was, rather, an association of industrious, well-behaved, self-disciplined men and women who, even while they were proudly conscious of the blessings that went with membership in a famous community, lived private lives and pursued private affairs in which the government had no right or cause to interfere. Liberty was important to Hamilton because it was the natural, even God-given heritage of man. The "clear voice of natural justice" had always spoken, even in the darkest hours of man's pilgrimage, for personal rights and self-government, and he had measured respect for its message. There was not much point in laboring to build up a great society if the men who lived in it were serfs and slaves. His interest was in men who enjoyed "the common privileges of subjects under the same government," and who had a "share" in the conduct of this government.[95]

Serfs and slaves, even when led by men of genius, could never, in fact,

build a great society. If liberty was a natural blessing it was also a social
necessity. Only men who had a taste for its "sweets" could be moved to
make the kind of effort—persistent, intelligent, imaginative—out of which
social progress emerges. He had high hopes for the "unequaled spirit of
enterprise" of the American people,[96] and he knew perfectly well that
this spirit would flourish only under conditions of economic, political,
social, and religious liberty. For this reason, if for no other, he could "profess himself to be as zealous an advocate for liberty as any man whatever." [97]

He was, however, an advocate who knew that the tree of liberty bears
sour fruits as well as sweet. Liberty was the nursery of learning, prosperity,
and virtue; it was also the forcing-ground of faction, envy, and corruption.
An excessive concern for liberty in public men could lead to weakness,
disorder, and ultimately anarchy. An excessive pursuit of liberty by private
men could lead to licentiousness, the "mischiefs of opulence," and ultimately slavery.[98] Yet the gamble of freedom was eminently worth making.
To the "unmingled misery of a gloomy and destructive despotism" Hamilton preferred the "alternate sunshine and storms of liberty." [99]

Like the other sober-minded men of his time he set out the political and
cultural conditions for a successful gamble. The first was a sense of self-
discipline in the people at large, which might save them from the worst
extravagances of luxury and license.[100] The second was morality in their
manners and customs, on which republican institutions could be erected
with some hope of success. The third was religion, on which morality
depended in large part for its sanctions.[101] And the fourth was constitutionalism, what we still celebrate as "liberty under law." Even as an
advocate of resistance to Britain, Hamilton paid his respects to the "steady,
uniform, unshaken security of constitutional freedom," and he never
tired of reminding his readers that they must choose whether to be
governed by "LAW" or "FORCE." [102] If they chose "law," they also chose
"authority," which alone could provide "the security of liberty against the
enterprises and assaults of ambition, of faction, and of anarchy." [103] As he
wrote to John Dickinson in the mutinous troubles of 1783:

> The rights of government are as essential to be defended as the rights of
> individuals. The security of the one is inseparable from that of the other.
> And indeed in every new government, especially of the popular kind, the great
> danger is that public authority will not be sufficiently respected.[104]

Hamilton did not need to be told by the Jeffersonians that one man's idea
of "authority" could be another man's idea of "slavery." He knew that the

"perfect balance between liberty and power" would be hard to find and harder to keep.[105] He was anxious only to proclaim the necessity of the search, to spike the easy notion that the absence of authority meant the presence of liberty. Obedience, not disobedience, was the natural posture of the free man. "A sacred respect for the constitutional law," he wrote as Tully in 1794, "is the vital principle, the sustaining energy, of a free government." [106] It was the duty of the statesman to tutor the people in the ways of rational obedience, and Hamilton discharged this duty when he placed these words in the Farewell Address:

> This government, the offspring of your own choice, uninfluenced and unawed, completely free in its principles, in the distribution of its powers, uniting energy with safety, and containing in itself a provision for its own amendment is well entitled to your confidence and support. Respect for its authority, compliance with its laws, acquiescence in its measures, are duties dictated by the fundamental maxims of true liberty. The basis of our political systems is the right of the people to make and alter their constitutions of government. But the Constitution for the time, and until changed by an explicit and authentic act of the whole people, is sacredly binding upon all. The very idea of the right and power of the people to establish government presupposes the duty of every individual to obey the established government.[107]

While Hamilton never went into detail about the contents of this package labeled "liberty," we know that he was a stout believer in the right of qualified persons to vote, the right of all persons to the guarantees of due process, freedom from oaths and tests that might "wound the tender consciences" of men, freedom of religion in terms of organization as well as conscience, freedom of speech and press (which he served nobly in the Croswell trial and, in company with other men who should have known better, poorly in the fracas over the Alien and Sedition Acts), the right to own private property and to enjoy the fruits thereof, and what we may loosely call freedom of economic choice.[108] The "desire" for property, especially land, was "founded on such strong principles in the human breast" that property itself must be regarded as a universal appendage of man, regulated by law yet enjoyed by right.[109] For men like Hamilton property was an essential part of the definition of liberty. The fact that it was also a begetter of "influence" was one of the hard problems facing the makers of constitutions.[110]

I do not mean to paint too rosy a picture of Hamilton the libertarian. Like every last man of his time he looked upon the preservation of personal liberty as only one among several mighty goals of the American Republic; like every last man, certainly every last Federalist or Republican, he was more concerned about the "sacred rights" of his friends than the "shabby privileges" of his enemies. Certainly he was no exception to the rule that for every self-styled "friend of liberty" there is a point beyond which the claims of friendship simply cannot be honored. I have meant only to call attention to the easily forgotten fact that Hamilton made room in his political philosophy for the Whig idea of natural and civil liberty, and that the landscape of his image of the good society was dotted with self-respecting men pursuing their private ends in a state of rational freedom. While it cannot be denied that Hamilton, both as thinker and doer, was less dazzled than Jefferson by the concept of personal liberty, it must not be forgotten that Jefferson, too, put limits on the play of liberty in theory as well as in practice. It is, in any case, amusing and instructive to compare Hamilton's solicitude as trustee of Columbia that the "politics" of a prospective president "be of the right sort" with Jefferson's warning as patron of the University of Virginia that "in the selection of our law professor we must be rigorously attentive to his political principles." [111]

THREE questions have been so earnestly agitated by men who write about Hamilton and his times—and, more to the point, about Hamilton and our times—that I must give my own answers by way of conclusion to these two chapters on his political science. And the questions are: Was Hamilton an individualist or a collectivist? Was Hamilton a conservative—and, if he was, what kind? Of which great political theorists was Hamilton an intellectual kinsman?

To the first question one can give only the fuzzy-edged answer that those who go to Hamilton for support of a discreetly individualistic political philosophy will not be disappointed, those who go to him for support of an essentially social or communitarian point of view will be thoroughly gratified. He was no "credulous votary" of the all-powerful state; he was no doctrinaire prophet of rugged individualism. He was, rather, a man who searched persistently—and thought the search well worth making—for the line between liberty and authority, right and obligation, individual and society. The point of interest about this archetype of the "empirical collectivist" [112] is that he was clearly more prepared than most leading men of his time to shift the line by enlarging the area within which the state could act forcefully and creatively.

Hamilton was, as I have said, a political thinker interested in men as children of God and agents of natural right, and he believed that America would grow to glory only if its citizens were reasonably free to pursue their particular versions of happiness. At the same time, and in a brave attempt to have it both ways, he was interested in the community as a phenomenon with a life and character and even purpose of its own. Although he was respectfully aware of the power of private interests, he was unyielding in his insistence that a public good rose above, incorporated, and occasionally obliterated the interests of men as individuals. One of the persistent cravings of men, he argued, was to identify themselves with the community, and he had little understanding of the man—the outlaw, the anarchist, the hermit, the pigheaded eccentric—who looks upon life as an unending war with authority. I doubt that he was ever gripped by a sense of outrage when it came time to pay his taxes. More than that, he had an extraordinary faith in the capacity of political authority to guide men in their pursuit of happiness. The release of individual energies was so important to bring about that he preferred the open hand of authority rather than the hidden hand of chance to hold the lever. The spirit of enterprise, he was convinced, could be stimulated by "prudent aids and encouragements on the part of government"; and although he knew that rulers in the past had slowed down the wheels of progress more often than they had speeded them up, he seems to have had confidence that the government of the United States would lend a helping rather than deadening hand to the efforts of individuals to better themselves and, in the process, would invigorate the social order.

All that I have said should go far to answer the subsidiary question whether Hamilton the political economist was a mercantilist, as most historians seem to think, or an exponent of *laissez faire,* as Professor Hacker has insisted in a dissenting opinion.[113] The answer, once again, is that he was both, that his eclectic, undogmatic mind had room for the best teachings of both Colbert and Adam Smith. If he was a mercantilist, he was one who was supple and new-fashioned; if he was a laissez-faire economist, he was one who dealt in expediency rather than ideology. No one would ever have caught him, at any time in American history, arguing for protection or free trade in doctrinaire terms. The "prosperity of commerce" depended on the "spirit of enterprise and competition";[114] it also depended on an alert, informed, adventurous use of political authority. As he wrote in his Report on Manufactures:

There is, at the present juncture, a certain fermentation of mind, a certain activity of speculation and enterprise which, if properly directed, may be made subservient to useful purposes; but which, if left entirely to itself, may be attended with pernicious effects.[115]

To suppress the pernicious effects of free enterprise, Hamilton called in, neither simple-mindedly nor queasily, the power of the state.

He had, in sum, no mystique of collectivism or individualism, of mercantilism or *laissez faire,* of protection or free trade, of liberty or authority. As a citizen of the great Republic he saw rising up on the American continent, he was not afraid to have the best of both possible worlds, that is, to live in the real world of eternal contradiction. He was a mixed-economy pragmatist as political economist, a community-minded individualist as political scientist.

The revival of self-conscious conservatism as a political and cultural phenomenon in the postwar years has sent both advocates and students of this point of view rummaging through the past in search of models of American conservatism. Having gone on this search myself, I can say with a conviction born of experience that Hamilton is one of a handful of famous men in our history with whom conservatives and critics of conservatism alike must make their peace.

This is not, however, an easy thing to do. I have tried it myself on four occasions,[116] and in my labors I have been confused, if also enlightened, by the many conflicting judgments passed on the quality of Hamilton's conservatism. Russell Kirk finds him to have been too much a mixture of backward-looking mercantilist and forward-looking exponent of industrialism to be classed with Burke and Adams. "Eminently a city-man," Hamilton "never penetrated far beneath the surface of politics to the mysteries of veneration and presumption."[117] Raymond English, on the other hand, considers his "ideas" a "base" for modern American conservatism as "solid as granite," Louis Hacker believes him to have been a "real conservative," and John C. Livingston salutes him as "that national figure who stands out above all others as the architect of a native American conservatism."[118]

My own opinion is that, while Hamilton was unquestionably a man of the Right, he cannot be listed, certainly not without a half-dozen major qualifications, among the undoubted heroes of American conservatism. I call him a man of the Right because in his politics and social attitudes, as in his tastes and prejudices, he was at home in the company of "the wise and good and rich," and because he hoped that such men would be called upon to rule republican America. While his "only client" may have been, as Professor Mitchell asserts, "the whole country,"[119] he served the whole country by first of all serving the men on or near the top of the heap. He had no special affection for the mass of farmers and workers, and he certainly gave his energies without stint to the vain task of keeping their leaders out of the seats of political power.

A man on the Right, however, is not necessarily a conservative, and if Hamilton was a conservative, he was the only one of his kind. He had, to be sure, many of the political and philosophical credentials of the conservative. He subscribed to a secular version of the doctrine of Original Sin, put a high value on law, order, and obedience, assumed the existence of classes and put his measured trust in the class at the top, spoke with feeling of the role of religious sentiment in man and organized religion in society, and voiced the standard conservative approval of prudence.[120] He despised ideologues, condemned the "rage for innovation," and declared himself more willing to "incur the negative inconveniences of delay than the positive mischiefs of injudicious expedients." [121] Always on his guard against the preachers of an "ideal perfection," certain that he would never see "a perfect work from imperfect man," he was prepared to leave much to chance, and thus presumably to the workings of prescription, in the social process.[122] He was never so eloquent as when he declaimed on the favorite conservative theme of the mixed character of all man's blessings. "The truth is," he wrote to Robert Morris in 1781, "in human affairs there is no good, pure and unmixed." " 'T is the lot of every thing human," he lectured Rufus King in 1791, "to mingle a portion of evil with the good." And some years later he restated this theme:

'T is the portion of man, assigned to him by the eternal allotment of Providence, that every good he enjoys shall be alloyed with ills, that every source of his bliss shall be a source of his affliction.[123]

Hamilton gave full vent to his conservatism, which in this instance went beyond mere opportunistic Rightism, in his reactions to the excesses of the French Revolution. He reads exactly like Burke or Adams in his attacks on "The Great MONSTER" for its impiety, cruelty, and licentiousness, for its spawning of an anarchy that had led straight to despotism, for its zeal for change and assaults on property, for its imposition of "the tyranny of Jacobism, which confounds and levels every thing." [124] He was enraged by the presumptuousness of the Directory in holding out "to the world a *general invitation* and *encouragement* to *revolution* and insurrection, under a promise of *fraternity* and *assistance*," [125] and was one of the first of a long line of publicists, which stretches down to this generation, to insist that a clear distinction be drawn between the French and American Revolutions in terms of inspiration, aspiration, character, and consequence.[126] Himself a victim of the passions unleashed by the French Revolution,[127] he had philosophical as well as pragmatic reasons for the horror he felt at the sight of liberty run amuck.

Having said all this, I must again insist that he was not a model for the average conservative to imitate. His bold plans for economic development, his genuine confidence in the uses of political power, his indifference to the established order in Virginia and points south, his impatience with traditions and loyalties that got in his way, his willingness to sweep away the states, his easy identification of plutocracy with aristocracy, the bias in his political philosophy toward economics, and above all his vision of the industrial society to come—these were not, surely, the marks of an American conservative of the 1790's. He was conservative and radical, traditionalist and revolutionary, reactionary and visionary, Tory and Whig all thrown into one. He is a source of inspiration and instruction to modern conservatives, but so is he, if they are not afraid to go to him, to modern liberals. Let us leave this point with the observation that his growing reputation is due in no small part to his ability to defy classification. Indeed, he may well be the most unclassifiable man of pronounced views in all the history of American thought and politics.

It is a common practice among intellectual historians to bracket Hamilton's name with that of one of the giants of political theory. In one study or another we may find proclaimed his kinship with everyone from Plato to Adam Smith by way of Locke and Rousseau. The names dropped most often are those of Hobbes and Machiavelli, and there seems to be a disposition among learned men who have a visceral as well as intellectual preference for Jefferson to put Hamilton in his place by labeling him "the American Hobbes" or, somewhat less often, "the American Machiavelli." [128]

This is, I think, to treat him both carelessly and arrogantly. While he, like all political thinkers of sense and courage, made grateful use of many of the insights of these two brilliant teachers, he was a man who simply could not have written either *The Prince* or *Leviathan*. Even in his toughest moments he was too old-fashioned a moralist to be called a Machiavellian, even in his most despairing moments too committed a constitutionalist to be called a Hobbesian. The only suitable title of this sort that one might bestow upon him is "the American Hume," for almost every quality or element of his political science that suggests the influence of Hobbes or Machiavelli can be found in a reworked and quite palatable form in Hume's political writings. Although all four of these celebrated men are classed among the "realists" of Western political thought, Hume and Hamilton, perhaps to their credit and certainly to our confusion, let so much idealism creep in by the back door that one ends up not knowing just where to place them on this spectrum.

Yet even Hamilton's debt to Hume, or intellectual kinship with him, was of such a nature that we must judge him finally to have been his own master. Experience was his dearest teacher; he went to Hume and others to have his crude ideas sharpened, polished, and reinforced. He was, indeed, one of a kind, a man who spilled out of the channels of convention, who went hunting for answers to questions that other leading minds of his time had not even thought to ask, who made an exceptional attempt to have the best of the two possible worlds of liberty and authority. In the process, I would maintain, he made a half-dozen contributions to our political thought that place him in the front rank of American thinkers with Madison, Adams, Jefferson, Lincoln, and Calhoun.

That, we must admit ruefully, still does not place him in the front rank of Western thinkers with Hobbes, Machiavelli, Locke, Hegel, and Rousseau. For reasons that we either know too well or do not know at all, America has never produced a man who could be assigned without hesitation to the company of famous political theorists, and Hamilton was not a Hobbes any more than Jefferson was a Locke, Calhoun an Aristotle, or, for that matter, Daniel De Leon a Marx. He asked some of the right questions, but not quite enough of them, and he was either too busy or too practical-minded to labor painstakingly over his answers. One likes to think that he could have written his great work, and that it would have been as much better than *The Federalist* as *The Federalist* is better than anything else ever written on politics in America, but one cannot be sure. Perhaps the very qualities that he displayed as the builder of a nation would have made it impossible for him ever to be the source of either a new departure or a grand consolidation in political theory. Perhaps, to go one step farther, there is something about a creative event in the world of reality like the writing of the American Constitution that makes it impossible for any mind, however fresh and profound, to match the event in the world of ideas. It may be more than coincidental that the practical success of the American polity has been matched by a speculative failure of the American political mind. The essence of the failure, in which Hamilton shares with Jefferson and the rest, is our continuing inability to understand the workings of constitutional democracy and to communicate this understanding in the universal language of politics. Or, as I have already asked by implication, has there been something in the nature or circumstances or timing of the American experiment that ordained this failure, that would have compelled even Aristotle or Hobbes, had he lived among us, to labor the obvious and to speak in contradictions?

It may be that I have been too demanding of the American political thinker and too unmindful of the majestic dimensions of American political thought. It may be that all the right questions have been asked and answered by one thinker or another, and that sooner or later a man of genius will come forward (later, let us hope, since it will probably signal our decline as a civilization) to absorb and restate the universally applicable lessons of the American trial of constitutional democracy. When he does come forward, he will turn, I trust, in gratitude to Hamilton. In the insights and convictions that Hamilton expressed so forcefully under the rubrics of passion, interest, public good, honor, order, power, confidence, and energy, this voice of America will find precious materials for his instruction and use. They are the more precious because he is not likely to find many of them in any other of the eminent sources of the American political tradition. Hamilton's contribution to this tradition was as exceptional as it was oracular.

SIX

HAMILTON'S CONSTITUTIONAL LAW

AND THEORY

> *"Every power vested in a government is in its nature* sovereign, *and includes . . . a right to employ all the* means *requisite and fairly applicable to the attainment of the* ends *of such power."*
>
> Hamilton to Washington, in the Opinion on the Constitutionality of the Bank of the United States, February 23, 1791

THE hard core of the American political tradition is a belief in the necessity of constitutional government. When the thoughtful American pledges his allegiance to democracy, he means constitutional democracy, a system of popular government in which power is diffused by means of a written constitution and the wielders of power are held in check by the rule of law. When he sings the praises of liberty, he means constitutional liberty, a condition of ordered freedom whose terms are set down for all men to read in the fundamental law. So ascendant is the principle of constitutionalism in our best and oldest schemes of political values that a man must honor it in his own scheme of values, even when he dishonors it in practice, or be counted as a dissenter from the American tradition.

In this matter, as in so many others in which neglect or malice has distorted our view of the guiding principles of his career, Alexander Hamilton was a full-blooded American. I state this point clearly at the beginning of an exposition of the principles of Hamilton's constitutionalism, for there are many who doubt that he was enough a constitutionalist to be credited with having any such principles. He was, it is assumed, so obsessed with power that he was willing to let it be used, if placed in the right hands, without restraint and without reckoning; he was so committed to action that he scorned all delays in the decision-making process.

To anyone who takes time to study Hamilton's career with an objective eye this assumption must seem as unfair as it is unoriginal. If he was never as painstaking a constitutionalist as Madison or as zealous a one as Adams, he was, by any standard, a firm advocate of the double-barreled principle that the governors of men should think, explain, and bargain before they act, and that they should act only through established procedures in making, administering, and enforcing public policy.[1] The government he recommended to his fellow citizens was to be decisive but not arbitrary, energetic but not oppressive, enterprising but not untrammeled; and he never for a moment believed that the rising nation, a community of men with no special exemption from the sanctions of the laws of human nature, would endure more than a few years without a skillfully written charter and a widespread devotion to it. He was not content with Hobbes merely to hope that men of power would act sanely; he went in search of rules of law that might restrain such men without paralyzing them, that would balance the energy of the government and the safety of the people in a working equation for political and social freedom.

Hamilton was, as we have already learned, a recognizable type (although hardly the archetype) of the American Whig, and his mind was therefore as thoroughly committed to the necessity of constitutionalism as it was to the sanctity of the natural law. One finds in his writings no word of contempt or ridicule for the standard principles and techniques of Whig constitutionalism. One discovers, to the contrary, that he was at least as quick as Jefferson or Marshall to salute the principles and advocate the techniques. Again and again he expressed his fear of concentrated and unfettered power—*"the essence of despotism"*—and warned his audience of the dangers that lurked in "the impetuous vortex of legislative influence."[2] Again and again he pointed to the stoutest of all defenses against the abuse of power: those "most approved and well-founded maxims of free government, which require that the legislative, executive, and judicial authorities should be deposited in distinct and separate hands."[3] Convinced by experience of "the insufficiency of a mere parchment delineation of the boundaries" between any two agencies of power,[4] he joined with John Adams, although with none of Adams's fervor, in the search for techniques with which to check power with power and to balance ambition against ambition.* In defending the independence of the judiciary in 1802 he set down the general rules for a system of checks and balances:

The means held out as proper to be employed for enabling the several departments to keep each other in their proper places are: 1. To give to each such an *organization* as will render them essentially independent of one another. 2. To secure to each a *support* which shall not be at the discretionary disposal of any other. 3. To establish between them such *mutual relations of authority* as will make one a check upon another, and enable them reciprocally to resist encroachments, and confine one another within their proper spheres.[5]

All in all, Hamilton is to be understood as a man who subscribed, for the most part uncritically, to the "conventional wisdom" of his generation about constitutions and constitutionalism, and who was thankful for the legacy of the Anglo-American effort to establish the rule of law, to secure the liberties of individuals, and to reduce the discretion of rulers to sensible dimensions. No advocate of federalism, he nonetheless recognized, although often to his chagrin, that the vertical distribution of power was a "double security to the people," and thus as potent a technique of constitutionalism as was the horizontal distribution.[6] No lover of the people, he nonetheless knew that no constitution could endure for long unless it was the creation of their will and guardian of their liberties.[7] He was therefore doubly concerned, as were both Madison and Adams, that the sense of the majority—the cutting edge of republican government—be solicited carefully and expressed soberly.[8] Like all American constitutionalists, he was anxious for the sake of liberty—and also, being Hamilton, anxious for the sake of authority—that the decision-making majority be clear-cut and coolheaded on all occasions, extraordinary on extraordinary occasions, and powerless on occasions when the consciences of men were at issue. He had abundant faith in "the regular deliberations and decisions of a respectable majority," no faith at all in those of an unfettered, whimsical, "overbearing majority." [9] As he wrote in *The Federalist* in support of those clauses that give firmness to the Presidency:

The republican principle demands that the deliberate sense of the community should govern the conduct of those to whom they intrust the management of

* Bemused as he was by the misleading but magisterial teachings of Montesquieu, Hamilton was no more understanding than any other Framer of the true nature of constitutional developments in eighteenth-century Britain.[10] Had he been able to look a hundred years into the future and watch the operations of parliamentary government under Gladstone and Disraeli, it is possible that he would have urged the union rather than the separation of the executive and legislative powers.

their affairs; but it does not require an unqualified complaisance to every sudden breeze of passion, or to every transient impulse. . . . When occasions present themselves in which the interests of the people are at variance with their inclinations, it is the duty of the persons whom they have appointed to be the guardians of those interests to withstand the temporary delusion in order to give them time and opportunity for more cool and sedate reflection.[11]

This is Hamilton the constitutionalist, and also Hamilton the political scientist, at his best and most judicious. The one hope for popular government, he seems to be saying, is the spirit and techniques of constitutionalism, which are in the end the only guarantee that the sovereign people will choose, check, encourage, chastise, and reward their governors through safe, sober, and predictable methods. Popular government must be "moderate government" or explode under the pressures of passion and interest, and for moderation the first requisite is "the fabric of a fixed and definite Constitution." [12] As he wrote in an exposition of his financial policies:

It is the part of wisdom in a government, as well as in an individual, to guard against its own infirmities; and, having taken beforehand a comprehensive view of its duty and interest, to tie itself down by every constitutional precaution to the steady pursuit of them.[13]

Having said all these nice things, which are also true things, about Hamilton the constitutionalist, we must remind ourselves of the known facts about the character of the man and the circumstances in which his constitutionalism was tested, that is to say, in which his constitutional theory became constitutional law. Three points are worth making in this regard. First, for him as for every man with whom he worked or struggled (indeed, for every American who has ever so much as thought about the Constitution), constitutional principles were primarily instruments of political purposes; and Hamilton's overriding purpose was to build the foundations of a new empire rather than to tend the campfires of an old confederation. Second, for him as for every man, his constitutional principles were in large part reflections of a political philosophy, of a rather more deeply held set of convictions about the nature of man, the structure of society, and the limits of politics; and Hamilton's political philosophy incorporated the prophetic notion of a well-mounted, energetic, guiding government. And third, throughout most of his career he was cast as an "in" rather than an "out"—and an "in" of a very special type. His fondest hopes were pinned upon the national government; he plied the executive rather than the legislative trade; he was a man whose political purposes beckoned him to be up and doing. All these were reasons enough for him to cherish principles of constitutionalism somewhat different from those of Jefferson and Madison, even of Adams and Jay.

Yet the situation of the 1790's was only one of the forces that shaped Hamilton's brand of constitutionalism. The style and temper of the man, which must surely have transcended time and circumstance, worked their influence, too. He was by nature and nurture a mover and shaker: an actor rather than a critic, a creator rather than a preserver, a man of the bold future rather than of the pleasant or at least endurable past. Even if he had been out of power for years on end, he would have been uncomfortable mouthing the rhetoric of strict construction; even if he had been a Senator with seniority, he would have refused to be pedantic about the separation of powers, and thus would have looked to the executive for leadership of the legislative process. Hamilton's constitutionalism was as natural to a dashing visionary as was Jefferson's to a peace-loving Arcadian or Madison's to a fussy eclectic. He wanted his constitutionalism and his energy, too. I think it can be shown that, as cleverly and successfully as any important constitutional thinker in American history, he ended up having the best of both these attractive worlds.

IT is not so much Hamilton's constitutional theory as his interpretation of the Constitution of 1787 that is our concern in this chapter, and I know no better way to bridge the gap between theory and law than to expound his rule for construing the clauses of this or of any other constitution. To this rule he remained faithful at all but the most desperate, isolated moments of his career. It was a natural projection of the purposes, circumstances, political principles, and character of the man, and together with its corollaries it gave direction to his prophetic interpretation of some of the most controversial clauses of the Constitution. It was, indeed, the essence of his style both as constitutional theorist and constitutional lawyer.

This rule of Hamiltonian constitutionalism can be reduced, not merely to one phrase, but to one word: *liberality*. To him the Constitution was more properly viewed as a grant of powers than as a catalogue of limitations. He searched in it almost always for encouragement rather than dissuasion, for ways to get things done rather than ways to keep things from being done. Energy was on his mind as he sat in his study, energy on his lips as he sat across the table from Washington. Energy was therefore the quality he sought most diligently to extract from the inert words of the Constitution. If the Constitution were to be converted into a source of energy, it would have to be interpreted broadly, loosely, liberally; and that is how Hamilton chose to interpret it. Long before there was the Constitution, and long after he had surrendered hope of ever again interpreting it as a responsible officeholder, Hamilton was one of that "description of men . . . disposed to do the essential business of the nation, by a liberal construction of the powers of government." [14] In a passage from his forceful argument in behalf of the constitutionality of the Bank, he reminded Washington of "this sound maxim of construction" of the words of a constitution:

namely, that the powers contained in a constitution of government, especially those which concern the general administration of the affairs of a country . . . ought to be construed liberally in advancement of the public good. This rule does not depend on the particular form of a government, or on the particular demarcation of the boundaries of its powers, but on the nature and objects of government itself. The means by which national exigencies are to be provided for, national inconveniences obviated, national prosperity promoted, are of such infinite variety, extent, and complexity, that there must of necessity be great latitude of discretion in the selection and application of those means. Hence, consequently, the necessity and propriety of exercising the authorities intrusted to a government on principles of liberal construction.[15]

From this guiding rule of Hamilton's constitutional theory flowed several corollaries—what Madison was still complaining about in 1829 as his "broad and ductile rules of construction" [16]—to which he resorted in his struggles with the political enemy. All were approaches to the problem of constitutional interpretation that came naturally to a man who looked upon the fundamental law as a launching pad rather than a roadblock.

The first rule was that a constitution should be interpreted "reasonably"—as if it meant what it said, and as if what it said in one place was consistent with what it said in other places. In commenting on the Repeal Act of 1802 he wrote:

There is no rule of interpretation better settled than that different provisions in the same instrument, on the same subject, ought to be so construed as, if possible, to comport with each other, and give a reasonable effect to all.[17]

The second was that a constitution should be interpreted in such a way as to encourage rather than to discourage action. In the course of his argument before the Supreme Court in support of the validity of the carriage tax he put the matter in words I have already quoted:

No construction ought to prevail calculated to defeat the express and necessary authority of the government.

It would be contrary to reason, and to every rule of sound construction, to adopt a principle for regulating the exercise of a clear constitutional power which would defeat the exercise of the power.[18]

And the third, which was really the first two in negative dress, was a warning not to "torture" the straightforward, frugal words of the fundamental law by approaching it in a "narrow," "rigid," "pedantic" frame of mind.[19] A law, he wrote to William Seton in his activist phase of 1792, "is not to be so literally construed as to involve *absurdity* and oppression." [20]

Next, construers of constitutions should always remember, he reminded Washington in 1791, that they were dealing with a unique phenomenon called "government," and that *"inherent* in the very *definition* of government" was "this *general principle":*

That every power vested in a government is in its nature *sovereign,* and includes, by *force* of the *term,* a right to employ all the *means* requisite and fairly applicable to the attainment of the *ends* of such power, and which are not precluded by restrictions and exceptions specified in the Constitution, or not immoral, or not contrary to the *essential ends* of political society.[21]

He had already announced this guiding principle of construction in his discussion of the war powers in *The Federalist* in the form of one of his "simple" and "universal" axioms: that "the persons from whose agency the attainment of any *end* is expected ought to possess the *means* by which it is to be attained." [22] In short, the "end" or "object" was the only real limit that could be fixed upon "discretionary powers" granted in a constitution. If the "end" or "object" was itself unlimited—for example, the defense of the nation in a brutal war of survival—so must be the powers.[23]

Finally, although he was a Framer himself, Hamilton looked with distaste upon those who based their interpretations of some clause in the Constitution on the words and attitudes, real or alleged, of the delegates at Philadelphia. From time to time he could not resist the temptation, so natural to the insider, to buttress a constitutional argument with a knowing reference to the "intent" of the Framers.[24] For the most part, however, he felt that each generation of Americans should shape the clauses of the Constitution to its own needs rather than try to read the thoughts of men who had passed from the scene—and whose thoughts, in any case, had been tentative or ill-formed about many crucial words in that charter.[25]

As a lawyer and a political scientist, and thus as a constitutionalist, Hamilton had as many scruples as the next man, whether Madison or Jefferson or Marshall, about manipulating the Constitution in a cynical way. He demonstrated a clear "unwillingness to chicane the Constitution"; [26] he would never have asked, even in his most hard-driving moments, "What's the Constitution among friends?" He was especially alert to the danger— even as he violated this rule in the passion of a political crisis *—of setting questionable precedents for wicked men to follow when they came to power.[27] Yet he was, plainly, one of those constitutionalists who despise "minute restrictions" and feel that constitutions should "consist only of general principles," [28] who insist that these principles neither be designed nor interpreted in such a way as to hamstring men called upon to serve the nation in unimagined circumstances, and who expect a constitution to grow with the country or be rendered obsolescent. Bemused as he was with the notion of economic and social growth, he looked upon the Constitution of 1787 as "a fabric which can hardly be stationary, and which will retrograde if it cannot be made to advance." [29] For this reason, if for no other, it must always be interpreted in a clear, untortured, reasonable, liberal manner, and never, as his friend Ames said in derision of the constitutionalism of Jefferson, with the aid of "captious pleas of abate-

---

* The most unbecoming moment of a generally spotless career as constitutionalist is revealed in his letter to Governor Jay, May 7, 1800, in which he proposed a scheme that would have set aside the results of the New York election of 1800 by calling the old, Federalist-dominated legislature into special session to alter the electoral law and thus prevent the newly elected, Republican-dominated legislature from choosing electors pledged to Jefferson. Two paragraphs from this letter are worth quoting, for they prove that Hamilton, like every other American who has faced a desperate political situation, could break out of the limits of his commitment to constitutionalism and propose an action that would have desecrated the principles of due process, fair play, and orderly government. They prove, too, that he thought it highly important to describe (and no doubt to think of) his proposal as "legal" and "constitutional."

"I am aware that there are weighty objections to the measure, but the reasons for it appear to me to outweigh the objections; and in times like these in which we live, it will not do to be over-scrupulous. *It is easy to sacrifice the substantial interests of society by a strict adherence to ordinary rules.*"

"In observing this, I shall not be supposed to mean that any thing ought to be done which integrity will forbid, but merely that the scruples of delicacy and propriety, as relative to a common course of things, ought to yield to the extraordinary nature of the crisis. They ought not to hinder the taking of a *legal* and *constitutional* step to prevent an atheist in religion, and a fanatic in politics, from getting possession of the helm of state." [30]

Jay, to his credit as both constitutionalist and politician, rejected this proposal and endorsed the letter: "Proposing a measure for party purposes which it would not become me to adopt."

ment." [31] Only thus interpreted could it serve as a guide to the nation along the shortest and yet safest road to glory. "We must bear in mind," he told his audience in *The Federalist,*

that we are not to confine our view to the present period, but to look forward to remote futurity. Constitutions of civil government are not to be framed upon a calculation of existing exigencies, but upon a combination of these with the probable exigencies of ages, according to the natural and tried course of human affairs. Nothing, therefore, can be more fallacious than to infer the extent of any power proper to be lodged in the national government from an estimate of its immediate necessities. There ought to be a CAPACITY to provide for future contingencies as they may happen; and as these are illimitable in their nature, it is impossible safely to limit that capacity.[32]

A constitution for the ages—this is what Hamilton hoped to make out of the imperfect Constitution of 1787, and his hope set the style for all his interpretations and manipulations.

THE Constitution, we noted in chapter 3, was an invitation to controversy. The directions of the Framers were general rather than precise, suggestive rather than didactic; it was left to future wielders of power (of whom the Framers expected to be the first and most influential) to make what they could out of phrases like "supreme law of the land," "executive power," and "necessary and proper." In playing his own part as one of the first wielders of power, in doing what he could to move the "more perfect Union" along the road to glory, Hamilton made a great deal out of these wonderfully inexact and pregnant words. While his struggles with Jefferson and Madison were political, economic, and social in character and consequence, they were also constitutional, and out of them emerged a bundle of constructions and understandings that we may properly style his "constitutional law." His constitutional theory was that of an American Whig more concerned to act creatively than to delay timidly; his constitutional law was the consequence of a consistent application of the principles of this theory to the problems of the new nation. Since his career as interpreter of the Constitution was a short one, and since he had neither the desire nor the opportunity to let his imagination play on every disputed word and clause in it, he had nothing to say as constitutional lawyer about many problems of vital interest to us today. On four problems, however, he had much to say, and since each was the kind that will be with us to the end, the dimensions of his constitutional law were, to say the very least, impressive. These problems were: 1) the division of authority between the nation and the states, 2) the nature and reach of the powers of Congress, 3) the nature and reach of the powers of the President, and 4) the role of the courts as guardians of the fundamental law. Let us turn now to review his interpretations of the Constitution in each of these areas.

The most unequivocal nationalist of the age in sentiment, interest, and political purpose, Hamilton was the most expansive nationalist in his view of the Constitution. This view, which even 160 years after his death would be considered "advanced" and indeed "dangerous" by some timid Americans, was the point of departure for almost every development in his constitutional law. Whether he was conjuring up the authority of a sovereign legislature out of the delegated powers in Article I, proclaiming the responsibility of the President to maintain law and order throughout the land, asserting the power of the Supreme Court to sit in judgment upon the constitutionality of state laws, or assuming the common-law jurisdiction of the federal courts, Hamilton set off on his influential career as interpreter of the Constitution from grounds that Jefferson and his friends looked upon as wholly untenable. To them the Constitution was the charter of a new model of confederacy; to him it was the charter of a nation. While he wished that this issue had been resolved more forcefully, and more favorably to the claims of the nation, in the Constitution, he was always ready in deed and word—as Secretary of the Treasury and also as Tully—to remedy this deficiency by reading its critical clauses with the eyes of a continentalist.

The intense nationalism of Hamilton's view of the Constitution arose in the first instance out of three deeply rooted if somewhat contradictory convictions, to each of which the Jeffersonians took sharp exception: that the Union was not at all the creation of the states; that the states were at best anachronisms, at worst "artificial beings," in the sight of history;[33] and that the federal system was an invitation to a contest for supremacy in which the states held better cards than the nation.

Hamilton never got his far-ranging thoughts on the origin of the Union into any sort of order, yet we do learn from one of his speeches in the New York Assembly in 1787 that he looked upon "Union" and "Independence" as twin offspring of the Declaration of July 4, 1776. Not only did the nation, in his opinion, have "full power of sovereignty" from this very first moment; the Articles of Confederation were "in fact an abridgment"—and an unfortunate one—of "the original sovereignty of the Union."[34] Whether the Constitution of 1787 was also such an abridgment he never had occasion to say. In any case, whoever or whatever might have created the Union, it most certainly was not Virginia and her twelve oddly assorted sisters.

We have already reviewed the evidence on the second of these points,[35] and the evidence is overwhelming that Hamilton was the least "federal" of all those heroic figures who laid the foundation for the first and most successful of federal systems. Despite his repeated protestations in public and private that the balance between states and nation was a stout defense of the liberties of the people, and that it was ridiculous to accuse him of fomenting "any combination to prostrate the State governments," [36] he never really gave Virginia and Massachusetts, or even New York and Connecticut, the place in the American system that they had always held in the minds and plans of the other men who professed to "think continentally." Even when he strained himself to acknowledge that the state governments might yet "prove useful and salutary," he set two large "ifs" as the conditions of this prospect: "if" they could be "circumscribed within bounds, consistent with the preservation of the national government," and "if" they were "all of the size of Connecticut, Maryland, or New Jersey." The truth of the matter is, as I pointed out in chapter 1, that Hamilton was the one "full-blooded American" alive in the early years of the Republic. Only such an American could have been so indifferent to the circumstances of his country and to the allegiances of his countrymen as to write ingenuously in 1799:

Happy would it be if a clause could be added to the Constitution, enabling Congress, on the application of any considerable portion of a State, containing not less than a hundred thousand persons, to erect it into a separate State. . . . *The subdivision of the great States is indispensable to the security of the general government, and with it of the Union.*[37]

Hamilton understood the realities of American politics and sentiment well enough to know that it would have been "inexpedient and even dangerous" to propose such an amendment openly, yet he could never understand why these realities were so tenacious, why, for example, a continentalist like Washington should feel so strongly about Virginia or one like his father-in-law feel the same way about New York.

As a result, he was never sanguine about the political and spiritual capacity of the nation to stand fast against the inroads of the ambitions, interests, traditions, and jealousies that grew so luxuriantly in the states, especially in the large ones. He held persistently to the worried opinion that the thrust of any federal system was "centrifugal" rather than "centripetal." [38] As early as 1781 he drew upon the "experience" of the ages and "the plainest principles of human nature" to demonstrate the validity of this opinion,[39] and even in his headiest days of power he stood by his mature reflections in *The Federalist,* number 17:

It will always be far more easy for the State governments to encroach upon the national authorities than for the national government to encroach upon the State authorities. The proof of this proposition turns upon the greater degree of influence which the State governments, if they administer their affairs with uprightness and prudence, will generally possess over the people. . . .

It is a known fact in human nature that its affections are commonly weak in proportion to the distance of diffusiveness of the object. Upon the same principle that a man is more attached to his family than to his neighborhood, to his neighborhood than to the community at large, the people of each State would be apt to feel a stronger bias towards their local governments than towards the government of the Union.[40]

Moved powerfully by this dual conviction—that the Union was the "rock" of "salvation" for America, and that the state governments were a standing threat to "sap the foundations of the Union" [41]—Hamilton sought anxiously to interpret the disputed clauses of the Constitution in favor of the wielders of national power. Having failed to persuade his colleagues at Philadelphia of the beauties of a truly national plan of government, and having thereafter recognized the futility of persuading the legislatures of three-fourths of the states to surrender even a jot of their privileges, he set out to remold the Constitution into an instrument of national supremacy. This he did, as he had promised to do in *The Federalist,* by instituting "a much better administration" in New York and Philadelphia than had ever been seen in Richmond or Albany,[42] by persuading men of substance and talent to move themselves and their ambitions to the center of the federal stage, and above all by inviting them to make creative use of the nebulous grants of power to Congress, President, and Supreme Court in the Constitution. Since we have already taken careful note, in chapter 3, of his manipulations of the Constitution as an administrator and a leader of legislation, and since we shall shortly be reviewing the arguments he drew upon in the most influential of these manipulations—those in which he persuaded Congress to be unstinting in the use of its own powers—it will suffice here to make the general point that Hamilton applied his major and minor rules of construction to the supremacy clause with zest and consistency.

His own draft constitution of 1787, a forceful instrument of nationalism, had incorporated a supremacy clause,[43] and as Publius he was quick to refute the "virulent invective and petulant declamation" that had greeted the appearance of Article VI, section 2. His argument was that of the clever constitutional lawyer who cuts the ground from under the critics of a clause by pointing out that the clause is merely declaratory of a palpable truth. "The clause which declares the supremacy of the laws of the Union," he wrote almost sententiously, "only declares a truth which flows immediately and necessarily from the institution of a federal government." [44] And in a passage that expressed his stoutest convictions both as a constitutional lawyer committed to national supremacy and as a political scientist enamored of energy, he put the matter forcefully:

A LAW, by the very meaning of the term, includes supremacy. It is a rule which those to whom it is prescribed are bound to observe. This results from every political association. If individuals enter into a state of society, the laws of that society must be the supreme regulator of their conduct. If a number of political societies enter into a larger political society, the laws which the latter may enact, pursuant to the powers intrusted to it by its constitution, must necessarily be supreme over those societies and the individuals of whom they are composed. It would otherwise be a mere treaty, dependent on the good faith of the parties, and not a government, which is only another word for POLITICAL POWER AND SUPREMACY.[45]

Although he went on from this point to deny quite properly that "invasions of the residuary authorities of the smaller societies" could ever "become the supreme law of the land," he had already made plain in word and deed, and was soon to make even plainer, that the "residuary authorities" of the states were few and unimportant. When he wrote to Washington in 1792 that there were "some things" which the "general government" had "clearly a right to do," others which it had "clearly no right to meddle with," and "a good deal of middle ground, about which honest and well-disposed men" might "differ," [46] he had already demonstrated that, so far as his own honesty and good disposition were concerned, all this "middle ground" was an area to which the nation had a superior claim—and in which it had every right to expect that its duly enacted laws would run unchallenged. Although he never went on record explicitly about the extreme techniques with which proponents of states' rights were beginning to toy, it is not hard to imagine what he would have thought of the doctrines of interposition, nullification, and secession.[47] Yet we must, for all the certainty we may entertain on this score, confine ourselves to imagination. As a constitutional lawyer who did not go looking for trouble, and also as a statesman more interested in acting than in theorizing, Hamilton had almost nothing to say about the meaning or wisdom of Amendments X and XI. To this most committed of nationalists the former, certainly as interpreted by Jefferson, must have been a standing affront to common

sense, history, and patriotism, the latter a "torturing" of the original meaning of the Constitution,[48] but he was probably too circumspect to say so
in public and too unconcerned to complain in private.

Hamilton waited until he was some years out of power, and indeed
beyond all reasonable expectation that he would ever hold power again,
to make his most impressive assertions of national supremacy under the
Constitution. He responded to the challenge of the Virginia and Kentucky
Resolutions by writing his famous letter to Jonathan Dayton, in which he
brushed aside the legal niceties of the Republican chieftains and then proposed steps to "extend the influence and promote the popularity" of the
national government.[49] He responded to President Jefferson's fulsome
praise of the state governments in his message to Congress of December 7, 1801 by writing a series of articles as Lucius Crassus, in the
ninth of which he laid bare that consuming allegiance to the national
government which shaped his every view of its authority. In refutation
of Jefferson's candid assertion that "the states themselves have principal
care of our persons, our property, and our reputation, constituting the
great field of human concerns," he wrote with equal candor:

> To the care of the Federal Government are confided . . . those great, general
> interests on which all particular interests materially depend: our safety in
> respect to foreign nations; our tranquillity in respect to each other; the foreign
> and mutual commerce of the States; the establishment and regulation of the
> money of the country; the management of our national finances. . . . In fine,
> it is the province of the General Government to manage the greatest number
> of those concerns in which the provident activity and exertion of *government*
> are of most importance to the people; and we have only to compare the state
> of our country antecedent to the establishment of the Federal Constitution,
> with what it has been since, to be convinced that the most operative causes
> of public prosperity depend upon that Constitution.[50]

For a politician and lawyer who believed this, as Hamilton surely did,
it was the most natural thing in the world to take the side of the nation in
those controversies over the nature of the federal system which agitated
American minds in his age far more furiously than in ours. If he came in
time to realize that the states were a fact of life with which he had to live
in peace, indeed that the government in Washington could "no more
abolish the State governments than they (could) dissolve the Union," * he
never gave them more than a secondary place in his schemes for distribut-

---

* It could, however, in the opinion of Camillus, adjust the boundaries of states that
bordered upon other nations or colonies by means of a treaty and without their
"special consent." [51]

ing the total power of the people. He was from first to last the most nationalist of all nationalists in his interpretation of the clauses of our federal Constitution. He considered it an "absurdity" to give "a government the direction of the most essential national interests" unless it were also given "the authorities which are indispensable to their proper and efficient management," [52] and he was morally certain that the government of the United States was not intended to be an absurdity.

THE most fateful contest over the meaning of the Constitution in the first years of its long and generally happy life centered upon those clauses which vest "all legislative powers herein granted" in the two houses of Congress. In his dual capacity as chief adviser to the President and willing servant of Congress, Hamilton was the acknowledged leader of the interests that were pressing for a "liberal" interpretation of those clauses, and he was also the leader of the forces of national supremacy. It was recognized by everyone—from the most meticulous Jeffersonian (probably Jefferson) to the most expansive Hamiltonian (certainly Hamilton)—that the authority of the new government would make its first and principal impact upon the people in the form of legislation. As the powers of Congress were construed, men agreed, so would the nature of the Union be shaped.

Hamilton's primary concern, of course, was to institute a financial, economic, and military program that would move an ever more perfect Union along the road to splendor, and, unlike such natural-born constitutionalists as Adams and Madison, he would have been happy if he had never had to give a thought to Article I, section 8 of the Constitution. As history would have it, however—the natural history of a free people under a written constitution—he had to give repeated thought to it. He learned through the hardest kind of experience that it is just as essential for an American to prove the constitutionality of a creative piece of legislation as it is to prove its importance for the cause of liberty and justice.

If he had had his way in 1787, there would have been no need for him to demonstrate his undoubted talents as constitutional lawyer in the debate with Madison and Jefferson over the propriety of a national bank. As we listen to the arguments of the Hamilton of 1791, we should keep in mind that the Hamilton of 1787 was prepared to make Congress the sovereign legislature of a united nation. While it is not surprising to learn that his plan of June 18 gave the national legislature the "power to pass all laws whatsoever," one does feel a small sense of astonishment in reading the opening words of Article VII of the more carefully digested draft constitution that he handed to Madison in September:

The legislature of the United States shall have power to pass all laws which they shall judge necessary to the common defense and safety and to the general welfare of the Union.*

Thwarted in his desire, which he knew to be both unfashionable and unattainable, to endow Congress directly with "a general legislative authority," [53] Hamilton spent the rest of his years in an attempt to give it such authority by construing the Constitution broadly. He did this principally by proclaiming the famous doctrine of "implied powers." Nation-minded men such as Hamilton, Madison, and James Wilson had stumbled upon this doctrine as early as 1781 in their attempts to extend the authority of the old Congress,[54] but it was left to Hamilton to convert it into the fortress of logic from which John Marshall was able to beat off the assault of the strict constructionists in *McCulloch* v. *Maryland*.

While the chief source of the mature doctrine of implied powers is Hamilton's Opinion on the Constitutionality of the Bank of February 23, 1791, one finds elaborations of this doctrine throughout his writings as Secretary of the Treasury. And the sum of all his thoughts on this matter was that Congress, if it were to be truly the legislature of a nation, must have authority to pursue the ends set down for it in the Constitution by employing "all the *means* requisite and fairly applicable to the attainment" of these ends.[55] "It is conceded," he wrote,

that *implied powers* are to be considered as delegated equally with *express ones*. Then it follows, that as a power of erecting a corporation may as well be *implied* as any other thing, it may as well be employed as an *instrument* or *means* of carrying into execution any of the specified powers, as any other *instrument* or *means* whatever. The only question must be in this, as in every other case, whether the means to be employed, or, in this instance, the corporation to be erected, has a natural relation to any of the acknowledged objects or lawful ends of the government. Thus a corporation may not be erected by Congress for superintending the police of the city of Philadelphia, because they are not authorized to *regulate* the *police* of that city. But one may be erected in relation to the collection of taxes, or to the trade with foreign countries, or to the trade between the States, or with the Indian tribes; because it is the province of the Federal Government to *regulate* those objects, and because it is incident to a general *sovereign* or *legislative* power to *regulate* a thing, to employ all the means which relate to its regulation to the best and greatest advantage.[56]

---

* In another section of this article Hamilton placed standard restrictions on his proposed legislature by forbidding it to pass bills of attainder and ex post facto laws, to grant titles of nobility, or to establish a church.[57]

No one, least of all the Madison of *The Federalist,* number 44, could deny that Congress had been given an extra dose of power by the decision to tack on the "necessary and proper" clause to Article I, section 8. The question on which Hamilton parted company from his old friend, and indeed from all those men who were beginning to rally around Jefferson, was very simply the size of this dose. To put the matter as succinctly as possible, what Hamilton extracted from the doctrine of implied powers was a broad competence to use the enumerated powers of Article I, section 8 in a grand manner. This he did, as we might expect, by applying all his major and minor rules of constitutional interpretation to the words "necessary and proper." Jefferson had argued for a highly restrictive interpretation of this phrase, and especially of the first word in it. "It has been urged," he wrote to Washington in a powerful attempt to prompt a presidential veto,

that a bank will give great facility or convenience in the collection of taxes. Suppose this were true: yet the Constitution allows only the means which are *"necessary,"* not those which are merely "convenient" for effecting the enumerated powers. If such a latitude of construction be allowed to this phrase as to give any non-enumerated power, it will go to every one, for there is not one which ingenuity may not torture into a *convenience* in some instance *or other,* to *some one* of so long a list of enumerated powers. It would swallow up all the delegated powers, and reduce the whole to one power.[58]

To which Hamilton, who was rightly suspected of wanting to "reduce the whole to one power," made reply:

It is essential to the being of the national government that so erroneous a conception of the meaning of the word *necessary* should be exploded.

It is certain that neither the grammatical nor popular sense of the term requires that construction. According to both, necessary often means no more than *needful, requisite, incidental, useful,* or *conducive to.* It is a common mode of expression to say that it is *necessary* for a government or a person to do this or that thing, when nothing more is intended or understood than that the interests of the government or person require, or will be promoted by, the doing of this or that thing. The imagination can be at no loss for exemplifications of the use of the word in this sense. And it is the true one in which it is to be understood as used in the Constitution. The whole turn of the clause containing it indicates that it was the intent of the Convention, by that clause, to give a liberal latitude to the exercise of the specified powers. The expressions have peculiar comprehensiveness. . . .

To understand the word as the Secretary of State does, would be to depart from its obvious and popular sense, and to give it a restrictive operation, an idea never before entertained. It would be to give it the same force as if the word *absolutely* or *indispensably* had been prefixed to it.[59]

"Such a construction," he added, "would beget endless uncertainty and embarrassment." Having had his fill of uncertainty and embarrassment under the Articles of Confederation, he was determined to construe this clause, and almost every clause in Article I, in such a way as to set Congress free to act in the national interest. Hamilton's Opinion on the Constitutionality of the Bank was an attempt to persuade his countrymen, many of whom were appalled to hear him argue in this sweeping vein, that it was "the manifest design and scope of the Constitution to vest in Congress all the powers requisite to the effectual administration of the finances of the United States." [60] It is plain that, in terms of legitimacy, he made no real distinction in his own mind between a power that was specifically delegated ("to lay and collect taxes" or "to borrow money") and a power that could be reasonably implied from this delegation (to incorporate a bank). In *The Federalist,* number 31 he had insisted that "a government ought to contain in itself every power requisite to the full accomplishment of the objects committed to its care," [61] and in the Opinion of 1791 he forged the essential link between this expansive concept of sovereign authority and the restrictive concept of delegated powers—between, in a phrase, the energy and the limits of a constitutional government.

With the aid of the doctrine of implied powers Hamilton converted the most important of the twenty-odd powers enumerated in Article I, section 8 into firm foundations for whatever prodigious feats of legislation Americans might need to perform in the unimagined circumstances of the future. Since he was never compelled, he never bothered to subject them to the kind of analysis that Marshall devoted to the commerce clause in *Gibbons* v. *Ogden.* He was more interested in using these powers expansively than in analyzing them rigorously, as he proved by rattling off a half-dozen as authority for incorporating a national bank. Such an incorporation, he "affirmed" grandly,

has a relation, more or less direct, to the power of collecting taxes, to that of borrowing money, to that of regulating trade between the States, and to those of raising and maintaining fleets and armies.[62]

And as if these "specified powers" were not enough, he threw in "the provision which authorizes the making of all *needful rules and regulations* concerning the *property* of the United States."

In this area, as in every other to which he gave any thought, his constitutional law was a collection of broad propositions that he fired off almost casually in his debates with the Jeffersonians. Yet he said enough about three of these powers to convince historians that, if he had ever been placed on the Supreme Court, he would have out-Marshalled even the Marshall of *McCulloch* v. *Maryland*.

The first was the power to "lay and collect taxes . . . to pay the debts and provide for the common defense and general welfare of the United States," and it should not surprise us to learn that he argued for an almost unlimited authority in Congress to tax and also to spend for the public good. His philosophy of taxation was proclaimed in the Pough-keepsie Convention, and from it this assessor of taxes on whisky and car-riages never wandered.

The great leading objects of the federal government, in which revenue is concerned, are to maintain domestic peace and provide for the common defense. In these are comprehended the regulation of commerce, that is, the whole system of foreign intercourse, the support of armies and navies, and of the civil administration. It is useless to go into detail. Every one knows that the objects of the general government are numerous, extensive, and important. Every one must acknowledge the necessity of giving powers, in all respects and in every degree, equal to these objects. . . . Where ought the great resources to be lodged? Every rational man will give an immediate answer. To what extent shall these resources be possessed? Reason says, as far as possible exigencies can require; that is, without limitation. A constitution cannot set bounds to a nation's wants; it ought not therefore to set bounds to its resources. Unex-pected invasions, long and ruinous wars, may demand all the possible abilities of the country. Shall not your government have power to call these abilities into action? The contingencies of society are not reducible to calculations; they cannot be fixed or bounded, even in imagination.[63]

It seems certain that Hamilton would have affixed a certificate of con-stitutionality, if not one of wisdom, to every last tax with which we now summon up "all the possible abilities" of this giant country. While he might not have liked the idea of an income tax, he would have been the last man, whether in 1861 or 1895 or 1964, to doubt its constitutional pro-priety.

Hamilton took a large view of the power of Congress to tax because he took a large view of its power to spend. We have already learned in chapter 3 about the falling-out he had with Madison and Jefferson over the authority that Congress might extract from the opening words of Article I, section 8. The occasion was the proposal in the Report on Manufactures to pay "pecuniary bounties" to producers of vital articles, and Hamilton seized upon it to make an unprecedented claim for the "general welfare," which Congress is instructed to "provide for" through its power to "lay and collect taxes." "A question has been made," he wrote, "concerning the constitutional right . . . to apply this species of encouragement, but there is certainly no good foundation for such a question." Except for the specific qualifications listed in Article I, section 8—that taxes be "uniform throughout the United States," that direct taxes be apportioned, and that "no tax" be laid on "articles exported from any state"—he continued:

The power to raise money is plenary and indefinite, and the objects to which it may be appropriated are no less comprehensive than the payment of the public debts, and the providing for the common defense and general welfare. The terms "general welfare" were doubtless intended to signify more than was expressed or imported in those which preceded; otherwise, numerous exigencies incident to the affairs of a nation would have been left without a provision. . . .

It is, therefore, of necessity, left to the discretion of the National Legislature to pronounce upon the objects which concern the general welfare, and for which, under that description, an appropriation of money is requisite and proper. And there seems to be no room for a doubt that whatever concerns the general interests of learning, of agriculture, of manufactures, and of commerce, are within the sphere of the national councils, as far as regards an application of money.[64]

Thus with a flourish did Hamilton convert the fuzzy words about the "general welfare" from a "sort of caption," as Madison described them, into a grant of almost unlimited authority to enact programs that would divert the growing riches of the American people into schemes for social and economic development. Indeed, the "only qualification" of this clause that seemed to him "admissible" was "that the object" of any appropriations "be general, and not local," that its "operation" extend "in fact or by possibility throughout the Union" and not be "confined to a particular spot." [65]

The second of the enumerated powers to which he applied the rules of broad construction was that which calls upon Congress "to regulate commerce with foreign nations, and among the several states." He had, to be sure, very little to say about a power whose uses would not be fully apparent to the American people until a more advanced stage of economic and social growth, but he said enough to leave us in no doubt that he would have approved the constitutional logic of Marshall in *Gibbons* v. *Ogden,* of Taft in *Stafford* v. *Wallace,* and of Hughes in *N.L.R.B.* v. *Jones and Laughlin.*[66] The commerce power was one of the six hooks of delegated power upon which he hung the implied power of Congress to incorporate a bank, and he, like most of the other nation-minded men of his time, seems to have used the word "commerce" as an all-inclusive label for the economic activities of the society.[67] A legislature empowered to "regulate commerce" was a legislature empowered to police, tax, and encourage—and, if necessary, to discourage—all those undertakings covered by the words "trade," "manufacturing," "finance," and even "agriculture." As a federal legislature it was, moreover, empowered to extend its sway over aspects of "internal" commerce that were mixed up with the "external" commerce of any state. Indeed, Hamilton seemed to ask in the Opinion of 1791, what meaningful line could ever be drawn between the two?

What regulation of commerce does not extend to the internal commerce of every State? What are all the duties upon imported articles, amounting to prohibitions, but so many bounties upon domestic manufactures, affecting the interests of different classes of citizens, in different ways? What are all the provisions in the Coasting Act which relate to the trade between district and district of the same State? In short, what regulation of trade between the States but must affect the internal trade of each State? What can operate upon the whole but must extend to every part? [68]

Since the Congress of the United States was plainly authorized to "operate upon the whole," it was authorized, in the opinion of this uncompromising nationalist, to "extend" its benevolent power "to every part" of the nation. It is hard to imagine that Hamilton would have brooked any limits, save those of equity and generality, upon the right of Congress to deal with any economic or even social problem that might arise in the course of our progress to industrial might.

The third of the enumerated powers to which Hamilton turned his attention in passing was that aggregate of clauses 1, 10, 11, 12, 13, 14, 15, and 16 of Article I, section 8—and also of the opening words of Article II, section 2—which Lincoln was later to describe simply and grandly as "the war power" of the United States. Since he could not imagine the dimensions of a modern war, Hamilton could not imagine the kinds of authority that Lincoln, Wilson, Roosevelt, Truman, and their Congresses would be able to carve out of these clauses; and once again we discover that he had only random comments to make on one of the mighty grants of power in the Constitution. Yet once again—and in this instance with a particular sense of awe at the prophetic nature of these comments—we must give him credit for having established a general framework of authority within which other men could work out the details of a constitutional law that placed emphasis upon national competence and national supremacy.

He did this, interestingly enough, in the twenty-third number of *The Federalist,* in which Publius spoke, like the old soldier he was, with a bluntness that gives the lie to those who accuse him of an unbecoming sensitivity to the prejudices of his audience. Aware that America might live forever in a world at war, anxious to arm it constitutionally for any military effort that it might be forced to make, Hamilton created— apparently out of whole cloth—a theory of the war power that has never been matched for grandeur and realism. "The authorities essential to the common defense," he wrote, "are these":

to raise armies; to build and equip fleets; to prescribe rules for the government of both; to direct their operations; to provide for their support. These powers ought to exist without limitation, *because it is impossible to foresee or define the extent and variety of national exigencies, or the correspondent extent and variety of the means which may be necessary to satisfy them.* The circumstances that endanger the safety of nations are infinite, and for this reason no constitutional shackles can wisely be imposed on the power to which the care of it is committed. This power ought to be coextensive with all the possible combinations of such circumstances. . . .

Whether there ought to be a federal government intrusted with the care of the common defense is a question in the first instance open to discussion; but the moment it is decided in the affirmative, it will follow that that government ought to be clothed with all the powers requisite to complete execution of its trust. And unless it can be shown that the circumstances which may affect the public safety are reducible within certain determinate limits; unless the contrary of this position can be fairly and rationally disputed, it must be admitted as a necessary consequence that there can be no limitation of that authority which is to provide for the defense and protection of the community in any matter essential to its efficacy—that is, in any matter essential to the *formation, direction,* or *support* of the NATIONAL FORCES.[69]

We can only speculate what implied powers Hamilton was prepared to extract from the pregnant phrase "to provide for their support." We do know that he fell back upon the war power as one of the foundations of the Bank, and that he recommended the establishment of government-owned "manufactories of all the necessary weapons of war"; * and we may therefore be certain that he would have been even less squeamish about

---

* "There appears to be an improvidence," he counseled in words to which we have paid perhaps too little attention, "in leaving [the] essential implements of national defense to the casual speculations of individual adventure." [70]

stretching the words "raise and support armies" to the limits of reason and ingenuity than he was about stretching the words "provide for . . . the general welfare." *

When one recalls the activities in which Hamilton persuaded the infant government of the United States to engage, then adds to these the other activities that he recommended in vain—whether to build munitions factories, encourage the growth of industry, stimulate "enterprise and experiment" in agriculture, establish a national university, afford "nutriment" to the "higher branches of science," "improve" all the means of "communications," and handle the problem of sedition (especially as practiced by "renegade aliens") even more vigorously than it had been handled in the Alien and Sedition Acts [71]—one must conclude that he took the most sweeping view of the powers of Congress of any political and legal figure in our first century and a half under the Constitution. He construed each of the enumerated powers singly in the broadest possible manner; he gave each of them an extra measure of vitality by lumping it together with all the others in an "aggregate view"; [72] and he converted the doctrine of implied powers into an ever-flowing, all-encompassing source of statutory authority. And as if these creative exercises in constitutional interpretation were not enough, he explored yet another source upon which future Congresses might draw. "It is not denied," he wrote in a remarkable aside in the Opinion on the Constitutionality of the Bank,

that there are *implied,* as well as *express powers,* and that the *former* are as effectually delegated as the *latter.* And for the sake of accuracy it shall be mentioned that there is another class of powers, which may be properly denominated *resulting powers.* It will not be doubted that if the United States should make a conquest of any of the territories of its neighbors, they would possess sovereign jurisdiction over the conquered territory. This would be rather a result from the whole mass of the powers of the government, and

* It is noteworthy that Hamilton took an equally expansive view of the power of the United States to make peace. Writing as Phocion in 1784 he had this to say in defense of the authority of the old Congress to make a detailed treaty of peace with Britain:

"The common interests of humanity, and the general tranquillity of the world, require that the power of making peace, wherever lodged, should be construed and exercised liberally; and even in cases where its extent may be doubtful, it is the policy of all wise nations to give it latitude rather than confine it. The exigencies of a community, in time of war, are so various and often so critical, that it would be extremely dangerous to prescribe narrow bounds to that power by which it is to be restored. The consequence might frequently be a diffidence of our engagements, and a prolongation of the calamities of war." [73]

from the nature of political society, than a consequence of . . . powers specially enumerated.[74]

Since he never followed up this tantalizing reference to a "class of powers" that belonged to the entire government (and thus, in the first instance, to Congress) simply because the United States was a full-fledged "political society," we cannot know what other kinds of activity he would have been prepared to justify under this rubric. It would appear that the stillborn doctrine of resulting powers had its chief application in the field of foreign affairs, and it is interesting to hear the faint echo of this Hamiltonian doctrine in Justice Sutherland's memorable opinion of 1936 in *U.S.* v. *Curtiss-Wright Export Corp.*[75]

The truth is, of course, that Hamilton felt no need to draw upon this controversial source in his attempts to bolster the self-confidence of Congress. In the enumerated and implied powers, as he read them, the gentlemen of Congress could find an unchallengeable sanction for just about any tax, scheme, program, or reform they were called upon by thoughtful majorities to initiate for the public good. There was, as Hamilton wrote near the end of the Opinion of 1791, "no parsimony of power" in the words of Article I, section 8. There was, indeed, that "general legislative authority" which, in his advanced opinion, ought to have been granted to Congress in the first place. Subject only to the limits of equity and generality and to specific prohibitions against such crudities as bills of attainder, Hamilton's Congress seems to have had the "power to pass *all laws whatsoever.*"

As the creative genius of the first administration under the Constitution, Hamilton was as determined to pile up the precedents of a strong Presidency as he was to untie the hands of a strong Congress. In his political science, and thus in his constitutional law and theory, there was no contradiction between these two designs. A legislature was "strong" if it grappled with problems of economic growth and national security by interpreting its mandate loosely and enacting far-ranging laws. It displayed not strength but indecorum when it followed its natural bent and tried to do the job of the executive. The executive, in its turn, was "strong" if it called attention to problems and suggested workable remedies, made use of the discretionary powers granted by the legislature, and guarded against invasions of its own area of constitutional responsibility. The balance between legislature and executive was one that changed with changing circumstances, yet the latter was always intended, in Hamilton's opinion, to be "one up" in the mixed pattern of co-operation and contention ordained in the Constitution. At the outset of his long search for the charter of a more perfect Union, in the letter of 1780 to Duane, he set the style for all subsequent thoughts on this matter:

Another defect in our system is want of method and energy in the administration. This has partly resulted from the other defect, but in a great degree from prejudice and the want of a proper executive. Congress have kept the power too much into their own hands, and have meddled too much with details of every sort. Congress is properly a deliberative corps, and it forgets itself when it attempts to play the executive.[76]

Hamilton had a healthy bias in favor of the Presidency (and would probably have had it even if he had spent his public life in Congress) because he was obsessed with energy, and because both reason and experience had persuaded him as far back as Valley Forge that energy was peculiarly the quality of the executive branch. If "energy in the executive" was not the sum of "good government," it was certainly "a leading character in the definition" of such government.[77] Writing first as Publius in 1788, then as Metellus in 1792, Hamilton summed up this article of his political faith:

A feeble executive implies a feeble execution of the government. A feeble execution is but another phrase for a bad execution; and a government ill executed, whatever it may be in theory, must be, in practice, a bad government.[78]

The success of every government—its capacity to combine the exertion of public strength with the preservation of personal right and private security, qualities which define the perfection of a government, must always naturally depend on the energy of the executive department.[79]

Hamilton's countrymen were not interested in "every government," but in republican government, and he therefore had to go further to prove that the "executive impulse" was not "inconsistent with the genius" of such government.[80] This he tried to do in theory in *The Federalist*, numbers 70-77 and in practice as constitutional adviser to Washington, and few will deny that he succeeded remarkably well. If the Presidency inherited by Adams and then by Jefferson was eminently a constitutional office, it was in part because Hamilton had worked so imaginatively in support of his own President to give it the right blend of power and limits or, as he wrote, of "energy" and "safety." Let us examine the law and theory of the Hamiltonian Presidency with the aid of his own statement of the problem in *The Federalist*, number 70:

The ingredients which constitute energy in the executive are unity; duration; an adequate provision for its support; and competent powers.

The ingredients which constitute safety in the republican sense are a due dependence on the people, and a due responsibility.[81]

Of the many wrong turns his colleagues might have taken at Philadelphia in 1787, the wrongest of all, in Hamilton's opinion, would have been to create a two-man or three-man executive, or even a single executive forced to share important powers with a standing council; and he must have felt a peculiar sense of relief and righteousness when he made his famous case for unity in *The Federalist,* number 70.[82] He was pleased, he acknowledged, with Article II not merely because its designation of a single chief executive was a boon to "vigor and expedition" and therefore "conducive to energy," but because it would thwart the tendency of "plurality in the executive" to "conceal faults and destroy responsibility." "All multiplication of the executive is rather dangerous than friendly to liberty," he asserted forcefully; "it is far more safe there should be a single object for the jealousy and watchfulness of the people." It could be argued, to be sure, that in the course of his earnest activity, first as the chief hustler in Washington's administration and then as the largest fly in Adams's ointment, he made his own inroads on the unity of the Presidency. Yet it would be fairer, I think, to judge him as a politician so committed to a large design, and so certain of the road that led to it, that he was not always meticulous in respecting a constitutional principle to which he was firmly attached. By and large, we may set him down as a man who, once the larger question of unity had been settled in Article II, was disturbed by the thought of any official or group—that is to say, the Vice-President or Cabinet—"treading close upon the heels" of the President.[83] He would have been distressed by the trend toward plurality under Madison and Monroe; he would have understood, even though he might have found the affair personally unpleasant, the decision of Jackson to reassert the political and moral supremacy of the President over the members of his Cabinet.

Hamilton was not quite so pleased with the solution of Article II to the problem of duration in the executive, for he made clear at Philadelphia, in both the plan of June 18 and the draft constitution of September, that the president of his model republic would serve, as Justices of the Supreme Court in fact serve, "during good behavior"[84]—in other words, for life. Yet four years were better than one or two or three, and he could console himself with the thought that the absence of any prohibition against re-eligibility would make it possible for at least some Presidents—

those not much less worthy than Washington and a good deal less intent upon retirement [85]—to enjoy a kind of permanent tenure. No one, incidentally, was more sorry than he that Washington declined to serve more than two terms. In any event, he put the case for indefinite re-eligibility as sensibly as it has ever been put, and those Americans who think Amendment XXII was a mistake can find confirmation of their fears in *The Federalist,* number 72.* As he wrote in conclusion to his argument for re-eligibility (or, more accurately, his argument against ineligibility):

> There is an excess of refinement in the idea of disabling the people to con-
> tinue in office men who had entitled themselves, in their opinion, to approbation
> and confidence, the advantages of which are at best speculative and equivocal,
> and are overbalanced by disadvantages far more certain and decisive.[86]

The one thing that Hamilton could never endure in political scientists or constitutional lawyers was "an excess of refinement." He was against littering up a constitution with unnecessary restrictions; he was for constitutional clauses that meant what they said, said a great deal, and said it in as few words—and thus with as few cautions—as possible. "It is more wise to observe the principle of rotation in practice," he argued in speaking to this issue in 1789, "than to make it one of the fundamentals of a constitution." [87]

Hamilton had very little to say in *The Federalist,*[88] and nothing at all in later years, about the third "ingredient" of "energy in the executive": an "adequate provision for its support." He did make clear that, as Americans had learned to their delight in the long years of conflict with royal governors, the separation of powers would be "merely nominal" and the executive be rendered "obsequious" in the absence of the stipulation that guarantees the President a steady compensation. This was the sort of clause, one that cut straight through a messy possibility with a few austere words, that he liked to see in a constitution.

HAMILTON's approach to the powers of the Presidency was the same as his approach to those of Congress. While he wished that Article II had been more generous in bestowing authority, he was prepared to remedy its deficiencies by construing it broadly and loosely. As he told McHenry in 1800, he was just as prepared to "claim the exercise of implied powers" for the President as for Congress.[89] He was anxious, especially when

---

* Hamilton spoke forcefully against a resolution proposing just such an amendment in the Poughkeepsie Convention, July 22, 1788.[90]

he was on the outside looking in at Jefferson, that "the first officer of the government . . . respectfully acquiesce in the spirit and ideas of that instrument under which he is appointed," [91] but he, after all, had done more than any man of the age to make the spirit of the Constitution lively and the ideas comprehensive. He was never a constitutional lawyer, even in his most downcast moments in 1802, to "torture" the words of Article II into a patch of "*anti*-executive maxims." [92] One of the few points, in his own mind, that recommended Jefferson for the Presidency was that, "while we were in the administration together, he was generally for a large construction of Executive authority and not backward to act upon it in cases which coincided with his views." [93]

Hamilton was usually quick with constitutional advice to Washington, Adams, and even Jefferson (not that the last two asked for it) to use their powers authoritatively. He took the spacious view of the veto power, which was designed to serve not merely as "a shield to the executive," but as "an additional security against the enaction of improper laws" and "against the effects of faction, precipitancy, or of any impulse unfriendly to the public good"; [94] he took the same view of the power to enforce the laws in the teeth of resistance and rebellion; [95] and he rarely missed an opportunity, as we learned in chapter 3, to give the President a free if not irresponsible hand in the conduct of foreign affairs. Occasionally he made what we would consider a bad or merely too cautious guess about some untried aspect of presidential authority—for example, his offhand association of the Senate with the power of removal in *The Federalist,* number 77 *—but for the most part he gave the President the benefit of any doubt that crossed his mind. In his manual of constitutional law the President was an official clothed with vast discretion, whether to take personal command of the armed forces "as first general and admiral of the Confederacy," [96] to direct these forces to answer war with war even in the

---

* It must have caused Hamilton no little embarrassment to hear Publius quoted in support of this "sentiment" in the famous debate over the location of this power in the House of Representatives in 1789, especially since by this time he must have agreed unreservedly with Madison that the power to remove department heads had been effectively vested in the President alone. It was, incidentally, his friend William Smith of South Carolina who tossed him into the debate—and in this manner: "A publication of no inconsiderable eminence in the class of political writings on the constitution, has advanced this sentiment. The author, or authors, (for I have understood it to be the production of two gentlemen of great information) of the work published under the signature of *Publius,* has these words:" Whereupon he quoted the critical passage in *The Federalist,* number 77. Madison, in reply, disposed of Publius neatly without revealing which of the "two gentlemen of great information" had made this slip. [97]

absence of a declaration,[98] to proclaim "temporary suspensions of hostilities" without the approval of Congress,[99] to provide Congress with forceful leadership in the enactment of legislation that had been requested specifically and in detail,[100] to accept from Congress (on an emergency basis) a decisive share of its most fateful power,* to reject requests by Congress for personal papers,[101] or to disburse public monies with an unpalsied hand.[102]

The high point in Hamilton's interpretation of the powers of the Presidency was reached, as we know, in the first of his seven papers as Pacificus in 1793, in which he denied that Washington had "stepped beyond the bounds of his constitutional authority and duty" in affirming the neutrality of the United States in the war between royal Britain and republican France.[103] Not only did he make a broad case for the ascendancy of the Presidency as the "organ of intercourse between the nation and foreign nations" and thus the "interpreter of the national treaties"; he grounded his case upon the broadest possible constitutional bases: the power to "take care that the laws be faithfully executed," the power of "command and disposition of the public force," and, most significantly, the "executive power" that is "vested" in the President by the opening words of Article II.

Hamilton had steered clear of this last power, if power it was, in his discussion of the Presidency in *The Federalist,* but by 1793 he was ready, and indeed had the encouragement of Madison's "liberal" interpretation of it in the debate over the removal power in 1789,[104] to make more of the phrase "executive power" than the other Framers had intended. He was, in short, ready to do with the opening words of Article II what he had already done with the opening words of Article I, section 8: to convert them from a gratuitous prologue to the enumeration of powers that followed into a grant of power in its own right. After quoting these words and then listing some of the specific powers granted to the President, he went on in his best style as constitutional lawyer:

It would not consist with the rules of sound construction, to consider this enumeration of particular authorities as derogating from the more compre-

---

* In a letter of January 26, 1799, Hamilton wrote to his friend Otis in Congress: "I should be glad to see, before the close of the session, a law empowering the President, at his discretion, in case a negotiation between the United States and France should not be on foot by the first of August next, or being on foot should terminate without an adjustment of differences, to declare that a state of war exists between the two countries, and thereupon to employ the land and naval forces of the United States in such manner as shall appear to him most effectual for annoying the enemy, and for preventing and frustrating hostile designs of France." [105]

hensive grant in the general clause, further than as it may be coupled with express restrictions or limitations. . . . The difficulty of a complete enumeration of all the cases of executive authority would naturally dictate the use of general terms, and would render it improbable that a specification of certain particulars was designed as a substitute for those terms, when antecedently used. The different mode of expression employed in the Constitution, in regard to the two powers, the legislative and the executive, serves to confirm this inference. In the article which gives the legislative powers of the government, the expressions are: "All legislative powers herein granted shall be vested in a Congress of the United States." In that which grants the executive power, the expressions are: *"The executive power* shall be vested in a President of the United States."

In making this distinction, still one of the most effective shots in the locker of advocates of the strong Presidency, the Hamilton of 1793 went far beyond the Madison of 1789 (and even farther beyond the vague intentions of his colleagues of 1787) in tapping the limitless potential of the so-called "vesting clause." [106] "The enumeration," he continued,

ought therefore to be considered as intended merely to specify the principal articles implied in the definition of executive power; leaving the rest to flow from the general grant of that power, interpreted in conformity with other parts of the Constitution, and with the principles of free government.

The general doctrine of our Constitution, then, is, that the *executive power* of the nation is vested in the President; subject only to the *exceptions* and *qualifications* which are expressed in the instrument.

The only exceptions that he could find—and these were "to be construed strictly" because they were in the nature of limitations rather than grants—were the association of the Senate in "the appointment of officers, and in the making of treaties," and "the right of the Legislature" to declare war. "With these exceptions," he concluded firmly, "the *executive power* of the United States is completely lodged in the President." [107] Just what were "executive acts" Hamilton did not find necessary or politic to say. A proclamation of neutrality was certainly such an act, no matter how insistently Madison and Jefferson might deny it, for it involved not the "enacting" of "some new law" but the determining and declaring of "a *fact,* with regard to the *existing state* of the nation." [108] If this were such an act, what act forced upon the President by the pressure of events would not be? The Louisiana Purchase, the destroyer deal of 1940, the seizure of the steel industry in 1952—all these, surely, were reasonable uses of the "executive power" for "the public good."

Two final points should be made about Hamilton's sweeping view of the powers of the President, which in fact was a sweeping view of the capacity of the nation to shape its own destiny. The first is that he made room in his constitutional law for the controversial doctrine of emergency powers. Having lived all his mature life in a country that seemed to move from one crisis to another, he was tough-minded in his expectation that it would be moving from one to another, perhaps by way of longer intervals of peace and plenty, until the end of time. His public and private writings are studded with references to the prospect, even for blessed America, of "emergencies," "extremities," "exigencies," "calamities," "crises," "public necessities," and "embarrassments," of "maladies as inseparable from the body politic as tumors and eruptions from the natural body." [109] In several places he seems to be warning his fellow countrymen that they must expect future Presidents and Congresses to "resort to first principles" and thus move outside the boundaries of the Constitution in their efforts to save the nation from destruction; in several others he seems to be saying that the Constitution, if interpreted correctly, can justify even the most extraordinary acts. It is the latter view, I think, that he would have advised us to take, for as he argued cogently at the end of *The Federalist,* number 25:

Nations pay little regard to rules and maxims calculated in their very nature to run counter to the necessities of society. Wise politicians will be cautious about fettering the government with restrictions that cannot be observed, because they know that every breach of the fundamental laws, though dictated by necessity, impairs that sacred reverence which ought to be maintained in the breast of rulers towards the constitution of a country, and forms a precedent for other breaches where the same plea of necessity does not exist at all, or is less urgent and palpable.[110]

Hamilton was well aware of the dangers to liberty that lurked in the concept of emergency powers. He was conversant with the history of the constitutional dictatorship of republican Rome; [111] he had heard men talk loosely of a "dictatorship" in the hard days of 1780; [112] he knew what could happen to the best of constitutional arrangements—for example, the attempt to draw an exact line between the civil and military powers—in time of national alarm.[113] Yet he did not flinch from the unpleasant consequences of his crudely developed yet candid theory of crisis government. One can certainly imagine him as a Justice of the Supreme Court taking an indulgent view of an emergency delegation of power from Congress to President or a resort by a desperate President to the "executive power" of Article II. As he wrote in *The Federalist* of poll taxes, so he could have written of martial law:

As little friendly as I am to the species of imposition, I still feel a thorough conviction that the power of having recourse to it ought to exist in the federal government. There are certain emergencies of nations in which expedients that in the ordinary state of things ought to be foreborne become essential to the public weal. And the government, from the possibility of such emergencies, ought ever to have the option of making use of them.[114]

And as he wrote during the "calamity" of the Whiskey Rebellion:

In emergencies, great and difficult, not to act with an energy proportioned to their magnitude and pressure, is as dangerous as any conceivable course. . . . [It] would be to sacrifice [the] laws, and with them the Constitution, the Government, the principles of social order, and the bulwarks of private right and security.[115]

The second point is that Hamilton interpreted the treaty-making power of the President and Senate as liberally as he did the other disputed clauses of the Constitution, and that within the framework of co-operation between these two organs he gave first place by a wide margin to the President. There is no reason to question the sincerity of his argument in *The Federalist,* number 75 against vesting this power in the President alone,* for he had made a place for "the *advice* and *approbation* of the Senate" in the treaty-making process in his plan of June 18, 1787.[116] Yet he never doubted the right of the President to give a strong lead to the Senate, whether in negotiating new treaties or suspending the operation of old ones.[117] Moreover, he was certain—much too certain, one might say—that the House of Representatives was under "constitutional, legal, and moral obligation" to make an appropriation of money that had been pledged by the United States in a duly ratified treaty.[118]

Whatever adjustments might be made from time to time in the delicate relations of President and Senate, their joint power to make treaties was "great"—and "necessarily so, else it could not answer those purposes of national security and interest . . . for which it is designed."[119] It could "reach and embrace" all objects "upon which the legislative power is authorized to act," and thus "must necessarily repeal an antecedent law contrary to it." "The organ of the power of treaty," he insisted, "is as truly the organ of the will of a nation as that of its legislative power."[120]

---

* "The history of human conduct," he wrote, "does not warrant that exalted opinion of human virtue which would make it wise in a nation to commit interests of so delicate and momentous a kind, as those which concern its intercourse with the rest of the world, to the sole disposal of a magistrate created and circumstanced as would be a President of the United States."[121]

The treaty power could also reach, he seemed to imply in a confidential message to Washington in 1795, objects other than those upon which Congress had been authorized to act. "A treaty cannot be made," he conceded, "which alters the constitutions of the country, or which infringes any express exceptions to the power of the Constitution." And yet, he added, "it is difficult to assign any other bounds to the power." It must be interpreted as a power "commensurate with the variety of exigencies and objects of intercourse which occur between nation and nation," a power able "to manage with efficacy the external affairs of the country in all cases in which they must depend upon compact with another nation," a power equal to negotiations on all "proper subjects of compacts with foreign nations." [122] Hamilton never did take that last step in the direction of *Missouri* v. *Holland*—the breath-taking case in which Justice Holmes, in effect, converted the treaty-making power into a constitutional basis for laws that Congress was not otherwise authorized to enact [123]—but since in his own mind he had extended a "general legislative authority" to Congress, he would have considered such a step to be superfluous.

I do not mean to leave an image of a lawyer who was prepared to find authority in the Constitution for any act the President might want to take, or who regretted the extent to which the President was dependent upon the House and Senate for the most effective use of his vast powers.[124] Hamilton had not been at war with himself when he had caused Publius to proclaim the necessity of "safety in the republican sense," and he had rejoiced to find it in the "due dependence" of the President "on the people" and in his "due responsibility." Not merely as critic of Adams and Jefferson but also as colleague of Washington, he had counsel to give in behalf of responsibility. He advised Washington to acknowledge the "right" of all Senators to have *"individual* access on matters relative to the *public administration,"* so that the people could be sure that there was "some body of men in the state" who were in "continual communication with the President." [125] He granted Congress full discretion, "by a collective act, to pronounce the non-operation or nullity of a treaty," [126] denied the power of the President "to appoint an envoy extraordinary, without the concurrence of the Senate," [127] and affirmed the right of the Senate to take a second look at a duly confirmed treaty from which an article had subsequently been struck.[128] Perhaps most interesting of his interpretations of a limiting nature was the letter he sent to McHenry May 17, 1798, in which he confessed misgivings about the President's constitutional power to authorize acts of "reprisal" against French ships, asserted his belief that "no doubtful authority ought to be exercised by the President," and hoped that Adams would go to Congress for the kind of assistance that would "remove all clouds as to what" he might be forced to do.[129]

Yet if he was often a man of propriety, he was always a man of energy, and he was anxious above all to establish the Presidency as a strong, dignified, legitimate agency of the national will. "Dependence on the people," in his opinion, worked both ways: to them the President owed the homage due a sovereign,[130] yet from them he drew, in the last resort, the authority to act as a sovereign in their behalf, not least because they had a vital role to play in his election.[131] Although Hamilton never did conjure up the Jacksonian formula of the President as tribune of the people,* he did supply one of its major ingredients by insisting, in effect, that the executive was better situated than the faction-ridden legislature to identify and express "the public good," and thus to be "the representative of the people." [132] And although he did not catch sight of the modern Presidency, he did as much as any man of his age except Washington to amass precedents and arguments upon which modern Presidents can draw with gratitude. In his own mature view, the Presidency seems to have been a nonrepublican institution come to cure republicanism of its worst diseases,[133] and one must applaud the campaign he waged to make it both sword and shield of the American Republic.

THE last of the four major problems to which Hamilton devoted his attention as constitutional lawyer was the role of the courts, especially the Supreme Court, in the American system of government. Here again we have an institution whose structure and authority were set forth in the Constitution in delphic language—so delphic indeed that the oracles themselves, the authors of Article III, understood only dimly the implications of their prophecy—and here again we find Hamilton prepared to read the words of the Constitution as if he, the Framer with the most continental and high-toned of minds, had written them himself. From Article III, as from Articles I and II, he extracted a constitutional law that was designed to serve the ends of a mighty nation launched on a voyage to empire. Having lived, to his distress, in a state whose courts

---

* To the extent that Hamilton talked of the President as a "man of the people," he did it in order to make clear that he was *not* a "man of the states." He broke with many of his Federalist friends to support Amendment XII because, at least in the form in which it was first proposed, it would strengthen "the connection between the Federal head and the people." "It has ever appeared to me as sound principle," he wrote to Gouverneur Morris, "to let the federal government rest, as much as possible, *on the shoulders of the people,* and as little as possible on those of the State Legislatures." [134]

were feeble and in a nation that had no courts at all,[185] he worked tirelessly and imaginatively for the independence, supremacy,* and power of the
national judiciary. Such a judiciary was necessary to any plan of free and
orderly government, especially a government for a continent. He had little
fear of what some Americans—on the far Left in the 1930's, on the far
Right today—have insisted upon calling "judicial tyranny." He knew even
before the Supreme Court had become a reality that "from the nature of
its functions" it would "always be the least dangerous" of the three
branches to liberty.

The executive not only dispenses the honors but holds the sword of the
community. The legislature not only commands the purse but prescribes the
rules by which the duties and rights of every citizen are to be regulated.
The judiciary, on the contrary, has no influence over either the sword or the
purse; no direction either of the strength or of the wealth of the society,
and can take no active resolution whatever. It may truly be said to have neither
FORCE nor WILL but merely judgment; and must ultimately depend upon the
aid of the executive arm even for the efficacy of its judgments.[136]

He also knew—and a shrewd bit of prophecy it has proved to be—that
only through a "union" with one of the other branches could the judiciary
put limits upon the cherished liberties (and, conversely, upon the ill-begot-
ten privileges) of any group of people.[137] For this reason if for no other
his ideal judiciary was "distinct" from the executive and legislature.

Hamilton made two contributions to the arsenal of constitutional logic
with which we are now accustomed to defend the independence of judges.
The first was the famous number 78 of *The Federalist,* in which he tied
together the independence of the courts with their power to sit in judgment on the constitutionality of acts of the legislature.[138] Only judges who
were secure against being "overpowered, awed, or influenced" by the
elected representatives of the people could, in his opinion, be expected or
trusted to wield the critical power of judicial review, and only if they had
a permanent tenure would they feel thus secure. To Publius "the standard
of good behavior for the continuance in office of the judicial magistracy"
appeared to be "one of the most valuable of the modern improvements in
the practice of government."

In a monarchy it is an excellent barrier to the despotism of the prince;
in a republic it is a no less excellent barrier to the encroachments and op-
pressions of the representative body. And it is the best expedient which can

* "Supremacy," that is to say, over the courts of the states.

be devised in any government to secure a steady, upright, and impartial administration of the laws.[189]

Independence of the will of the legislature was essential if the courts were to be the "bulwarks" of the Constitution against the depredations of the legislature; it was "equally requisite to guard . . . the rights of individuals" against "ill humors in the society," whether these might be displayed by legislators, administrators, or merely private citizens. Independence, in short, was the stoutest guarantee of the courage, integrity, moderation, and erudition, and steadiness of the courts. It was "the citadel of the public justice and the public security."

Hamilton's second contribution to the American doctrine of judicial independence is to be found in the eight articles in which, writing as Lucius Crassus, he castigated Jefferson for proposing to undo the good work done in the Judiciary Act of 1801.[140] His rhetoric, as we know, was unavailing: the act was repealed; the new federal courts it had established were wiped out with one stroke of Jefferson's pen; and the "midnight judges" were, in effect, removed from office. In contending vigorously that the undoubted right of Congress to "change or abolish inferior courts" did not permit it to "abolish the actual judges," which is exactly what the Repeal Act was intended (and managed) to do, Hamilton made a memorable statement in behalf of "the real and substantial independence of the courts and judges" against meddling executives and covetous legislatures. Although by 1802 there was nothing new for any American to say about the independent judiciary as "a precious shield to the rights of persons and property" and as a "counterpoise" to "all the momentum of popular favor," [141] he did sum up the conventional wisdom on this subject in words that would have graced the pages of *The Federalist*. He did not, unfortunately, elaborate on the one touch of novelty in the argument—that an independent judiciary was, in one sense, an "auxiliary" of the executive in its endless struggle to keep from being sucked down in "the impetuous vortex of legislative influence" [142]—and we are left to wonder what he might have made of this interesting idea. Since he had written elsewhere of his fear that "a dangerous combination might by degrees be cemented between the executive and judiciary departments," [143] he plainly did not mean to suggest that there should be active political co-operation between the two. Like the other men of his time he had to learn through experience—the experience, for example, of Jay's polite rebuff to Washington in 1793—how aloof the Supreme Court must hold itself from the day-to-day business of the other branches.

In these same articles Hamilton also proclaimed the "objects which were designed to be accomplished" by Article III,[144] and these were, needless to say, the "objects" that would seem important to a man whose first thoughts were of the nation. The federal judiciary, like the army, was a "cement of Union." Were it to perform all the functions of independent courts and yet read the supremacy clause in a niggardly manner, it would not be the judiciary for which men who thought continentally had hoped and sacrificed in the painful years under the old Congress. The courts antic-ipated in Article III, above all the Supreme Court, were to interpret the laws of Congress, support the exertions of the President, and police the boundaries of the federal system in such manner as to strengthen the Union upon which the "salvation" of America rested. Although Hamilton never worked out the details of this concept of the judiciary as bulwark, not merely of order against anarchy, property against licentiousness, and constitutionalism against demagoguery, but of the nation against the states, he did establish the outlines of the general theory of the Constitu-tion which, to the distress of all the heirs of the constitutional Jefferson, makes the Supreme Court the "balance-wheel of federalism" by making it first of all an agency of national supremacy. Indeed, if he had had his way, whether in 1787 or 1800, there would have been few conflicts of jurisdiction between the courts of the nation and those of the states, prin-cipally because the latter, to the extent to which they were permitted to function at all, would have been converted into appendages to a far-reaching system of national justice. Hamilton, it is certain, was playing the part of the shrewd family lawyer rather than of the candid constitu-tional lawyer when he took a tolerant view of the jurisdiction of the state courts in *The Federalist,* number 82. Yet even in this area of delicacy (and in this moment of crisis) he left no doubt in the minds of his audience that he thought first of the Union. He made clear that Congress had power to set up a system of appeals from the decisions of state courts not merely to the Supreme Court but to the "subordinate courts" in the federal structure.[145]

Both the independence and the supremacy of the federal courts rested, in the last resort, on their power "to declare all acts contrary to the manifest tenor of the Constitution void," and with the word "acts" Hamil-ton meant to cover laws and resolutions of Congress, treaties negotiated by the President and confirmed by the Senate, and laws of the state legisla-tures that were in "contravention of the articles of Union." [146] Judicial review of national and state legislation was a prominent feature of his constitutional law, and the seventy-eighth number of *The Federalist,* in which he first demonstrated the existence of this power, ranks with the Opinion of 1791 and the first number of Pacificus as one of the great creative essays of American constitutionalism. To him must go the primary credit for converting the vague Whig assumption that some laws are not laws at all because they are unconstitutional into the clear-cut American doctrine that the courts have a special responsibility to refuse to enforce such laws.[147] The explicitness of Hamilton's exposition of judicial review in *The Federalist*, number 78 stands in astonishing contrast to the fuzziness of all previous flirtations with this doctrine (including those of Hamilton) [148] and to the almost studied refusal of the members of the Philadelphia Convention (including Hamilton) * to consider the possibility that it might emerge as the crowning check in their system of checks and balances. American constitutional law has never been the same since the publication of this number on May 28, 1788.

This exposition defies condensation, and every student of American constitutional history must read it for himself.[149] In describing the Constitution as the charter of a "limited" government, in identifying it as a "fundamental law" that could be interpreted and enforced like statutory law, in asserting its superiority in all instances of "manifest" conflict with such law, and in designating the judiciary as the agency licensed by "the nature and reason of the thing" to resolve such conflicts in favor of the Constitution, Hamilton led the way inexorably to acceptance of this mightiest of the unwritten principles of American constitutional law. Most important of all, he grounded the doctrine of judicial review on the sovereignty of the people. In one of the most audacious lines of argument of an audacious career as constitutional lawyer, he turned his fire on those who "imagined" that "the doctrine would imply a superiority of the judiciary to the legislative power." Since the authority of Congress had been "delegated" in the Constitution, and since "every act of a delegated authority, contrary to the tenor of the commission under which it is exercised, is void," a "legislative act" that ran "contrary" to the Constitution plainly could not be "valid."

To deny this would be to affirm that the deputy is greater than his principal; that the servant is above his master; that the representatives of the people are

---

* No specific provision for judicial review was made in either the plan of June 18, 1787 or the draft constitution of September. There was, to be sure, provision for a "negative" on "all laws about to be passed" in any particular state by the "Governor" or "President" of the state, who was, in both of Hamilton's schemes, to be *"appointed by the* General Government." [150]

superior to the people themselves; that men acting by virtue of powers may do not only what their powers do not authorize, but what they forbid.

"If there should happen to be an irreconcilable variance" between "a particular act proceeding from the legislative body" and "a prohibition in the Constitution," he continued, the courts were bound to give effect to the law of "superior obligation and validity" and thus to declare the former null and void. "The Constitution ought to be preferred to the statute, the intention of the people to the intention of their agents."

Nor does this conclusion by any means suppose a superiority of the judicial to the legislative power. It only supposes that the power of the people is superior to both, and that where the will of the legislature, declared in its statutes, stands in opposition to that of the people, declared in the Constitution, the judges ought to be governed by the latter rather than the former.

And so, he concluded in his most weighty manner, "Whenever a particular statute contravenes the Constitution, it will be the duty of the judicial tribunals to adhere to the latter and disregard the former." *

Hamilton was an advocate of judicial review, not of judicial supremacy. He had too expansive a view of the powers of Congress to tolerate any "torturing" of the Constitution in an effort to frustrate the legislative intent. The "limitations" he expected the courts to "preserve" against "legislative encroachments" were the "specified exceptions" like the prohibitions on bills of attainder and ex post facto laws. He most certainly did

---

* This is the way Hamilton summed up his first exposition of judicial review in *The Federalist* many years later, in the attack on Jefferson by Lucius Crassus, March 9, 1802:

"The essence of the argument is, that every act of a delegated authority, contrary to the tenor of the commission under which it is exercised, is void; consequently that no Legislative act, inconsistent with the Constitution, can be valid. That it is not a natural presumption that the Constitution intended to make the legislative body the final and exclusive judges of their own powers; but more rational to suppose that the courts were designed to be an intermediate body between the people and the Legislature, in order, among other things, to keep the latter within the bounds assigned to its authority. That the interpretation of the laws being the peculiar province of the courts, and a *Constitution* being in fact a *fundamental law,* superior in obligation to a *statute,* if the Constitution and the statute are at variance, the former ought to prevail against the latter; the will of the people against the will of the agents; and the judges ought in their quality of interpreters of the laws, to pronounce and adjudge the truth, namely, that the unauthorized statute is a nullity." [151]

From here he went on to quote his own words about judicial review as an institution that "supposes" not the *"superiority* of the judicial to the legislative power," but of the "power of the people . . . to both."

not expect judges to go fishing for constructions that would permit them to substitute their own wills for those of legislators, and by nature he looked forward more eagerly to those "solemn decisions" of the Supreme Court which would give the "most complete and comprehensive sanction" to the creative use of Article I than to those which would tie the hands of Congress.[152] His assertion of the doctrine of judicial review must always be read in conjunction with his interpretation of Article I, section 8 as a bestowal of "general legislative authority."

It must also be read in conjunction with his doctrine of national supremacy, which conspired with his long-standing distrust of popular majorities in state legislatures to make him rather less reserved about the Supreme Court's power to declare state laws null and void. For laws that encroached upon the authority of the national government, as for laws that invaded the rights of property, Hamilton had the most severe contempt, and he expected the Court to knock them down without mercy. It may be of interest to note that, as a New York lawyer asked for a written opinion in 1796 by several purchasers of the Yazoo lands, he pointed the way to both major conclusions of Marshall's opinion in *Fletcher* v. *Peck*: that a state law making a grant of land or some other privilege was a "contract" within the meaning of Article I, section 10, clause 1; and that the courts of the United States had a clear duty to declare a law revoking such "contracts" null and void. This duty flowed from "the terms of the Constitution in their large sense" as well as from "the first principles of natural justice and social policy." [153] It is certain that Hamilton would have looked with favor on the holding in *Fletcher* v. *Peck* and on most other cases in the nineteenth century in which the Court exercised a stern power of judicial review over state laws that meddled with property rights.[154] As a politician he might have disapproved of the blow struck for national supremacy, judicial review of state laws, and defense of civil liberties in *Near* v. *Minnesota* and its dozens of progeny, but as a constitutional lawyer he would have been bound to acknowledge that his own principles were full of life.[155]

The doctrine of judicial review has been considerably refined since Hamilton first asserted it openly in *The Federalist*, number 78. Yet his brilliant paragraphs remain the most forceful exposition ever made of this doctrine. Certainly no one, neither the most commanding of judges nor persuasive of scholars, has managed to set judicial review on any firmer foundations than those he constructed in the spring of 1788 out of almost no precedents whatever. By "deducing" judicial review not "from any circumstance peculiar to the plan of the convention, but from the general theory of a limited Constitution," * and by insisting that it was essentially an instrument of "the power of the people," [156] Hamilton gave a legitimacy to this extraordinary "check and balance" that has carried it through some of the most violent storms in American political history. It was a stroke of genius, even if also an exercise in guile, that turned a restraint upon the will of the people inside out and made it an expression of their sovereignty.

IT remains only to be said by way of conclusion that there were perhaps fewer inconsistencies in Hamilton's mature view of the Constitution than in that of almost any other noted American who has been asked to interpret it in a variety of circumstances as judge, legislator, or administrator. No conflict existed in his own mind between any two of the four major propositions that he laid once and for all before the American people. To the contrary, what John Beckley, who hated him, said of his financial program—that "all his measures," like the "links of a chain," were "dependent on each other" and acquired "additional strength by their union and concert" [157]—could also be said of his constitutional law. Men of later generations might set his theory of the forceful Congress against his theory of the energetic Presidency or the doctrine of judicial review against the doctrine of national supremacy, but only because they failed to make the distinctions he had made in expounding the principles of his constitutional law. If we remember that he read the powers of Congress broadly in order to produce far-ranging laws for energetic heads of department to administer, that he expected the Court to confine its power of judicial veto to such palpable invasions of constitutional propriety as bills of attainder, and that he always considered the Presidency as first among equals, we should have no more trouble than he did in linking his interpretations of Articles I, II, and III into an unbreakable chain. Indeed, we should have no trouble at all if we remember that the strongest link in the chain was the transcendent doctrine of national supremacy. Hamilton read every clause in the Constitution with the eyes of a man who put the Union first on his list of political goods. He was an advocate of "a liberal and efficient exercise of the powers of the national government" because, in flat opposition to his enemies in the other camp, he was certain that it was *"the only solid and rational expedient for preserving republican government in the United States."* [158] His was the constitutional law of a man of energy and purpose, a man with plans for building a mighty nation.

* It was out of this theory that Hamilton extracted his assumption that the state courts, too, enjoyed the power of judicial review even in the absence of specific authorization.[159]

SEVEN

THE RELEVANCE OF HAMILTON

"Mine has been an odd destiny."
Hamilton to Gouverneur Morris,
February 27, 1802

IN 1806, "as an expression of their affectionate Regard to his Memory," some grieving admirers erected a handsome monument on the dueling ground in Weehawken where Hamilton had held his fatal "interview" with Aaron Burr. In 1820, on the "complaint" of a number of "citizens in the vicinity," the monument was dismantled and dumped into the Hudson River. The reason for this apparently uncharitable action was not, we are told, political malice, for some of the citizens of Weehawken were themselves admirers of Hamilton and all of them knew a handsome monument when they saw one. It was a question, quite simply, of the "bad moral effect" of this memorial, which had lured romantic youths from all over the country to come and "expose their lives" on the spot where "that great man fell from all his glory and usefulness." [1] The lives of some of these youths had, quite predictably, ended there, and the monument had become a "bloody beacon to posterity." It was therefore decided to offer up the memory of Hamilton as a sacrifice to the interests of law and order. Since his own passion had been law and order—since, moreover, he had condemned the custom of dueling as "in the highest degree criminal" [2]—it was doubtless assumed that he would have approved the decision.

The wry story of the raising and leveling of the monument in Weehawken is a fitting introduction to an attempt to assess the importance of Hamilton for this generation of Americans. The citizens of Weehawken were neither the first nor the last of his countrymen to find the memory of this extraordinary man too hot to handle, and thus to take the easy way out by dumping it, whether gladly, reluctantly, or carelessly, into the river of oblivion. Hamilton has had perhaps the most checkered posthumous career of any famous American, not even excluding John C. Calhoun and Jefferson Davis, and even today we have trouble deciding whether to raise more monuments to his memory or to dismantle those raised in the past. Other heroes have had their ups and downs as America has moved from one stage to the next in its spectacular march to power, but Hamilton, a center of controversy in death as he was in life, often seems to have been moving up and down at the same time.

For the most part, and for reasons that will occur readily to readers of this book, his reputation has suffered more downs than ups. For more than a century this has been a Jeffersonian country, one in which democracy has held sway as a secular religion and Thomas Jefferson has been acknowledged as its high priest. There have been a few scholars and public men who have disliked Jefferson openly, just as there have been a few periods since his death when his reputation among the people was fuzzy or shaky, but most Americans, whether scholars, public men, or ordinary citizens, now give all the thanks a democratic posterity might be thought to owe to the first great spokesman for American democracy.[3] Since Jefferson and Hamilton were the fiercest of opponents in the formative years of the Republic, and since it is convenient to write about an episode in history (and amusing to read about it) as a clash between giant antagonists, the intellectual and emotional decision to be kind to Jefferson has forced most Americans to be harsh to Hamilton. The history of this country, I repeat, has been presented to most of us as a vast Manichean struggle between hope and fear, freedom and oppression, equality and privilege, democracy and oligarchy—in a familiar phrase, between the Good Guys and the Bad Guys—and Hamilton has been cast too easily and often as the Baddest Guy of All to be admitted even by the back door into the inner circle of American heroes. Having sampled the judgments of American historiography and the rhetoric of American politics with all the objectivity I can muster, I would guess that for every one "Hamiltonian" in scholarship and public life there are now at least ten "Jeffersonians,"

Because we are taught about such matters by our historians (or by teachers taught by these historians), and because our politicians do their best to reflect our tastes and prejudices, I would guess that a random sample of Americans would also choose Jefferson over Hamilton by a ten-to-one margin.

The problem of what then to do with the memory of Hamilton, the heroic anti-hero, has been handled by those who inform and express our sentiments in one of four ways: by disliking him, by underestimating him, by misinterpreting him, or, easiest of all for some kindly persons, by passing him by on the other side. Each of these approaches was given a full test in the lowest period of Hamilton's reputation, which extended in almost unbroken line from the day after his funeral to the eruption of Theodore Roosevelt as a national figure, and each continues to have its uses even today when we have all become more clear-eyed in taking the dimensions of the leading men of our past.

It is not easy to be stirred to anger by a man who lived more than a hundred and fifty years ago, yet the dead Hamilton seems to have some of the unique ability of the live one to arouse what Charles A. Beard described as "choking emotions in the bosoms of all 'right thinkers'" who refuse to look beyond the Jeffersonian tradition.[4] Most American history, Samuel Eliot Morison reminds us,[5] is now being written by such men, and one result has been a show of hostility toward Hamilton on the part of some of our most respected historians. The style was set dramatically by Henry S. Randall in his three-volumed *Life of Thomas Jefferson* (1858), of which a reviewer in the *New York Tribune* complained, with some justice, that it exalted Jefferson "into a demigod" by debasing "his antagonists into demons."[6] It was followed by Henry Adams in his influential *History* (1889), which treated Hamilton with respect but also with a thinly veiled antipathy. ("I dislike Hamilton. . . . From the first to the last words he wrote," Adams put the matter squarely to Hamilton's champion Senator Lodge, "I read always the same Napoleonic kind of adventuredom."[7]) And it has been carried on by a host of twentieth-century historians who pass lightly over Jefferson's shabby politics and yet are outraged by Hamilton's[8]—the former, after all, fought for "freedom" and the latter for "privilege"—and who make their case principally by quoting, quite out of context, the most eloquent of Hamilton's strictures on the fickleness of democracy. While most of these warmhearted Jeffersonians have been decent or careful enough not to top off the assault upon Hamilton with the apocryphal words about the people as a "great *beast*," a few have been unable to resist this doubtless overpowering temptation, and I expect that we shall be stumbling over it in our history books until the memory of Hamilton and Jefferson is no more.[9]

The second well-established approach to the problem of Hamilton leads by way of discomfort in his presence—a sensation readily distinguishable from that of active dislike—to a solution that puts him in his place simply by lowering that place two or three notches. It is impossible, of course, to ignore the evidence that has now piled up in Hamilton's favor and thus to write him off as a secondary figure in the grand events of the first two decades under the Constitution. Yet if he is not shoved discourteously away from the center of the stage upon which Washington, Jefferson, Franklin, Marshall, John Adams, and Madison are seen standing around and (all but the hair-shirted Adams) chatting self-confidently, he is often left waiting well over to one side. Some historians, of whom the authors of several prominent college texts are perhaps the most cavalier in their treatment, seem to think that to welcome Hamilton cheerfully into this group is somehow to embarrass Jefferson, and thus to break faith with the democracy of which he is "the true and sure symbol." The heroes of a great democracy, it appears, must all be democrats, or at least not conspicuous anti-democrats, and Hamilton must therefore be treated with cool respect rather than warm enthusiasm. These historians have much respect, to be sure, for the achievements of Hamilton the financier and administrator, but not for those of Hamilton the diplomat, politician, constitutionalist, and patriot. And what, after all, is the founding of a national bank or funding of a national debt compared with the winning of a revolution, the fathering of a constitution, the authoring of a bill of rights, the founding of a popular party, or the rescuing of liberty from the designs of spiteful autocrats? There is, I am bound to say, a depressing sameness about the Hamilton whom historians present for the instruction of American college students—and a sameness, too, about their Jefferson. Since the dimensions of the latter are almost always larger than life, the dimensions of the former are almost always smaller.[10]

Both the feeling of hostility toward Hamilton and the tendency to depreciate him have a close cousin in the urge, which sometimes seems almost willful, to give a distorted interpretation of his aspirations and achievements. Despite the mighty deeds that he did for the Constitution, some authors have ripped his anguished remark about "the frail and worthless fabric" out of context in order to denounce him as a man who despaired faintheartedly when he ought to have hoped nobly.[11] Despite the palpable fact that he was a man so obsessed with the future as to be a restless visionary, some others persist in echoing Randall's easy judgment that his "wisdom" was like the stern light of a ship, casting "all its light backward, over the course already passed over, and not a ray forward." [12] And despite the equally palpable fact that he was goaded principally by the "love of fame," still others have portrayed him as a caricature of Hobbesian man, as someone caught up in a "perpetual and restless" pursuit of power that ceased "only in death." [13] His ambition, pride, officiousness, and pessimism are painted in searing colors, his courage, industry, integrity, patriotism,[14] and vision in pastels. He was, it is now conceded, a necessary man, perhaps even a great one—but how sad that a great and necessary man of that golden age should have been so much less noble than Washington, less kindly than Franklin, less virtuous than Adams, and less hopeful than Jefferson. Why, oh why, one can almost hear the teachers of American history asking sorrowfully, did so important a Founding Father behave so often like a premature John Bircher? [15] The answer, of course, is that almost none of these teachers has ever taken the dimensions of the man on the same scale of compassionate understanding that is used to measure Jefferson.

For some historians, especially those who do not have to worry themselves about unpleasant realities like banks and armies, the easiest way out has been the way of the citizens of Weehawken: to deal with Hamilton by consigning him to oblivion, to solve the problem he presents by acting as if the problem did not exist at all. Thus, by ignoring Hamilton, Ralph Barton Perry can give us a picture of what is "characteristically American" that we can understand without a guide, Carl Becker can set up the tension between "freedom and responsibility" in such a manner as to make it bearable, Dexter Perkins can celebrate "the American approach to foreign policy" in a mood of undiluted liberalism, and Hans Kohn can, in effect, assure a race of sentimental Jeffersonians that the ideals of American patriotism owe nothing to the likes of Hamilton.[16] While it is, to be sure, becoming more difficult for intellectual historians to look right through Hamilton in their search for the sources of the American tradition, there is no doubt that Woodrow Wilson's formula—a "great man" but "not a great American" [17]—will continue to have an appeal for those who find the effort to digest the real Hamilton too much for their stomachs.

I DO not mean to give too cheerless an impression of Hamilton as a despised, underrated, misunderstood, and ignored figure out of our past who finds defenders only among angry men who have some compelling reason to attack Jefferson. More and more Americans with unimpeachable credentials as democrats are coming to understand and thus to describe Hamilton as an authentic giant—and I mean Hamilton in his own right and not just as a foil to Jefferson. His reputation has been on the slow rise ever since the turn of this century, and one can anticipate further gains for his name in the three worlds of scholarship, politics, and popular esteem. If the Hall of Fame for Great Americans in New York were being founded today, Hamilton would not have to wait quite so long as he did for election to the club. It is, incidentally, a fairly accurate indication of his stature at the turn of this century that Washington, Franklin, Adams, Jefferson, Marshall, Lincoln, Clay, Webster, Grant, Lee, Story, and even his young friend James Kent were elected in the first quinquennial ballot in 1900, the younger Adams, Madison, and General Sherman in 1905, Andrew Jackson and a host of literary luminaries in 1910—and that he finally got past the front gate in 1915 in company with Daniel Boone, Charlotte Saunders, and Mark Hopkins (whose log was doubtless used to knock the gate down). Whether it would have given him comfort to have been elected before Patrick Henry and James Monroe is hard to say, but at least he does not have to endure the presence of Aaron Burr.[18]

The nineteenth century was a time of almost unrelieved neglect for Hamilton's reputation. Historians with open contempt for Jefferson— Richard Hildreth, John Bach McMaster, and Hermann von Holst are perhaps the most distinguished examples[19]—might present him as a man with "the same rare and lofty qualities" as Washington or as "the most brilliant and versatile" of the Founding Fathers. His flesh-and-blood descendants, spurred by his widow (who outlived him by fifty years) and led by his indefatigable son John C. Hamilton, might plead his cause fiercely in a hundred quarrels with the political and literary heirs of Jefferson—and in the process come perilously close to deifying him (and thus presumably themselves).[20] And politicians of conservative bent might pause for a moment in their ceaseless efforts either to destroy Jefferson or to kidnap him and recall the benefits Hamilton had bestowed upon the men of property in America—or at least upon those in the northeastern part of it. Daniel Webster, in particular, paid a public tribute to Hamilton in words calculated to stir the emotions of all right-thinking Americans:

He smote the rock of the national resources, and abundant streams of revenue gushed forth. He touched the dead corpse of the Public Credit, and it sprung upon its feet. The fabled birth of Minerva, from the brain of Jove, was hardly more sudden or more perfect than the financial system of the United States, as it burst forth from the conceptions of Alexander Hamilton.[21]

Yet the financier got most of the scraps of admiration that were tossed at Hamilton,[22] and the whole man was almost lost from popular view as America rushed headlong into its love affair with democracy. Old John Quincy Adams expressed the sense of the matter in an entry in his diary for April 8, 1837:

I read this morning in the manuscripts of Mr. Madison the report of the speech of Alexander Hamilton in the Convention of 1787 upon presenting his plan for a Constitution of the United States. The speech occupied a whole day, and was of great ability. The plan was theoretically better than that which was adopted, but energetic, and approaching the British Constitution far closer, and such as the public opinions of that day never would have tolerated. Still less would it be endured by the democratic spirit of the present age—far more democratic than that; for, after half a century of inextinguishable wars between the democracy of the European race and its monarchy and aristocracy, the democracy is yet in the ascendant, and gaining victory after victory over the porcelain of the race. If Hamilton were now living, he would not dare, in an assembly of Americans, even with closed doors, to avow the opinions of this speech, or to present such a plan even as a speculation.[23]

Lesser folk had no need to go rummaging in "the manuscripts of Mr. Madison." They knew for a certainty that Hamilton had given his whole life to the fight against democracy, and they wasted no time celebrating his memory.

Even in the grim hour of his vindication, the victorious war fought by the North and West to preserve the Union, he was a largely forgotten man. To the best of my knowledge, Lincoln never once invoked Hamilton's name in any of his intellectual or emotional arguments for the Union.[24] And even when a solid man like Representative James A. Garfield of Ohio could express his delight publicly that "the fame of Jefferson" was "waning" and that of Hamilton "waxing," [25] there were many other solid men in those days, as there were many in the days of the New Deal (and are many in these), who found Hamilton unpalatable because he had been so strenuous a champion of an energetic national government.[26] Most Republicans in the era of Garfield and McKinley would have agreed with a leading spokesman for present-day ultra-conservatism that Hamilton, for all his fine qualities, was "at his worst a prototype of the 'modern Republican'—a modern 'liberal' under wraps." [27] Since all Democrats were forbidden to have anything to do with Hamilton, this left him, as James Bryce pointed out from the unique perspective of an Englishman who had bothered to study America before writing about it, the one important

Founding Father to whom "subsequent generations of Americans" had simply "failed to do full justice." [28]

Responding with a will to Bryce's gentle scolding, a number of eminent Americans did their best in the first years of the twentieth century to do justice to this neglected hero. By far the most eminent was Theodore Roosevelt, who had been instructed in the virtues of Hamilton by Henry Cabot Lodge and John T. Morse, and who was delighted to find support for his exalted view of this "gallant" and "dashing" figure in the remarkable biography published by another Englishman, Frederick Scott Oliver, in 1906.[29] Although Roosevelt was too wise politically to say so in public, he thought of Jefferson as a "slippery demagogue." "Thank heaven," he wrote to Oliver in a letter of tribute to the latter's book,

> I have never hesitated to criticize Jefferson; he was infinitely below Hamilton; I think the worship of Jefferson a discredit to my country; and I have as small use for the ordinary Jeffersonian as for the ordinary defender of the house of Stuart.[30]

Whether it was Roosevelt exhorting his friends, Gertrude Atherton writing romantically of Hamilton as *The Conqueror*, Nicholas Murray Butler paying the tribute of Columbia to her most successful son, Edward Channing carrying on the good work of Hildreth and McMaster, or James Brown Scott taking the measure of Hamilton the lawyer,* the leaders of this modest revival of Hamilton's reputation were still feuding with the ghost of Jefferson.[31] Even Herbert Croly, one of the masters of Progressive thought, did not seem to realize that if one man's good name could only be purchased at the price of the other's, Hamilton stood no chance of being a hero to more than a handful of Americans. Yet Croly's famed *The Promise of American Life* (1909) did an immense service to the historical Hamilton by presenting him soberly as a man whose "policy was one of energetic and intelligent assertion of the national good," whose concern it was "to protect and encourage liberty, just as far as such encouragement was compatible with good order," and whose tradition of a national leadership committed to "a conscious and indefatigable attempt . . . to promote the national welfare" was readily convertible to popular ends.[32] Croly, it could be said, was the first American to make the connection in words,

---

* And finding him not only a lawyer without a peer but "the greatest single intellectual force in the history of the United States." To Scott, himself a distinguished international lawyer, it was "abundantly clear" that Hamilton "made the American nation." As for that other man, the "archpriest of states-rights," Scott wrote, "let those who have a stomach for it pay tribute to Jefferson." [33]

which Roosevelt had already sought to make in deeds, between Hamiltonian means and Jeffersonian ends.*

While Hamilton has had his troubles with posterity in the past fifty years—especially, as we have seen, with authors of standard texts in American history—his reputation has never again sunk to the sorry state in which it was left through most of the hundred years after his death. Thanks to Republicans who have learned to quote him with circumspection,[34] New Dealers and New Frontiersmen who have forgiven him his trespasses against Jefferson out of respect for his idea of a balanced and guided (and perhaps even planned) economy,† biographers who have succumbed to his manly charm and capacity for creative leadership,[35] and historians of such special aspects of our history as foreign policy, economic development, and public administration, he has been gaining steadily in both scholarly and political favor over the past quarter-century. He will never become a folk hero, never rank in popular esteem with Washington, Lincoln, Jefferson, and Franklin. But he will henceforth receive more respect than all but these four supreme heroes of the American tradition, and, what is more to the point, he may be listened to as attentively as any of them.

He will never become a folk hero for three good reasons. The first is that, as I wrote above, the United States is (or thinks it is) a Jeffersonian country, that it has as powerful and uncritical an ideological commitment to Jefferson as the Communists have to Marx. We believe with George Bancroft that Jefferson "was able with instinctive perception to read the soul of the nation, and, having collected its best thoughts and noblest feelings, to give them out in clear and bold words, mixed with so little of

* Yet even in making this connection, Croly felt that a final choice had to be made between Jefferson and Hamilton, and it was for Hamilton that he made his own choice. "The alliance between the two principles," he wrote, "will not leave either of them intact; but it will necessarily do more harm to the Jeffersonian group of political ideas than it will to the Hamiltonian. The latter's nationalism can be adapted to democracy without an essential injury to itself, but the former's democracy cannot be nationalized without being transformed."

Most other intellectuals of the Progressive movement found Croly's choice interesting but bizarre. To the extent that they paid any attention at all to Hamilton, they preferred to adapt him to Jefferson rather than Jefferson to him.[36]

† Franklin Roosevelt did his own part by telling the Democratic faithful at the Jackson Day dinner in 1940 that Hamilton was a "hero" to him "because he did the job which then had to be done—to bring stability out of the chaos of currency and banking difficulties." He was careful, however, to qualify his praise by scolding Hamilton for "his position that the nation would be safer if our leaders were chosen exclusively from persons of higher education and of substantial property ownership"—all of which must have been confusing to at least a few friends and critics who recalled that Roosevelt was just such a person.[37]

himself that his country, as it went along with him, found nothing but what it recognized as its own." [38] We believe with James Parton that "if Jefferson was wrong, America is wrong. If America is right, Jefferson was right." [39] And we are not going to be argued out of these beliefs by professors who can demonstrate that many of our institutions and patterns of behavior violate some of the most apposite of Jefferson's instructions, and who therefore bid us look back, if look back we must, to other men as sources and symbols of the American way of life. Democracy is the essence of that way of life, and Jefferson is the source and symbol of that democracy: for this reason, if for no other, the man who fought with all his might against the living Jefferson can never take rank with him in American mythology. One really must—I am forced to admit it on the basis of the most intense personal experience—make an emotional (if not intellectual) choice between Hamilton and Jefferson, and one has to be an eccentric soul to share the American commitment to democracy and still like Hamilton better than Jefferson.

If the admittance of Hamilton into the inner circle would strain the devotion of most Americans to the comforting ghost of Jefferson, it could also strain our devotion to the admonishing ghost of Washington; and that, too, is a development we would hardly welcome. Hamilton did his most important work for this country as Washington's lieutenant, and some interpreters of our early years have sought to make him, whether with good or bad intent, a foil for Washington as well as for Jefferson.[40] The quality and consequences of the alliance between Hamilton and his "essential Aegis" will continue to be debated among serious students of our history, but if the price of crying up the reputation of Hamilton is to cry down the reputation of Washington (as Solon if never as Cincinnatus), few Americans will pay attention to the debaters. What is true of the masses of Americans who cherish the memory of Washington is also true of the smaller groups who like to remind us of the notable achievements of Marshall, Madison, and John Adams. Hamilton was so deeply and anomalously involved, whether as guiding friend or thwarting foe, in the careers of all three of these famous men that it is next to impossible to celebrate one of them without finding some fault with Hamilton—or to celebrate Hamilton without implying that one of them has fewer credentials for secular sainthood than his champions would have us believe. It is unfortunate but true that the biographer of Hamilton finds himself locked willy-nilly in tense if polite combat with the biographers of almost every major figure among the Founding Fathers—unfortunate for Hamilton and unfortunate for him.

The third reason is the problem of Hamilton himself and the deeds for which he is best remembered. While there is much to admire in his character, he was, quite obviously, a far "pushier" person than either Washington or Jefferson, and this one failing has been enough to discourage a widespread cult of Hamilton. Dixon Wecter was doubtless right when he pointed out that most Americans who meet Hamilton get a first impression of an arrogant man, and that arrogance is the one quality we cannot suffer in our folk heroes.[41] And while there is much to be admired in the record of Hamilton's achievements, his best-known deeds had something to do with money. Money can buy almost anything in the United States except the affections of the people. The fact that he was himself quite indifferent to personal gain—or that the debt, the bank, and the tariff were only means to the greater end of national glory—cannot save Hamilton from the fate to which he has been assigned by the makers and consumers of our myths. He will henceforth be acknowledged, perhaps even by historians deeply in love with Jefferson, as "one of this country's really prodigious figures," [42] but he will always be, as he thought of himself in his darkest hours, an "exotic" to whom the last door is barred firmly. In death as in life, Hamilton's has been an "odd destiny." [43] "He stands, in reputation, among the giants," his most meticulous and admiring biographer has written, "but his head is not in the clouds." [44]

THE Hamilton of this book, the man of the Constitution, has been the most neglected Hamilton of all. My intention is therefore to account for the opinion, which I formed somewhat unexpectedly in the course of this study, that his works and words have been more consequential than those of any other American in shaping the Constitution under which we live. I have neither the patience nor the skill to do credit to the whole Hamilton; I shall be content if this single Hamilton henceforth receives a more enthusiastic presentation by historians and interpreters of our fundamental law. He will be given such a presentation, I am convinced, by all fair-minded men who take the trouble to look with fresh eyes upon the services he rendered directly to the Constitution during his own life, the influence he had upon its development in the years immediately after his death, and the relevance of his teachings for the present and future course of the Constitution.

I have said all that is necessary to say on the first of these subjects, and readers may turn back to the end of chapter 3 for my estimate, which I confess to be highly enthusiastic, of the importance of Hamilton in creating that supple instrument of nation-building, the Constitution inherited by

Jefferson and his friends in 1801. For those who dislike to look back through books, let me restate the opinion that Hamilton's influence was persuasive when the Constitution was anticipated, prominent when it was written and ratified, commanding when it was put to work, and decisive when it was put on trial, and that his services as marriage broker, midwife, guardian, and teacher were the most splendid rendered to the Constitution by any man of the first generation. Let me also make explicit a point that was left largely implicit in that chapter and, indeed, throughout this book: that as teacher Hamilton had no equal among the men who chose to interpret the Constitution as a reservoir of national energy. This is, to be sure, largely a matter of circumstantial evidence, for one searches in vain through the papers of all the Federalists from Washington and Jay to King and Wolcott for votes of thanks to the mettlesome (and meddlesome) Hamilton for having taught his friends how to read the Constitution.[45] (One searches equally in vain for a word of protest, for even the smallest sign that one of them was disturbed by his "broad and ductile rules of construction.") These friends were already disposed to read the Constitution "liberally in advancement of the public good," yet there is little doubt that they first learned the details of their constitutional law in the official papers of the Secretary of the Treasury, the unofficial opinions of Publius, Pacificus, and Camillus, and the unrecorded conversations—of which there must have been hundreds—between Hamilton and one of his band of brothers. Whether as adviser to the troubled Washington, soother of a doubting public, advocate in *Hylton* v. *United States,* or willing tutor to Smith, Sedgwick, Boudinot, Ames, and the other Federalists in Congress, Hamilton was the chief source of inspiration for the view of the Constitution that was ascendant in the councils of the first and most critical of administrations. His assertions as constitutional lawyer as much as his exertions as politician and financier led the opposition to describe him satirically as the "King of the Feds," the master of "the gladiators" of monarchy, the captain of "the crew of the Hamilton galley," the "man who moves the puppets," the sun among its "satellites," and the "old jockey" whose "haloo" could set "the whole pack" to yelping "in chorus," [46] and led his own friends to think of him, even in the period of his poorest behavior, as a *"Father confessor"* to whom they could render "the homage" of "veneration and respect." [47] When Rufus King promised Hamilton "assistance" to whatever "measures and maxims" he would "pursue," when Colonel Carrington assured him that he did "most heartily re-echo" his "opinion," when Stephen Higginson predicted that "we shall now perfectly coincide, as to all great points" of the Constitution, they were expressing the sentiments of all the Federalists—or of all except crusty John Adams.[48] In public law as in private law, Hamilton was recognized by his friends and even many of his enemies as, in Edward Rutledge's admiring words, "perfect master of the subject." [49]

Hamilton's influence on the development of the Constitution by no means ended abruptly in 1801 or 1804. He had done his work as financier and administrator so thoroughly—and with such an intuitive feeling for the future needs of the nation—that the victorious Jeffersonians could do little more than pick up where he had left off and carry on manfully. Like the Republicans who came after Franklin D. Roosevelt, this other breed of Republicans might curse the memory of the archfoe, but they could not or would not undo the work he had done. That they could not is plain in a letter from Jefferson to Du Pont de Nemours in 1802:

> When this government was first established, it was possible to have kept it going on true principles, but the contracted, English, half-lettered ideas of Hamilton, destroyed that hope in the bud. We can pay off his debt in 15 years: but we can never get rid of his financial system. It mortifies me to be strengthening principles which I deem radically vicious, but this vice is entailed on us by the first error.[50]

And that they would not is even plainer in the conduct of affairs by Albert Gallatin throughout his twelve years as Secretary of the Treasury under Jefferson and Madison. This gifted and dedicated man was as essential to the success of Jefferson's administration as Hamilton had been to Washington's, and he was essential because, despite an occasional complaint about the "mystifying and useless machinery" of the Treasury Department,[51] he bore himself like a Republican Hamilton.[52] If I may tie these two points together with the help of a masterful judgment by Henry Adams:

> The true ground of Hamilton's great reputation is to be found in the mass and variety of legislation and organization which characterized the first Administration of Washington, and which were permeated and controlled by Hamilton's spirit. . . . The results—legislative and administrative—were stupendous and can never be repeated. A government is organized once for all, and until that of the United States fairly goes to pieces no man can do more than alter or improve the work accomplished by Hamilton and his party.
> What Hamilton was to Washington, Gallatin was to Jefferson, with only such differences as circumstances required.[53]

If the "first error" had been financial and administrative, it had also been constitutional. If the Bank was a fact of life with which the new men of power must now make the best peace they could, so was the view of the Constitution that had discovered a bank in the words of Article I, section 8. Here, too, it was impossible for Jefferson and his friends to roll back the years and act as if Hamilton had never existed. Indeed, the Jefferson of the Louisiana Purchase and the Embargo Act would have astounded the Jefferson of 1791 and 1793, and the Madison of the Seventh Annual Message to Congress (December 5, 1815) was a throwback to the Madison of the 1780's. Having already made clear his belief that "the question of the constitutional authority" of Congress to charter a Bank of the United States had been "precluded" by more than twenty years of precedent—and by the "concurrence of the general will of the nation" in the "validity of such an institution" [54]—Madison now gave his public endorsement to the movement to incorporate a second national bank. In addition, he made some rather Hamiltonian observations on the usefulness and constitutional propriety of schemes to encourage manufactures, build roads and canals, and create a national university. "It is a happy reflection," he told the members of Congress in words that revived a formula of persuasion more than once used by Hamilton, "that any defect of constitutional authority which may be encountered can be supplied in a mode which the Constitution itself has providently pointed out." [55] While we may smile tolerantly over Madison's refusal, in which he persisted to the end of his life,[56] to admit that he may have been wrong and Hamilton right in the constitutional debate of 1791, and may smile ironically over Josiah Quincy's comment that Madison, under pressure from the exuberant nationalists in Congress, had "out-Federalized Federalism," * we ought to recall that it was a national bank approved by Madison, not a national bank proposed by Hamilton, which Marshall rescued in *McCulloch* v. *Maryland*. No one can follow the harried Madison through the struggle that led to his signing of the bill creating the Second Bank April 10, 1816, or read through the reluctantly Hamiltonian rhetoric of Henry Clay as he announced his intention to vote for this bill,[57] without feeling the hand of Hamilton in the affairs of men who had known him as their enemy. His reading of the Constitution, a rather fortunate "first error" which "the general will of the nation" now seemed eager to repeat, prevailed in these critical days for American nationalism. Ambrose Spencer, who had fought many a good fight against Hamilton in the courts and at the polls of New York, was one fair-minded Republican who could testify that "hundreds of politicians and

---

* A comment echoed at the other end of the political spectrum by John Randolph, who complained that Madison's administration "out-Hamilton's Alexander Hamilton." [58]

statesmen" in the days of Jefferson and Madison got "both the web and woof of their thoughts from Hamilton's brains." [59]

WHILE the Constitution of Hamilton held subtle and unacknowledged sway over the comings and goings of Jefferson, Madison, and their Congresses, it held firm (yet also largely unacknowledged) sway over the work of the Supreme Court. I speak here, of course, of the prodigious achievement of John Marshall, about which enough has been written to fill a small library,[60] and also of the influence of the living and dead Hamilton upon Marshall, about which almost nothing has been written. The reason for this silence upon so important a subject is not a lack of charity or zeal on the part of the hundreds of historians, political scientists, and constitutional lawyers who have taken the measure of Marshall, but simply a lack of substantial evidence in the documents of the period.*

Almost everyone seems to agree that Hamilton was first into the field with most of the principles and methods of constitutional interpretation to which Marshall turned in his notable decisions, and that Marshall's mind had absorbed completely the logic and even the phrasing of Hamilton's writings on the Constitution. We know that these two kindred spirits met at Valley Forge in the heroic winter of 1777-1778 and remained admiring if never close friends.[61] We have peripheral evidence that Marshall ranked Hamilton second only to Washington among the "greatest men" to have appeared "in the public councils of the United States." [62] We can read in Marshall's unfortunate *Life of Washington,* which began to appear in 1804, that he was fully conversant (as was no other man save Hamilton himself) with the arguments on each side of the principal constitutional debates in Washington's Cabinet,[63] and that, despite the studied impartiality of his narrative, he was squarely on the side of Hamilton.[64] We can lay the second part of *Marbury* v. *Madison* side by side with *The Federalist,* number 78,[65] the first part of *McCulloch* v. *Maryland* side by side with the Opinion on the Constitutionality of the Bank, the observations of *Fletcher* v. *Peck* on the contract clause of the Constitution side by side with Hamilton's opinion for the purchasers of the Yazoo lands [66]—and see for ourselves how much Marshall must have relied on Hamilton.[67] We may even note the interesting circumstantial evidence that Marshall had never

---

* This lack of evidence did not seem to trouble Justice Holmes, who made a unique if offhand claim for the influence of Hamilton in an address on John Marshall Day, February 4, 1901. "I should feel a . . . doubt," he declared in the presence of some of the great men of Massachusetts, "whether, after Hamilton and the Constitution itself, Marshall's work proved more than a strong intellect, a good style, personal ascendancy in his court, courage, justice and the convictions of his party." [68]

said a word about judicial review before being elected to the Virginia Convention of 1788, that the seventy-eighth number of *The Federalist* first appeared in the second volume of the McLean edition on May 28, that fifty-two copies of this volume were sent off at once to the Federalists at Richmond,[69] and that Marshall arose on June 20 to assert the power of judicial review in words taken from the mouth of Publius.[70] Yet hardly a shred of direct and conclusive evidence exists on this or any other point of contact between the two men as interpreters of the Constitution. One cannot find in Marshall's papers a single public or private expression of gratitude to the man who had taught him to read the Constitution as a charter "adapted to the various crises of human affairs." [71]

This is not, I feel certain, a case of ingratitude, whether studied or casual, but of a man in whom style and circumstance joined to mask the sources of his principal ideas from the scrutiny of history. Marshall's style as a friend was to be casual, as a correspondent to be noncommittal (when, indeed, he bothered to write at all), and as a judge to argue from self-evident premises to logical conclusions with almost no visible aid from learned authorities. Never given to writing or citing,* he was made even more reticent by the political situation throughout his long years on the Court. He had troubles enough with the "Jacobins" without asking for more by tossing the name of the fiercest anti-Jacobin into the arena; he had every reason to be grateful to John Adams and thus to shun the label of "Hamiltonian." In all Marshall's five hundred-odd opinions there is not a single undisguised reference to Hamilton or to any of his constitutional writings, only a handful of references—most of them inconsequential—to a "work entitled to great respect" called *The Federalist.*†

The most consequential reference is to be found in *Cohens* v. *Virginia,* the case in which Marshall affirmed the supremacy of the federal judiciary. In so doing he made extended use of Hamilton's argument for the appellate jurisdiction of the Court over the state courts "in all the enumerated cases of federal cognizance." Although he knew that his enemies in Virginia knew who had written this eighty-second number of *The Federalist,*

---

* Or, for that matter, to saving letters from friends. The extant correspondence of Hamilton and Marshall consists of exactly four letters.[72]

† Marshall was almost as reticent in his private writings as in his public announcements. In a series of twenty-six staunchly Federalist letters to Story between 1819 and 1834 he drops the names of Washington, Jefferson, and Madison often, the name of Hamilton not once, and in an autobiographical sketch written in 1827 for Story he makes only one passing reference to Hamilton. In describing the strong feelings aroused against him during the crisis of 1793, he says: "I was attacked with great virulence in the papers and was so far honored in Virginia as to be associated with Alexander Hamilton, at least so far as to be termed his instrument." [73]

he tried to make it look as if Madison and Hamilton had co-authored each paper. "The opinion of the *Federalist*," he wrote magisterially,

has always been considered as of great authority. It is a complete commentary on our constitution; and it is appealed to by all parties in the questions to which that instrument has given birth. Its intrinsic merit entitles it to this high rank; and the part two of its authors performed in framing the Constitution, put it very much in their power to explain the views with which it was framed. These essays having been published while the Constitution was before the nation for adoption or rejection, and having been written in answer to objections founded entirely on the extent of its powers, and on its diminution of State sovereignty, are entitled to the more consideration when they frankly avow that the power objected to is given, and defend it.[74]

The exact influence of Hamilton upon Marshall must remain a subject of speculation, yet one suspects that if Marshall himself, a fair-minded man, had been pressed for an opinion, he would have been happy to acknowledge Hamilton as the most forceful of his teachers.[75] One suspects, too, that Hamilton, another fair-minded man, would have been the staunchest of Marshall's supporters in the stormy public debates that followed hard upon most of the famous decisions, and would have recognized the special talents that Marshall brought to his task. As Marshall needed Hamilton to set the political and intellectual stage for *Marbury* v. *Madison, Fletcher* v. *Peck, McCulloch* v. *Maryland,* and *Cohens* v. *Virginia,* so Hamilton needed Marshall to seize upon a series of fortuitous opportunities—several of which an impetuous Chief Justice might have mishandled badly or passed by carelessly—and give the stamp of unquestioned legitimacy to the principles of national supremacy, broad construction, and judicial review. Yet if Marshall, in Edward S. Corwin's judgment, "founded American Constitutional Law," [76] Hamilton provided the materials with which he was able to found it. If, in Chief Justice Warren's words, it "fell to the lot of John Marshall to translate our Constitution" into the "real life" of judicial decisions,[77] it had fallen earlier to the lot of Hamilton to translate it into the even more real life of statutes, orders, and ordinances. So long as we take the broad view that the law of our Constitution includes the practices of executives and decisions of legislatures as well as the precedents of courts, Hamilton's place as a co-founder of this law will be secure. It is no discredit to Marshall to say that he could not have done half as well as the creative Hamilton during the tense days that produced the Opinion of 1791 or the first number of Pacificus, no discredit to Hamilton to say that he could not have done half as well as the shrewd Marshall in forging and hurling the splendid thunderbolts of *Marbury* v. *Madison* and *McCulloch*

v. *Maryland.* There is glory enough for both men in the conclusion that neither could have worked his huge influence on the development of a strong, flexible, living Constitution without the help of the other.[78]

Marshall was not the only man of bench and bar to display the Hamilton touch in the course of this thirty-year labor to convert the statutes and practices of Washington's administration into the precedents of case law. Bushrod Washington of Virginia, who had a unique opportunity to study the manuscripts of Hamilton's communications to his uncle, supported Marshall for almost three decades and with almost perfect fidelity. Brockholst Livingston of New York, with whom Hamilton had been associated years before in *Rutgers* v. *Waddington,* did all that could be expected of a judge appointed by Jefferson.[79] And William Johnson of South Carolina, who also owed his place on the Court to Jefferson, went down the line for Hamiltonian principles (if not for Hamilton) in such cases as *McCulloch* v. *Maryland, Cohens* v. *Virginia, Anderson* v. *Dunn,* and *Gibbons* v. *Ogden.*[80] All these judges were reminded every year of the principles of the departed Hamilton by the distinguished advocates who appeared before them. Old followers of Hamilton like William Pinkney and Robert Goodloe Harper, old opponents like Luther Martin and William Wirt, younger men like Daniel Webster who knew him only by reputation—all came sooner or later before the Court to argue causes that would have enlisted Hamilton's sympathies, and did it more or less knowingly in Hamilton's own words.[81] And if any member of the Court had doubts about the right way to think in one of these causes, Marshall was always there to instruct him in the beauties of broad construction and national supremacy.

Next to Marshall the most important figures on the bench in these years were James Kent and Joseph Story, both of whom were Hamiltonians and both of whom worked a lasting influence on American law as judges, scholars, and teachers. Kent, as we know, was a devoted follower of Hamilton, and he molded his conduct and principles consciously on the example of a man whom he considered not only the finest lawyer he had ever seen in action, but the "pride and glory of our country." [82] Although he never caught the full splendor of Hamilton's vision of a great nation, and although his confinement to the stage of New York law and politics seemed to narrow his own vision as the years went by and the democracy of Jackson swept over him, Kent made his famous *Commentaries* (1826–1830) a repository of Hamiltonian principles of order and justice,[83] and generations of lawyers who barely knew Hamilton's name were led subtly into the paths he had trod.

Story never met Hamilton, and in his years at Harvard (1795–1798) he would probably have struck the "King of the Feds" as a shameless Jacobin. Yet in the course of the astounding pilgrimage from 1811, when he was appointed to the Court by Madison as a counterweight to Marshall,[84] to 1845, when he died after years of throwing his weight behind rather than against the illustrious Chief Justice, Story became the most Hamiltonian of judges. He construed the powers of Congress liberally; he upheld the supremacy of the nation doggedly; he even found the Alien and Sedition Laws constitutional in retrospect.[85] And he did all this as an open-eyed disciple of Hamilton. Even before he was elevated to the Court, he had come around to the view—which he was careful not to voice publicly—that Hamilton was "a high and ennobled spirit," indeed "one of the greatest men of the age"; once he had paused for a "solemn" half hour in Trinity Churchyard to lament that "the city feels not the value of the dust it encircles." [86] And from his citadel amidst the storms of Jacksonian democracy he looked back to salute Hamilton as a "giant" to whom, along with the "grave and sober" man who had named him to the Court, "we are mainly indebted for the Constitution of the United States." [87] Story's famous *Commentaries on the Constitution,* which were first published in 1833, could almost as easily have been entitled *Commentaries on Alexander Hamilton's Commentaries on the Constitution.* His exposition of the implied powers of Congress goes back beyond *McCulloch* v. *Maryland* to the *"unanswerable"* Opinion of 1791,[88] from which it also draws the notion of resulting powers; his observations on the Presidency are borrowed wholesale from *The Federalist,* which is cited repeatedly; and much of his chapter on the judiciary is simply a collection of passages from *The Federalist,* numbers 78–83, which are, in Story's respectful opinion, so "clear and satisfactory" as to render condensation impossible and unworthy.[89] One cannot, indeed, look into any part of Story's celebrated treatise without recognizing that this was the principle vehicle for disseminating Hamilton's ideas among the legal elite—or at least among that part of it educated in the North—during the middle years of the nineteenth century. Since Marshall, too, has a place of honor in the *Commentaries,*[90] the total effect is one of an intensely conservative and yet far-seeing nationalism.

Toward the end of this century, as the leaders of American industry felt the first stirrings of federal regulation of their enterprises, the overt influence of all three of these constitutional nationalists—Story, Marshall, and Hamilton—declined sharply. As defenders of private property and exponents of judicial review, indeed as men who had never made peace with the progressives of their own day, they were held in the highest esteem, but as men who had asserted the supremacy of the national government and had interpreted the powers of Congress liberally, they went under a cloud of suspicion. The contrast between Story's *Commentaries,* in which Hamilton is presented as a giant, and the treatises of such laissez-faire jurists as Christopher G. Tiedeman and Thomas M. Cooley, in which Hamilton is either patronized or ignored,[91] is a measure of the drastic shift from power to limitations as the primary concern of American constitutional law in the years between the peak of Marshall's influence and the peak of Stephen J. Field's. Not until the final victory of the New Deal did the principles of nationalism and broad construction expounded by Hamilton and his disciples regain the high place they had once held in American constitutionalism. It was one of the ironies of American history—or was it rather the logic?—that these principles should have been salvaged to serve the reforming urges of a popular movement that Hamilton would probably have fought with the passion of the politician of 1800. Whether he would have himself departed from these principles and raised his voice with the Liberty League in praise of the restrictive constitutionalism of Jefferson is a question about which we may debate endlessly if somewhat idly,[92] yet it is hard for me, as I have said several times, to imagine a man of Hamilton's character, energy, political philosophy, and vision ever abandoning the dynamic view of the Constitution.

WHILE the principles of Hamilton have governed the development of American constitutional law since the middle of the 1930's, the name of Hamilton the constitutional lawyer has been saluted in only the most desultory fashion. As I wrote in the opening chapter, one searches to little purpose in constitutional histories,[93] commentaries and casebooks on constitutional law,[94] the *Reports* of the Supreme Court,* and debates in Congress for instances of clear-cut recognition of his unique role as maker, manipulator, and interpreter of the Constitution of his day and as prophet of the Constitution of ours. His unfortunate reputation as anti-hero, the brooding figure of Marshall, our obsession with cases (as contrasted with statutes, executive actions, and customs) in the study of constitutional law, and the

---

* The direct uses of Hamilton by the Court in this century have been few and scattered. Three famous cases in particular were dramatic vindications of several of his most advanced interpretations: *Myers* v. *U.S.* (1927), in which Chief Justice Taft read the opening words of Article II with the help of Pacificus; *U.S.* v. *Curtiss-Wright Export Corp.* (1936), in which Justice Sutherland staged a modest revival of the doctrine of resulting powers; and *Helvering* v. *Davis* (1937), in which Justice Cardozo—who was, to tell the truth, merely finishing off the work of Justice Roberts in *U.S.* v. *Butler* (1936)—gave the Court's unqualified sanction to Hamilton's generous view of the power of Congress to tax and spend for the "general welfare." [95]

very fulfillment of his prophecies with the passing of the years—all these facts stand obstinately between Hamilton the constitutionalist and the kind of esteem he deserves but rarely gets.

In the end, the relevance rather than the influence of this remarkable Hamilton must earn him at least a decent portion of this esteem. About his influence on the Constitution of the 1960's there is nothing very meaningful that one can say, because who can measure the influence of a single man on a broad pattern of government a century and a half after his death? As a living and creating man of ideas and achievements, Hamilton has long since vanished into the vast structure for which he helped to lay the foundation, and too many other men have now contributed their talents to the upbuilding of the structure for us to put our finger upon any part of it and say, "This is Hamilton's." The myth of a man may often, to be sure, work an influence on later generations that is more visible than his achievements as a living person, but the myth of Hamilton will never, I repeat, be one to compete with those of Washington, Franklin, Jefferson, and Lincoln.

About his relevance, however, one can say a good deal that is meaningful, and I propose to top off what I have said about it in these pages by restating my conviction that we live today—and will live indefinitely, if we live at all—under a Hamiltonian Constitution, a fundamental law that is interpreted in a style of which he has been the most spirited advocate in American history. In a world in which political energy is a major spur to progress and political power is the key to survival, this constitutionalist who talked incessantly of energy and power makes the kind of sense to posterity that he could never quite make to his own age. While his posterity, the American people, may not be aware of the fact, his rules of interpretation, the four elements of his constitutional law, and the spirit of his constitutional theory are the essence of American constitutionalism in the 1960's.

His rules of interpretation, let us remind ourselves, were summed up in the memorable advice to Washington in 1791 that "the powers contained in a constitution of government, especially those which concern the general administration of the affairs of the country . . . ought to be construed liberally in advancement of the public good." Although we may perpetrate our own petty brands of "torture" on some parts of the Constitution, our Presidents and Congresses now use and our Justices now interpret the power-giving clauses of the Constitution in the "liberal" and "reasonable" frame of mind of which he was the first and least equivocal exponent. We shun constructions "calculated to defeat the . . . necessary authority of the government"; we shape our "means" grandly to our "ends"; we seem intent upon proving that this "fabric" can "advance" with us indefinitely, guiding us while it admonishes us, on the road to an ever higher civilization. In short, we read the Constitution, as he asked us to read it, in such a way as to "provide for national exigencies," "obviate national inconveniences," and "promote national prosperity." [96]

The first of the major elements of his constitutional law, the principle of clear and uncompromised national supremacy, is more ascendant today—as well it ought to be—than at any time in our history. The slogans of states' rights are shouted vehemently in at least one part of the land, men in every part quote Jefferson sorrowfully on the dangers of big government in faraway Washington, and it is certain that every long step toward regulation or welfare for generations to come will be resisted in the name of Amendment X. Yet resistance, in order to be successful, will have to be political in character, for the Constitution has now been converted into an effective instrument of national supremacy. The misguided attempts of states'-righters (prodded and fed by "states'-wrongers") to reverse the course of history by constitutional amendment are, in one sense, a tribute to the success of this conversion.[97] In any case, the actions taken by our last four Presidents (including Mr. Eisenhower), the laws passed by our last fifteen Congresses (including the Eightieth), and a chain of judicial decisions that would have appalled the constitutional Jefferson (*U.S.* v. *Curtiss-Wright Export Corp.,* *N.L.R.B.* v. *Jones and Laughlin Steel Corp., Steward Machine Co.* v. *Davis, U.S.* v. *Darby, Wickard* v. *Filburn, Case* v. *Bowles, Brown* v. *Board of Education, Griffin* v. *Illinois, Baker* v. *Carr*) [98] are proof enough that the Constitution has kept pace, and should be able to keep pace indefinitely if left to its own prescriptive devices, with our political, economic, social, and spiritual progress toward a "more perfect Union." While our system is still more "federal"— and wisely so—than Hamilton wanted it to be, it is "national" enough to be saluted as a "more perfect Union." This is one area in which his prophetic fears have not been realized, for, thanks not least to a full generation of men who have read the supremacy clause as he advised them to read it, the centripetal forces in our federal system now overmatch the centrifugal by a healthy margin. Most Americans now approach the Constitution as men convinced that "the most operative causes of public prosperity" depend upon its being read as the charter of a nation.

The second of the major elements, the notion of the broadest construction of the powers of Congress consistent with the teachings of "reason and experience," is no less ascendant. The formula of congressional authority today reads: the commerce power + the war powers + the power to tax and spend for the general welfare × the loosest possible reading of the words "necessary and proper"—and what seems to come out at the other end is an unchallengeable authority to pass laws dealing with almost any problem that appears to be national in scope, including problems of agriculture, health, education, conservation, morals, welfare, and civil rights. If Congress now virtually has what Hamilton proposed that it should have—"a general legislative authority"—this is largely because it has accepted, knowingly or unknowingly, his prophetic contributions to this formula. While I would not claim the first part of it primarily for Hamilton (although he helped clear the ground for John Marshall's interpretation of the commerce clause), I would insist that the other three parts find their purest sources in, to take them in order, *The Federalist,* number 23, the Report on Manufactures, and the Opinion on the Constitutionality of the Bank.[99] If any part of the Constitution is thoroughly Hamiltonian today, it is Article I, section 8.

Yet so also is Article II, which he read so grandly and creatively as Publius, Pacificus, and Secretary of the Treasury that Edward S. Corwin found "the modern theory of presidential power" to be "the contribution primarily of Alexander Hamilton."[100] Other men, responding to the challenge of mighty events, have made the Presidency the splendid instrument of constitutional democracy it is today; other men, attempting to find a pattern of constitutional logic in these responses, have piled construction upon construction to give the theory of the Presidency a content far more detailed than he was able to work out. Yet all these responses and all these constructions have been, in one sense, merely an elaboration of the principle he first announced as Pacificus: "that the *executive power* of the nation is vested in the President; subject only to the *exceptions* and *qualifications* which are expressed in the instrument."[101] No matter how loudly our latter-day Whigs may protest, the "Stewardship Theory" of Theodore Roosevelt expresses the realities of presidential power in a government committed to vast responsibilities at home and abroad, and that theory may be traced back in unbroken line to Hamilton's teachings.

Hamilton's reading of Article III as the foundation of a judiciary whose characteristics were to be independence, supremacy, and power has won overwhelming approval in the twentieth century, as indeed it has ever since John Marshall finished his work. The independence of the Supreme Court, to which Hamilton devoted some of his best thoughts as Publius and Lucius Crassus, has been confirmed dramatically in the past quarter-century against the assaults of both the eager Left and the angry Right.

The supremacy of the Court,* which was only one aspect of his commitment to the Union, has been confirmed in decisions such as *Nelson* v. *Pennsylvania, Griffin* v. *Illinois,* and *Moore* v. *Michigan.*[102] And the power of judicial review of acts of Congress, having been strained beyond the limits of common sense in the days of *U.S.* v. *Butler,*[103] is now being used sparingly, as he thought it should be used, as a final defense against palpable invasions of constitutional propriety.[104] We cannot say for certain what Hamilton the constitutional lawyer would have thought of the use of Amendment XIV (in conjunction with Amendment I) to chop down state laws and ordinances that segregate public facilities or authorize prayers in public schools or compel children to salute the flag, for this development of recent years would have forced him, in effect, to make a choice between his doctrine of national supremacy and his doctrine of prudence in the use of the power of judicial review. One has the feeling, although it can be no more than a feeling, that in this instance, too, he would have made his choice for national supremacy.

Finally, the purposeful spirit that pervaded Hamilton's view of the Constitution seems to have conquered forever the cautious mood that colored Jefferson's. To us today, as to him one hundred and seventy years ago, the Constitution appears as a grant of splendid powers rather than a catalogue of niggling limitations. We go to it for support rather than admonition, for encouragement rather than dissuasion, for ways to get things done rather than to keep things from being done. We are intent as any generation of Americans upon preserving the spirit and practices of constitutionalism, but that spirit has been infused, as he hoped it would be, by a new confidence in the uses of political power; and those practices—open and orderly methods of making decisions, honest and well-contested elections, the techniques of procedural due process, restraints upon improper violations of liberty and deprivations of opportunity—are recognized as the real substance of constitutional government. Because this generation has been forced willy-nilly to use power on a grand scale to reclaim the wastelands of industrialism and to defend the nation against first one and then another relentless foe, his expansive teachings have become the essence of American constitutionalism in the 1960's—and will continue to be as far as the eye of imagination can reach.† The

* "Supremacy," I again point out, over the courts of the states, not over the President or Congress.

† To those who might wish to point out that the chief business of the Supreme Court today lies in an area—civil liberties and civil rights—in which Hamilton the constitutionalist had almost nothing to say, I would make two answers: first, there is more to American constitutional law than the decisions of the Supreme Court;

relevance of Hamilton the constitutionalist is as certain today as his influence was decisive one hundred and seventy years ago. If we will school ourselves in his rules and interpretations and soak ourselves in his spirit, we can keep the Constitution a living presence in a country whose dimensions and difficulties even he could not have imagined.

IF Hamilton is the most relevant of all Americans as constitutionalist, he is one of the most relevant four or five as political thinker. Engaged as we seem to be in an effort to save our dominant liberal tradition from the defects of its own virtues, and also to extend its range to new social and economic problems, we are rummaging in the past for political thinkers who can help us to perform this critical task. The new respect one finds in standard texts of American political thought for Madison, Adams, Calhoun, and Lincoln is a sign of how far this rescue operation has been pushed, and one can expect that it will go even farther in the next few years—although not, one hopes, so far as to persuade us to abandon our liberal tradition. If it is pushed with prudence and imagination, one can expect that Hamilton, too, will be offered a new measure of respect. It is high time, in my opinion, that our understanding of his gifts as a political scientist was infused with a touch of the enthusiasm of one of his eulogists in 1804, the editor of the *Utica Patriot:*

> With talents profound and active, with genius acute and penetrating, with learning deep and extensive, he made unwearied researches in political science, and has left as a rich legacy to his countrymen, a luminous view of the most correct principles in civil policy and government.[105]

His political principles were not as "correct" for the United States, in his time or in ours, as were those of Jefferson and Madison. No one who has studied and cherished the American political tradition would identify Hamilton as its First Source, and thus look to him for expression of the basic ideals of American democracy. He was too skeptical a judge of men and too harsh a censor of democracy ever to be allowed to stand alone as our teacher. Yet he did speak brilliantly to a number of questions that most of his contemporaries preferred to ignore, and his answers have never seemed more relevant than at this very moment. They are relevant not only because they teach us to deal more imaginatively with the hard problems of a high civilization, but because they are as fully convertible to the uses of committed democrats of the twentieth century as are the

_____

and second, it is exactly because these issues of the supremacy of the nation and the powers of Congress have been solved in a Hamiltonian manner that the Court can now turn its attention to other matters.

principles of his constitutional law. The lessons we learn from Hamilton the political thinker will reinforce and energize the liberal tradition, not sap or corrupt it. And the best of those lessons would seem to be:

Men are driven to strive and to achieve by their "passions," of which the most politically significant are the desire for esteem, the anticipation of gain, and the love of power.

Men also wish to preserve and advance their "interests," which are the physical and psychological fruits, real or merely hoped for, of their strivings.

It is next to useless to preach to men about their duty as citizens to control their passions and rise above their interests.

There is, however, a variety of political techniques through which passions can be steered into channels of healthy creativity and interests can be secured against the assaults of fear and envy.

The test of a sound and viable government is its ability to use old techniques and invent new ones that can harness the passions of men and enlist their interests in the service of the common ends of society.

Encompassing the mass of private interests, yet rising above them to live a life of its own, is the interest of all men in the pursuit of these ends—the general welfare, the common felicity, the public good.

No society can survive and prosper unless its citizens understand the commands of the public good and can generally, whether lured by carrots or threatened by sticks, be made to obey them.

No society can survive and prosper unless it has ways to nurture "choice spirits," men of uncommon virtue and talent, and to place them in positions of responsible authority.

As the opinions of the people are the decisive force in the political process, so the confidence of the people is the principal support of government.

Confidence is inspired chiefly by an honorable, dignified, efficient administration of public affairs.

It is also inspired, up to a point, by the sounds and appearances of such an administration.

The worst of social ills are disorder, violence, instability, and unpredictability—in a phrase, "the hydra Anarchy."

The worst of political ills is a weak government unable to cope with the convulsions of anarchy, because the next stop beyond anarchy is not chaos but despotism.

The most likely candidates for the role of despots are demagogues.

In a disordered world, there is more to be feared from a dearth of political power than from an overdose of it.

The cutting edge of power is energy—the use of power imaginatively and forcefully in the public interest—which is the indispensable quality of good government.

The executive is the chief source of political energy.

An energetic executive is as necessary to the success of democratic government as it is to any other kind.

The happiness of men in a civilized society depends to a critical extent upon the capacity of government, not merely to keep order and to protect them in the enjoyment of their rights and property, but actively to promote social, economic, and cultural growth.

Banks, factories, and armies are as important for the freedom and progress of civilized men as schools and churches. The authors of constitutions for those who aspire to be such men will make room in their planning for these instruments of society.

This is not, be it remembered, the whole of Hamilton's political thought, for he had many other things to say on many other subjects. Nor is the whole of his thought, I repeat, a political philosophy for American democracy. But this is a catalogue of opinions and judgments of which he was the first and most explicit exponent among the Founding Fathers—in several instances the only exponent—and Americans may go to it confidently for instruction in the problems and possibilities of twentieth-century statecraft. Hamilton the political scientist, like Hamilton the constitutionalist, is both the teacher and the property of the whole nation. He speaks to the Right but also to the Left, and speaks perhaps most intelligibly to those who mill about in the middle and seek for ways to save both America and American democracy. He is a useful man to know because he tells us harsh truths that we are not told by Jefferson, useful because democracy needs skeptics to warn as well as enthusiasts to acclaim. Hamilton the political thinker was a skeptic who was honest, acute, and specific about his doubts and fears, and as such a thinker he has a message of unique perception for this generation of Americans. As Eliphalet Nott warned in 1804, if this government of ours, the "illustrious fabric" on which Hamilton's "genius" was "impressed," should ever fall, "his prophetic declarations will be found inscribed on its ruins." [106]

IN conclusion, let us look again at the whole Hamilton, whose relevance for our times goes well beyond his teachings as constitutional lawyer and political scientist. It is not alone our indulgent Constitution and energetic government that should remind us daily that he lived and achieved and prophesied, nor even our mixed, balanced, productive, regulated, and occasionally guided economy. It is, rather, the very existence of America as a nation that spreads its sway over most of a continent and its influence over much of the world. We have achieved the power and glory he foretold in his most hopeful hours because we have become a far more perfect Union than all his enemies and even most of his friends wanted us to be. Men who distrust the authority of the Union, like the governors of Alabama and Mississippi,* and men who would seek to destroy it, like the leaders of the U.S.S.R. and Communist China, are all faced with the enduring fact of its existence. This fact above all others makes Hamilton—the constitutionalist, the political scientist, the American—a man of immense consequence for our age.

Whether he is, as a few men of good will and good judgment have insisted, even more consequential than Jefferson is a question I would prefer not to answer, for I believe that an American democrat can listen to both these men with immense profit and with surprisingly few feelings of tension. If one must, as I wrote above, make an emotional choice between them, one need not be either a full-blooded Jeffersonian or full-blooded Hamiltonian in politics and ideology.[107] It may seem odd that a book about Hamilton—and in praise of Hamilton—should end by refixing half our attention on his great antagonist. Yet it does this not so much through choice as through compulsion, that is to say, in obedience to the obstinate truth that the mighty figure of Jefferson stands forever between Hamilton and the unrestrained applause of the American people. In death, as they were in life, these two men are perpetual contestants for the allegiance of their countrymen,[108] and since the country proposes to remain a democracy, the eager democrat will always win out over the reluctant republican.† As Rosemary and Stephen Vincent Benét wrote of "H., the stripling Colonel" in their *Book of Americans:*

> He could handle the Nation's dollars
> With a magic that's known to few,
> He could talk with wits and scholars

---

* To the pretensions of such men Hamilton made the "retort classical" on the floor of the Convention at Philadelphia: "But as States are a collection of individual men, which ought we to respect most, the rights of the people composing them, or of the artificial beings resulting from the composition? Nothing could be more preposterous or absurd than to sacrifice the former to the latter." [109]

† Even if the country becomes something else, the choice, one suspects, will still be for Jefferson, for his rhetoric is too deeply implanted in our national consciousness to be easily uprooted. As has been often said, if an authoritarianism of Left or Right ever comes to America, it will doubtless come with all the trappings and slogans of democracy.

And scratch like a wildcat, too.
And he yoked the States together
With a yoke that is strong and stout.
(It was common dust that he did not trust
And that's where J. wins out).[110]

I have tried to show that there were other Hamiltons as well as other Jeffersons, and I hope that in time Americans will learn to notice which Hamilton and which Jefferson are bidding for their favor. While most Americans, even those who "like" Hamilton better than Jefferson, will choose the democrat over the republican, and indeed the man of culture and science over the man not much interested in art and music or in anthropology and architecture, perhaps they will learn to be not quite such easy Jeffersonians when confronted with each of these pairs: the anxious states'-righter and the uncompromising nationalist, the natural-born legislator and the natural-born executive, the politician who thought locally and the politician who thought continentally, the peaceful agrarian and the bustling sponsor of industry,[111] the political scientist who feared an overdose of power and the political scientist who feared a dearth, the statesman who praised a wise and frugal government and the statesman who recommended a wise and active one, the statesman who sought peace by talking of peace and the statesman who sought peace by studying war, the man who worshiped liberty and the man who hated anarchy, the man of contemplation who could have lived forever in Monticello and the man of action who "anticipated" Pittsburgh, and, most important of all for this study, the lawyer who took a narrow, rigid, almost suffocating view of the Constitution and the lawyer who meant it to be the obliging charter of a republican empire.[112]

I do not see how anyone can study this list thoughtfully and deny that, in most of the issues it encompasses, Hamilton is the more relevant of the two men. In a dozen ways that count heavily, this is clearly and perhaps even fortunately a Hamiltonian rather than a Jeffersonian country. Accustomed as we now must become to thinking in terms of a progressive industrial society served by an energetic national government under the liberating Constitution of a sovereign Union, we are bound—even the committed Jeffersonians among us—to pay homage to the man who first set this image before the American people.

SHORT TITLES AND ABBREVIATIONS USED

IN THE NOTES

Adams: C. F. Adams, ed., *The Works of John Adams,* 10 vols. (Boston, 1851)

AHR: American Historical Review

Ames: Seth Ames, ed., *Works of Fisher Ames,* 3 vols. (Boston, 1854)

Annals: The Debates and Proceedings in the Congress of the United States (Washington, 1834–), generally known by the short title *Annals of Congress.* In these notes the Roman numeral following each citation refers to the number of the particular Congress.

APSR: American Political Science Review

ASP: American State Papers

Cabot: H. C. Lodge, *Life and Letters of George Cabot* (Boston, 1878)

Coleman: William Coleman, *A Collection of the Facts and Documents, Relative to the Death of Major-General Alexander Hamilton* (1804) (Boston, 1904)

Constitution Annotated: Edward S. Corwin, ed., *The Constitution of the United States of America: Analysis and Interpretation,* Sen. Doc. 170, 82nd Congr., 2nd sess. (1953)

Elliot: Jonathan Elliot, ed., *The Debates in the Several State Conventions on the Adoption of the Federal Constitution,* 2nd ed., 5 vols. (Philadelphia, 1876)

Farrand: Max Farrand, ed., *The Records of the Federal Convention of 1787,* 4 vols. (New Haven, 1911, 1937)

Federalist: Clinton Rossiter, ed., *The Federalist Papers* (New American Library, New York, 1961)

Fitzpatrick: J. C. Fitzpatrick, ed., *The Writings of George Washington,* 39 vols. (Washington, 1931–1944)

Gallatin: Henry Adams, ed., *The Writings of Albert Gallatin,* 3 vols. (Philadelphia, 1879)

A. M. Hamilton: Allan M. Hamilton, *The Intimate Life of Alexander Hamilton* (New York, 1911)

History: John C. Hamilton, *History of the Republic of the United States of America, as Traced in the Writings of Alexander Hamilton and of His Cotemporaries,* 7 vols. (New York, 1857–1864)

Hume: C. W. Hendel, ed., *David Hume's Political Essays* (New York, 1953)

Jay: Henry P. Johnston, ed., *The Correspondence and Public Papers of John Jay,* 4 vols. (New York and London, 1890–1893)

Jefferson (Ford): P. L. Ford, ed., *The Writings of Thomas Jefferson,* 10 vols. (New York and London, 1892–1899)

Jefferson (Lipscomb): A. A. Lipscomb, ed. in chief, *The Writings of Thomas Jefferson,* "Monticello Edition," 20 vols. (Washington, 1903)

Journals: W. C. Ford and others, eds., *Journals of the Continental Congress, 1774–1789,* 34 vols. (Washington, 1904–1937)

Kent: William Kent, *Memoirs and Letters of James Kent* (Boston, 1898)

King: Charles R. King, *The Life and Correspondence of Rufus King,* 6 vols. (New York, 1894–1900)

L of C: Library of Congress

Letters: E. C. Burnett, ed., *Letters of the Members of the Continental Congress,* 8 vols. (Washington, 1921–1936)

Madison (1867): *Letters and Other Writings of James Madison,* 4 vols. (Philadelphia, 1867)

Madison (Hunt): Gaillard Hunt, ed., *The Writings of James Madison,* 9 vols. (New York and London, 1910)

McHenry: B. C. Steiner, *The Life and Correspondence of James McHenry* (Cleveland, 1907)

MHS: Massachusetts Historical Society

NYHS: New-York Historical Society

NYPL: New York Public Library

Papers: Harold C. Syrett and Jacob E. Cooke, eds., *The Papers of Alexander Hamilton,* 6 vols. through 1962 (New York and London, 1961–)

Pickering: Octavius Pickering and C. W. Upham, *The Life of Timothy Pickering,* 4 vols. (Boston, 1867–1873)

PSQ: Political Science Quarterly

Stat.: United States Statutes at Large

Tansill: C. C. Tansill, ed., *Documents Illustrative of the Formation of the Union of the American States* (Washington, 1927)

U.S.: United States Supreme Court Reports, which in earlier years bore the name of the reporter—Dallas, Cranch, Wheaton, Peters, Howard, Black, or Wallace

WMQ: William and Mary Quarterly

Works (JCH):   John C. Hamilton, ed., *The Works of Alexander Hamilton*, 7 vols. (New York, 1851)

Works: Henry Cabot Lodge, ed., *The Works of Alexander Hamilton*, "Constitutional Edition," 12 vols. (New York and London, 1904)

NOTE: The problem of citing Hamilton's writings is complicated by the fact that this book appears while the publication of *Papers* is in progress. As a general rule, I have cited *Papers* for all writings before Sept. 1, 1790 (the cut-off point for the last volume to appear before this book went to the printer), and either *Works, Works* (JCH), or various MS. collections for all writings after that date. Since neither J. C. Hamilton nor Lodge was as reliable an editor as he might have been, I have checked all passages taken from these two collections against the original sources, without, however, making corrections unless these seemed absolutely necessary—necessary, that is, to an accurate rendering of Hamilton's sentiments.

NOTES

CHAPTER ONE

THE MANY HAMILTONS AND THE ONE

1. Evidence of the durability of the Manichean view of the struggle between Jefferson and Hamilton is to be found in Dumas Malone, *Jefferson and the Rights of Man* (Boston, 1951), xx–xxii, 286, 305, 314, 329, 341, 352. Although Professor Malone took a more respectful view of the great antagonist of his beloved Jefferson in "Hamilton on Balance," *Proceedings of the American Philosophical Society,* CII (1958), 129, 134–135, he has restated the theme of Hamilton as the Child of Darkness in *Jefferson and the Ordeal of Liberty* (Boston, 1962), esp. chaps. 2, 5, 6, 11, 16. Perhaps the most popular and influential of all works in this vein has been Claude G. Bowers, *Jefferson and Hamilton* (Boston, 1925), a lusty story whose theme was set by the subtitle, *The Struggle for Democracy in America.* See also his *Jefferson in Power* (Boston, 1936). One might also mention the poem on Hamilton in Rosemary and Stephen Vincent Benét, *A Book of Americans* (New York, 1933), 42–43, which begins:

> Jefferson said, "The many!"
> Hamilton said, "The few!"
> Like opposite sides of a penny
> Were these exalted two.

2. The best studies of Hamilton are Broadus Mitchell, *Alexander Hamilton,* 2 vols. (New York, 1957–1962), which surpasses all others in documentation; John C. Miller, *Alexander Hamilton* (New York, 1959); Nathan Schachner, *Alexander Hamilton* (New York, 1946); and, still as useful a special introduction to Hamilton as Lord Charnwood's biography is to Lincoln, Frederick Scott Oliver, *Alexander Hamilton* (London, 1906). Other biographies are cited in these notes.

The quotation in the preface may be found in Marquis de Talleyrand-Périgord, *Étude sur la République des États-Unis d'Amérique* (New York,

1876), 192; Duc de Broglie, ed., *Memoirs of the Prince de Talleyrand* (New York, 1891), I, 181–187.

3. To those who still insist on quoting Hamilton out of context to the effect that a "national debt" is a "national blessing" (*Papers,* II, 635; *Works,* VIII, 259 ff.), I recommend a careful reading of his words in *Papers,* VI, 106; *Works,* II, 411, 445–446; III, 40–45, 261–265; IV, 126; VIII, 160, 223.

4. These particular steps were perhaps the least successfully taken. See J. C. Miller, *The Federalist Era, 1789–1801* (New York, 1960), 60–61.

5. See especially the measured yet admiring judgments in Bray Hammond, *Banks and Politics in America* (Princeton, 1957), chaps. 4–5; J. T. Holdsworth, *The First Bank of the United States* (Washington, 1910).

6. D. R. Dewey, *Financial History of the United States* (New York, 1922), chaps. 4–5, a useful summary of Hamilton's financial measures; A. B. Hepburn, *A History of Currency in the United States* (New York, 1915), 19–20, 41–45; A. S. Bolles, *The Financial History of the United States* (New York, 1879), I, 92, 93; II, 6, 7, 175–181; E. C. Kirkland, *A History of American Economic Life* (New York, 1932), 304; H. R. Smith, *Economic History of the United States* (New York, 1955), 88–92; R. C. McGrane, *The Economic Development of the American Nation* (Boston, 1942), 144; Fred A. Shannon, *Economic History of the People of the United States* (New York, 1934), 331–338; Fritz Redlich, *The Molding of American Banking* (New York, 1947), I, 26–29; Paul Studenski and H. E. Kroos, *Financial History of the United States* (New York, 1952), chap. 5, a mixed judgment; Joseph Dorfman, *The Economic Mind in American Civilization* (New York, 1946–1959), I, 288 ff., 404–417.

7. Clarence L. Ver Steeg, *Robert Morris: Revolutionary Financier* (Philadelphia, 1954), 120, 199; Miller, *Hamilton,* 86–87. A letter from Hamilton to Morris dated Nov. 9, 1790, New Hampshire Historical Society, makes clear that the Secretary of the Treasury drew on Morris's financial experience during the formative years of the new government.

On the much argued question of Hamilton's sources, see C. F. Dunbar, "Some Precedents Followed by Alexander Hamilton," *Quarterly Journal of Economics,* III (1888–1889), 32, which emphasizes English precedents, especially the financial measures of William Pitt; J. O. Wettereau, "Letters from Two Business Men to Alexander Hamilton," *Journal of Economic and Business History,* III (1930–1931), 667, which points to the importance of home-grown advice—in this instance, that of William Bingham—which was in turn inspired by the English experience. Page Smith, *James Wilson* (Chapel Hill, 1956), 158, makes a case for Wilson's influence on Hamilton.

On the possible but not very probable influence of Tench Coxe (whose papers remain closed to scholars), see Harold Hutcheson, *Tench Coxe* (Baltimore, 1938), viii, 21 ff., 99–101; Mitchell, *Hamilton,* I, 151–152, who denies flatly that Coxe had anything but a helping hand in preparing the Report on Manufactures. The most important of Coxe's writings in a Hamiltonian vein are *An Enquiry into . . . a Commercial System for the United States* (Philadelphia, 1787); *Observations on the Agriculture, Manufactures and Commerce of the United States* (New York, 1789); *A View of the United States* (Philadelphia, 1794).

8. Report from the Secretary of the Treasury, Dec. 9, 1828, *Sen. Doc.*, No. 7, 20th Congr., 2d sess., p. 9. Rush went on to praise Hamilton's "comprehensive genius, looking into futurity, and embracing in its survey all the interests that go to make up the full strength and riches of a great empire." Hamilton's major papers as Secretary of the Treasury may be found in *American State Papers, Finance* (Washington, 1832), vol. I, and in Samuel McKee, Jr., ed., *Alexander Hamilton's Papers on Public Credit, Commerce and Finance* (New York, 1957), which has a useful index.

9. L. D. White, *The Federalists* (New York, 1948), 125–126, 507 ff.; L. K. Caldwell, *The Administrative Theories of Hamilton and Jefferson* (Chicago, 1944), 230, 241; Richard B. Morris, ed., *The Basic Ideas of Alexander Hamilton* (New York, 1957), xv; Louis M. Hacker, *Alexander Hamilton in the American Tradition* (New York, 1957), 145.

10. *The Federalists*, 127. Caldwell, *Administrative Theories of Hamilton and Jefferson*, 3–10, 230–234, gives a balanced judgment of Hamilton's quality as administrator.

11. Hans J. Morgenthau, *In Defense of the National Interest* (New York, 1951), 14–18, and "The Mainsprings of American Foreign Policy," *APSR*, XLIV (1950), 833, 840; Adrienne Koch, *Power, Morals, and the Founding Fathers* (Ithaca, 1961), 78. A. H. Bowman, "Jefferson, Hamilton, and American Foreign Policy," *PSQ*, LXXI (1956), 18, spoils an interesting case for Jefferson as the "realist" and Hamilton as the "unrealist" by overstating it grotesquely. Support for Professor Morgenthau is offered by Felix Gilbert, *To the Farewell Address* (Princeton, 1961), 111–114, who writes that "eighteenth-century power politics . . . spoke authoritatively and decisively through the voice of Alexander Hamilton."

12. *Works*, IV, 464, 321–325, 457–465, 469; VI, 226–227, 236; VIII, 212. One of the first to call attention to Hamilton's importance as the apostle of diplomatic realism was Charles A. Beard, *The Idea of National Interest* (New York, 1934), 43–49. For a quick review of some of the literature on this point, see Bowman, *PSQ*, LXXI (1956), 18–19 n.

13. *Works*, VIII, 161–165; X, 200, 249, 256, 266, 276–277, 288; IV, 332, 336, 374–375; VII, 11; VIII, 185, 210–212; VI, 207; *Papers*, V, 68. And see his excellent advice to "young and weak nations" in *Works*, VI, 106–107.

14. Remarks on the Independence of Vermont, March 28, 1787, *Papers,* IV, 128, 132–133; (New York) *Daily Advertiser,* April 5, 1787.

15. Works, IV, 325, 463, 465.

16. Draft of speech for Washington, Nov. 6, 1793, *Works,* VIII, 106; V, 266–267.

17. Hamilton was the first choice of most Federalists for this delicate mission, and from first to last he took so active a role in its initiation and ratification that Samuel F. Bemis, *Jay's Treaty* (New York, 1923), 271, suggests that it might well be "more aptly . . . called Hamilton's Treaty." I disagree with Bemis (pp. 218–231, 269) that Hamilton hurt Jay's chances for a stronger treaty by passing soothing information to George Hammond, the British Minister to the United States. I agree with Miller, *Federalist Era,* 12–13 n., that Alexander De Conde, *Entangling Alliance: Politics and Diplomacy under George Washington* (Durham, 1958), 505–511, overstates Hamilton's influence in the diplomacy of the young Republic.

18. Despite the work of Morgenthau and others, Hamilton continues to get clearly less than his due in such standard histories of American foreign affairs as S. F. Bemis, *A Diplomatic History of the United States,* 3rd ed. (New York, 1950), 89 ff.; Thomas A. Bailey, *A Diplomatic History of the American People,* 4th ed. (New York, 1950), 53–54, 61–64, who tags Hamilton much too casually as a "deep-dyed conservative"; Nelson M. Blake and Oscar T. Barck, *The United States in Its World Relations* (New York, 1960), 43–62; L. E. Ellis, *A Short History of American Diplomacy* (New York, 1951), 62–72; Robert H. Ferrell, *American Diplomacy: A History* (New York, 1959), 33–34, 36, 42; John H. Latané, *A History of American Foreign Policy* (Garden City, 1927), 76–78, 90, 93; Julius W. Pratt, *A History of United States Foreign Policy* (Englewood Cliffs, N.J., 1955), 72–83.

19. Not, however, without some kind words for the "cultivation of the earth" as "a state most favorable to the freedom and independence of the human mind." *Works,* IV, 74, 103.

20. Works, IV, 70–198; (Philadelphia) *Gazette of the United States,* Sept. 10, 1791; *New-York Journal,* Sept. 14, 1791; A. H. Cole, ed., *Industrial and Commercial Correspondence of Alexander Hamilton* (Chicago, 1928), 191–199, which also presents many of the letters and documents sent to Hamilton from all parts of the nation in 1791 for his enlightenment in drawing up the Report on Manufactures. Of the Report it has been eloquently said: "The city, the factory, the whole, indeed, of our complex industrial civilization, lay in embryo within the stately body of this document." R. G. Tugwell and J. Dorfman, "Alexander Hamilton: Nation-Maker," *Columbia University Quarterly,* XXIX (1937), 209; XXX (1938), 59, 62. On the question of authorship of the S.U.M. prospectus, see Mitchell, *Hamilton,* II, 181; Miller, *Hamilton,* 300; Schachner, *Hamilton,* 278.

21. See generally Joseph S. Davis, *Essays in the Earlier History of American Corporations* (Cambridge, 1917), I, 349 ff.

22. Americanus, Feb. 8, 1794, *Works,* V, 87.

23. To the House of Representatives, March 16, 1792, *Works,* II, 413–414.

24. Report on Manufactures, *Works,* IV, 116.

25. To Robert Morris, April 30, 1781, *Papers,* II, 617–618.

26. *Basic Ideas of Hamilton,* xix; Douglass C. North, *The Economic Growth of the United States, 1790 to 1860* (Englewood Cliffs, N.J., 1961), 46; Victor S. Clark, *History of Manufactures in the United States* (Washington, 1916–1928), I, 625; George Soule and Vincent P. Carosso, *American Economic History* (New York, 1957), 105–113.

27. Bower Aly, *The Rhetoric of Alexander Hamilton* (New York, 1941), 182–197.

28. Harrison Gray Otis, *Eulogy on Alexander Hamilton* (1804), reprinted in Frank Moore, *American Eloquence* (New York, 1895), I, 563; James Kent, *An Address . . . before the Law Association of the City of New-York* (New York, 1836), 16, 19 ff.; *Commentaries on American Law,* 3rd ed. (New York, 1836), I, 62–64; III, 20; Kent, 290–295, 317–318, 321–325; Nathan Schachner, ed., "Narrative of Colonel Robert Troup," *WMQ,* 3rd ser., IV (1947), 213, 221; W. D. Lewis, ed., *Great American Lawyers* (Philadelphia, 1907), I, 357–432.

29. For evidence, see the fantastic grasp of detail in *Works,* VI, 483–487; VII, 3–225.

30. "Anthony Pasquin" (John Williams), *The Hamiltoniad* (Boston, 1804), 28.

31. To James Duane, Sept. 30, 1780, *Papers,* II, 407.

32. To the Convention at Poughkeepsie, June 27, 1788, *Papers,* V, 98; Elliot, II, 351.

33. For examples of the way in which Hamilton's strictly political thought is given short shrift in the standard texts, see F. W. Coker, *Democracy, Liberty, and Property* (New York, 1947), 343–346, 468; R. G. Gettell, *History of American Political Thought* (New York, 1928), 168–172; A. P. Grimes, *American Political Thought* (New York, 1955), 130–143; J. M. Jacobson, *The Development of American Political Thought* (New York, 1932), 179–186; A. T. Mason and R. H. Leach, *In Quest of Freedom* (Englewood Cliffs, N.J., 1959), 144–188; C. E. Merriam, *A History of American Political Theories* (New York, 1920), 100–122; A. M. Scott, *Political Thought in America* (New York, 1959), 96–97, 152–154; F. G. Wilson, *The American Political Mind* (New York, 1949), 152–160. Caldwell, *Administrative Theories of Hamilton and Jefferson,* chap. 2, is a uniquely respectful and respectable short treatment of Hamilton's political

thought. Lord Acton, *Essays on Freedom and Power* (Boston, 1948), 50, 201 ff., described Hamilton and Burke as "the best political writers" of the eighteenth century, but most of Acton's large audience seem to have dozed off at this point.

34. Woodrow Wilson, *The New Freedom* (New York, 1913), 55. The leading historian of nationalism, Hans Kohn, has a low opinion of Hamilton's dedication and influence. His *The Idea of Nationalism* (New York, 1944), 288, describes Hamilton as a "pioneer in the field of economic nationalism," but denies that his "ideological foundation" was "characteristically American"; his *American Nationalism* (New York, 1961), 32, 51, 196, gives him even less credit or consideration. A much more understanding appraisal of Hamilton as nationalist is W. S. Culbertson, *Alexander Hamilton* (New Haven, 1911), 3, which insists that "the idea of nationality . . . dominated every phase of his political and economic thinking."

35. Works, VIII, 193. Washington in fact put it a good deal less strongly in his own first draft. Fitzpatrick, XXXV, 56.

36. Oliver, *Hamilton,* 450, a judgment echoed by Miller, *Hamilton,* 119.

37. Works, X, 90, 425–426.

38. McHenry to Hamilton, Sept. 4, 1800, McHenry Papers, L of C; *Works,* VII, 327; X, 426; *Adams,* IX, 290, 277, 295; X, 125–126.

39. For representative comments of Hamilton on England, see *Papers,* I, 129–130 (America's debt to the mother country); IV, 184, 192, 200; *Works,* II, 462 (the excellence of the British constitution); *Papers,* IV, 276 (the possibility of reunion); *Works,* IV, 335–336 (the possibility of alliance); VIII, 410 ff. (the appeal to English legal precedent); X, 294 (the refusal to knuckle under to England). See also the notes of a conversation with George Beckwith, Oct., 1789, *Papers,* V, 483, which have Hamilton saying, *"we think in English,* and have a similarity of prejudices, and predilections." Bradford Perkins, *The First Rapprochement* (Philadelphia, 1953), 14, 23, makes clear the importance of Anglo-American commerce in Hamilton's broad scheme for economic development.

40. His strongest denial of the accusation, in which Adams joined with Jefferson, that he was "leader of a British faction" is in *Works,* VII, 357–362.

41. Henry Cabot Lodge, *Alexander Hamilton* (Boston, 1891), 161–162.

42. Robert Troup to Hamilton, Jan. 19, 1791, Hamilton Papers, L of C.

43. Dec. 16, 1796, *Works,* X, 217.

44. The Farmer Refuted (1775), *Papers,* I, 84.

45. Bradford to Hamilton, July 2, 1795, Hamilton Papers, L of C. Perhaps Bradford's observation had been prompted by a letter from Hamilton discussing

Jay's Treaty, in which he admitted, "You see I have not entirely lost my appetite for Politics," then added quickly: "You must not infer that I have not a very good one for law." June 13, 1795, Bradford Papers, Historical Society of Pennsylvania.

46. *Charleston Courier,* Aug. 7, 1804, reprinted in Coleman, 178.

47. Lucius Crassus, Feb. 23, 1802, *Works,* VIII, 313, a bit of lamentable rhetoric; to King, June 3, 1802, *Works,* X, 440.

48. *Papers,* I, 56, 93.

49. Publius, Nov. 16, 1778, *Papers,* I, 580.

50. Oct. 2, 1798, *Works,* X, 321. And to Theodore Sedgwick he wrote Feb. 27, 1800 that "America, if she attains greatness, must creep to it. Will it be so? Slow and sure is no bad maxim. Snails are a wise generation." *Works,* X, 362–363.

51. July 10, 1804, *Works,* X, 458, 445. As far back as 1797 he had been hearing talk of secession from Federalist extremists in New England, as witness the zealous letter of Uriah Tracy of Connecticut, April 6, 1797, Hamilton Papers, L of C. That he was disturbed by such talk, especially in 1804, is made clear in the documents assembled or referred to in Henry Adams, ed., *Documents Relating to New-England Federalism. 1800–1815* (Boston, 1877), 145, 148, 169; Mitchell, *Hamilton,* II, 518–523, 757–758; L. W. Turner, *William Plumer of New Hampshire* (Chapel Hill, 1962), 141–143; *King,* IV, 346–360; A. Hoops to James Hamilton, March 30, 1829, Hamilton Papers, L of C, which records a conversation of 1804 in which Hamilton equated disunion with the destruction of "civil liberty"; *History,* VII, 822–823, which has Hamilton saying to John Trumbull five days before his death: "You are going to Boston. You will see the principal men there. Tell them from ME as MY request, for God's sake, to cease these conversations and threatenings about a separation of the Union. It must hang together as long as it can be made to." For Madison's testimony to Hamilton's loyalty to the Union, see his letter to J. Q. Adams, Feb. 24, 1829, *Madison* (Hunt), IX, 340–341.

52. Camillus (July 25, 1795), *Works,* V, 206; *Federalist,* 33.

53. To Washington, April 14, 1794, *Works,* V, 97, 105.

54. *Papers,* III, 557.

55. June 26, 1787, *Papers,* IV, 218; Farrand, I, 424.

56. *Federalist,* 33.

57. *Papers,* III, 556; *Works,* VII, 234; *Papers,* III, 557. For other appeals to the idea of mission, see *Papers,* V, 67; *Works,* V, 408; VI, 425; VIII, 192, 207; *Federalist,* 72, 91, 224. On this concept, see generally Clinton Rossiter, "The

American Mission," *American Scholar,* XX (1950–1951), 19; E. M. Burns, *The American Idea of Mission* (New Brunswick, 1957), esp. chaps. 1, 4.

58. Farrand, III, 381–382. These memorable words were first reported by Gouverneur Morris in his *Oration, upon the Death of General Washington* (New York, 1800).

59. To Thomas Mifflin, Aug. 7, 1794, *Works,* VI, 394.

60. Miller, *Hamilton,* 473.

61. Tully, Aug. 28, 1794, *Works,* VI, 423; III, 268–269; IV, 102, 309; V, 316; VIII, 95; *Federalist,* 85–91.

62. Papers, II, 63.

63. Works, VIII, 296, 183, 193–199; *Papers,* II, 665; III, 425–426; IV, 91–92; *Works,* II, 465; IX, 513; *Papers,* III, 256.

64. The Continentalist, July 4, 1782, *Papers,* III, 106.

65. Federalist, 105, and 33, 36–37, 53–76, 84–105, 366, 517–521, 526–527.

66. A. Hoops to James Hamilton, March 30, 1829, Hamilton Papers, L of C.

67. Federalist, 97–99.

68. May 26, 1792, *Works,* IX, 513.

69. Examination of Jefferson's Message, Dec. 17, 1801, *Works,* VIII, 246–247; X, 440.

70. The Continentalist, July 12, 1781, *Papers,* II, 651.

71. Notes for draft of Farewell Address, *Works,* VIII, 185, 207–212.

72. See especially his memorable reports and messages to Congress on securing the public credit (*Papers,* VI, 51–110; *Works,* II, 337–351; III, 199–301), establishing a national bank (*Works,* III, 388–442), and encouraging manufactures (*Works,* IV, 70–198). William Hill, "The First Stages of the Tariff Policy of the United States," *Publications of the American Economic Association,* VII (1893), 88, makes clear that Hamilton "stood almost alone among the statesmen of first rank in advocating commercial regulations as a necessary and desirable thing in themselves."

73. Papers, VI, 105; *Works,* II, 436; *Papers,* II, 606; *Works,* VIII, 94, 184, 206–207, 445–451. His most forceful argument in behalf of the public credit is in *Works,* III, 294–301. A summing-up of his system is in *Works,* VII, 259.

74. To McHenry, June 21, 1799, *McHenry,* 395.

75. John Quincy Adams, *Jubilee of the Constitution* (New York, 1839), 107; Otis, *Eulogy,* 563, who said of his friend that his "heart exulted in 'the tented field.'"

76. Miller, *Hamilton,* xi.

77. *Federalist,* 153.

78. *Papers,* I, 94; *Works,* VIII, 195; *Papers,* III, 451; *Works,* X, 75; *Federalist,* 67–71, 115, 170–174, 521.

79. *Federalist,* 166, 173–174, 182–187. See the exchange of letters in 1790 with Aedanus Burke of South Carolina on Hamilton's supposed low opinion of the militia, in *Papers,* VI, 333–337, 357–358.

80. To Washington, March 8, 1794, *Works,* X, 63; to Duane, Sept. 3, 1780, *Papers,* II, 402, 410–411.

81. June 18, 1783, *Papers,* III, 378–397.

82. *Federalist,* 166. For a respectful view of Hamilton's place in the American military tradition, see Russell F. Weigley, *Towards an American Army* (New York, 1962), chap. 2.

83. (Philadelphia) *Aurora,* Feb. 25, 1799.

84. *Works,* VII, 179–186, 48; VIII, 218; X, 382; Sidney Forman, *West Point* (New York, 1956), 14–19.

85. Draft of a letter from Washington to McHenry, Dec. 13, 1798, *Works,* VII, 11.

86. *Works,* IV, 168.

87. To John Adams, Sept. 25, 1798, Fitzpatrick, XXXVI, 460–461.

88. Otis, *Eulogy,* 563; *Ames,* II, 256–264, a fascinating "sketch" of Hamilton's "character" by an intimate friend deeply moved by his death; McHenry to Hamilton, Jan. 3, 1791, *McHenry,* 129, only one of many letters in which a friend expresses altogether sincerely his "esteem" and "love" for Hamilton; Henry Lee to Hamilton, May 6, 1792, *Works* (JCH), V, 507; William Vans Murray to Hamilton, Oct. 9, 1800, *Works* (JCH), VI, 476; Caleb Gibbs to Hamilton, Sept. 10, 1792, Hamilton Papers, L of C. The friends of Hamilton wrote to one another, as well as to him, of their "love" and "esteem" of this dazzling leader, as witness Christopher Gore to Rufus King, Dec. 24, 1793, King Papers, NYHS; Theodore Sedgwick to Van Schaack, Dec. 17, 1794, Sedgwick Papers, MHS; George Cabot to John Lowell, July 18, 1804, *Cabot,* 348–349; Rufus King to Christopher Gore, Feb. 14, 1795, *King,* II, 4–5.

89. Otis, *Eulogy,* 564.

90. An act of incivility further compounded by his letter of explanation to General Schuyler, Feb. 18, 1781, *Papers,* II, 563–568, which proves that the first draft of this letter was even two or three degrees hotter than the final version.

91. *Works,* II, 453–454. For a survey of Hamilton's program that emphasizes (or perhaps the word should be overemphasizes) the seamy side, see Irving Brant, *James Madison* (Indianapolis, 1948–1956), III, chaps. 23, 24, 28.

92. Works, VII, 229–306.

93. Letter from Alexander Hamilton Concerning the Public Conduct and Character of John Adams, Esq., President of the United States (New York, 1800), in *Works,* VII, 309–364. Even his good friend Cabot was "bound" to tell Hamilton that "some very worthy and sensible men" found this famous pamphlet an exercise in "egotism" and "vanity." Cabot to Hamilton, Nov. 29, 1800, *Cabot,* 41; Ames to Hamilton, Nov., 1800, *Ames,* I, 283–285. For a view of Hamilton "through the eyes of John Adams"—and therefore a rather unpleasant sight—see Page Smith, *John Adams* (Garden City, 1962).

94. To John Jay, May 7, 1800, *Works,* X, 371–374, a proposal that even Lodge, *Hamilton,* 227, labels a "fraud." See above, p. 192.

95. Works, VII, 369–479. For a judicious summary of the whole affair, see Mitchell, *Hamilton,* II, chap. 21.

96. Papers, II, 675; III, 69–70, 192; *Works,* X, 444, 457; to Richard Peters, Dec. 29, 1802, Harvard University Library.

97. Mitchell, *Hamilton,* I, xii. For a contrary view of Hamilton's program as a projection of the "trickle-down theory of economic welfare," see Merle Fainsod, Lincoln Gordon, and J. C. Palamountain, *Government and the American Economy,* 3rd ed. (New York, 1959), 94–96.

98. July 29, 1798, *Works,* X, 301.

99. Pickering to Lafayette, July 23, 1828, Pickering Papers, MHS.

100. See his youthful complaint to Edward Stevens, Nov. 11, 1769, *Papers,* I, 4; IV, 252–253, 72–73; *Works,* II, 427; III, 178–179; X, 60–66, 364. His concern for military reputation, of which some biographers have made too much, is evident in *Papers,* II, 509, 568, 594–595, 636–638; III, 461–462. There is no doubt that, like any average Romantic, his idea of soldiering was "some employment" that would enable him "to get knocked in the head in an honorable way." To John Laurens, May 22, 1779, *Papers,* II, 52.

101. Adrienne Koch, *Power, Morals, and the Founding Fathers,* 66–75, finds the "pursuit of power" to have been the essence of Hamilton's political style, an interpretation with which I must flatly disagree. Just as flatly must I disagree with Dumas Malone, *Jefferson and the Rights of Man,* xxii, who makes a "lust" out of a "pursuit." Nor do I find Brant, *Madison,* III, 361–362, convincing in his assertion, based on one bit of marginal evidence and an animus toward Hamilton, that his "deepest motive was his own hidden ambition to be President." (The evidence is an unpublished letter to "Aristides," 1792, in Hamilton Papers, L of C, vol. XVIII, p. 2476.) Hamilton would doubtless have liked to be President—who but Washington in that age wouldn't have?—but it seems to have been an ambition not only well hidden but held in rigid control. A rare mention of Hamilton as a likely man for the Presidency is John Nicholas to McHenry, May 3, 1799, *McHenry*, 389. See also the disclaimer of his friend William Smith, *The Politicks and Views of a Certain Party, Displayed* (1792), 35–36, and the affidavit of Noah Webster, July 13, 1797, H. W. Warfel, ed., *Letters of Noah Webster* (New York, 1953), 160–161.

102. *Papers*, V, 260.

103. To Henry Lee, Dec. 1, 1789, *Papers*, VI, 1. The inquiring letter from Lee that prompted this declaration is in *Papers*, V, 517.

104. *Works*, III, 178–179, 199.

105. The Reynolds Pamphlet, VII, 373. It is almost pitiable to observe him pressing for his pay as major general in 1798–1799, in *Works*, VII, 50–53, 103–105. For conclusive evidence of his commitment to "large policies of government" rather than to "personal interests"—and of the essential honesty of the commitment—see Charles A. Beard, *An Economic Interpretation of the Constitution of the United States* (1913) (New York, 1948), 100–114; Forrest McDonald, *We the People* (Chicago, 1958), 48–49.

106. Troup to Hamilton, May 11, 1795, Hamilton Papers, L of C; Hamilton to Troup, April 13, 1795, Yale University Library; Otis, *Eulogy*, 564; Wolcott to McHenry, July 16, Aug. 2, 1804, *McHenry*, 529–532; "Sketch of the Character of Alexander Hamilton," 1804, *Ames*, II, 259, 262, only one of many recognitions by his close friends that "he did not thirst for power," that "no man held wealth cheaper," and that the "fame" for which he "thirsted" was fame "which virtue would not blush to confer." See also *Papers*, V, 419; VI, 449.

107. *Works*, VII, 378–379.

108. For evidence that he had more than his share of such bouts, see *Works*, V, 61; X, 69, 132, 190, 256, 275, 343, 458.

109. H. G., March 19, 1789, *Papers*, V, 305.

110. *Papers*, I, 373, 390. The pay book is to be found in the Hamilton Papers in the Library of Congress. For a useful little edition and judicious appraisal, see E. P. Panagopoulos, *Alexander Hamilton's Pay Book* (Detroit, 1961).

111. Hamilton to Robert Morris, Aug. 13, 1782, *Papers*, III, 139.

112. Sept. 21, 1795, *Jefferson* (Lipscomb), IX, 309–310.

113. For examples of his restless urge to do the work, and thus guide the conduct, of other men, see *Works*, IV, 205 ff., 313 ff., 343 ff., 408 ff.; V, 97 ff., 115 ff., 138 ff.; VI, 201 ff., 394 ff.; VII, 22 ff.; VIII, 120 ff., 153 ff., 161 ff.; X, 92 ff., 104 ff., 117 ff., 145 ff., 224 ff.; *Papers*, VI, 493 ff.

114. At Washington's request, to be sure. May 5, 1789, *Papers*, V, 335–338; Fitzpatrick, XXX, 319 ff.

115. See generally *Works,* X, 241 ff.; Stephen G. Kurtz, *The Presidency of John Adams* (Philadelphia, 1957), 260–283, which makes clear that McHenry and Wolcott were far more pliable instruments of Hamilton's will than was Timothy Pickering. The value of Kurtz's study is lessened by his largely unproved assertions about Hamilton's "militarism" (and military aspirations) in the crisis of 1798–1800.

116. Bayard to Hamilton, Aug. 11, 1800, Bayard Papers, NYPL; *McHenry,* 291–295. To the readers of the (Philadelphia) *Aurora,* May 9, 1799, Hamilton was "the man who moves the puppets." For examples of the eagerness with which Hamilton's opinion was sought by men in office, see Pickering to Hamilton, March 26, 1797, March 25, 1798, Otis to Hamilton, Dec. 21, 1798, Wolcott to Hamilton, June 18, July 28, Sept. 26, Oct. 6, 1795; *Works* (JCH), VI, 7, 24, 39, 41, 154, 215, 272, 273, 377, 379; George Gibbs, *Memoirs of the Administrations of Washington and John Adams* (New York, 1846), I, 211, 219, 225, 247, 254, 261, 263, 265.

117. *Adams,* X, 127, 155, 162, as well as the even more tart complaint about Hamilton as major general in *Adams,* IX, 435.

118. *Works,* X, 97, 171, 398–399.

119. March 17, 1798, *Works,* X, 275.

120. Lodge, *Hamilton,* 278.

121. To Jefferson, June 30, 1789, *History,* IV, 47 n.; *Madison* (1867), I, 480.

122. Hamilton was never reluctant to press Washington to do his duty, especially to stand for the Presidency again and again. See *Works,* X, 7–10, 180–182; *Papers,* V, 201–202, 220–222.

123. To Tobias Lear, Jan. 2, 1800, *Works,* X, 357.

124. Washington to John Adams, July 16, 1798, Fitzpatrick, XXXVI, 453, 460–461. It was Timothy Pickering's opinion that, almost alone among Washington's "family," Hamilton maintained an independence of judgment, thanks largely to his "correct and elevated mind." Pickering to John Marshall, Feb. 14, 1827, Pickering Papers, MHS. It was also his opinion that Hamilton's writing had served as a "model" for Washington, who learned a good deal about spelling, grammar, and punctuation with the subtle aid of his youthful aide-de-camp. Pickering to Richard Peters, Jan. 5, 1811, *Pickering,* II, 96.

There is still no more perceptive judgment of Hamilton's influence as penman for Washington, and of Washington's final responsibility for his own words, than Jared Sparks, ed., *The Writings of George Washington* (Boston, 1837), XII, app. 3. The best modern judgments of the over-all relationship of these two great men are Oliver, *Hamilton,* 70 ff., 109; Broadus Mitchell, "Hamilton's Quarrel with Washington," *WMQ,* 3rd ser., XII (1955), 199, and *Hamilton,* I, 113 ff., 240–241; II, 373 ff., 388 ff., 427, 462 ff.; Lodge, *Hamilton,* 14–18;

Miller, *Hamilton,* 22, 35, 66 ff.; R. B. Morris, "Washington and Hamilton: A Great Collaboration," *Proceedings of the American Philosophical Society,* CII (1958), 107, perhaps the best judgment of all, leaving little more to be said.

The extreme view of Washington as Hamilton's aging dupe is presented, somewhat obliquely to be sure (and thus, oddly enough, with telling force), in Joseph Charles, *The Origins of the American Party System* (Williamsburg, 1956), 38–53; the extreme view of Washington as a man with ideas of his own (and of Hamilton as an expounder of these ideas) in Curtis P. Nettels, *The Emergence of a National Economy, 1775-1815* (New York, 1962), 104–108, as well as Rose C. Engelman, "Washington and Hamilton," Cornell Univ. Ph.D. thesis, 1948.

125. See the letters to Hamilton cited below, p. 294, n. 107.

126. Washington to Pickering, July 11, 1798; to Hamilton, July 14, Oct. 21, 1798; to Knox, July 16, Aug. 9, 1798; to John Adams, Sept. 25, 1798, Fitzpatrick, XXXVI, 323, 329, 345, 396, 453, 500.

127. Harold W. Bradley, "The Political Thinking of George Washington," *Journal of Southern History,* XI (1945), 469, is, I think, much too offhand in its dismissal of Hamilton's purely intellectual influence on Washington.

128. The Adams Controversy (1800), *Works,* VII, 339. For Hamilton's influential role in shaping the Farewell Address, see *Works,* VIII, 181–214; Fitzpatrick, XXXV, 48, 51–61, 178, 190, 198, 204; V. H. Paltsits, *Washington's Farewell Address* (New York, 1935), esp. 25, 53–54, 75; Mitchell, *Hamilton,* II, 388–395; Miller, *Federalist Era,* 196–197, and the works cited at 197 n.; Brant, *Madison,* III, 356, 440 ff., which is a useful reminder of Madison's role. Once again the extreme view of Hamilton's influence over Washington is taken by Charles, *Origins of the American Party System,* 48. A valuable corrective to the perhaps too condescending judgment of Hamilton's contribution made so authoritatively by Paltsits is Gilbert, *To the Farewell Address,* chap. 5, and pp. 165–169, who points out, I think most convincingly, that "Hamilton's contribution went beyond an execution of Washington's instructions and added a new intellectual element."

129. Feb. 23, 1791, *Works,* III, 445–493.

130. William Branch Giles, Nov. 20, 1792, *Annals,* II, 706.

CHAPTER TWO   **HAMILTON AND THE CONSTITUTION: 1780–1788**

1. Feb. 27, 1802, *Works,* X, 425. In the *Anas,* his autobiographical notes of the period 1791–1809, Jefferson recorded a conversation of Oct. 1, 1792 with Washington in which he told the President that Hamilton had called the Constitution a "shilly shally thing, of mere milk and water, which could not last, and was only good as a step to something better." *Jefferson* (Ford), I, 204.

2. Despite the partisan vigor with which it belabors the ghost of John Fiske and celebrates the achievements, real or imagined, of the government under the Articles of Confederation, Merrill Jensen, *The New Nation* (New York, 1950), is much the best chronicle of events in these years. See also his *The Articles of Confederation* (Madison, 1940). For the course of events in New York, see E. W. Spaulding, *New York in the Critical Period, 1783–1789* (New York, 1932), and Allan Nevins, *The American States During and After the Revolution* (New York, 1924), esp. chap. 7.

3. *Papers*, II, 400–418. Jensen, *The New Nation*, 50, describes this letter as "the outstanding expression of the nationalists' political philosophy in 1780, the program they wanted, and the methods they were ready to use to establish themselves."

4. For evidence of his early concern for the "feeble, indecisive, and improvident" actions of Congress, see his letter to George Clinton from Valley Forge, Feb. 13, 1778, *Papers*, I, 425–428. Although he had become known (and known as a very bright and industrious young man) to the leading men in New York as early as March, 1777—when he undertook to act as a sort of military correspondent to the Revolutionary legislature (*Papers*, I, 207 ff.)—Hamilton seems to have had nothing to do with the New York Constitution of 1777. For the writing of this generally admirable plan of government (by John Jay with an assist from Gouverneur Morris and R. R. Livingston), see Frank Monaghan, *John Jay* (New York, 1935), 89–98; Nevins, *American States*, 158–164; C. Z. Lincoln, *The Constitutional History of New York* (Rochester, 1906), I, chap. 2, esp. pp. 495–499. For Hamilton's early and unenthusiastic views of it, which he wrote in his most "democratic" stage, see his letters to Gouverneur Morris, May 7, 19, 1777, *Papers*, I, 248, 254. For his later and more respectful views, see *Papers*, V, 120; *Federalist*, 170.

5. *Papers*, II, 407.

6. For evidence that Hamilton was already gaining a considerable reputation in Congress, see *Journals*, XV, 1391; XVIII, 1138, 1156; *Letters*, IV, 539–541, 546–547.

7. *Journals*, XIX, 31, 57, 125–128; E. C. Burnett, *The Continental Congress* (New York, 1941), 489–493; E. P. Alexander, *A Revolutionary Conservative: James Duane of New York* (New York, 1938), 144–145.

8. To take up these claims in order:
    1) Having proposed a "continental conference" to frame a "Continental Charter" in *Common Sense* (1776), Paine then took "the opportunity of renewing"

his "hint" in a pamphlet published December 30, 1780. He must therefore certainly be given credit for getting into print with the first general proposal to replace the Articles of Confederation with a more suitable plan of government. P. S. Foner, ed., *The Complete Writings of Thomas Paine* (New York, 1945), I, 28–29; II, 332.

2) Rutledge wrote to R. R. Livingston in August, 1776, when the Articles of Confederation were being framed, that a "special Congress to be composed of new Members" ought to frame a charter for the United States. *Letters*, II, 54–56.

3) B. J. Lossing, *The Life and Times of Philip Schuyler* (New York, 1872), II, 432–433, makes an assertion (which is certainly not documented in Schuyler's papers) of his early influence on Hamilton in this and other matters. Schuyler wrote to Washington Jan. 21, 1781 that the "Eastern States" should "join in a Convention" for a number of purposes, one of them "to invest Congress" with "extensive" powers, and made clear that he had already been pressing his views upon colleagues in the New York Senate. Jared Sparks, ed., *Correspondence of the American Revolution* (Boston, 1853), III, 213.

4) Nathanael Greene wrote to Jeremiah Wadsworth from Morristown May 8, 1780 that "many Members of Congress" were so disillusioned with "the present plan of confederation" that a motion would soon be brought in "to call a Convention of the States" with authority "to form a plan of confederation upon such liberal principles as shall give" the national government "powers of general jurisdiction and control over individual States . . . where the general interest is concerned." Knollenberg Collection, Yale University Library. See generally F. V. Greene, *General Greene* (New York, 1893), 308–310; Theodore Thayer, *Nathanael Greene* (New York, 1960), 273.

5) Henry Laurens wrote two letters in 1779, one July 5 to William Livingston proposing "a grand council composed of men renowned for Integrity and Abilities from each state—to take under their consideration the state of the nation," the other October 4 to John Adams proposing "a grand convention" for unstated purposes. *Letters*, IV, 298, 469.

6) John Sullivan, who may or may not have been shown Hamilton's letter, wrote to Meshech Weare Oct. 2, 1780 about the necessity of calling together "a Convention of the Several States to Declare what powers Congress is to possess and to vest them with authority" to coerce recalcitrant states. *Letters*, V, 398. There is no doubt that there was talk of a constitutional convention in and around Congress in 1780.

See also Noah Webster to Madison, Aug. 20, 1804, to James Kent, Oct. 20, 1804, Warfel, *Letters of Noah Webster*, 255–256, 257–262; Peletiah Webster, *A Dissertation on the Political Union and Constitution of the Thirteen United States* (Philadelphia, 1783).

There may, of course, be other and earlier proposals for a constitutional convention hidden away in the mass of unpublished papers stored in our universities, historical societies, and state and federal archives, but I was unable to find any that antedated those of Hamilton and Paine.

9. Burnett, *Continental Congress,* 487–488. See Charles Warren, *The Making of the Constitution* (Boston, 1928), 6–15, for a review of the major proposals for a convention in the years 1780–1786. For glimpses of Hamilton's concern in his private letters, see *Papers,* I, 425–426; II, 422, 472; III, 108, 292, 462. It must be remembered that the other twelve states had to wait two full years for stubborn Maryland to ratify the Articles of Confederation March 1, 1781. See *Journals,* IX, 932–935; XIII, 150, 186–188, 236; XIX, 138–139, 186, 208–214.

10. To Washington, Feb. 13, 1783, *Papers,* III, 253, 254.

11. For his case against the Articles of Confederation, in his opinion a prize example of "constitutional imbecility," see *Papers,* II, 400–418, 649–652, 654–657, 660–665, 669–674; III, 75–82, 99–106, 110–113, 268–274, 420–430; V, 16–23, 43–45, 52–54; *Works,* III, 31; IX, 3–5; *Federalist,* 105–152.

12. He was elected to the delegation July 22, 1782, commissioned by Governor Clinton October 25, took his seat November 25, was appointed to his first committee November 26, and was active until July, 1783. *Journals,* XXIII, 750, 757; XXIV, 369, 422, 440; V, 623; *Papers,* III, 117, 188, 198–430.

13. *Papers,* III, 245–247, 252–253, 261–262, 401–402, 420–426, 410–411, 399–400, 397–398, 403–407; *Journals,* XXIII, 855–856; XXV, 848, 868–869, 870, 872, 884–885, 901, 902–903, 906, 907, 910, 919, 932, 937, 952. S. F. Bemis, *The Diplomacy of the American Revolution* (New York, 1935), 167, gives Hamilton much credit for the "anti-entanglement" resolution of June 12, 1783 (*Journals,* XXIV, 394), which was a forerunner of Washington's foreign policy in the 1790's.

14. *Journals,* XXIII, 745, 748, 759–760, 761, 783–784, 786, 789, 790, 797, 811, 821, 825, 836, 838, 875, 882; XXIV, 3, 37, 45, 93, 95, 106, 116, 140, 145, 153, 170, 181, 188, 190, 203, 230, 277, 283, 334, 383, 405, 416; XXV, 613, 714, 722, 911, 916, 986; *Papers,* III, 378–397.

15. *Journals,* XXIV, 38, 45, 46, 95, 117, 142, 170, 192, 209, 212, 230, 242, 254, 264, 267, 274, 306, 312, 321, 322, 326, 334–335, 383, 403, 413, 415, 421; XXV, 722–744 (his sensible and yet, for that time, much too daring proposals for a peacetime army).

16. *Journals,* XXIII, 783–784, 811, 818, 868; XXIV, 140, 201, 313–315, 371, 411 ff., 422; XXV, 901, 907, 919; *Papers,* III, 264, 283.

17. Brant, *Madison,* II, chaps. 25–26.

18. *Journals,* XXIV, 422 ff.

19. 1779? 1780?, *Papers,* II, 234–251, a letter thought by some historians to have been written to General John Sullivan. See Miller, *Hamilton,* 52–56, for the case for Schuyler; Mitchell, *Hamilton,* I, 190, for the case for Morris; Schachner, *Hamilton,* 97–98, for the case for Sullivan; *Papers,* II, 234–236, for a review of the whole problem.

20. April 30, 1781, *Papers,* II, 604–635. See also Washington's letter to Joseph Reed of May 28, 1780 (Fitzpatrick, XVIII, 434–440), which Mitchell, *Hamilton,* I, 186, 552, ascribes largely to Hamilton. The editor of *Papers,* II, 331, seems to disagree, since the letter is simply calendared, and Douglas S. Freeman, *George Washington* (New York, 1948–1954), V, 166–167, treats it as entirely Washington's.

21. *New York Packet,* July 12, 19, Aug. 9, 30, 1781; April 18, July 4, 1782, in *Papers,* II, 649, 654, 660, 669; III, 75, 99. In these six papers he developed many of the themes about human nature, political energy, and federalism that he was to dwell upon six years later in *The Federalist.*

22. July 20, 21, 1782, in *Papers,* III, 74, 110–113, 115. For the politics of this resolution, which was adopted unanimously by both houses, see Schachner, *Hamilton,* 148–149.

23. *Papers,* II, 630.

24. *Journals,* XXV, 952; *Papers,* III, 314.

25. *Journals,* XXIV, 285; XXV, 532.

26. *Papers,* III, 420–426.

27. See, for example, his "notes for argument" in the Rutgers case, in A. M. Hamilton, 461. Evidence of the "nationalizing" influence of his argument in this case (in behalf of the supremacy of a law or treaty of Congress over state laws) can be found in a letter of Jefferson to John Adams, Feb. 23, 1787, *Jefferson* (Lipscomb), VI, 98, as well as in resolutions of Congress, March 21, 1787, and a circular letter of April 13, 1787, in *Journals,* XXXII, 124–125, 177–184.

28. McHenry to Hamilton, Oct. 22, 1783, *Papers,* III, 472, who "recollected with pleasure" Hamilton's "homilies" in Congress.

29. Otis, *Eulogy,* 560.

30. Tansill, 38; *Papers,* III, 665–666.

31. *Works,* I, 335–339; Tansill, 39–43; *Papers,* III, 686–689; Brant, *Madison,* II, chap. 24; Mitchell, *Hamilton,* I, chap. 22.

32. *Journals,* XXXII, 71–74; Tansill, 44–46.

33. *Papers,* IV, 1–153.

34. *Journal of the Assembly of the State of New York,* 10th sess. (New York, 1787), 20–21, 55, 68, 71, 82–84, 166, 171; *Journal of the Senate of the State*

of New York, 10th sess. (New York, 1787), 35, 44–45; *Papers,* IV, 93, 101, 108, 147.

35. John A. Krout, "Alexander Hamilton's Place in the Founding of the Nation," *Proceedings of the American Philosophical Society,* CII (1958), 124, 125. See the balanced opinion of Madison in a letter to Noah Webster, Oct. 12, 1804, *Madison* (Hunt), VII, 162–167.

36. Robert Troup to Timothy Pickering, March 17, 1828, Hamilton Papers, L of C.

37. These events are described in detail by Jensen, *The New Nation,* chap. 3. For a fresh perspective on Jensen, and indeed on the whole problem of the historiography of the 1780's, see Stanley Elkins and Eric McKitrick, "The Founding Fathers: Young Men of the Revolution," *PSQ,* LXXVI (1961), 181.

38. Works, II, 192–223. The importance Hamilton attached to this one act (as a stimulus to the calling of a "general convention") is plain in the letter from Robert Troup to Timothy Pickering, March 17, 1828, Hamilton Papers, L of C. For the details of the long struggle in New York over this measure, see C. E. Miner, *The Ratification of the Federal Constitution by the State of New York* (New York, 1921), 16–39; Spaulding, *New York in the Critical Period,* 171, 176–180.

39. To Charles Thomson, April 7, 1784, *Jay,* III, 125.

40. To John Jay, Jan. 10, 1784, Jared Sparks, *The Life of Gouverneur Morris* (Boston, 1832), I, 266–267.

41. Farrand, III, 89.

42. Still the most useful guides through the maze (more apparent than real) of the Convention are Max Farrand, *The Framing of the Constitution of the United States* (New Haven, 1913), and Warren, *Making of the Constitution.* For the documentary history of Hamilton's participation, see *Papers,* IV, 158–274.

43. See the noncommittal message with which Clinton passed on the Congressional resolution of Feb. 21, 1787 to the legislature, in C. Z. Lincoln, ed., *Messages from the Governors* (Albany, 1909), II, 270.

44. For two rare (and meaningless) occasions on which Yates and Lansing differed, and on which Hamilton therefore found himself in a majority, see J. R. Strayer, ed., *The Delegate from New York* (Princeton, 1939), 77, 83, the note-taking delegate in this instance being Lansing. The notes of Yates are, of course, hardly less important for the period of his attendance than are those of Madison. Hamilton's own sketchy notes were brought together and published in *American Historical Review,* X (1904), 97–109, and may now be found in *Papers,* IV, 161–176.

45. Tansill, 59–60; *Journal of Assembly* (1787), 84.

46. Strayer, *Delegate from New York,* 85, in which Lansing records Hamilton as favoring a nine-year term for the upper house.

47. *Papers,* IV, 192, 193, 199–200; Farrand, I, 288, 289, 299, 300.

48. Farrand, I, 2, 4, 6; Strayer, *Delegate from New York,* 22, 22 n.

49. Farrand, I, 27, 31 (36), 85, 94 (98, 107), 95 (104), 107, 128, 193 (202), 241.

50. Farrand, I, 246.

51. *Works,* I, 381–403; Farrand, I, 282–304; *Papers,* IV, 187–207; Strayer, *Delegate from New York,* 61–68. His notes for this speech are in *Works,* I, 370–378; Farrand, I, 304–311; *Papers,* IV, 178–187.

52. *History,* III, 283–284.

53. *Works,* I, 347–350; *Papers,* IV, 207–211; Farrand, I, 291–293 (300–301); III, 426, 434–435, 524, 533–534, 551, 617–619; Tansill, 979–988, which, with Strayer, *Delegate from New York,* 119–122, gives us six separate but (in all important essentials) similar versions of Hamilton's plan. See generally Mitchell, *Hamilton,* I, 625; J. F. Jameson, "Studies in the History of the Federal Convention of 1787," in *Annual Report of the American Historical Association* (1902), I, 143–150, who discusses two additional versions.

54. Hamilton's subsequent public defense of this rule (Sept. 11, 1792) is in *Works,* VII, 246.

55. Evidence that Hamilton liked to think of this plan as a trial balloon in later years can be found in the editorial of the *New York Evening Post,* Feb. 24, 1802. And see also the record of a conversation between Rufus King and Thomas Hart Benton in 1824, in Benton, *Thirty Years' View* (New York, 1866), I, 58, in which King seems to have convinced his young friend from Missouri that Hamilton's plan was "offered for consideration, and to bring about opinions," and "ought not to be quoted" against him.

56. Farrand, I, 355 (363, 366).

57. Farrand, I, 463 (471); W. T. Read, *Life and Correspondence of George Read* (Philadelphia, 1870), 453–454. It is possible that Rufus King, who is said to have been much influenced by Hamilton in the Convention, would have agreed with Read. See his letter of July 11 to Henry Knox in which he wished he "had returned to New York with . . . our very able and segacious Friend Hamilton." Farrand, IV, 68.

58. An exact rendering of Hamilton's plan, which may well have been communicated to the printer by Yates or Lansing, was published in *Propositions of Colonel Hamilton, of New-York, in the Convention for establishing a Constitutional Government for the United States* (Pittsfield, Mass., 1802), 3–5, in which he is accused of having pointed all his subsequent "measures" toward achieving the goal of "limited Monarchy" thus marked out in 1787.

59. Farrand, I, 463 (471).

60. *Papers,* IV, 220–221; Farrand, I, 465–467, 472–474, 477, 479.

61. Strayer, *Delegate from New York,* 96.

62. *Papers,* IV, 223–225; Farrand, III, 53–54.

63. July 10, 1787, Fitzpatrick, XXIX, 246; Farrand, III, 56–57.

64. (New York) *Daily Advertiser,* July 21, 1787; *Papers,* IV, 229–232.

65. Strayer, *Delegate from New York,* 107 n. See their undated letter of explanation to Governor Clinton in Farrand, III, 244–247.

66. Farrand, II, 265 (268); to King, Aug. 20, 28, 1787, *Papers,* IV, 235, 238.

67. Hamilton's attendance record may be found summarized in Farrand, III, 588. Manasseh Cutler, then on the road lobbying for the Ohio Company, noted that Hamilton was in Philadelphia July 13, but there is no evidence that Hamilton attended the Convention on that day. Cutler, *Life, Journals, and Correspondence* (Cincinnati, 1888), I, 254.

68. And yet not so moderate as to abandon the "advanced" notions of a general legislative authority in Congress and a veto of state laws by governors "appointed under the authority of the United States." *Works,* I, 350–369; Farrand, III, 619–630; *Papers,* IV, 253–274.

69. Farrand, II, 524-525 (530–531), 553, 558 (559), 560 (562, 563), 585, 645, 665.

70. Farrand, II, 547, 553, 554.

71. *Papers,* IV, 253; Farrand, II, 645–646. See also his statement of September 6, as recorded by James McHenry: "He does not agree with those persons who say they will vote against the report because they cannot get all parts of it to please them—He will take any system which promises to save America from the dangers with which she is threatened." Farrand, II, 530–531. Madison's tribute of 1831 to Hamilton's capacity for compromise in this moment of crisis is recorded in *Madison* (Hunt), IX, 454.

72. *Works,* I, 418; Farrand, II, 553; *Papers,* IV, 244, 274.

73. On Hamilton's failure to contribute much of anything to Article II, see C. C. Thach, *The Creation of the Presidency, 1775–1789* (Baltimore, 1922), 92–94, 120. On his possible influence over the final outlines of the treaty-making power, see W. S. Holt, *Treaties Defeated by the Senate* (Baltimore, 1933), 3.

74. Farrand, I, 31 (36), 85, 94 (98, 107), 128, 193 (202), 323–325 (328, 329), 358–359 (364), 362 (366, 368), 376 (381–382), 390 (394), 434–435, 452; II, 268, 524–525 (530–531), 553, 558, 559, 560, 562, 563.

75. John P. Roche, "The Founding Fathers: A Reform Caucus in Action," *APSR*, LV (1961), 799.

76. Smith, *James Wilson*, 233, 234, who also suggests that Hamilton's speech of June 18 may have helped in an odd way to win acceptance for the Virginia Plan by making it appear a kind of "middle ground" between the two possible extremes of confederation and consolidation. See Brant, *Madison*, III, 156–158, and Farrand, *Framing of the Constitution*, 196 ff., for judicious attempts to give the proper amount of applause to each of the notable Framers.

77. To Robert Walsh, Feb. 5, 1811, Farrand, III, 418; Sparks, *Life of Gouverneur Morris*, III, 260; Anne C. Morris, ed., *The Diary and Letters of Gouverneur Morris* (New York, 1888), II, 523, an altogether fascinating letter about Hamilton's opinions and contributions.

78. (New York) *Daily Advertiser*, July 29, 1788; *Journals*, XXXIV, 378 n.

79. To Madison, April 3, 1788, *Papers*, IV, 644.

80. E. W. Spaulding, *His Excellency George Clinton* (New York, 1938) is especially useful for its balanced espousal of Clinton's side in the many battles the Governor fought with Hamilton.

81. March 4, 1825, Resolution of Board of Visitors of the University of Virginia on "Political Science," Saul K. Padover, ed., *The Complete Jefferson* (New York, 1943), 1112. The College of Rhode Island (Brown) was using *The Federalist* as a standard text well before 1810. *The Works of Alexander Hamilton* (New York, 1810), I, v n.

82. A bouquet of early appeals to *The Federalist* (some of them in flat opposition to Hamilton's programs and interpretations as Secretary of the Treasury) may be found in *Annals*, I, 474; II, 1941; *Madison* (Hunt), VI, 151; Otis, *Eulogy*, 561; Brant, *Madison*, III, 259, 378; Miller, *Federalist Era*, 181 n.; *Penhallow* v. *Doane*, 3 Dallas 54, 67 (1795); *Calder* v. *Bull*, 3 Dallas 386, 391 (1798), in which Justice Chase saluted Publius as a lawyer "superior" to Blackstone for "his extensive and accurate knowledge of the true principles of government." For examples of Hamilton's own use of *The Federalist*, see *Works*, VI, 186; VIII, 337.

83. The first foreign publication of *The Federalist*—and also the first anywhere after the McLean edition of 1788—was in Paris in 1792. An outstanding foreign interpretation of *The Federalist*, in which Hamilton looms almost larger than life, is A. Garosci, *Il Pensiero Politico degli Autori del "Federalist"* (Milan, 1954). Richard Rush quotes the French historian Guizot as having told him in 1849 that *The Federalist* was "the greatest work known to him" in the "application of elementary principles of government to practical administration." Note in Rush's hand at end of copy of vol. II of Hamilton's *Works* (1810) in the Boston University Library.

84. Aug. 28, 1788, Fitzpatrick, XXX, 66. See also his opinions in Fitzpatrick, XXIX, 308, 323–324, 331, 404, 407, 466. For letters of Hamilton to Washington and Madison during this period (and concerning *The Federalist*), see *Papers,* IV, 306–307, 644, 649–650; V, 2–4, 10, 35, 91, 140–141, 147–148, 177–178, 201–202.

85. For evidence on this point, see Madison's letter to Jefferson, Aug. 10, 1788, *Madison* (Hunt), V, 246.

86. For years it has been assumed that Hamilton fired two ranging shots October 1 and 17 in the (New York) *Daily Advertiser* under the pseudonym of Caesar, but Jacob E. Cooke and Frederick Mosteller, each in his own way, have proved beyond a doubt that no shred of evidence exists for attributing these two peppery pieces to Hamilton. See p. 316, n. 36 of this book.

A useful guide to the literary war in New York is Miner, *Ratification of the Constitution by New York,* chap. 3. Of particular importance were the letters of George Clinton (only thinly disguised as Cato) in the *New-York Journal,* Sept. 27, Oct. 11, 25, Nov. 8, 22, Dec. 16, 1787, and Jan. 3, 1788, reprinted in P. L. Ford, ed., *Essays on the Constitution* (Brooklyn, 1892), 245–278.

87. Other men who were asked to help were Gouverneur Morris, William Duer, and perhaps James Duane. Mitchell, *Hamilton,* I, 415–416, 631; *Papers,* IV, 288.

88. Among them Washington, who was informed cryptically by Madison in a letter of Nov. 18, 1787, *Madison* (Hunt), V, 55, and directly by Hamilton in a letter of Aug. 13, 1788, *Papers,* V, 201; and Jefferson, who got the word from Madison in a ciphered letter of Aug. 10, 1788, *Madison* (Hunt), V, 246.

89. (Philadelphia) *Freeman's Journal,* Jan. 30, 1788. See also (Edenton) *North-Carolina Gazette,* Dec. 19, 1787, in which "an old Spy" confesses that "the sublime reasonings" of "Hamlinton" and several other Federalists "seem to bear down the lame arguments of their opposers"; S. B. Webb to Joseph Barrell, Jan. 13, 1788, to Miss Hogeboom, June 26, 1788, W. C. Ford, ed., *Correspondence and Journals of Samuel Blachley Webb* (New York, 1893–1894), III, 90, 108, which gives full credit for *The Federalist* to Hamilton.

90. For the exact dates and vehicles of publication, see Jacob E. Cooke, ed., *The Federalist* (Middletown, Conn., 1961), xiii–xv, and the footnote to each paper, and for a mass of definitive information on *The Federalist,* see *Papers,* IV, 287–301.

91. Monaghan, *Jay,* 290. Jay must be given credit for his persuasive pamphlet *An Address to the People of the State of New York* (New York, 1788), reprinted in *Jay,* III, 294–319.

92. Brant, *Madison,* III, 161, 170, 185.

93. New York Evening Post, March 25, 1817; H. B. Dawson, ed., *The Foederalist* (New York, 1863), xxvii; Mitchell, *Hamilton,* I, 419–420; *Papers,* IV, 295–296, which finds this list "suspect." In *Port Folio* (Philadelphia),

Nov. 14, 1807, there appeared yet another list, which was said to have been found by the executors of Hamilton's will in his own copy of *The Federalist* and placed in the New York Public Library. Its assignment of the various papers was identical with the so-called "Benson list" published by Dawson. This is not true, however, of still a third list, which was placed by James Kent in his own copy of *The Federalist,* now in the Columbia University Library.

On this whole difficult question, which unreconstructed partisans will doubtless be arguing about for centuries to come, see Douglass Adair, "The Authorship of the Disputed *Federalist Papers*," *WMQ,* 3rd ser., I (1944), 97, 235; Cooke, ed., *The Federalist,* xix–xxx, 601–606; the works by Lodge, P. L. Ford, J. C. Hamilton, Dawson, and Baily cited by Cooke at pp. 601, 606; E. G. Bourne, "The Authorship of the *Federalist*," *AHR,* II (1897), 443, on whom Adair drew heavily in making his case; B. F. Wright, ed., *The Federalist* (Cambridge, Mass., 1961), 8–10; Mitchell, *Hamilton,* I, 418–420; Brant, *Madison,* III, 183–184. For an overly optimistic attempt to bury this controversy forever, see Brant's note in *AHR,* LXVII (1961), 71. That the controversy will continue is plain in the reserved judgments of the editors of *Papers,* IV, 292–301. Indeed, so reserved are their judgments that they still cannot bring themselves to give number 51 to Madison with no strings attached! *Papers,* IV, 497.

Perhaps I in my turn am being overly pessimistic—now that the machine has been asked to resolve this squabble among men. In any case, I find Frederick Mosteller and David L. Wallace, "Inference in an Authorship Problem," a paper delivered Sept. 9, 1962 at the statistical meetings in Minneapolis, altogether convincing in its support of the Bourne-Adair conclusions. The Mosteller-Wallace method of feeding "marker" words and "color" words from the disputed papers into a computer along with large chunks of the established writings of each man is a hard one to fault, even by scholars who are terrified by the sight of a computer.

94. Wolcott to Hamilton, April 4, 1800, Hamilton Papers, L of C, in which Wolcott pressed Hamilton to reveal "whether any and if any which of the numbers of *Publius* were written by Mr. Madison"; Hamilton to Wolcott, April 7, 1800, Wolcott Papers, Connecticut Historical Society, in which Hamilton refuses and adds: "You will be sensible that I ought to be peculiarly circumspect with regard to this Gentleman."

95. For the extreme view of its influence on the struggle over ratification, see Charles Warren, *Congress, the Constitution, and the Supreme Court* (Boston, 1925), 8.

96. June 14, 1789, *The Journal of William Maclay* (New York, 1927), 73–74, to which might be added the comment of the (Springfield, Mass.) *Hampshire Chronicle,* Dec. 25, 1787, that Publius was a match for John Trotter, "a Scotch preacher who was as remarkable for the length of his sermons as for their insignificance."

97. The reprinting of the first few numbers in Richmond seems to have been done at the suggestion of Washington, who in his turn had been spurred into action by Madison. Madison to Washington, Nov. 18, 1787, *Madison* (Hunt), V, 53–55; Washington to David Stuart, Nov. 30, 1787, and to Madison, Dec. 7, 1787, Fitzpatrick, XXIX, 323–324, 331.

98. Hamilton to Madison, May 11, 19, June 8, 1788, *Papers,* IV, 648, 649; V, 3; Kent, 302. A letter of Charles Thomson to James McHenry, April 19, 1788, McHenry Papers, L of C, makes clear that at least a few men of influence were rushing copies of *The Federalist* to friends of the Constitution in other states.

99. See especially A. T. Mason, "The Federalist—A Split Personality," *AHR,* LVII (1952), 625, who preaches persuasively, as do all exponents of this point of view, from a text by John Quincy Adams, *An Eulogy on the Life and Character of James Madison* (Boston, 1836), 31–32. It is interesting to note that at a key point in his argument (pp. 635–636) Mason takes the Hamilton of June 18, 1787, off the bench and sends him in as a substitute for the Hamilton of *The Federalist.* Another example worth noting is Herbert W. Schneider, *A History of American Philosophy* (New York, 1946), 89–99.

100. Not to mention "sophistry" and, in the case of Madison, something "perilously near to falsehood." W. W. Crosskey, *Politics and the Constitution* (Chicago, 1953), I, 8–11, 220–221, 509 n.; II, 711–712. I am bound to say that the malice Crosskey bears toward Madison conspires with his assumption that the Framers knew exactly what they were doing to blur the essential message (and to mock the prodigious researches) of these volumes.

101. Jefferson was one of the first to see that Publius was not happy with every detail of the new Constitution. Writing to Madison from Paris Nov. 18, 1788, he noted that "in some parts . . . the author means only to say what may best be said in defense of opinions, in which he did not concur." *Jefferson* (Lipscomb), VII, 183.

102. *Papers,* IV, 275–277.

103. *Papers,* IV, 281.

104. To Washington, Oct. 30, 1787, *Papers,* IV, 306.

105. *Journals,* XXXIII, 549. Nine men who had just signed the Constitution, including Madison and King, were among those resolving unanimously to submit the Constitution to the states and ultimately to the people. That the unanimous vote was a small tour de force is evident in the only other recorded vote on this issue, which is at p. 542.

106. Elliot, II, 205–206.

107. (New York) *Daily Advertiser,* June 3, 4, 6, 7, 14, 1788; *New-York Journal,* June 5, 1788; Spaulding, *New York in the Critical Period,* 203; Kent,

303; O. G. Libby, *The Geographical Distribution of the Vote of the Thirteen States on the Federal Constitution* (Madison, 1894), 18–26, 80–82, 114, whose figures are for the final vote in the Convention rather than the election of delegates.

108. June 8, 1788, *Papers,* V, 3.

109. June 19, 1788, *Papers,* V, 10.

110. Hughes to John Lamb, June 17, 1788, Lamb Papers, NYHS. One day later Hughes wrote to Lamb that the "well born" leaders of the Federalists were feeling out of place in the Convention.

111. Clinton to John Lamb, June 28, 1788, Lamb Papers, NYHS; Hamilton to Madison, June 25, 27, 1788, *Papers,* V, 80, 91.

112. The best studies of this Convention are Spaulding, *New York in the Critical Period,* chaps. 11–14; Mitchell, *Hamilton,* I, chaps. 26–27; Miner, *Ratification by New York,* chaps. 4–5; George Dangerfield, *Chancellor Robert R. Livingston* (New York, 1960), 219–233, who goes too far, in my opinion, in treating the whole course of events at Poughkeepsie as a "pre-determined event" that could have had only one possible outcome; and Jackson T. Main, *The Antifederalists* (Chapel Hill, 1961), 233–242, who gives Hamilton too little credit.

113. To John Lamb, June 21, 1788, Lamb Papers, NYHS.

114. June 21, 1788, Elliot, II, 262.

115. Elliot, II, 216, 222; *Papers,* V, 13. The original copy of this resolution in the New-York Historical Society is, significantly, in the hands of both Livingston and Hamilton.

116. The most important are: 1) the stenographic report taken by Francis Childs, published as *The Debates and Proceedings of the Constitutional Convention . . . Assembled at Poughkeepsie* (New York, 1788), reprinted in Elliot, II, 205–414, which is excellent up until July 4, when Childs seems to have run out of steam (or had a big night from which he never recovered); 2) *Journal of the Convention of the State of New-York* (Poughkeepsie, 1788), which gives some of the motions and votes and all the official documents; 3) the newspapers of New York, Poughkeepsie, and other towns and cities, the most useful of which is the (New York) *Daily Advertiser;* 4) some official records and also notes assembled by John McKesson, a secretary at the Convention, which are in the New-York Historical Society; 5) some notes kept by R. R. and Gilbert Livingston, which are in the New-York Historical Society and New York Public Library respectively; and 6) some notes of Melancton Smith in the New York State Library. Most of these sources have now been assembled in *Papers,* V, 11–198.

117. Kent, 306.

118. See especially the peroration of his splendid speech of June 28, *Papers*, V, 124–125; Elliot, II, 370–371.

119. Lamb Papers, NYHS.

120. S. B. Webb to Joseph Barrell, July 1, 1788, *Correspondence of Webb*, III, 109.

121. Elliot, II, 207.

122. Elliot, II, 222.

123. Elliot, II, 356–360; *Papers*, V, 112–113.

124. Elliot, II, 376; *Papers*, V, 135–139; (New York) *Daily Advertiser*, July 4, 1788; (Philadelphia) *Pennsylvania Packet*, July 12, 1788.

125. (Annapolis) *Maryland Gazette*, July 17, 1788.

126. Hamilton to Washington, Oct. 11–15, 1787, *Papers*, IV, 248–253, 280–281, 284–285; *New-York Journal*, Sept. 20, 1787; (New York) *Daily Advertiser*, Sept. 15, 1787.

127. Oct. 18, 1787, Fitzpatrick, XXIX, 290–291.

128. *New York Packet*, July 8, 1788; *Country Journal and Poughkeepsie Advertiser*, July 8, 1788; *New-York Journal*, July 11, 1788; Jay to Mrs. Jay, July 5, 1788, *Jay*, III, 347–348.

129. *Works*, II, 3–91; *Papers*, V, 16 ff.; Elliot, II, 230–239, 251–259, 300–307, 315–321, 347–356, 360–371.

130. (Portsmouth) *New-Hampshire Spy*, July 5, 1788. The Convention at Poughkeepsie was surprisingly well reported in the press of other states, and much was made of the ability of "Col. Hamilton" to "draw tears" from "the audience" with his "eloquent and pathetic" arguments. *Norwich Packet*, July 31, 1788.

131. The opposite view on this last point is well (if not sympathetically) stated in Cecelia Kenyon, "Men of Little Faith," *WMQ*, 3rd ser., XII (1955), 3.

132. *An Oration. Commemorative of the Late Major-General Alexander Hamilton* (1804), reprinted in Coleman, 265.

133. Elliot, II, 321.

134. To John Lamb, June 21, 1788, Lamb Papers, NYHS.

135. Elliot, II, 322, 324; *Papers*, V, 34–35.

136. See his letters to Madison and to John Sullivan of New Hampshire, May 19, June 6, 8, 19, 1788, *Papers*, IV, 649; V, 2, 3, 10, as well as the exchange between Rufus King and John Langdon, June 4, 10, 21, 1788, King Papers, NYHS.

137. *Country Journal and Poughkeepsie Advertiser,* July 8, 1788; De Witt Clinton to Charles Tillinghast, July 2, 1788, Lamb Papers, NYHS.

138. Hamilton to Madison, June 8, 1788, *Papers,* V, 3; Abraham Yates to Abraham Lansing, May 28, 1788, Yates Papers, NYPL; G. Livingston, Notes on Debates, NYPL; *Papers,* V, 175–176; S. B. Webb to Miss Hogeboom, June 26, July 6, 13, 1788, *Correspondence of Webb,* III, 108, 111; Jay to Washington, May 29, 1788, *Jay,* III, 335; George Mason to John Mason, Sept. 2, 1788, Kate Mason Rowland, *The Life of George Mason* (New York, 1892), II, 299, 301.

139. Hamilton to Madison, July 2, 8, 1788, *Papers,* V, 140–141, 147.

140. *Journal of the Convention,* 42 ff.

141. See especially the notes on a speech of July 12 in the Melancton Smith Papers: "Mr. Hamilton," according to Smith, "rises with reluctance . . . because he wishes to conciliate." *Papers,* V, 159.

142. July 8, 19, 1788, *Papers,* V, 147–148.

143. July 20, 1788, *Papers,* V, 184–185. Hamilton read this letter on the floor July 24. *Papers,* V, 193.

144. (New York) *Daily Advertiser,* July 16, 1788; *New-York Journal,* July 17, 1788; *Papers,* V, 156–158.

145. *Journal of the Convention,* 37–39; *Papers,* V, 171–172.

146. "Upon the whole," Hamilton wrote Madison July 22, "our fears diminish." *Papers,* V, 187.

147. Elliot, II, 412.

148. Elliot, II, 412; *Journal of the Convention,* 70.

149. Elliot, II, 413. See the map and table in Spaulding, *New York in the Critical Period,* 282, 285–287. The vote of Jesse Woodhull of Orange County is wrongly recorded as opposed to ratification.

150. The declaration of rights may be found in *Journal of the Convention,* 71–74, the amendments in *Journal of the Convention,* 78–82, the circular letter in Elliot, II, 413–414. See also Tansill, 1034–1044.

151. Fitzpatrick, XXX, 63, 66, 96; *Madison* (Hunt), V, 244, 249–250, 253–254, 256, 264.

152. E. P. Smith, "The Movement toward a Second Constitutional Convention," in J. F. Jameson, ed., *Essays in the Constitutional History of the United States* (Boston, 1889), 46–115.

153. *Journals,* XXXIV, 56; *Papers,* IV, 492–493.

154. (Portsmouth) *New Hampshire Spy,* Aug. 12, 1788; Jonathan Patterson to James Duane, Sept. 22, 1788, Duane Papers, NYHS.

155. Journal of the Convention, 77–78; *Country Journal and Poughkeepsie Advertiser,* July 26, 1788.

156. For some of the high points of his service, see *Journals,* XXXIV, 383–388, 393, 397–399, 403–404, 415–417, 452, 456–458, 482–484, 502 n., 521–523, 527, 534–535.

CHAPTER THREE   **HAMILTON AND THE CONSTITUTION: 1789–1804**

1. On this point, see generally Charles A. Beard, *Economic Origins of Jeffersonian Democracy* (New York, 1915), 85 ff.; Hammond, *Banks and Politics,* 120, who points out that the Constitution "had not displaced rival principles or reconciled them but had become their dialectical arena"; Robert L. Schuyler, *The Constitution of the United States* (New York, 1923), chap. 5; Edward Elliott, *Biographical Story of the Constitution* (New York, 1910), 30–31; John A. Krout, "Hamilton's Contribution to the Constitution," *Outlook,* Feb. 16, 1927.

2. Papers, V, 201–202, 220–222, 225–226, 230–231, 233–234, 235–237; Fitzpatrick, XXX, 65–67, 109–112. The efforts of Madison's friends to have him elected to the Senate had been thwarted by Patrick Henry's vengeance. Brant, *Madison,* III, 236–242.

3. Journals, XXXIV, 522–523, a resolution on which Hamilton and Madison had the satisfaction of voting "aye."

4. Annals, I, 16–18, 25–29, 101–102; Freeman, *Washington,* VI, 163–166, 177–184, 187–198.

5. Annals, I, 106 ff.

6. Freeman, *Washington,* VI, 201–202. Hamilton's written opinion of May 5, 1789 on this matter is in *Papers,* V, 335–338, as is Washington's note of thanks in which he begs Hamilton to "permit" him to "entreat a continuation" of this kind of advice "as occasions may arise."

7. The New York Directory, and Register, for the Year 1789 (New York, 1789); I. N. Phelps Stokes, *The Iconography of Manhattan Island* (New York, 1915–1928), V, 1237, 1238, 1252; Mitchell, *Hamilton,* I, 332, 603; Brant, *Madison,* III, 246; Freeman, *Washington,* VI, 185, 189–196, 252–253.

8. John Quincy Adams asserted in 1819 that the Treasury Act of 1789 "was drawn up by A. Hamilton, who was himself to be the Secretary," but there is no substantial evidence to support this altogether logical judgment. See H. B. Learned, *The President's Cabinet* (New Haven, 1911), 109.

9. Brant, *Madison*, III, chaps. 19–22.

10. Annals, I, 2034–2035, 2183–2187, 2214–2215, 2231–2233, 2239–2255; I *Stat.*, 24–27, 27–28, 28–29, 49–50, 65–67, 73–93; Tansill, 1063–1065.

11. Annals, I, 383–392, 473–608, 614, 400–412.

12. G. A. Boyd, *Elias Boudinot* (Princeton, 1952), 168 ff., which makes clear that Hamilton must have had something to do with the drafting of the Treasury Act. In later years, Albert Gallatin wondered pointedly, in a note to Jefferson dated Nov., 1801, whether the laws setting up the Treasury Department had not been written purposefully and cleverly "in order to give Mr. Hamilton a department independent" of both executive and legislative "control." *Gallatin*, I, 67.

13. Miller, *Federalist Era*, 18; Brant, *Madison*, III, 246–254.

14. Madison to Jefferson, May 27, 1789, *Madison* (Hunt), V, 371 n.

15. Christopher Gore to Hamilton, Sept. 20, 1789, *Papers*, V, 392.

16. E. P. Oberholtzer, *Robert Morris* (New York, 1903), 237; W. G. Sumner, *The Financier and Finances of the American Revolution* (New York, 1891), II, 204, 209–210; *History*, IV, 29–31.

17. Even earlier than that, if the memory of his old friend (and college room-mate) Robert Troup can be trusted. "Washington," he wrote to Timothy Picker-ing March 31, 1828, "immediately after becoming President . . . and before Congress had passed a single act, called on Hamilton and told him it was his in-tention to nominate him in charge of the financial department of the Govern-ment, as soon as that department should be organized." Hamilton Papers, L of C. See also William Smith to Otho Williams, July 7, 1789, Williams Papers, Mary-land Historical Society ("Col Hamilton is spoke of . . . to fill the Secretary's office to the treasury"), and Christopher Gore to Rufus King, Sept. 13, 1789, King Papers, NYHS, which reads in part:

What causes the delay of appointing the executive officers? We have been in the expectation of hearing the appointments every post the week past—and such is the celebrity of Col. Hamilton's name in this part of the country that if he is appointed to the office of Secretary of the treasury, it will afford great joy to all.

For evidence of the satisfaction with which Hamilton's appointment was greeted, see McHenry to Hamilton, Oct. 27, 1789, *Papers*, V, 471.

18. Annals, I, 56, 80–81, 643, 2231–2233; *Papers*, V, 365.

19. For evidence of Hamilton's jet-propelled start as Secretary of the Treasury, see *Papers*, V, 366 ff.

20. Annals, I, 939.

21. To Theodore Sedgwick, Jan. 29, 1789, *Papers,* V, 250; Miller, *Hamilton,* 225; Charles Warren, *The Supreme Court in United States History* (Boston, 1947), I, 35.

22. Freeman, *Washington,* VI, 249–250. Washington did examine the report before it went to the House. J. C. Fitzpatrick, ed., *The Diaries of George Washington* (Boston, 1925), IV, 65.

23. Annals, I, 1079–1080.

24. June 25, 1789, *Annals,* I, 615–631.

25. Annals, I, 1080–1081.

26. Annals, I, 1092.

27. See Washington's testimony on this early harmony in his letter to Gouverneur Morris, Oct. 13, 1789, Fitzpatrick, XXX, 442.

28. That Hamilton sought to keep the partnership alive as long as possible is clear in a letter to Madison, Nov. 24, 1791, Univ. of Virginia, in which he asks his old comrade to "peruse" a draft of the Report on Manufactures and then to "converse on the subject of it." "It will not be disagreeable to me," he adds, "if after perusal you hand it over to Mr. Jefferson."

29. Annals, I, 1131–1141, 1169–1224, 1233–1239, 1247 ff., 1323 ff., 1753–1762 (the final votes); Brant, *Madison,* III, chaps. 23–24; Mitchell, *Hamilton,* II, 79–85; Malone, *Jefferson and the Rights of Man,* 297–305, 502. The essence of the "deal" was Hamilton's promise to work for the removal of the capital to Philadelphia and thence to the Potomac in exchange for enough Southern votes to put through the plans for funding and assumption. Madison, be it noted, refused to make one of these votes his own. He stood firm to the end against both funding and assumption, thus bringing down Hamilton's wrath upon him for his "perfidious desertion" of the principles they had shared. For a measurement of the gap that had suddenly opened between them, one may contrast Hamilton's letter to Madison of Oct. 12, 1789, in which he seeks confidential advice on the plans he is drawing up, and his letter to Carrington of May 26, 1792, in which he bewails Madison's "intrigues." *Papers,* V, 439; *Works,* IX, 462–463, 513–535. Most of our knowledge of the "deal" is gleaned from Jefferson's not entirely honest accounts in *Jefferson* (Ford), VI, 172–174, and *Jefferson* (Lipscomb), I, 272 ff.

30. Feb. 9, 1791, *Journal of William Maclay,* 376, as well as the observations on Hamilton's leadership of his "gladiators" at 136, 192, 202–203, 206, 221, 228, 252, 269, 282–283, 302, 321, 390, 392, 397, 400. In the midst of the struggle over assumption, March 8, 1790, Maclay took note of "the rendezvousing of the crew of the Hamilton galley. It seems all hands are piped to quarters."

31. Marshall, *The Life of George Washington* (Philadelphia, 1807), V, 244.

32. Brant, *Madison,* II, 233–234. Hamilton wrote Carrington in 1792 that Madison had agreed with him in 1787 on the "expediency and propriety of such a measure" under the terms of the Constitution they were then engaged in writing. *Works,* IX, 515.

33. Dec. 16, 23, 1790, in W. W. Hening, ed., *Statutes at Large of Virginia* (New York, Richmond, and Philadelphia, 1819–1823), XIII, 237; *Annals,* I, 1915; *ASP, Finance,* I, 90–91. Madison himself laid the Virginia protest before the House without comment.

34. To Thomas Dwight, March 8, 1792, to G. R. Minot, March 8, 1792, *Ames,* I, 114–115.

35. Papers, VI, 77.

36. Works, IX, 473–474. Hamilton must also—as was his habit—have alerted other friends throughout the Union, as one may deduce from a letter of Benjamin Lincoln to Hamilton, Dec. 4, 1790, Hamilton Papers, L of C, in which Lincoln comforts him by observing that the only result of the Virginia protest in Boston was to "confirm the doubtful in the importance of a firm energetic head to the Union, sufficiently strong to control the whole."

37. Nov. 28, 1790, *Jay,* III, 404, 409–411; Warren, *Supreme Court,* I, 52–53.

38. Annals, I, 1763, 1844, 1846–1847.

39. Works, III, 388-443.

40. Annals, I, 1903–1916, 1944–1945.

41. Federalist, 283–286; Brant, *Madison,* III, 330–331.

42. Annals, I, 1951–1952. Small wonder that Hamilton's closest friends now looked upon Madison as "a desperate party leader." Ames to Thomas Dwight, Jan., 1793, *Ames,* I, 126–127.

43. Works, III, 410.

44. Annals, I, 1791, 1922, 1935, 1940 ff., 2012. See the debate touched off by a Quaker memorial on the evils of slavery in the second session of the First Congress, in *Annals,* I, 1224–1233, 1239–1247, 1465–1466, 1500–1526.

45. Randolph's opinion, weak alike in conception and execution, is in Washington Papers, L of C, Letter Book No. 23, dated Feb. 12, 1791. The covering letter mentions "two conversations" on "this subject." Jefferson's opinion, a memorable source of states'-rights constitutionalism, is in *Jefferson* (Ford), V, 284–289.

46. Randolph to Washington, Feb. 12, 1791, Washington Papers, L of C.

47. Feb. 16, 1791, Fitzpatrick, XXXI, 215–216; *Works,* III, 443–444.

48. Printed in part in *Madison* (Hunt), VI, 42–43 n.

49. Works, III, 445–493, the so-called "second copy" in the Hamilton Papers, L of C, which is the best known of eight surviving MS. versions of this famous document. Lodge copied this version from *Works* (JCH), IV, 104–138, which in its turn was taken—with one small and unexplained deletion—either from the 1810 edition of Hamilton's writings or from the undated pamphlet described below, p. 340, n. 63. The editors of *Papers* are printing another version as the "final" copy most likely to have been sent to Washington, but the differences between the two are few and unimportant.

50. Works, III, 455.

51. (Philadelphia) *Gazette of the United States,* Feb. 26, 1791. For other newspaper discussion of the issue, see *New-York Daily Gazette,* Feb. 12, 1791; (Philadelphia) *Dunlap's American Daily Advertiser,* Feb. 16, 22, 1791; (Philadelphia) *Gazette of the United States,* Feb. 9, 23, 1791.

52. The Politicks and Views of a Certain Party, Displayed (1792), 18–20, a pamphlet so eloquently Hamiltonian in its defense of the Washington administration and its attack on Jefferson that it has occasionally been attributed to Hamilton himself. On Smith's association with Hamilton, see G. C. Rogers, *Evolution of a Federalist: William Loughton Smith of Charleston* (Columbia, S.C., 1962), esp. chaps. 11–12.

53. Works, III, 488.

54. Hamilton's proposal for such a tax, dated Dec. 13, 1790, is in *Works,* II, 337–351; the text of the act is in *Annals,* I, 2384–2405; I *Stat.,* 199–214; the House debate over it in *Annals,* I, 1875–1876, 1890–1900, 1901, 1905–1910, 1918–1932.

55. For example, William Branch Giles of Virginia, *Annals,* I, 1929–1930.

56. Jefferson (Ford), VII, 299; Adrienne Koch and Harry Ammon, "The Virginia and Kentucky Resolutions," *WMQ,* 3rd ser., V (1948), 145.

57. Excise Act of June 5, 1794, *Annals,* III, 1464–1471; I *Stat.,* 384–390.

58. Jan. 15, 1790, *Annals,* I, 1095.

59. Works, IV, 159, 156–157.

60. Works, IV, 150–152.

61. Annals, II, 1329–1332, 1364–1370; I *Stat.,* 259–263. The Tariff Act of 1792 was presented and passed as "a bill for raising a farther sum of money for the protection of the frontiers." *Annals,* II, 551, 560–572. See also the expansion of the tariff program in the Act of 1794, *Annals,* III, 1472–1473; I *Stat.,* 390–392.

62. Feb. 28, 1792, *Jefferson* (Ford), I, 177.

63. Annals, III, 362–401, esp. 386–389, 401; Madison to Edmund Pendleton, Jan. 21, 1792, *Madison* (1867), I, 545–546; Hamilton to Carrington, May 26,

1792, *Works,* IX, 526. For an interesting report on Madison's inconsistency in this matter, see Brant, *Madison,* III, 137–139.

64. Feb. 23, 1791, Fitzpatrick, XXXI, 224 n.

65. Oct., 1793, Fitzpatrick, XXXIII, 116–118, 121–122, 125–129, 130–131; *Works* (JCH), IV, 477–479; *Jefferson* (Ford), VI, 436; *Madison* (Hunt), VI, 199–203.

66. Cabinet opinion, Jan. 28, 1794, Freeman, *Washington,* VII, 151; *Works* (JCH), IV, 505–506.

67. April 14, 23, 1794, *Works,* V, 113, 115 ff. For the opposition's elaborate (and labored) view of the unconstitutionality of sending Jay on this mission, see (Philadelphia) *Dunlap's American Daily Advertiser,* May 12, 1794; *Madison* (Hunt), VI, 212; S. M. Hamilton, ed., *The Writings of James Monroe* (New York, 1898–1903), I, 293–296.

68. Hamilton to Washington, 1790, *Works* (JCH), IV, 13–15. See also his sensible letter to Washington, Feb. 2, 1795, National Archives, in which he interprets the President's statutory power "to authorize any person or persons at his discretion" to perform the duties of a sick or absent head of department.

69. See Hamilton's articles as Tully, Aug. 23, 26, 28, Sept. 2, 1794, *Works,* VI, 410–426; Freeman, *Washington,* VII, 186 ff.

70. Aug. 5, 1793, *Works,* V, 54–56.

71. March 8, 1794, *Works,* X, 63–65. Congress laid a thirty-day embargo in March, then gave the President temporary authority (June 4, 1794) to do the same in the absence of the Houses "whenever, in his opinion, the public safety shall so require." *Annals,* III, 75–76, 529–530, 1450; I *Stat.,* 372.

72. June–July, 1794. The exchange of views is in Fitzpatrick, XXXIII, 415, 420–422.

73. Freeman, *Washington,* VII, chaps. 2–4; Charles M. Thomas, *American Neutrality in 1793* (New York, 1931), which exaggerates Hamilton's partiality toward Great Britain; Charles S. Hyneman, *The First American Neutrality* (Urbana, 1934), which is especially useful for the study of Hamilton as an international lawyer.

74. To Madison, June 23, 1793, *Jefferson* (Ford), VI, 315.

75. April 19, 1793, *Jefferson* (Ford), VI, 217. The debate on this issue continued throughout the year, Jefferson and Randolph taking the restricted and Hamilton the expansive view of the President's right to "declare" on the "question of war or peace." See Freeman, *Washington,* VII, 141–142, and Washington's explanation to Congress, Fitzpatrick, XXXIII, 164–165.

76. Fitzpatrick, XXXI, 430–431. The unfortunate choice for drafting this document was Attorney General Randolph.

77. To Jefferson, June 19, 1793, Brant, *Madison*, III, 375.

78. Freeman, *Washington*, VII, 53.

79. "Pacificus is operating here," Stephen Higginson wrote Hamilton from Boston, "without interruption." July 26, 1793, *Works* (JCH), V, 570–571. Both Pacificus and Helvidius were reprinted in Philadelphia in 1796.

80. (Philadelphia) *Gazette of the United States*, June 29, July 3, 6, 10, 13, 17, 20, 1793; *Works*, IV, 432–489.

81. *Jefferson* (Ford), VI, 338.

82. (Philadelphia) *Gazette of the United States*, Aug. 24, 28, Sept. 7, 11, 14, 18, 1793; *Madison* (Hunt), VI, 138–188.

83. In addition, Hamilton had fallen sick with yellow fever during the course of Madison's rejoinder.

84. *Madison* (Hunt), VI, 150–151, 162, 175–176.

85. Theodore Sedgwick described Hamilton's "determination to resign" "as the most serious misfortune which has yet befell the government." To Williams, Dec. 2, 1794, Sedgwick Papers, MHS. The pertinent documents are in *Works*, X, 79, 84–85; *Works* (JCH), V, 55, 56, 73–75; Fitzpatrick, XXXIV, 109–110. See also the testimony of Joshua Coit of Connecticut recorded in C. M. Destler, *Joshua Coit* (Middletown, Conn., 1962), 71.

86. To Jefferson, July 30, 1793, *Madison* (1867), I, 588; July 18, 1793, *Madison* (Hunt), VI, 135.

87. William Bradford to Hamilton, July 2, 1795, Hamilton Papers, L of C; Warren, *Supreme Court*, I, 124–125; *History*, VI, 253; Smith, *James Wilson*, 372; Jay to Hamilton, April 19, 1798, Hamilton Papers, L of C; Hamilton to Jay, April 24, 1798, *Works*, X, 281; R. G. Harper to Hamilton, April 27, 1798, *Works* (JCH), VI, 282, which begins, "Could any thing prevail on you to take the War Department?"; Kurtz, *Presidency of Adams*, 301–302, which speculates on the astonishing possibility of Hamilton as Adams's Secretary of War. Attorney General Bradford's letter to Hamilton reads in part:

Your squabbles in New York have taken our Chief Justice from us—ought you not to find us another? I am afraid that department as it relates neither to War, finance nor Negotiation, has no charm for you: and yet when one considers how immensely important it is, where they have the power of paralizing the measures of the government by declaring a law unconstitutional, it is not to be limited to men who are to be scared by popular clamor or warped by feeble-minded prejudices.—I wish to heaven you would permit me to name you:—If not, what think you of Mr. Randolph?

The sluggish Supreme Court of the 1790's was, of course, no place for the effervescent Hamilton. It is questionable, in any case, whether Washington would have agreed with his Attorney General that Hamilton was the best man he could name to this job at this time, and he had already decided to seek out John Rutledge (who needed precious little seeking) even as Bradford was writing Hamilton. Washington to Rutledge, July 1, 1795, Fitzpatrick, XXXIV, 225–226.

Hamilton was almost constantly being proposed by friends as Governor or Senator. Sedgwick to Van Schaack, Dec. 17, 1794, Sedgwick Papers, MHS; James Gunn to Rufus King, Aug. 22, 1795, King Papers, NYHS.

88. Otis, *Eulogy,* 561.

89. To Carrington, May 26, 1792, *Works,* IX, 531. See Jefferson's concurring opinion in *Jefferson* (Ford), I, 174.

90. Mary L. Hinsdale, *A History of the President's Cabinet* (Ann Arbor, 1911), 19–22.

91. George Hammond, report of a conversation with Hamilton, Jan., 1795; Joseph Willard to Hamilton, Aug. 27, 1792, both in Hamilton Papers, L of C.

92. *Annals,* II, 835–841, 895, 899–955, 955–963 (which reveals that Madison voted "aye" on every last resolution), 1197 ff.; *ASP, Finance,* I, 192, 200, 202, 218; *Works,* III, 137–177, 178–179, 183–190, 199; D. R. Anderson, *William Branch Giles* (Menasha, Wisc., 1914), 20–25; Jane J. Boudinot, *The Life, Public Services, Addresses and Letters of Elias Boudinot* (Boston, 1896), II, 266–312; Malone, *Jefferson and the Ordeal of Liberty,* chap. 2.

93. *Annals,* I, 1012, 1014, 1026.

94. Hamilton's argument, dated May 28, 1790, is in *Papers,* VI, 433–439, Jefferson's in *Jefferson* (Ford), V, 175–178.

95. *Annals,* II, 111–112, 403 ff., 482–483.

96. Jefferson's opinion, dated April 4, 1792, is in *Jefferson* (Ford), V, 493–501. Washington's worries over this problem are described in Freeman, *Washington,* VI, 345–347; *Jefferson* (Ford), I, 192.

97. April 4, 1792, *Works,* VIII, 96–100.

98. Washington's message, dated April 5, is in *Annals,* II, 539; Fitzpatrick XXXII, 16–17. The act as finally passed (adopting the method of "rejected fractions") is in *Annals,* II, 1359; I *Stat.,* 253.

99. Z. Chafee, "Congressional Reapportionment," *Harvard Law Review,* XLII (1929), 1021.

100. Fitzpatrick, XXXIII, 15–19.

101. *History,* V, 304; *Works,* V, 16 n.; and Warren, *Supreme Court,* I, 109, all make this assertion without documentation, and the most careful search in the papers of Hamilton, Jay, Washington, Knox, and the other actors in this scene has turned up absolutely no substantiating evidence. Freeman, *Washington,* VI, 104 n., cites various notes of Jefferson to this effect, but he seems to have found something in *Jefferson* (Ford), I, 241–243, VI, 276 n., 344–345, which simply does not exist, that is, evidence that Hamilton and Knox concurred "reluctantly" with Jefferson's proposal to refer questions of neutrality to the Court.

102. Including this particular issue of neutrality. See the letters to Jay of Nov. 13, 1790, Sept. 3, 1792, and April 9, 1793, *Works*, IX, 473; X, 18–19, 39. Washington, too, turned naturally to Jay in the first years of his administration, as witness Hamilton to Jay, July 9, 1790, *Papers*, VI, 488.

103. See in particular the delicate phrasing of Jefferson's letter transmitting the questions to the Court, in *Jefferson* (Ford), VI, 351–352; *Jay*, III, 486–487. The questions as finally put were the joint product of Hamilton and Jefferson. *Jefferson* (Ford), VI, 352–354.

104. July 20, Aug. 8, 1793, *Jay*, III, 478–479.

105. Muskrat v. *U.S.*, 219 U.S. 346, 354 (1911); *Constitution Annotated*, 549–550.

106. His draft is in *Works*, V, 12–16. On the question of authorship of the final draft, see Thomas, *American Neutrality in 1793*, 148–149.

107. See, for example, Washington's pleas for assistance or opinion in Fitzpatrick, XXXIV, 226, 237, 241, 262, 295, 347, 362, 363, 404, 481; XXXV, 38, 48, 101, 190, 198, 204, 251, 255, 271, 287, 372. He was no less eager for Hamilton's advice in the events of 1798–1799, as witness Fitzpatrick, XXXVI, 271, 329; XXXVII, 136, 473.

The derisive label "King of the Feds" was pasted on Hamilton in a pamphlet published by "Tom Callender, Esq., Citizen of the World, *Letters to Alexander Hamilton, King of the Feds* (New York, 1802).

108. (New York) *Minerva*, July 22, 1795–Jan. 9, 1796, in *Works*, V, 189–491; VI, 3–197. There were thirty-eight articles in this series, ten of which were written by Rufus King under Hamilton's guidance (and with many additions and alterations from his pen). The first twenty-two numbers were issued as a book entitled *A Defense of the Treaty* (New York, 1795).

109. Works, VI, 160 ff.; V, 346, 351.

110. See the comment of his friend Fisher Ames in a letter to Jeremiah Smith, Jan. 18, 1796, *Ames*, I, 183.

111. Works, VI, 160–161.

112. The constitutional arguments of the opposition are summed up in *Works*, VI, 171–173.

113. Works, VI, 183, 179.

114. Cabot to King, July 27, 1795, *Cabot*, 81–83; *King*, II, 20; Pickering to J. Q. Adams, Sept. 10, 1795, *Pickering*, III, 202.

115. Sept. 21, 1795, *Jefferson* (Ford), VII, 31–33. Washington's gratitude to Camillus, whom he suspected at once to be Hamilton, was expressed in a letter to Hamilton of July 29, 1795, Fitzpatrick, XXXIV, 262–264.

116. See *Works,* VIII, 161–181, as well as the letters of March 10–April 15, 1796 to Washington, King, Smith, and Wolcott, *Works,* X, 145–160. Washington's formal invitation was sent March 22 (*Works,* X, 151), but no copy of it has ever been found. Hamilton, in any case, had already begun to give "much careful thought" to the problem (*Works,* X, 145) at the behest of Wolcott, who in turn had been prompted by Washington. See the latter's letter of March 3 to Wolcott, Fitzpatrick, XXXIV, 481–482.

117. *Annals,* IV, 400, 426 ff., 759–760. Edward Livingston's original motion of March 2 requesting the President's papers was passed by a vote of 62–37 March 24, the words "excepting such of said papers as any existing negotiations may render improper to be disclosed" having been added in the meantime.

118. (Boston) *Independent Chronicle,* April 21, 1796.

119. To Monroe, April 18, 1796, Madison Papers, L of C (a coded letter). Madison's most important speech on this subject, which was delivered April 6, is in *Annals,* IV, 772–781.

120. *Annals,* IV, 760–761; Fitzpatrick, XXXV, 2–5. The reaction of the House to this message is chronicled in *Annals,* IV, 762 ff. Washington's explanation (dated March 31) of why he did not use Hamilton's draft, for which he had waited with keen anticipation, is in Fitzpatrick, XXXV, 6–8.

121. *Annals,* IV, 782–783, 2191. On the freedom of Congress to make its own judgment in the case of treaties that are not self-executing, see *Constitution Annotated,* 418–420; S. B. Crandall, *Treaties, Their Making and Enforcement,* 2nd ed. (Washington, 1916), chaps. 11–12; and the dictum of the Court in *De Lima* v. *Bidwell,* 182 U.S. 1, 198 (1901).

122. March 8, 1796, 3 Dallas 171 (1796); Warren, *Supreme Court,* I, 146–149.

123. *Annals,* III, 120, 729–730 (in which Madison is recorded as protesting against the tax as an "unconstitutional" attempt to "break down one of the safeguards of the Constitution"), 1452–1454; Madison to Jefferson, May 11, 1794, *Madison* (1867), II, 14; I *Stat.,* 373–375.

124. John Taylor, *An Argument Respecting the Constitutionality of the Carriage Tax* (Richmond, 1795).

125. Taylor, *Argument,* 4–5. At p. 11 of this pamphlet Taylor appeals directly to "the celebrated author of the Federalist" for support of his definition of a direct tax.

126. David Hunter to Hamilton, July 7, 1796, and Hamilton's endorsement, Hamilton Papers, L of C.

127. Bradford to Hamilton, July 2, 1795, Hamilton Papers, L of C; Hamilton to Wolcott, Aug. 5, 1795, *Works,* X, 112; Wolcott to Hamilton, Jan. 15, 1796, *Works* (JCH), VI, 83–84.

128. To Mrs. Iredell, in G. J. McRee, *Life and Correspondence of James Iredell* (New York, 1858), II, 461–462, in which he also notes that Hamilton dined with him the next day. No one expected Justices of the Court and practicing attorneys to maintain a splendid isolation in those early days.

(Philadelphia) *Gazette of the United States,* Feb. 26, 1796, reported Hamilton's performance in these enthusiastic words:

Yesterday, in the Supreme Court of the United States, Mr. HAMILTON, late Secretary of the Treasury, made a most eloquent speech in support of the Constitutionality of the Carriage Tax—He spoke for three hours, and the whole of his argument was clear, impressive, and classical. The audience, which was very numerous, and among whom were many foreigners of distinction, and many of the members of Congress, testified, by their continual attention, the effect produced by the talents of this great orator and statesman.

129. See Iredell's opinion, 3 Dallas 181–182.

130. Works, VIII, 380.

131. (Poughkeepsie) *New-York Journal,* Oct. 19, 26, Nov. 16, 1778; *Papers,* I, 562, 567, 580.

132. 3 Dallas 177–178.

133. The basic literature of this subject is Charles G. Haines, *The American Doctrine of Judicial Supremacy,* 2nd ed. (New York, 1959), chaps. 5–8, E. S. Corwin, *The Doctrine of Judicial Review* (Princeton, 1914), chap. 1, and "The Rise and Establishment of Judicial Review," *Michigan Law Review,* IX (1910–1911), 102, 283; Charles A. Beard, *The Supreme Court and the Constitution* (New York, 1912); and Crosskey, *Politics and the Constitution,* II, chaps. 27–29, as useful as it is exasperating.

134. Federalist, 468. See the forecast of this doctrine in his speech to the New York Assembly, April 17, 1787, *Papers,* IV, 152, in which Cicero is used to good advantage.

135. See generally the contemporary pamphlet *Arguments and Judgment of the Mayor's Court of the City of New-York, in a Cause Between Elizabeth Rutgers and Joshua Waddington* (New York, 1784); Mitchell, *Hamilton,* I, 335–345; Crosskey, *Politics and the Constitution,* II, 962–965; H. B. Dawson, ed., *The Case of Elizabeth Rutgers versus Joshua Waddington* (New York, 1886); R. B. Morris, ed., *Select Cases of the Mayor's Court of New York City, 1674–1784* (Washington, 1935), 57–59, 302–327.

136. For Hamilton's use of Coke's notion of a "void" statute, see his "notes for argument" in this case, in A. M. Hamilton, 465.

137. Arguments and Judgment of . . . Rutgers and Waddington, 40.

138. See the remarks of James Wilson in the Pennsylvania convention Dec. 7, 1787, of Oliver Ellsworth in Connecticut Jan. 7, 1788, and of John Marshall in Virginia June 20, 1788 (above, pp. 240–241), in Elliot, II, 489, 196; III, 553; as well as the interesting letter of James Iredell to R. D. Spaight, Aug. 26, 1787, in reply to Spaight's letter (from Philadelphia), Aug. 12, 1787, McRee, *Life of Iredell,* II, 168–170, 172–176.

139. See, for example, the evidence assembled by Crosskey, *Politics and the Constitution,* II, 952–961, on the case of *Commonwealth* v. *Caton,* 4 Call (Va.) 5 (1782), as well as Corwin, *Doctrine of Judicial Review,* 71–75. The pros and cons of this particular aspect of the Rutgers case were thoroughly ventilated in the press of New York. See, for example, (New York) *Independent Journal,* Sept. 11, 1784; *New-York Gazetteer,* Sept. 10, 21, Oct. 26, 29, 1784; *New York Packet,* Sept. 13, Nov. 4, 1784.

140. Max Farrand, "The First Hayburn Case, 1792," *AHR,* XIII (1908), 281; Warren, *Supreme Court,* I, 69–72; *Annals,* II, 556–557, in which the House of Representatives took direct notice of this "first instance in which a court of justice had declared a law of Congress to be unconstitutional."

141. Smith, *Wilson,* chaps. 21–22; J. D. Andrews, ed., *The Works of James Wilson* (Chicago, 1896), I, 415–418.

142. A. C. McLaughlin, *The Courts, the Constitution and Parties* (Chicago, 1912), 19–301, and *Constitutional History of the United States* (New York, 1935), 312–313 n.; Haines, *American Doctrine of Judicial Supremacy,* chap. 7; Corwin, *Doctrine of Judicial Review,* 75–78. See the enthusiastic tribute to Hamilton's "full," "apposite," and "conclusive" "reasoning" in *Kamper* v. *Hawkins,* 1 Va. Cases 20 (1793).

143. Taylor, *Argument,* 4–5. For a summary of private and public opinions, many of them Jeffersonian, in support of some kind of judicial review, see Warren, *Supreme Court,* I, 253–268.

144. The replies of Rhode Island, New Hampshire, and Vermont explicitly affirmed the power of the courts to pass on the validity of laws alleged to violate the Constitution. See Elliot, IV, 533, 539. And see Madison's answer to these resolutions in *Madison* (Hunt), VI, 341–406.

145. 2 Dallas 304 (1795); 3 Dallas 171, 199 (1796); 3 Dallas 386 (1798). It is of interest to note that in the third of these cases Hamilton's essential argument in *Rutgers* v. *Waddington*—that the treaty of peace with Britain must prevail over state laws discriminating against Tories—was the basis of the Court's decision.

146. 18 Fed. Cases No. 10461, 3 N.C. 404 (1802). See also the debate in Congress in 1801 over the repeal of the Judiciary Act of 1801, *Annals,* VII, 26 ff., 510 ff.

147. The opinion was given in full in the *New York Evening Post,* March 23, 24, 1803.

148. Annals, I, 2248; I *Stat.,* 85–87. I must confess to have been totally unconvinced by Crosskey's nonconforming interpretation of section 25 in *Politics and the Constitution,* II, 1028–1035.

149. Dec. 17, 1801–April 8, 1802, *Works,* VIII, 246–373. See also his letter of Aug. 10, 1802 (in defense of Lafayette), *Works,* X, 441.

150. Miller, *Hamilton,* 551. See generally Allan Nevins, *The Evening Post* (New York, 1922), 9–37.

151. G. S. Hillard, ed., *Memoir and Correspondence of Jeremiah Mason* (Cambridge, 1873), 32–33. For corroborative evidence adduced by James Cheetham, a leading Republican editor, see Nevins, *Evening Post,* 29. Cheetham's own paper, the (New York) *American Citizen,* Nov. 23, 1801, saluted Coleman as the "Generalissimo of federal editors," while "Tom Callender, Esq.," *Letters to Alexander Hamilton,* 51, described him satirically as Hamilton's "principal typographer."

152. My own search through the letters and newspapers of the period confirms the conclusions of Warren, *Supreme Court,* I, 245–253. If there was an occasional Republican attack on Marshall's use of the power of judicial review (for example, the letters of "An Unlearned Layman" in the *Washington Federalist,* April 20, 22, 27, 1803), there was no Federalist rejoicing that the question left open in Article III of the Constitution had finally been answered—and answered correctly.

153. Below, p. 300, n. 168.

154. Nathan Schachner, *Thomas Jefferson* (New York, 1951), II, chaps. 52–53; Dangerfield, *Livingston,* pt. V; the still fresh and masterly account of Henry Adams, *History of the United States during the Administrations of Jefferson and Madison* (New York, 1889–1901), II, chap. 4; Brant, *Madison,* IV, chap. 11, which is hard on Livingston but good on the constitutional issue.

155. New York Evening Post, March 23, 24, 1803. See also (New York) *Chronicle Express,* March 7, 1803; (New York) *Commercial Advertiser,* March 5, 28, 29, 30, 1803; (New York) *Republican Watchtower,* March 9, 1803; (Washington) *Universal Gazette,* March 24, 31, 1803; (Washington) *National Intelligencer,* March 24, 25, 1803; (New York) *Spectator,* March 5, 9, 30, April 2, 16, 1803; *New-York Herald,* March 5, 23, 1803; (Philadelphia) *Aurora,* March 23, 24, 1803.

156. Works, VIII, 337–346, esp. 342–344.

157. For his two drafts of such an amendment, as well as the documents of his strategic retreat from the notion of acknowledging openly that he had "done an act beyond the Constitution" in order to "advance the good of the country," see *Jefferson* (Ford), VIII, 241–249.

158. To Wilson Cary Nicholas, who had none of Jefferson's painfully honest troubles in shrugging off fifteen years of strict construction, Sept. 7, 1803, *Jefferson* (Ford), VIII, 247–248.

159. Quoted in William Plumer, MS. Autobiography, L of C, p. 114.

160. See the reserved yet generally approving comments in the *New York Evening Post,* June 30, July 5, 11, 20, Nov. 7, 8, 1803, as well as the derisive poem (derisive, that is to say, about the role of Jefferson and his friends rather than about the territory acquired) in the issue of July 21. In the same issue an editorial speculates that the purchase might "turn out to be rather a costly one," yet goes on to observe that "on a grand national scale we are inclined to think well of it." There is, alas, an almost unbelievable dearth of useful and revealing private correspondence to and from Hamilton in these years.

161. Joseph Story, *Commentaries on the Constitution,* 3rd ed. (Boston, 1858), II, 167 (sec. 1282).

162. *Jefferson* (Ford), VII, 306. For the texts of the Virginia and Kentucky Resolutions, see Elliot, IV, 528, 540, 544, 580.

163. As indeed they seem to have been. James M. Smith's assumption of the unconstitutionality of the Sedition Act, in his excellent study *Freedom's Fetters* (Ithaca, 1956), is pretty thoroughly destroyed by Mark De Wolfe Howe in a review in *WMQ,* 3rd ser., XIII (1956), 573.

164. To Jonathan Dayton, 1799, *Works,* X, 329, 335–336; speech to the court in the Croswell case, 1804, *Works,* VIII, 421; James Kent MS. record of Croswell case, NYPL, pp. 59, 63. That this was the general view of men like him—including Jay, Ellsworth, Iredell, Paterson, Wilson, and others—is made clear in Warren, *Supreme Court,* I, 433–442. See the argument of Harrison Gray Otis in Congress July 10, 1798 as recorded in *Annals,* V, 2146–2151.

165. For Jefferson's strong opinion in this matter, see his letters to Edmund Randolph, Aug. 18, 1799, and Charles Pinckney, Oct. 29, 1799, *Jefferson* (Ford), VII, 383, 398. The Court's fateful decision that there are no common-law offenses against the United States, that only acts which Congress has forbidden (and to which it has fixed penalties for disobedience) are crimes, was made finally in *U.S.* v. *Hudson and Goodwin,* 7 Cranch 32, 33 (1812). See also *U.S.* v. *Coolidge,* 1 Wheaton 415 (1816), in which Story made clear his disagreement; *U.S.* v. *Britton,* 108 U.S. 199, 206 (1883); *Manchester* v. *Massachusetts,* 139 U.S. 240, 262–263 (1891); *U.S.* v. *Eaton,* 144 U.S. 677, 687 (1892). For an extreme view of the "destructive" consequences of the Hudson case (and a nationalistic view of the common law as part of the law of the United States in effect encompassed by the Constitution), see Crosskey, *Politics and the Consti-*

tution, II, 766–784, as well as I, 470–486, 560–561, 578–640; II, 871–902, 1165–1169. And see the remarks of Julius Goebel, Jr., in W. M. Jones, ed., *Chief Justice John Marshall* (Ithaca, 1956), esp. 113–114.

166. II *Stat.*, 89–100. See Max Farrand, "The Judiciary Act of 1801," *AHR*, V (1900), 682.

167. Still the best account of the struggle over the judiciary in these years is Warren, *Supreme Court*, I, chaps. 4–6. See also Felix Frankfurter and James M. Landis, *The Business of the Supreme Court* (New York, 1928), 21–30.

168. II *Stat.*, 132, as well as 156, 244. For the debate in Congress on the constitutional issue of tenure for the newly appointed judges, see *Annals*, VII, 28–184, 510–985.

169. 1 Cranch 299, 309 (1803). The Court confined itself in this case to the single issue of the constitutionality of circuit-riding.

170. *Works*, VIII, 246–373, esp. 271–283, 312–364. See also his letters to C. C. Pinckney and James A. Bayard, March 15, April, 1802, *Works*, X, 428, 432.

171. *Works*, VIII, 350.

172. A protest in the form of a petition of eleven of the judges was made to Congress, but the Jeffersonian majority saw to it that no relief was granted. See the petition, debates, and votes in *Annals*, VII, 30–32, 51–78, 427–441; *ASP, Miscellaneous*, I, 340; J. H. Morison, *Life of Jeremiah Smith* (Boston, 1845), 143–155. The hopes of the Federalists that this law might be challenged in the courts were dampened by the extraordinary statutory maneuver through which the Republicans managed to keep the Supreme Court legally adjourned from December, 1801 to February, 1803. II *Stat.*, 156. In a letter to Hamilton dated Feb. 22, 1802, Gouverneur Morris scolded him for opposing a petition of the New York bar to Congress asking for repeal of the Repeal Act. Hamilton's answer, which fails to explain his true motives, was the famous letter of Feb. 27, 1802 ("Mine is an odd destiny"). Sparks, *Life of Morris*, III, 161; *Works* (JCH), VI, 528; *History*, VII, 552–554; *Works*, X, 425. See also Hamilton to C. C. Pinckney, March 15, 1802, *History*, VII, 564.

173. In 1913 Congress abolished the Commerce Court, which had been set up in 1910, but thoughtfully provided for the redistribution of its judges among the Circuit Court of Appeals. See XXXVIII *Stat.*, 208, 219–221, for the pertinent provisions; Frankfurter and Landis, *Business of the Supreme Court*, 162–174, for a documented account of this event; W. S. Carpenter, *Judicial Tenure in the United States* (New Haven, 1918), for a review of the whole problem first raised by the Repeal Act of 1802. Story, *Commentaries*, 3rd ed., II, 476–478, was certain that this act was unconstitutional.

174. *Annals*, VI, 623, 643–649; (Philadelphia) *Aurora*, March 13, 22, 24, April 17, 1800; Warren, *Supreme Court*, I, 186; Hamilton to Jonathan Dayton, 1799,

Works, X, 329, 331–332. This bill was reported by Hamilton's good friend Robert Goodloe Harper. The evidence for ascribing it to Hamilton, while substantial, is mostly circumstantial. I have not been able, despite an assiduous search in the papers of Hamilton, Harper, and others, as well as in the records of the House of Representatives, to find a manuscript copy of the full bill.

175. 3 Johnson's Cases (N.Y.) 336 (1804). In addition to this report, the most important sources of information about the Croswell case are the MS. record of James Kent, NYPL; *The Speeches . . . in the Great Cause of the People, Against Harry Croswell* (New York, 1804), a contemporary pamphlet; M. W. Hamilton, *The Country Printer* (New York, 1936), 176–177, 187–188, 196–198; MS. note of Croswell (written in his later and cooler years) in his file of *The Wasp,* NYHS; and such highly interested newspapers as the (Hudson) *Balance,* July 19, 26, Aug. 2, 9, 16, 23, 30, 1803, Feb. 21, 1804; (Hudson) *Bee,* July 19, Aug. 2, 1803; *New York Evening Post,* Jan. 29, July 19, 20, 22, Sept. 2, 3, 13, 17, 1803, Feb. 18, 20, 24, 1804. Leonard W. Levy, *Legacy of Suppression* (Cambridge, 1960), esp. 297–300, puts this case in the perspective of the "emergence of an American libertarian theory" of freedom of speech and press. See also Professor Levy's "Liberty and the First Amendment: 1790–1800," *AHR,* LXVIII (1962), 22.

176. From the *New York Evening Post,* July 12, 1802. *The Wasp* appeared on thirteen occasions between July 7, 1802 and Jan. 26, 1803, and never failed to sting Jefferson (and every other Republican in sight) for "demagoguery," "detestible conduct," and loose morals. Croswell seems to have been especially incensed (Jan. 26, 1803) by the Republican taunt that Washington had been "a mere old woman, led about by the nose by general Hamilton."

177. Jefferson (Ford), VIII, 218–219.

178. Note to *King* v. *Withers,* 3 Term Reports 428 (1784); T. B. Howell, *State Trials* (London, 1816), XXI, 846, 1034–1042.

179. (Hudson) *Balance,* Feb. 21, 1804.

180. To Elizabeth Schuyler Hamilton, June 23, 1803, Hamilton Papers, L of C.

181. Kent MS. on Croswell case, NYPL, pp. 62–63. See also the admiring testimony to the "last effort" of "that wonderful man" in Jabez Hammond, *The History of Political Parties in the State of New York* (Cooperstown, 1846), I, 206–207; the tribute of Ambrose Spencer in A. M. Hamilton, 198; and Troup to Pickering, March 31, 1828, Hamilton Papers, L of C, in which the former wrote:

I attended court, and heard the arguments on both sides; and I have often said, of Hamilton's argument, that if it could go down to posterity, with all the advantages it possessed in the delivery, that he could not fail to be regarded, by the wise and virtuous, as one of the greatest and best of men.

182. Kent, 323–326.

183. We have three versions of Hamilton's address to the court: 1) *Works,* VIII, 387–425, which is taken from *The Speeches . . . in the Great Cause of . . . Croswell* (1804), 62–78; 2) 3 Johnson's Cases (N.Y.) 336, 352–361 (1804), which "was obligingly communicated to the reporter, by a person of great legal eminence"; 3) Kent MS. in Croswell case, NYPL, pp. 41–71. Hamilton's notes in the case—improperly labeled a "brief"—may be found in *Works,* VIII, 383–386.

184. Works, VIII, 396. That Hamilton had been made well acquainted with the arguments for a free press of the famous Thomas Erskine is plain in a letter of Samuel Paterson to Hamilton, Feb. 16, 1793, Hamilton Papers, L of C. See especially *The Rights of Juries Vindicated* (London, 1785), *The Resolutions of . . . the Friends to the Liberty of the Press* (London, 1793), and *The Genuine Trial of Thomas Paine* (London, 1793), in all of which Erskine's views are given full vent.

185. Kent MS. in Croswell case, NYPL, p. 57.

186. Works, VIII, 383, 389–390, 422.

187. For an unfriendly but essentially truthful account of Hamilton's pursuit of the (New York) *Argus* for having printed an outrageous libel, see Smith, *Freedom's Fetters,* 398–417.

188. Works, VIII, 390.

189. Works, VIII, 384–386, 391–394, 411–424. In this matter Hamilton and the men associated with him relied heavily on the British Libel Act of 1792, largely the work of Charles James Fox, which opened the way to greater participation by the jury in a trial for libel. 32 Geo. III c. 60; *The Statutes Revised* (London, 1950), II, 148–149.

190. Works, VIII, 385.

191. I *Stat.,* 596–597, esp. sec. 3. The legislative history of the Sedition Act may be found in Smith, *Freedom's Fetters,* chaps. 5–8, the text of the original bill (which incorporated neither of these protections and was, as Hamilton warned, a long stride toward "tyranny") in Manning Dauer, *The Adams Federalists* (Baltimore, 1953), app. 4. Hamilton's friends Bayard and Harper and a Republican from Tennessee, William C. C. Claiborne, seem to have been chiefly responsible for adding these protections to the bill. *Annals,* V, 2133–2138.

192. According to Kent, Hamilton was "proud," and indeed "gloried" in the fact, that truth had been made a defense in the Sedition Act. Kent MS. on Croswell case, NYPL, p. 52.

193. Works, VIII, 385, as well as 398, 403, 407, 421. On the origin of the doctrine of criminal libel, see W. L. Prosser, *Law of Torts,* 2nd ed. (St. Paul, 1955), 630.

194. Kent MS. on Croswell case, NYPL, pp. 59, 61. As counterpoint to his jibe at Jefferson, Hamilton engaged in a "eulogy on General Washington" that, according to the thoroughly smitten Kent, was "never surpassed—never equalled."

195. Croswell MS., NYHS, in which he complains of having been "harrassed for several years" after 1804; *Lansingburgh Gazette*, July 24, 1804.

196. B. Gardenier to Hamilton, Oct. 6, 1803, Hamilton Papers, L of C; *People* v. *Freer*, 1 Caine's (N.Y.) Reports 394, 485, 518 (1803); Hamilton, *Country Printer*, 177; N. B. Sylvester, *History of Ulster County* (Philadelphia, 1880), 144; M. Schoonmaker, *History of Kingston* (New York, 1888), 418–419; *Lansingburgh Gazette*, Feb. 21, 1804; *New York Evening Post*, Feb. 24, 1804.

197. *Laws of the State of New York* (1805), IV, 232–233. A new trial was awarded to Croswell on the basis of this act by the Supreme Court, but it seems that the whole matter was allowed to drop. In *Steele* v. *Southwick*, 9 Johnson's Cases (N.Y.) 213, 214 (1812), the Court went out of its way to acclaim Hamilton's definition of libel as one "drawn with the utmost precision."

198. *The Constitution of the State of New York* (Albany, 1894), 67. The present definition of libel in New York law, which is clearly developed from Hamilton's own definition, is to be found in *New York Penal Law*, sec. 1340.

199. *Reports of the Proceedings and Debates of the Convention of 1821* (Albany, 1821), 487–495, esp. 488; Kent MS. on Croswell case, NYPL, pp. 153–157.

200. See *Index Digest of State Constitutions*, 2nd ed. (New York, 1959), 682–683. On the whole question of the plea of truth as a defense (and the limitations on such a plea), see Charles Angoff, *Handbook of Libel* (New York, 1946), 2–4. It is interesting to note that British law did not catch up with American law in this matter of truth as a defense against libel until Lord Campbell's Act of 1843, 6 & 7 Vict. c. 96; *Statutes Revised*, IV, 684, 685. See generally W. A. Button, *Principles of the Law of Libel and Slander* (London, 1946), 16, 75 ff.

201. For attempts to assess Hamilton's influence, see A. Moses, "Alexander Hamilton's Influence on the American Law of Libel," *National Corporation Reporter*, XXVIII (1904), 692, 698; R. R. Ray, "Truth: A Defense to Libel," *Minnesota Law Review*, XVI (1931), 43, 47. For evidence of the leading role of New York law and precedents, see Bertram Harnett and John V. Thorton, "The Truth Hurts," *Virginia Law Review*, XXXV (1949), 425. And see the remarkable tribute of Thomas Cooper, one of the leading Republican editors to be prosecuted under the Sedition Act (and a man who in turn tried to have Hamilton prosecuted for libel against John Adams!), in his *Treatise on the Law of Libel* (New York, 1830), 78–83. This treatise, it must be admitted, was published in Cooper's later and more conservative days.

202. Hamilton's associate Van Ness made this exact point in his argument in the Croswell case, insisting that "to publish truth cannot be libellous in any country having a free and elective form of government." *Speeches . . . in the Great*

Cause of . . . Croswell, 7. For evidence that this process was well under way, and that Hamilton knew all about it, see the report (and editorial) about *People* v. *Tracy,* as well as the report of a new law of libel in Connecticut, both in *New York Evening Post,* June 9, 11, 14, 15, 1804.

203. For the facts of this famous duel, see W. M. Wallace, H. C. Syrett, and Jean G. Cooke, eds., *Interview in Weehawken* (Middletown, Conn., 1960).

204. Oliver Wolcott to Rufus King, July 12, 1804, King Papers, NYHS. Fisher Ames spoke of the "uncommonly profound public sorrow" occasioned by the news of Hamilton's death. *Ames,* II, 257.

205. Charleston Courier, Aug. 7, 1804, reprinted in Coleman, 169, 171.

206. A bouquet of such tributes may be found in Coleman, 44 (from the highly interesting eulogy of Gouverneur Morris, *New York Evening Post,* July 17, 1804), 58, 68, 124, 153, 159, 160, 190, 211, 244, 262–268. Harry Croswell's last grateful salute was fired in the (Hudson) *Balance,* July 24, 1804, reprinted in Coleman, 155–156. See also *New York Gazette,* July 13, 14, 16, 20, 1804; (New York) *American Citizen,* July 27, 1804; *New York Evening Post,* July 16, 18, 31, Aug. 3, 1804; and the pamphlets listed in P. L. Ford, ed., *Bibliotheca Hamiltoniana* (New York, 1886), 69–85.

207. See in particular the tributes of the (Utica) *Patriot,* (Philadelphia) *Gazette of the United States,* and *Albany Centinel,* all reprinted in Coleman, 184, 80, 216.

208. (Philadelphia) *Aurora,* Aug. 7, 1804; Gallatin to Jefferson, July 18, 1804, *Gallatin,* I, 200; "Anthony Pasquin," *The Hamiltoniad,* 4, 6, 10, 54, 56 ff., 73 ff.; (Boston) *Independent Chronicle,* Aug. 16, 20, 23, 27, 30, 1804, which offers an especially interesting assessment of Hamilton from the Jeffersonian point of view.

209. For evidence that he would have understood yet opposed the secessionist urges of his more extreme colleagues in New England, see the letter to Sedgwick, July 10, 1804, *Works,* X, 457–458.

210. In saying this I am entering at least a mild dissent to the full implications of the judgment of McLaughlin, *Constitutional History,* 234, that Hamilton "was not primarily burning candles before the altar of a disembodied principle of constitutional interpretation."

211. To J. K. Paulding, April, 1831, *Madison* (Hunt), IX, 454. See also the remarks of Gouverneur Morris in Coleman, 44.

CHAPTER FOUR **HAMILTON'S POLITICAL SCIENCE: MAN AND SOCIETY**

1. Jan. 16, 1801, *Works,* X, 415; Bayard to Hamilton, Jan. 7, March 8, 1801, *Works* (JCH), VI, 505, 522. On Bayard's role in this election, see Morton Borden, *The Federalism of James A. Bayard* (New York, 1955), chap. 7.

2. Hamilton to Pickering, May 15, 1800, Hamilton Papers, L of C.

3. *Federalist,* 178, 92; *Works,* VIII, 305.

4. Oct. 6, 1789, *Papers,* V, 425; *Works,* IX, 460; *Papers,* II, 649; V, 36-37; *Works,* II, 455; III, 6; *Papers,* II, 242; *Works,* III, 490; VIII, 305, 426, 448.

5. To Oliver Wolcott, June 8, 1797, *Works,* X, 271.

6. *Hume,* 101, 12.

7. *Federalist,* 72.

8. *Federalist,* 526, 474.

9. *Papers,* I, 177; VI, 435-436; *Works,* II, 343; *Papers,* III, 495, 550; *Works,* IV, 469; V, 242, 406, 425, 467; VIII, 287-288, 435; *Federalist,* 59, 193-194, 363, 476.

10. *Federalist,* 402; Camillus, *Works,* V, 406.

11. Kent, 327-328.

12. Kent, 328.

13. To Washington, Aug. 18, 1792, *Works,* II, 437.

14. Sept. 3, 1780, *Papers,* II, 418; Dec., 1779 (?), *Papers,* II, 251.

15. *Works,* II, 426.

16. June 6, 1797, *Works,* X, 270.

17. To Washington, May 10, 1796, *Works,* X, 165.

18. *Works* (JCH), I, 4; Miller, *Hamilton,* 46.

19. *Papers,* I, 87-88, 91, 106; III, 485, 533; *Works,* V, 319, 391, 407; VIII, 393-425; *Federalist,* 418, 419, 512.

20. Dumas Malone, *Jefferson the Virginian* (Boston, 1948), 62-74; Gilbert Chinard, *Thomas Jefferson* (Boston, 1939), 27-33.

21. Miller, *Hamilton,* 15, 49-51; *Papers,* I, 176-177, 254-256.

22. To J. B. Cutting, Oct. 2, 1788, in Julian P. Boyd, ed., *The Papers of Thomas Jefferson* (Princeton, 1950-), XIII, 649. In a letter to Madison, Feb. 17, 1826, he spoke with bitterness of the "honied Mansfieldism of Blackstone," which had lured "nearly all the young brood of lawyers" into "toryism." *Jefferson* (Ford), X, 376.

23. Speech in the Case of Harry Croswell (1804), *Works,* VIII, 399, 425.

24. Hamilton to Richard Harison, June 13–15, 1793, Harison Papers, NYHS.

25. *Works,* IV, 242 n., 313 ff., 369 ff.; V, 383, 359 ff; VI, 131 ff., 215 ff. And see his "notes for argument" in *Rutgers* v. *Waddington,* printed in A. M. Hamilton, app. H; the opinion of the Mayor's Court in *Arguments and Judgment . . . of Rutgers and Waddington,* 20–28, 30–41; and the MS. "Brief on the Trespass Act," Hamilton College Library.

26. The Continentalist, April 18, 1782, *Papers,* III, 77. The references in *Works,* I, 144, 148; *Papers,* I, 373 ff.; II, 595, give evidence of Hamilton's early acquaintance with Postlethwayt. See also Panagopoulos, *Hamilton's Pay Book,* viii–x, 4–7. Postlethwayt's two-volumed *Universal Dictionary of Trade and Commerce* (a translation and elaboration of the work of Jacques Savary Desbrulons) first appeared in London in 1751–1755 and went through three more editions before Hamilton came upon it. See also his *Britain's Commercial Interest Explained and Improved* (London, 1757), and *Great-Britain's True System* (London, 1757). The plagiarizing Postlethwayt was in turn plagiarized by Richard Rolt, *A New Dictionary of Trade and Commerce* (London, 1756), with which Hamilton was also familiar. J. C. Hamilton said (*History,* II, 514) that in 1783, while a member of Congress, Hamilton studied Smith with great care and wrote "an extended commentary upon his *Wealth of Nations,* which is not preserved." See E. G. Bourne, "Alexander Hamilton and Adam Smith," *Quarterly Journal of Economics,* VIII (1893–1894), 328. Jonathan Jackson wrote to Fisher Ames, Feb. 7, 1790, that he was "pleased" that Hamilton seemed to have "adopted so fully the sentiments of Adam Smith as he has." Sedgwick Papers, MHS. *Papers,* VI, 51–65 is an excellent review of possible and probable sources of the ideas in the Report on Public Credit.

27. *Papers,* I, 86–87, 101; IV, 184–185; V, 100, 150, 151; *Works,* V, 407; VI, 210; *Federalist,* 73, 466; A. M. Hamilton, app. H, esp. 465.

28. The only direct references to Locke I have been able to find in Hamilton's writings are the noncommittal comments in *Papers,* I, 86; *Works,* VIII, 381.

29. *Papers,* I, 94, 100; IV, 216; *Works,* III, 346; VIII, 459; *Federalist,* 526; *Papers,* II, 595; III, 77, 705; IV, 216, 217, 721.

30. A copy of Hume's *Essays* was in Hamilton's library. A. M. Hamilton, 74. Hume was not published in America until 1795, when his *History of England* appeared in six volumes. Hume himself wrote to a friend in 1775, "I am an American in my principles and wish we could let them alone to govern or misgovern themselves as they think proper." J. Y. T. Greig, ed., *The Letters of David Hume* (Oxford, 1932), II, 303. For a highly interesting attempt to measure the influence of Hume and Machiavelli on Hamilton's mind, see Alex Bein, *Die Staatsidee Alexander Hamiltons in Ihrer Entstehung und Entwicklung* (Munich and Berlin, 1927), 165–177.

31. Papers, I, 177, 178, 181; III, 484, 545.

32. Mitchell, *Hamilton,* I, 45–49; Boyd, *Boudinot,* 19 ff. Livingston's forceful views, along with those of his friends William Smith, Jr., and John Morin Scott, were first put on view in the *Independent Reflector,* which was published in New York in 1752–1753. See Dorothy R. Dillon, *The New York Triumvirate* (New York, 1949); Milton M. Klein, ed., *The Independent Reflector* (Cambridge, 1963).

33. Papers, I, 86.

34. Papers, IV, 212; *Works,* III, 291; V, 415.

35. Papers, I, 88; III, 533, 535, 548, 549; IV, 126; V, 117, 294; *Works,* II, 380; V, 415; *Federalist,* 204; Farrand, I, 477.

36. Papers, I, 88.

37. Papers, I, 87.

38. Papers, I, 87–88; *Works,* V, 416, 423.

39. Papers, I, 46, 62, 88, 96, 104, 121–122; III, 553–554; V, 117; *Works,* V, 46.

40. Papers, I, 47, 96; IV, 222; Farrand, I, 477.

41. Papers, I, 563; *Works,* IV, 465 n.

42. Papers, I, 121–122, 136; III, 550–551; *Works,* VI, 419; *Federalist,* 367; Hamilton to Isaac Homes, June 17, 1794, Wolcott Papers, Connecticut Historical Society, which makes the necessary distinction—so dear to all conservative Whigs—between "a nation" offering resistance to tyranny and "a small part of the citizens" undertaking to defy a duly enacted law.

43. Montesquieu, *The Spirit of the Laws* (T. Nugent, ed., New York, 1949), I, 20–21; P. M. Spurlin, *Montesquieu in America* (University, La., 1940), 218, 233, 250, 261–262. For a review of early American views on the importance of morality to freedom, see Clinton Rossiter, *Seedtime of the Republic* (New York, 1953), 429–437.

44. Works, VIII, 205; VI, 277; *Papers,* III, 495.

45. Papers, VI, 69; III, 485.

46. Cornelia Le Boutillier, *American Democracy and Natural Law* (New York, 1950), 110–116, argues that Hamilton's concept of natural law was "utilitarian" or "historical" or "empirical" rather than "metaphysical" or "transcendental" in character.

47. For examples of his lifelong use of the concept of natural law, see *Papers,* I, 47–48, 87–88 (quoting Blackstone), 90, 136, 440; III, 485, 486, 532, 548–551; V, 24; *Works,* II, 471; IV, 406, 441; V, 406, 421–423, 437, 443, 473; VIII, 385, 398, 403, 407, 421, 431, 464; IX, 480. For evidence that he could

make a distinction between "natural law" and "customary law," see *Works,*
V, 433.

48. Phocion, *Papers,* III, 548, 532.

49. Phocion, *Papers,* III, 549.

50. Aug. 27, 1790, *Papers,* VI, 573–574.

51. Defense of the Funding System (after 1795), *Works,* VIII, 431.

52. Phocion, *Papers,* III, 495; Camillus, *Works,* V, 425; *Federalist,* 193–194.

53. Works, VIII, 205; VI, 277; III, 6.

54. The Farmer Refuted, Papers, I, 87.

55. Fragment on the French Revolution, *Works,* VIII, 425–429; VI, 267, 275;
X, 244. See the proclamation of national thanksgiving he drafted for Washington
in *Works,* VIII, 120–122, as well as his advice to Pickering and others to make
use of days of "humiliation and prayer," in *Works,* X, 244, 248, 276. Other
references to God or, as he preferred, Providence are in *Papers,* V, 359; *Works,*
VI, 397; X, 456, 475. Although he seems to have grown more religious in his
later years, his most eloquent appeal to God was a product of his youth, in
the famous "hurricane letter" of 1772, *Papers,* I, 35–37. See generally Douglass
Adair and Marvin Harvey, "Was Alexander Hamilton a Christian Statesman?,"
WMQ, 3rd ser., XII (1955), 308.

56. To James A. Bayard, April, 1802, *Works,* X, 432–437. For Bayard's polite
rejection of this proposal, see his letter to Hamilton, April 25, 1802, *Works*
(JCH), VI, 543; Borden, *Bayard,* 128–131. Henry Jones Ford, *Alexander Hamilton* (New York, 1931), 347, did not exaggerate much when he described
the proposal as "claptrap."

57. Works, IV, 377, 446, 469, 473; V, 40, 382; VIII, 385.

58. Federalist, 57; *Papers,* I, 126; II, 249, 656; III, 150, 543, 554; V, 36, 121;
VI, 100; *Works,* III, 389, 490; IV, 104, 134, 139; V, 99, 190; VII, 185; VIII,
201, 288, 305; X, 80; *Federalist,* 54, 108, 138, 164, 169, 458.

59. Papers, I, 154; II, 18, 652; *Works,* IV, 130, 459; *Federalist,* 425. See generally
Panagopoulos, *Hamilton's Pay Book,* chap. 3, who makes much, perhaps too
much (esp. pp. 120–123), of Hamilton as a man of "pragmatic notions."

60. Pacificus, July 6, 1793, *Works,* IV, 459; VIII, 435; *Papers,* I, 46; *Federalist,*
186, 193, 496–497, 517.

61. Federalist, 68.

62. Papers, IV, 216; *Works,* IV, 246; III, 6. For characteristic references and
appeals to human nature, see *Papers,* I, 36 (in the famous "hurricane letter" of
1772), 141–142, 151; II, 388 (in a love letter of 1780 to his "saucy little
charmer" Betsy), 655; III, 468; IV, 82, 130, 191; V, 19, 42; *Works,* II, 342;

IV, 94; V, 99, 453; VII, 270, 285; VIII, 201, 220, 392, 426–427; X, 395; *Federalist,* 119, 399, 407, 472.

63. June 28, 1788, *Papers,* V, 120.

64. *Works,* VIII, 448–449.

65. *New-York Journal,* Feb. 25, 1792.

66. *The Farmer Refuted, Papers,* I, 94–95.

67. *Works,* III, 4; *Federalist,* 471.

68. *Papers,* I, 93–94, 126–127; III, 306; *Works,* III, 261; V, 190, 194; VIII, 196, 393, 443; IX, 517; X, 31; *Federalist,* 34, 54, 57, 59, 92, 175, 208, 426, 437–438, 451, 458; Thomas P. Govan, "The Rich, the Well-Born, and Alexander Hamilton," *Mississippi Valley Historical Review,* XXXVI (1950), 675.

69. *Federalist,* 54–65, 115–116.

70. *Works,* VIII, 443; *Federalist,* 208.

71. *Papers,* I, 50; II, 247, 649–652; III, 108; IV, 37; V, 102, 115; *Works,* VIII, 449; X, 416, 445; *Federalist,* 59, 108, 160, 208, 216, 432, 451, 455, 471, 523.

72. *Federalist,* 458.

73. *Papers,* V, 96.

74. *Federalist,* 458.

75. The Continentalist, July 4, 1782, *Papers,* III, 104; *Works,* VIII, 220, 448.

76. *Papers,* I, 51, 53, 95; III, 564; IV, 191; *Works,* VIII, 193; *Federalist,* 67, 72, 213, 217, 224, 426.

77. *The Farmer Refuted, Papers,* I, 156.

78. Eulogium on Major General Greene, July 4, 1789, *Papers,* V, 348.

79. Phocion, *Papers,* III, 484.

80. The Continentalist, Aug. 9, 1781, *Papers,* II, 660.

81. *Federalist,* 59, 192–193.

82. *Federalist,* 437, 57, 111, 114, 426; *Papers,* I, 141, 498; II, 660; *Works,* IV, 152; V, 108, 200, 447; IX, 480; X, 259.

83. *Hume,* 121; Smith, *Theory of Moral Sentiments* (1759), 6th ed. (London, 1790), I, 284.

84. *Papers,* II, 656; IV, 181, 216; *Works,* III, 261; IV, 103; VI, 303; VIII, 196, 437; *Federalist,* 34, 54, 105, 114, 451.

85. *Federalist,* 57.

86. *Papers,* I, 126, 127, 141–142, 498; IV, 189, 197, 216; *Works,* VIII, 204; *Federalist,* 54, 57, 111, 118–119, 163, 440, 443.

87. As he doubtless also looked upon habit. For his scattered comments on habit, see *Papers,* I, 569; V, 56; *Works,* IV, 104; VI, 319; *Federalist,* 176.

88. *Papers,* II, 660; *Works,* V, 190; X, 433; *Federalist,* 407, 426.

89. *Papers,* IV, 181; II, 611; *Federalist,* 451.

90. *Papers,* I, 126–127; *Works,* VI, 234, 303; VIII, 196, 393–394, 437; *Federalist,* 54, 119.

91. *Leviathan* (M. Oakeshott, ed., Oxford, 1955), 64.

92. *The Farmer Refuted, Papers,* I, 126.

93. Phocion, *Papers,* III, 542–543.

94. *Papers,* I, 51, 53–54, 60, 92; II, 431; III, 103, 494; IV, 216–217; V, 85; *Works,* II, 342; *Federalist,* 34, 112, 137, 426.

95. The Continentalist, July 4, 1782, *Papers,* III, 103.

96. *The Farmer Refuted, Papers,* I, 95.

97. June 22, 1787, *Papers,* IV, 216.

98. *Federalist,* 441, 445, 458.

99. *Federalist,* 217.

100. Hobbes, *Leviathan,* 109, 120; *Hume,* 20, 30, 34, 40, 85, 105, 135, 137. Book II of Hume's *Treatise of Human Nature* bears the title "Of the Passions."

101. For evidence of his reliance on "passion" and "the passions," see *Papers,* II, 656; III, 483–485; IV, 91, 181, 187, 189, 197, 277; *Works,* III, 272; IV, 109; V, 99–105; VI, 277; VIII, 201, 220; IX, 532; X, 259, 416, 433 ("the vicious are far more active than the good passions"); *Federalist,* 54, 56, 114, 116, 160, 176, 193, 379, 396, 400–401, 426, 456. "Prejudice," too, was a word he could use in both a pejorative and nonpejorative sense, as in *Papers,* I, 354; III, 428; V, 41; *Works,* VII, 144.

102. *Papers,* III, 428, 484; V, 41; *Works,* V, 99–100, 191, 212, 242, 251, 260, 439; X, 396.

103. *Papers,* I, 176.

104. April, 1802, *Works,* X, 433.

105. To King, Jan. 5, 1800, *Works,* X, 358; *Federalist,* 34.

106. *Federalist,* 375.

107. *Federalist,* 110–111, 56, 112, 396, 401, 456.

108. Camillus, July 25, 1795, *Works,* V, 200.

109. *Federalist,* 437.

110. *The Farmer Refuted, Papers,* I, 95.

111. Phocion, *Papers,* III, 494.

112. *Papers,* IV, 216–217.

113. *Papers,* II, 244. In the original of this letter, Hamilton spelled the operative word "monied." For other evidences of his concern for the interests of the "moneyed men," see *Papers,* II, 242, 415, 623; V, 43; *Works,* II, 346; III, 167, 419; *Journals,* XXV, 885.

114. *Works,* IV, 29; X, 332–333.

115. June 21, 1788, *Papers,* V, 43.

116. Defense of the Funding System (after 1795), *Works,* IX, 28.

117. *Works,* VIII, 284–291.

118. Report on Manufactures (1791), *Works,* IV, 138–140.

119. Phocion (1784), *Papers,* III, 494.

120. *A Full Vindication* (1774), *Papers,* I, 51.

121. For instructive examples of Hamilton's use of the word "class," see *Papers,* II, 612; III, 215, 318; IV, 200; V, 320; VI, 70; *Works,* II, 346, 352, 413, 421; III, 45; IV, 29, 76, 129; VIII, 206, 290, 468–473; *Federalist,* 33–34, 91, 105, 211–212, 217, 222, 367–368, 370–371, 522.

122. June 18, 1787, *Papers,* IV, 185, 192, 200; *Works,* IV, 109.

123. For an isolated reference, see *Papers,* V, 48.

124. A. Koch and W. Peden, eds., *Selected Writings of John and John Quincy Adams* (New York, 1946), xvi; *Adams,* V, 41, 458; VI, 10.

125. *Hume,* 128.

126. Despite his disclaimer in the Poughkeepsie Convention, in *Papers,* V, 41–42.

127. Miller, *Hamilton,* 228.

128. *Federalist,* 55.

129. To the Supervisors of the City of Albany, Feb. 18, 1789, *Papers,* V, 256.

130. May 28, 1790, *Papers,* VI, 439; April 14, 1794, *Works,* V, 114.

131. *Federalist,* 224; *Works,* VII, 252. See generally *Papers,* II, 605; III, 427, 486; IV, 192; V, 255–256; VI, 105, 439; *Works,* IV, 335, 386, 454; V, 114, 343, 377, 474; VI, 410, 457; VIII, 123, 376; X, 330; *Federalist,* 179, 470.

132. *Works,* V, 422, 433, 443; VI, 100; VIII, 200, 271; *Papers,* III, 91; *Federalist,* 140, 167.

133. *Works,* IV, 140; II, 437; V, 95; VII, 235; *Papers,* II, 651.

134. June 22, 26, 1787, *Papers,* IV, 218, 219; *Works,* VIII, 438.

135. *Works,* II, 342; IV, 87.

136. Catullus, Sept. 29, 1792, *Works,* VII, 272; to Carrington, May 26, 1792, *Works,* IX, 533; to Washington, Aug. 18, 1792, *Works,* II, 462.

137. Aug. 13, 1791, *Jefferson* (Ford), I, 169.

138. June 29, 1787, *Papers,* IV, 222; Farrand, I, 473.

139. *Papers,* II, 17–19; Mitchell, *Hamilton,* I, 176–177; Henry Laurens to Hamilton, April 18, 1785, *Papers,* III, 606–607. In the crisis of 1798–1800, however (and for reasons about which one can only speculate), he wrote to C. C. Pinckney, "I do not think it proper that men of color should be enlisted." April 21, 1800, Hamilton Papers, L of C. It is interesting to note that Hamilton's friend William Smith of South Carolina made a satirical attack on Jefferson's opinion of the natural inferiority of Negroes in his *Politicks and Views* (1792), 29.

140. *Papers,* I, 53; II, 18; V, 24, 351, 487; *Works,* V, 146, 148, 216–217.

141. *Papers,* III, 597, 604, 654; Schachner, *Hamilton,* 183, 449; A. M. Hamilton, 235.

142. *Papers,* V, 24; *Works,* V, 216.

143. Hamilton was thus admiringly described in a letter from Fisher Ames, Aug. 15, 1791, Wolcott Papers, Connecticut Historical Society. Ames, of course, used the word as a synonym for "nationalist," yet I doubt that he would object to my having borrowed it for this purpose.

144. Cecelia Kenyon, "Alexander Hamilton: Rousseau of the Right," *PSQ,* LXXIII (1958), 161.

145. *Hume,* 13, 20, 68, 145, 158.

146. These quotations may be found in *Papers,* II, 401; IV, 200; V, 56, 70, 269, 335; *Works,* III, 14; VII, 338; VIII, 100; *Federalist,* 191, 443. Others are in *Papers,* II, 36, 166, 413; III, 253; IV, 19, 139–140, 217; V, 166, 186, 221, 225, 231, 258, 318, 321, 433; VI, 436, 439; *Works,* III, 417, 427; IV, 461; VI, 457; VII, 115; VIII, 161, 474; X, 10, 160, 301; *Federalist,* 35, 97, 148, 194, 406, 445, 474; A. M. Hamilton, 457, 462.

147. *Papers,* I, 51, 74, 90, 99, 104; III, 269, 484, 489, 540; IV, 139, 187, 197; V, 81, 219; *Works,* II, 335, 379; III, 16, 249, 484; IV, 161; VI, 399; VIII, 431; IX, 517; X, 14, 256; *Federalist,* 110, 111, 190, 191, 210, 364.

148. Tully, Aug. 26, 1794, *Works,* VI, 414–415.

149. *Federalist,* 524–525.

150. Feb. 24, 1783, *Papers,* III, 269.

151. June 22, 1787, *Papers,* IV, 217; Farrand, I, 376, 381.

152. *Works,* VIII, 184, 185, 196–197, 200–204.

153. Federalist, 171, 427, 484; *Works,* VIII, 203. For instances in which he used the word "party" nonpejoratively and in a modern vein, see *Papers,* V, 258, 319; *Works,* VIII, 203, 422; X, 26.

154. Papers, I, 84; V, 85; *Works,* VI, 163, 414–415; VIII, 200; X, 31.

155. De Cive (S. P. Lamprecht, ed., New York, 1949), 149; *Leviathan,* 155.

156. Hume, 77–78, 15, 23, 43, 47, 53, 69, 70, 76, 80, 86, 153–154.

157. Works, VIII, 184, 196, 200, 422; *Federalist,* 71, 175, 396–397, 401, 452, 462, 484; Farrand, I, 434–435.

158. Tully, Aug. 26, 1794, *Works,* VI, 414–415.

159. Papers, IV, 73; V, 56, 256, 319; *Works,* V, 194, 197, 262, 460; VI, 163; VIII, 185, 196, 197, 201, 269; X, 31; *Federalist,* 34, 72, 171; James Kent MS. record of Croswell case (1804), NYPL, pp. 59, 62–63.

160. June 25, 1788, *Papers,* V, 85; Elliot, II, 320.

161. Speech in the Case of Harry Croswell, 1804, *Works,* VIII, 422.

162. June 18, 1787, *Papers,* IV, 188; Farrand, I, 284; to Clinton, Feb. 24, 1783, *Papers,* III, 272. Other samples of Hamilton's concern about "confidence" may be found in *Papers,* II, 242; III, 221–222; IV, 188; V, 95; VI, 436; *Works,* II, 436; III, 255, 281, 428; V, 102; VI, 201–202; VII, 266.

163. June 18, 1787, *Papers,* IV, 189; Farrand, I, 284.

164. Works, III, 255; VII, 266.

165. Federalist, 120.

166. Catullus to Aristides, Sept. 29, 1792, *Works,* VII, 264.

167. Papers, II, 655; IV, 181, 220–221; V, 43, 101–102; VI, 421; *Works,* VIII, 293–294; X, 331–334; *Federalist,* 119–120, 151.

168. Federalist, 116.

169. Nov. 11, 1794, *Works,* VI, 457, 427.

170. For a classic example of his concern to enlist public opinion (in this instance in support of the implementation of Jay's Treaty), see Kurtz, *Presidency of Adams,* 53 ff.; and for a classic example of his willingness to bow to it, I quote from a letter to John Marshall, Oct. 2, 1800, which was kindly made available to me by its owner, the Hon. Alex H. Sands, Jr., of Richmond. "Of one thing I am sure," he writes in reaction to news that France may be relaxing its rigid stand toward America, "if France will slide into a state of Peace *de facto,* we must meet her on that ground. The actual posture of European Affairs and the opinions of our people demand an accomodating course."

Hamilton was always assiduous in having his own writings (as well as the writings of friends and colleagues) reprinted widely. All the great Reports were published immediately upon delivery to Congress, while his letters as Phocion (1784) were given almost simultaneous publication in New York, Philadelphia, Boston, and Newport. The Report on Manufactures was printed in Dublin in 1792 and in London in 1793.

171. Papers, IV, 19, 130; *Federalist,* 71.

172. Papers, V, 36; I, 499; *Works,* III, 388; IV, 332–334; X, 280, 340; *Federalist,* 177, 514–515, 517. See the interesting if perhaps too imaginative article of Douglass Adair, "A Note on Certain of Hamilton's Pseudonyms," *WMQ,* 3rd ser., XII (1955), 282.

173. To Washington, Sept. 15, 1790, *Works,* IV, 332–335.

174. Papers, II, 238, 630; V, 36; VI, 97; *Works,* IV, 332–334; VII, 100, 195; IX, 135; X, 280; *Federalist,* 429, 514.

175. Feb. 2, 1799, *Works,* X, 340. Sedgwick, a stout New England Federalist, was obviously going to do nothing *in* Virginia.

176. Works, VIII, 158.

177. Papers, VI, 96–97.

178. To ?, Dec., 1779–March, 1780, *Papers,* II, 242.

179. Jan. 28, 1791, *Works,* IV, 45–46, 53–54.

180. Dec., 1799, *Works,* VII, 188; IV, 29, 45, 54; VI, 420. *Papers,* II, 242, 244–245; VI, 97.

181. Churchill, *My Early Life* (*A Roving Commission*) (London, 1959), 64.

182. 1779–1780, *Papers,* II, 247.

CHAPTER FIVE **HAMILTON'S POLITICAL SCIENCE: THE PATTERN AND PURPOSE OF GOVERNMENT**

1. To Carrington, May 26, 1792, *Works,* IX, 533, 534; anonymous letter to Hamilton, Aug. 30, 1793, Hamilton Papers, L of C. See also his protests in *Works,* II, 459–463; VII, 244–246; X, 446–448, 450–455; *Papers,* I, 426; the editorials in *New York Evening Post,* Feb. 19, 24, 1802; and the correspondence in Farrand, III, 353–354, 368–369, 395–396, 397–399, 409–410, and *History,* III, 256, 339–353. This whole subject is reviewed exhaustively, and favorably to Hamilton, in Louise Dunbar, *A Study of "Monarchical" Tendencies in the United States from 1776 to 1801* (Urbana, 1922), 82–98, 124–126.

2. To Pickering, Sept. 18, 1803, *Works,* X, 446.

3. Jefferson (Ford), I, 165, 160, 164, 168–169; IX, 269, 295–296; X, 305–316, 330–332.

4. To ?, Dec., 1779–March, 1780, *Papers*, II, 238; V, 37.

5. Jan. 6, 1799, *Works*, X, 337, as well as Feb. 21, 1799, *Works*, X, 343–345, in which he sketches an autocratic system of government for Santo Domingo, an island which "no regular system of liberty will at present suit." For this idea in Hume, see *Hume*, 134.

6. Papers, IV, 130.

7. Papers, IV, 218, 192, quoting Necker; *Works*, II, 462, in which he described his opinion of 1787 as "theoretical" and "abstract."

8. For his most extensive consideration of forms of government, see his notes for a speech of July 12, 1788, in *Papers*, V, 149–151.

9. Papers, V, 45, 49, 67; Elliot, II, 259, 301; Lamb Papers, NYHS.

10. Sept. 18, 1803, *Works*, X, 448.

11. Works, VIII, 240; *Jefferson* (Ford), VIII, 3; Clinton to Hamilton, March 6, 1804, *Works* (JCH), VI, 561–565.

12. May 26, 1792, *Works*, IX, 534; *Papers*, V, 77.

13. June 18, 1787, *Papers*, IV, 192; Farrand, I, 288. By the time he had come to write numbers 9 and 28 of *The Federalist*, he seems to have changed his mind (at least publicly), probably under Madison's tutelage. See *Federalist*, 73, 181; *Papers*, V, 99–100.

14. June 18, 1787, *Papers*, IV, 193, 201; *Works*, IV, 481; VI, 158, 216; VII, 312; VIII, 185; *Federalist*, 148–150, 412.

15. June 18, 1787, *Papers*, IV, 193.

16. May 2, 1797, *Works*, X, 259; June 3, 1802, *Works*, X, 439.

17. Papers, II, 651–652; IV, 193, 200.

18. June 21, 1788, *Papers*, V, 38–39; Elliot, II, 253–254; *Federalist*, 71; and the confirming testimony of Gouverneur Morris in a letter to Robert Walsh, Feb. 11, 1811, Sparks, *Life of Morris*, III, 260–261.

19. June 25, 1788, *Papers*, V, 82; Elliot, II, 317; *Federalist*, 56–57, 111–112, 175, 360–361, 401, 456.

20. June 27, 1788, *Papers*, V, 96; Elliot, II, 349.

21. Papers, III, 553; IV, 73; V, 256; *Federalist*, 152.

22. June 18, 1787, *Papers*, IV, 200, 185; I, 105.

23. June 21, Sept. 8, 1787, *Papers*, IV, 213, 244; V, 36; Farrand, I, 358–359, 361, 364; II, 553–554.

24. *Papers,* IV, 254, 256, 259. And see his common-sense remarks on property qualifications delivered to the New York Assembly, Jan. 27, 1787, *Papers,* IV, 25–29.

25. Dec. 29, 1802, *Works,* X, 445. See also *Works,* X, 458; *Papers,* III, 135; IV, 202.

26. Aug. 18, 1792, *Works,* II, 460–461; III, 5; VIII, 200; IX, 535; *Papers,* IV, 185; *Federalist,* 35, 521, 527.

27. Catullus to Aristides, Sept. 29, 1792, *Works,* VII, 266.

28. Camillus, July 22, 1795, *Works,* V, 190–191.

29. Unsubmitted Resolution Calling for a Convention, July, 1783, *Papers,* III, 421; *Federalist,* 401.

30. *Papers,* IV, 185; Farrand, I, 309.

31. June 24, 1788, *Papers,* V, 68; IV, 193; Elliot, II, 301.

32. *Papers,* IV, 188, 251; V, 38, 45, 51, 151, 154; *Federalist,* 117, 156, 180, 197, 203, 367, 372, 412, 430, 467–469.

33. *Papers,* I, 176–177, 569; III, 102; IV, 193, 200; V, 68; *Works,* III, 262; V, 191; VII, 266; X, 329–330, 384, 440.

34. *Federalist,* 58.

35. *Papers,* IV, 222; III, 484; V, 37, 68, 261; *Works,* IV, 481; V, 195, 209; VI, 163, 265, 427; VII, 300; X, 44, 359; *Federalist,* 367.

36. *Papers,* III, 150; *Works,* VII, 353. Critics who make perhaps too much of Hamilton's anti-popular feelings rely heavily on the two unhappy letters of Caesar printed in the (New York) *Daily Advertiser,* Oct. 1, 17, 1787, and reprinted by P. L. Ford, who ascribed them to Hamilton, in *Essays on the Constitution,* 279–291. Most of Hamilton's keen biographers (*e.g.,* Miller, *Hamilton,* 184–189; Mitchell, *Hamilton,* I, 406; Schachner, *Hamilton,* 208) accept the fact of Hamilton's authorship, but Jacob E. Cooke, "Alexander Hamilton's Authorship of the 'Caesar' Letters," *WMQ,* 3rd. ser., XVII (1960), 78, raises such serious doubts—as does the very style of the letters themselves—that one can no longer ascribe them confidently or fairly to Hamilton. Cooke's case is questioned but in no way refuted by Adrienne Koch, *Power, Morals, and the Founding Fathers,* 64. I am happy to report that Cooke's conclusions are supported vigorously by Professor Mosteller's machine (above, p. 281, n. 93), which cannot, however, tell us who wrote a disputed piece quite as easily as it can tell us who did *not* write it.

37. "Notes on Virginia," Query XIX; to Madison, Dec. 20, 1787; to John Adams, Oct. 28, 1813, in *Jefferson* (Ford), III, 269; IV, 479–480; IX, 428, 429.

38. *Federalist,* 277, 342.

39. Theophilus Parsons, Jr., *Memoir of Theophilus Parsons* (Boston, 1859), 109–110; Adams, *History of the United States,* I, 109.

40. *Works,* VIII, 246–267; X, 415, 440.

41. Fragment on the French Revolution, *Works,* VIII, 427.

42. *Papers,* I, 88, quoting Blackstone; IV, 126–127; *Works,* III, 410; V, 414–415; VIII, 42–43; *Federalist,* 120, 423.

43. The Continentalist, April 18, 1782, *Papers,* III, 76–79.

44. Address to the Electors of the State of New York, 1801, *Works,* VIII, 241–242, 295.

45. *Papers,* III, 105; *Works,* IV, 70 ff., 168; VIII, 214–223, 261–263, 294–295; X, 204–205.

46. *Papers,* V, 95; III, 553; *Works,* VI, 422.

47. June 18, 1787, *Papers,* IV, 200; *Works,* VII, 285.

48. Lucius Crassus, Dec. 24, 1801, *Works,* VIII, 262–263.

49. June 29, 1787, Strayer, *Delegate from New York,* 94.

50. *Papers,* V, 74; *Works,* VI, 418, 422; VII, 267; VIII, 375; IX, 534; *Federalist,* 35, 71–72, 113, 137, 148, 156, 169, 178, 362, 401, 412, 423, 527; *Papers,* I, 177.

51. *Federalist,* 71, a polished version of a passage in The Continentalist, July 12, 1781, *Papers,* II, 651.

52. To Carrington, May 26, 1792, *Works,* IX, 534–535; II, 460–461. The rest of this passage reads: "That there are men acting with Jefferson and Madison who have this in view, I verily believe; I could lay my finger on some of them. That Madison does not mean it, I also verily believe; and I rather believe the same of Jefferson, but I read him upon the whole thus: 'A man of profound ambition and violent passions.' "

53. Aug. 18, 1792, *Works,* II, 460; VIII, 422; *Papers,* IV, 11–12; James Kent MS. record of Croswell case (1804), NYPL, p. 61.

54. The Continentalist, July 12, 1781, *Papers,* II, 651.

55. *Journals,* XXIII, 808; *Papers,* III, 221–222.

56. As reported by Yates, June 19, 1787, Farrand, I, 329.

57. *Federalist,* 136–137.

58. *Works,* VIII, 201; *Papers,* III, 556–557; Fitzpatrick, XXXV, 226.

59. To Duane, Sept. 3, 1780, *Papers,* II, 401.

60. *Papers,* V, 94; Elliot, II, 347.

61. *Papers,* V, 95, 68, 81; Elliot, II, 348.

62. July, 1783, *Papers,* III, 424; *Works,* VI, 397; VIII, 200; *Federalist,* 35, 87, 108, 140, 148, 153–157, 169, 223–224, 423–424; *Journals,* XXV, 872.

63. *Federalist,* 35; *Papers,* III, 557.

64. Jan. 19, 1787, *Papers,* IV, 11; *Works,* VIII, 15–16.

65. June 29, 1787, *Papers,* IV, 222, 221; Farrand, I, 473.

66. *Federalist,* 87.

67. *Federalist,* 423 ff., 431, 435–436, 463; *Papers,* V, 73–74; I, 255.

68. The Continentalist, Aug. 30, 1781, to Robert Morris, April 30, 1781, *Papers,* II, 671, 629.

69. *Federalist,* 188.

70. June 29, 1798, *Works,* X, 295.

71. The Continentalist, July 4, 1782, *Papers,* III, 100, 104; Report on Manufactures (1791), *Works,* IV, 161–163.

72. June 25, 1788, *Papers,* V, 81; II, 651; III, 221–222; Elliot, II, 316; *Works,* VII, 285; Farrand, I, 434–435.

73. March 12, 1778, *Papers,* I, 440–441; III, 91, 305, 447, 486, 492, 556; *Works,* IX, 525–526; II, 345; IV, 331, 342, 387, 417; V, 9, 88, 244, 287; VI, 299; VII, 235–236; VIII, 464; X, 158, 254, 266; *Federalist,* 107; *Journals,* XXV, 884, 942.

74. May 13, 1797, *Works,* X, 266.

75. The Warning, Feb. 21, 1797, *Works,* VI, 243–245. In *Works,* VI, 313 n., he makes this interesting distinction between petty blackmail by "Algerines and Indians" and massive blackmail by the French Directory: "It is the general practice of civilized nations to pay barbarians; there is no point of honor to the contrary. But between civilized nations, the payment of tribute by one to another, is, by the common opinion of mankind, a badge of servitude."

76. To Washington, Sept. 15, 1790, *Works,* IV, 342.

77. Defense of the Funding System (after 1795), *Works,* IX, 31.

78. To McHenry, March 18, 1799, *Works,* X, 349, a remark prompted by the Fries rebellion. See *Works,* IV, 413, for an expression of his belief that weakness is no excuse for a government to plead when accused of "infractions of its duty toward foreign nations."

79. *Papers,* VI, 67–68; IV, 91; III, 355, 371; *Works,* V, 405; VIII, 265–270, 431, 464; IX, 525–526; X, 89–90.

80. Vindication of the Funding System, 1791 (?), *Works,* III, 13–14, 17, 266, 286–287; *Papers,* II, 629.

81. Camillus, Oct. 23–24, 1795, *Works,* V, 439; A. M. Hamilton, 457.

82. Camillus, Nov. 5–11, 1795, *Works,* V, 467, 347, 438; IV, 463; X, 114, 159.

83. June 6, 1797, *Works,* X, 268; IV, 331; V, 9, 205; VI, 201, 416; VIII, 149; *Papers,* V, 335; III, 371; *Federalist,* 107.

84. Enclosure with letter of April 10, 1797, Hamilton Papers, L of C.

At the height of the crisis of the "naval quarantine" of Cuba in 1962 the following dispatch appeared in the *New York Times,* Oct. 25, 1962, p. 23, under the headline "Boarding Rule Outlined by Hamilton in 1790":

WASHINGTON, Oct. 24—The "delicate relationship" of a United States officer with the crew of a vessel being boarded was underlined 171 years ago by Alexander Hamilton.

Hamilton, as Secretary of Treasury, wrote the following regulation in 1790 for the Revenue Marine, predecessor of the Coast Guard. The language has been widely quoted and applied in all naval services.

"While I recommend in the strongest terms to the respective officers, activity, vigilance, and firmness, I feel no less solicitude that their deportment may be marked with prudence, moderation and good temper. Upon these last qualities, not less than the former, must depend the success, usefulness and consequently continuance of the establishment in which they are included.

"They cannot be insensible that there are some prepossessions against it, that the charge with which they are entrusted is a delicate one, and that it is easy by mismanagement to produce serious and extensive clamour, disgust, and alarm."

85. Camillus, Aug. 21, 1795, *Works,* V, 287.

86. Hume, 12.

87. Federalist, 414.

88. Federalist, 404; *Papers,* II, 404.

89. July, 1783, *Papers,* III, 424.

90. The Continentalist, July 12, 1781, *Papers,* II, 649. See White, *The Federalists,* chap. 37, for evidence of the "rudimentary" state of "the administrative art" in the early Republic.

91. White, *The Federalists,* 127.

92. Papers, II, 404–405, 649; III, 102, 424; IV, 186; *Works,* III, 420, 421; VII, 180; VIII, 220–221; *Federalist,* 218–219, 391, 404, 414, 423–424, 435–436, 437, 447, 455, 517–520.

93. White, *The Federalists,* 478.

94. Oliver, *Hamilton,* 262–263.

95. Jan., April, 1784, Phocion, *Papers,* III, 487, 545. Hamilton's early thoughts on liberty may be sampled in *Papers,* I, 47, 53, 76, 104, 156, his mature thoughts in *Federalist,* 35, 37, 67, 72, 164, 168, 372, 375, 430, 440, 466, 469–470, 510–515, 521. See generally Maynard Smith, "Reason, Passion and Political Freedom in *The Federalist," Journal of Politics,* XXII (1960), 525.

96. *Federalist,* 85, 88.

97. June 26, 1787, *Papers,* IV, 218; Farrand, I, 424.

98. *Papers,* II, 401, 617; III, 495; V, 68; *Works,* IV, 386; VII, 266; VIII, 390–391, 438–439; X, 46.

99. *Works,* VIII, 439.

100. *Papers,* I, 58, 152; V, 42; VI, 100; *Works,* III, 407; VIII, 206.

101. *Works,* VI, 277; VIII, 205–206.

102. *Papers,* I, 76; *Works,* VI, 418–422; VIII, 447.

103. *Federalist,* 423.

104. *Papers,* III, 451–452; *Federalist,* 168.

105. June 24, 1788, *Papers,* V, 81.

106. *Works,* VI, 418–419; *Papers,* I, 48; III, 451–452.

107. *Works,* VIII, 199.

108. *Papers,* I, 68, 173; III, 553–554; IV, 23–24, 28; V, 321–322; VI, 435–436; *Works,* IV, 29–30; VII, 266; VIII, 238–239, 284 ff., 383 ff.; X, 295, 341; *Federalist,* 510–515. On his orthodox behavior (orthodox, that is, for a Federalist) in the conflict over the Alien and Sedition Acts, see James M. Smith, "Alexander Hamilton, the Alien Law, and Seditious Libels," *Review of Politics,* XVI (1954), 305, and *Freedom's Fetters,* 153–155, 407–417. His dislike of oaths and tests is recorded in *Papers,* III, 543–546; IV, 22–24.

109. *Works,* IV, 103; V, 414–415; IX, 15. His close identity of property with liberty is apparent in *Federalist,* 67, 120, 423, 521.

110. Jan. 27, 1787, *Papers,* IV, 29.

111. To Bayard, Aug. 6, 1800, *Works,* X, 385; *Jefferson* (Ford), X, 367.

112. Although given no credit for his pioneering efforts in either C. V. Shields, "The American Tradition of Empirical Collectivism," *APSR,* XLVI (1952), 104, or F. W. Coker, *Recent Political Thought* (New York, 1934), chap. 20.

113. Miller, *Hamilton,* 290; Dorfman, *Economic Mind,* I, 410; Studenski and Kroos, *Financial History of the United States,* 45; Wright, ed., *The Federalist,* 21; Mitchell, *Hamilton,* I, 245–248; Russell Kirk, *The Conservative Mind* (Chicago, 1953), 68–69; Amaury de Riencourt, *The Coming Caesars* (New York, 1957), 103–104; Hacker, *Hamilton,* 10–13, 73, 166–170.

114. To ?, Dec., 1779–March, 1780, *Papers,* II, 250. As Phocion he wrote that "all monopolies, exclusions, and discriminations, in matters of traffic, are pernicious and absurd." April, 1784, *Papers,* III, 555.

115. *Works,* IV, 142.

116. In *Conservatism in America* (New York, 1955), 112–113; "The Giants of American Conservatism," *American Heritage,* VI (1955), 56; *Conservatism in America,* rev. ed. (New York, 1962), 105–110; and, drawing heavily on the results of the third attempt, in this book. I trust that my judgments in the first two instances will not be quoted against me. They are, quite simply, those of a man who has changed his mind as a result of new evidence and fresh thoughts.

117. Kirk, *The Conservative Mind,* 65–70; *A Program for Conservatives* (Chicago, 1954), 258.

118. English, "Conservatism: The Forbidden Faith," *American Scholar,* XXI (1952), 393, 401; Hacker, *Hamilton,* ix–x, 247–251; Livingston, "Alexander Hamilton and the American Tradition," *Midwest Journal of Political Science,* I (1957), 209; Bower Aly, ed., *Alexander Hamilton* (New York, 1957), xii; Saul K. Padover, *The Genius of America* (New York, 1960), 69 ff.

119. Mitchell, *Hamilton,* I, xii.

120. *Works,* III, 398, 430; IV, 393; V, 101; VIII, 196; X, 248; *Federalist,* 162, 177, 197, 200, 203, 400, 448, 491, 527.

121. *Papers,* II, 242, 650; III, 272, 383; V, 36; *Works,* II, 455; III, 6, 490; VII, 203, 266; VIII, 200, 231, 271, 305, 426, 448; *Federalist,* 443–444, 469. For one of his rare direct arguments for change, see *Papers,* II, 416–417. He professed to steer a middle course between "the love of innovation" and "a spirit of blind deference to authority and precedent." *Works,* VII, 203.

122. *Works,* VIII, 305; *Federalist,* 118, 173, 196, 401, 509, 523.

123. *Papers,* II, 618, 619; III, 82; *Works,* III, 402; VIII, 438–439, 474; IX, 485.

124. *Works,* IV, 386–387; V, 202; VI, 267; VIII, 225–228, 231, 245, 425–429; X, 244, 275. See generally the enclosure accompanying his letter of April 10, 1797 (*Works,* X, 256), Hamilton Papers, L of C.

125. *Works,* IV, 402, 451; VI, 234, 259–260; X, 244.

126. *Works,* IV, 473; V, 75 ff., 94–95; X, 45–46, 255.

127. See the interesting argument in Lodge, *Hamilton,* 154, 250–271.

128. I do not include Professor Mitchell in this group. He makes a thoughtful but, I fear, quite unconvincing case for Hamilton as Hobbes in his *Hamilton,* I, 385–387. The extreme view of Hamilton as "outstanding among the champions of Hobbes" in America, which is joined with an extreme view of Hobbes as an absolutist, is to be found in C. M. Wiltse, *The Jeffersonian Tradition in American Democracy* (Chapel Hill, 1935), 22, 99–101. The first of many references to Hamilton as "the greatest Machiavel in America" is in "Callender," *Letters to Alexander Hamilton* (1802), 18.

CHAPTER SIX **HAMILTON'S CONSTITUTIONAL LAW AND THEORY**

1. "Mr. Hamilton declared the constitution to be their creed and standard, and ought never to be departed from"—to the New York Assembly, Jan. 24, 1787, *Papers*, IV, 22.

2. Papers, I, 100; *Works*, VIII, 202, 333, 336; *Federalist*, 403, 442, 518.

3. July, 1783, *Papers*, III, 421; V, 151; *Works*, VIII, 332–339 (in which the Hamilton of 1802 quotes the Madison of 1788); *Federalist*, 72, 151–152, 401–402, 449–450, 466.

4. Federalist, 167, 442.

5. Lucius Crassus, *Works*, VIII, 341–342, as well as *Papers*, IV, 185, 193; V, 151; *Federalist*, 72, 181, 401–402, 442, 457, 465–466. For an earlier and doubtless undigested view, see the letter to Gouverneur Morris, May 19, 1777, *Papers*, I, 255.

6. The Continentalist, July 19, 1781, *Papers*, II, 654–655; IV, 83; V, 43, 57, 101–102; *Federalist*, 180–181, 516, 521, 526.

7. Phocion (1784), *Papers*, III, 550; *Works*, VIII, 199.

8. Federalist, 146–148.

9. Federalist, 148, 367, 443.

10. See the Provision (Article II, section 8) calculated (like Article I, section 6, clause 2 of the Constitution) to frustrate the rise of parliamentary government in his draft constitution of 1787, *Papers*, IV, 256. And see the evidence presented by Thach, *Creation of the Presidency*, 93.

11. Federalist, 432; *Papers*, IV, 185.

12. Papers, IV, 219; III, 549–550; *Works*, VIII, 172.

13. Defense of the Funding System (after 1795), *Works*, VIII, 451.

14. To Washington, Aug. 18, 1792, *Works*, II, 459. For his broad, one might say latitudinarian, view of the powers of the old Congress, see the letter to Duane, Sept. 3, 1780, *Papers*, II, 400–402.

15. Works, III, 455; VII, 273.

16. To W. C. Rives, *Madison* (1867), IV, 3–4.

17. Feb. 23, 1803, *Works*, VIII, 318; VI, 178, 441.

18. Works, VIII, 380.

19. To Washington, Aug. 18, 1792, *Works*, II, 459; III, 5; VIII, 100, 122, 152; *Papers*, III, 547.

20. June 26, 1792, *Works*, IX, 540.

21. *Works,* III, 48, 446, 454 ff.

22. *Federalist,* 153, 194.

23. To Duane, Sept. 3, 1780, *Papers,* II, 402.

24. For an example, and a useful one, see his argument as Camillus, Jan. 9, 1796, *Works,* VI, 183. And see Madison's comment on Hamilton's appeal to the "intent" of the Framers, Jan. 25, 1826, *Madison* (1867), III, 515.

25. *Works,* III, 463.

26. To McHenry, May 17, 1798, *Works,* X, 282.

27. To King, July 5, 1792, to G. Morris, April 6, 1802, *Works,* X, 4, 430.

28. Aug. 13, 1787, *Papers,* IV, 234; V, 118.

29. To King, Jan. 5, 1800, *Works,* X, 359.

30. *Works,* X, 371–374; *Jay,* IV, 270–272.

31. Ames to Thomas Dwight, Jan. 30, 1792, *Ames,* I, 111–112.

32. *Federalist,* 207; *Papers,* V, 97–98.

33. June 29, 1787, *Papers,* IV, 222.

34. *Papers,* IV, 77–79. See also his notes for the argument in the Rutgers case, in A. M. Hamilton, 459–461. His youthful contribution to the American effort to construct a "dominion theory" of the British empire may be found in *Papers,* I, 90 ff.

35. Above, pp. 13–15, 19–21.

36. To Carrington, May 26, 1792, *Works,* IX, 533–534.

37. To Jonathan Dayton, 1799, *Works,* X, 335.

38. To Washington, March 24, 1783, *Papers,* III, 304.

39. The Continentalist, July 19, 1781, *Papers,* II, 655. See also *Papers,* II, 402–403, 654–657; IV, 82–83, 188–190, 202; V, 26, 70–71, 100–102; *Works,* VIII, 293–294; IX, 28, 478, 533.

40. *Federalist,* 119, 163, 197, 203.

41. *Works,* VIII, 183; *Federalist,* 203.

42. *Federalist,* 119, 174.

43. *Papers,* IV, 270.

44. *Federalist,* 201, 204–205.

45. *Federalist,* 204.

46. Aug. 18, 1792, *Works,* II, 458.

47. See his sharp letter to Isaac Homes, Collector at Charleston, about the "attempt of a part of the Citizens of Charlestown to overrule" a decision of

President Washington on the applicability of certain articles of a treaty with Sweden. June 17, 1794, Wolcott Papers, Connecticut Historical Society.

48. The event that produced Amendment XI was, of course, *Chisholm* v. *Georgia,* 2 Dallas 419 (1793), in which the Supreme Court entertained a suit against Georgia by a citizen of another state. Hamilton had denied this possibility in *The Federalist,* number 81 (pp. 487–488), as had Marshall in a speech in the Virginia Convention (Elliot, III, 555), but neither could have been displeased with the decision or the opinions in the Chisholm case. Fisher Ames invited—but did not get—Hamilton's opinion on this case. Aug. 31, 1793, *Works* (JCH), V, 581–582.

49. 1799, *Works,* X, 329–336.

50. *Jefferson* (Ford), VIII, 120; Lucius Crassus, Jan. 18, 1802, *Works,* VIII, 294–295.

51. *Papers,* V, 84–85; *Works,* V, 346.

52. *Federalist,* 157.

53. *Federalist,* 497, which is an excellent example of Hamilton's ability to suppress his own natural urges in the act of crying up the Constitution.

54. *Papers,* II, 245, 400–402; III, 219; *Journals,* XX, 469; XXIII, 798–810; Brant, *Madison,* II, 108 ff., 119–120, 217 ff.; III, 331; Andrews, *Works of James Wilson,* I, 556 ff.; Smith, *Wilson,* 151–153; Margaret C. Klingelsmith, "Two Theories in Regard to the Implied Powers of the Constitution," *American Law Register,* LIV (1906), 214.

55. *Works,* III, 446.

56. *Works,* III, 450.

57. *Papers,* IV, 207, 268.

58. *Jefferson* (Ford), V, 287.

59. *Works,* III, 452–453.

60. *Works,* III, 489.

61. *Federalist,* 194.

62. *Works,* III, 473–474.

63. June 27, 1788, *Papers,* V, 97–98; *Federalist,* 188 ff., 207–211. See his excoriation of Jefferson in 1801 for proposing to "abandon . . . all the internal revenue of the country," *Works,* VIII, 252 ff., esp. 262–263, and see his draft of a taxation act for New York in *Papers,* IV, 40 ff.

64. *Works,* IV, 151–152.

65. *Works,* IV, 152.

66. 9 Wheaton 1 (1824); 258 U.S. 495 (1922); 301 U.S. 1 (1937).

67. *Works,* III, 481; *Federalist,* 143–145, 155. See generally Crosskey, *Politics and the Constitution,* I, chaps. 4–7; W. H. Hamilton and D. Adair, *The Power to Govern* (New York, 1937), 55 ff. It is safe to say that Hamilton would have agreed unreservedly with the broad definitions of "commerce" one finds in the writings of his assistant Tench Coxe. See, for example, the excerpts in Crosskey, *Politics and the Constitution,* I, 87–89, 109–110, 229 n.

68. *Works,* III, 481–482. "The truth is," he had written in 1782, "that no federal constitution can exist without powers that, in their exercise, affect the internal police of the component members." *Papers,* III, 216.

69. Federalist, 153–154.

70. Report on Manufactures (1791), *Works,* IV, 168; VIII, 222.

71. Report on Manufactures (1791), *Works,* IV, 143 ff.; VIII, 214–223; X, 329–336.

72. Works, III, 489.

73. Phocion (1784), *Papers,* III, 540.

74. Works, III, 449.

75. 299 U.S. 304, 316–317 (1936). And see the remarkable forecast of this opinion in Sutherland's little book *Constitutional Power and World Affairs* (New York, 1919), 51–52, in which he quotes with approval Hamilton's assertion of the existence of *"resulting* powers." One of the few commentators on the Constitution to accept this category was W. W. Willoughby, *The Constitutional Law of the United States* (New York, 1910), I, 65–66, who credited it, however, to Marshall, *American Insurance Co.* v. *Canter,* 1 Peters 511, 542–543 (1828), and Story, *Commentaries,* sec. 1256. See the variations on this theme cited in *Constitution Annotated,* 72–73.

76. Sept. 3, 1780, *Papers,* II, 404.

77. Federalist, 423.

78. Federalist, 423.

79. Oct. 24, 1792, *Works,* VII, 285.

80. To Washington, March 8, 1794, *Works,* X, 67; *Federalist,* 423.

81. Federalist, 424.

82. Federalist, 424–431, 447. For his early and late preference for single administrators, see *Papers,* II, 246 n., 404–405, 472, 673–674; *Works,* VIII, 231; X, 240–241.

83. Works, VII, 285 ff., 338; X, 397; *Papers,* V, 236; *Federalist,* 436; White, *The Federalists,* chaps. 3–4. On the question of the special position of the Secretary of the Treasury as servant of both President and Congress, see Learned, *The President's Cabinet,* 100–105, and the amusing testimony of

Jefferson recorded in the "Anas," *Jefferson* (Ford), I, 189–190, which has Hamilton attempting "to place himself subject to the House when the Executive should propose what he did not like, and subject to the Executive, when the House should propose anything disagreeable."

84. Papers, IV, 208, 262.

85. That Hamilton understood the political utility of having a President delay announcing his decision to retire until the last possible moment is clear in his pleading letter to Washington, July 5, 1796, *Works,* X, 181–182.

86. Federalist, 440.

87. To the Electors of New York, April 7, 1789, *Papers,* V, 325; to William Short, Sept. 1, 1790, *Works,* IV, 302. For somewhat contrary thoughts on the issue of rotation in office, see *Works,* III, 420 ff.; *Papers,* III, 219.

88. Federalist, 441–442.

89. March 21, 1800, *Works,* VII, 205.

90. Papers, V, 188–189.

91. Lucius Crassus, Jan., 1802, *Works,* VIII, 281.

92. To King, Feb. 15, 1797, *Works,* X, 238.

93. To Bayard, Jan. 16, 1801, *Works,* X, 413.

94. Federalist, 442–447; to Washington, April 14, 1794, *Works,* V, 112.

95. To Washington, Sept. 1, 1792, *Works,* VI, 341, 344, 393, 398; draft of letter of Governor Mifflin, Aug. 30, 1794, *Works,* VI, 427–441; draft of proclamation, Sept. 25, 1794, *Works,* VI, 442–445.

96. Federalist, 68, 418, 447; to Washington, Sept. 9, 1792, *Works,* VI, 344, which was contrary to the opinion he had expressed—or, rather, been constrained to express—in 1787 and 1788, in *Papers,* IV, 263; V, 169.

97. Federalist, 459; *Annals,* I, 383, 474, 480–482. This whole debate is summarized in James Hart, *The American Presidency in Action, 1789* (New York, 1948), 155–214; E. S. Corwin, *The President's Removal Power under the Constitution* (New York, 1927), 10–23. Hamilton's mature view of the removal power was stated by Pacificus in 1793, *Works,* IV, 439. See the footnote in the edition of *The Federalist* of 1802 (published in New York), p. 202, to which Madison refers somewhat snidely in a letter to W. C. Rives, Jan. 10, 1829, *Madison* (1867), IV, 5. The note reads simply: "This construction has since been rejected by the legislature; and it is now settled in practice, that the power of displacing belongs exclusively to the president."

For another bad guess as Publius that he was later to correct as Washington's chief adviser, see his unthinking comments on the power to receive ambassadors in *Federalist,* 420. The correction was also made by Pacificus, who asserted quite soundly that this power "includes that of judging, in the case of a revolution of government in a foreign country, whether the new rulers are competent organs of the national will, and ought to be recognized or not." *Works,* IV, 441.

98. Lucius Crassus, Dec. 17, 1801, *Works,* VIII, 247–252; to McHenry, May 17, 1798, *Works,* X, 281–282, which makes clear that Hamilton did not regard the President's discretionary power to repel aggression as unlimited.

99. To Marshall, Oct. 2, 1800, cited above, p. 313, n. 170.

100. To Washington, April 14, 1794, *Works,* V, 112; to Pickering, March 22, 1797, *Works,* X, 246; to Washington, Oct. 24, 1793, *Works,* VIII, 110–113; R. V. Harlow, *The History of Legislative Methods in the Period before 1825* (New Haven, 1917), 140 ff.; White, *The Federalists,* chap. 5.

101. Above, pp. 92–93.

102. To McHenry, March 21, 1800, *Works,* VII, 203–206; VIII, 304–312, a sweeping assertion of executive discretion in spending public funds; X, 289–290; White, *The Federalists,* chap. 26.

103. June 29, 1793, *Works,* IV, 432–444.

104. *Annals,* I, 480–482. Jefferson seems to have at least toyed with this notion in a written opinion on the power of the Senate (which he denied) to "negative the grade" of persons appointed by the President to diplomatic posts, April 24, 1790, *Jefferson* (Ford), V, 161–162. Hamilton's grateful recognition as Pacificus of the precedent set in 1789—that is, the refusal of Congress to intrude upon the President's power of removal in any of the acts establishing the first executive departments—is recorded in *Works,* IV, 439.

105. *Works,* X, 338.

106. Corwin, *Removal Power,* 68–70, is doubtless correct in asserting that the Convention probably "did not regard the opening clause of Article II as constituting a grant of powers." At the same time, there is no evidence to support the contrary view that it regarded these words as purely and simply supererogatory. As is usually the case in such disputes over the meaning of some word or clause in the Constitution, the silence of the Framers—whether studied or casual—thunders. Madison, writing as Helvidius, refused to argue this point with Hamilton by simply denying that the powers to make war and peace were executive in nature. *Madison* (Hunt), VI, 143 ff.

107. *Works,* IV, 437–439, 443.

108. *Works,* IV, 440–444.

109. *Federalist,* 148, 167, 178, 223, 423, 439, 446; *Works,* II, 411; III, 14–17, 252, 394, 413, 454; IV, 136; V, 473; VI, 397; *Papers,* I, 48–49, 50–51; III, 173, 540, 549; IV, 131–132; V, 107, 352; VI, 436.

110. *Federalist,* 167.

111. Federalist, 423.

112. Burnett, *Continental Congress,* 458–460; *Letters,* V, xv, xii, 175, 305, 363, 452; Schuyler to Hamilton, Sept. 10, 16, 1780, *Papers,* II, 425, 433.

113. To William Livingston, April 21, 1777, *Papers,* I, 235–236.

114. Federalist, 223.

115. Draft of letter to Governor Mifflin, Aug. 7, 1794, *Works,* VI, 397.

116. Papers, IV, 208, 263.

117. Pacificus, June 29, 1793, *Works,* IV, 442; to Wolcott, Aug. 10, 1795, *Works,* X, 113–114.

118. Works, VIII, 166–167, 171–179; above, pp. 92–93.

119. Works, VIII, 177.

120. Camillus, Jan. 6, 1796, *Works,* VI, 174; VIII, 166, 169; X, 150.

121. Federalist, 449–454.

122. July 9, 1795, *Works,* V, 138, 158–159; VI, 174; VIII, 167–170.

123. 252 U.S. 416 (1920).

124. Federalist, 464.

125. May 5, 1789, *Papers,* V, 337.

126. Draft of message for Washington, March 20, 1796, *Works,* VIII, 176; X, 168.

127. To Washington, July 5, 1796, *Works,* X, 180.

128. Washington to Hamilton, July 3, 14, 1795, Fitzpatrick, XXXIV, 228, 241–242; Bradford to Hamilton, July 2, 1795, Hamilton Papers, L of C.

129. Works, X, 281–282.

130. See his comment in *Federalist,* 429, on the "restraints of public opinion" as a check upon the executive.

131. Federalist, 411–415, 464, which makes clear that Hamilton expected the electors of the President to be "chosen by the people."

132. June 21, 1788, *Papers,* V, 38; *Works,* VI, 179; VIII, 169.

133. June 18, 1787, *Papers,* IV, 193, 200.

134. To Morris, March 4, April 6, 1802, *Works,* X, 427–428, 429–432. He had taken the same view, in the Convention of 1787, of the constituency of the House of Representatives. Above, p. 48. On June 22, 1787 Hamilton "pressed the distinction," according to Madison, "between state governments and the people." *Papers,* IV, 215. For his draft of this amendment, see *Works* (JCH), VII, 836.

135. For Hamilton's early view of the importance of courts in a sound social order, see *Papers*, I, 167–168; III, 421. His despair over the failure of the Articles of Confederation to establish a judiciary is recorded in *Federalist*, 150–151.

136. Federalist, 465.

137. Federalist, 466; *Works*, VIII, 335–336; *Papers*, IV, 97. For an interesting Southern comment on this aspect of Hamilton's theory of the judiciary, see S. J. Ervin, Jr., "Alexander Hamilton's Phantom," *Vital Speeches*, XXII (1955), 23.

138. Federalist, 464–472.

139. Federalist, 465.

140. Dec. 29, 1801–March 20, 1802, *Works*, VIII, 271–283, 312–364.

141. Works, VIII, 334, 336.

142. Works, VIII, 333.

143. Federalist, 446–447.

144. Works, VIII, 272–273.

145. Federalist, 491–495.

146. Federalist, 466, 475–476, 482–483; *Works*, VIII, 179, in which he acknowledges the right of the House of Representatives to "pause in the execution" of a controversial treaty "until a decision on the point of constitutionality in the Supreme Court of the United States shall have settled the question."

147. For examples of Hamilton's own use of this "vague Whig assumption," see *Papers*, I, 110; III, 488–497, 530–556; IV, 30, 73, 78; *Federalist*, 205, 406.

148. In addition to his argument in *Rutgers* v. *Waddington* (above, pp. 95–96), Hamilton expounded something akin to the doctrine of judicial review in a speech to the New York Assembly in 1787, *Papers*, IV, 152. It is interesting to note that he went out of his way to avoid making a flat assertion of this doctrine in the earlier essays of Publius. See *Federalist*, 117, 203, 205. He was probably moved to write number 78 by the dark picture of judicial review painted by Yates as Brutus in the *New-York Journal*, Jan. 31, 1788.

149. Federalist, 466–469, as well as the other remarks on judicial review at pp. 117, 482–483. See also his later (and entirely consistent) allusions in *Works*, VIII, 173, 179, 342–345, in which, with becoming modesty, he quotes his argument in *The Federalist*, number 78 at length.

150. Papers, IV, 209, 265–267, 270–271.

151. Works, VIII, 344–345.

152. Camillus, Sept. 18, 1795, *Works*, V, 384.

153. Hamilton's opinion, dated March 25, 1796, is used and reprinted in Robert Goodloe Harper, *The Case of the Georgia Sales on the Mississippi* (Philadelphia, 1799), 37–38, 88–89, where it is incorrectly dated 1795. Another opinion, undated and titled "Opinion for Constable on the Yazoo Affair," is in the Hamilton Papers, L of C. Harper appeared before the Court as counsel for the purchasers, and pressed Hamilton's views upon Marshall and his colleagues. On Hamilton's role, see B. F. Wright, *The Contract Clause of the Constitution* (Cambridge, 1938), 21–22, 28, 244; Warren, *Supreme Court,* I, 396–397.

154. For his scattered observations on the courts as guardians of the rights of property "against fraudulent and oppressive laws of particular states," see *Works,* III, 410; VIII, 273; *Papers,* VI, 434 ff.

155. 283 U.S. 697 (1931), for which the way was prepared in *Gitlow* v. *New York,* 268 U.S. 652, 666 (1925), and *Fiske* v. *Kansas,* 274 U.S. 380 (1927). In his one pointed remark on "due process," Hamilton insisted that these words "have a precise technical import, and are only applicable to the process and proceedings of courts of justice; they can never be referred to an act of legislature." To the New York Assembly, Feb. 6, 1787, *Papers,* IV, 35. He was speaking in this instance of a clause in the New York Constitution of 1777.

156. Federalist, 482, 468. See generally E. V. Rostow, "The Democratic Character of Judicial Review," *Harvard Law Review,* LXVI (1952), 193, 196.

157. To Madison, Oct. 17, 1792, Madison Papers, NYPL. Beckley also warned Madison—as if the latter did not already know to his chagrin—that there was "no inferior degree of sagacity in the combinations of this *extraordinary* man," that he went about his frightful business "with a comprehensive eye, a subtle and contriving mind, and a soul devoted to his object."

158. Catullus, Sept. 29, 1792, *Works,* VII, 273.

159. Federalist, 482–483.

CHAPTER SEVEN   **THE RELEVANCE OF HAMILTON**

1. New York Gazette and General Advertiser, June 3, 1831; Stokes, *Iconography of Manhattan,* III, 877, plate 20A; V, 1587, 1623, 1703; C. H. Winfield, *History of the County of Hudson, New Jersey* (New York, 1874), 221–223; P. Stansbury, *A Pedestrian Tour of Two Thousand Miles* (New York, 1822), 14. The plaque from this monument is preserved in the New-York Historical Society.

2. Statement on "expected interview" with Burr, 1804, *Works,* X, 471, 474; Wolcott to Mrs. Wolcott, July 11, 1804, A. M. Hamilton, 405; Morris, *Diary of Gouverneur Morris,* II, 456.

3. On the fascinating topic of the posthumous career of Jefferson, see the instructive study (to which I am greatly indebted) of Merrill D. Peterson, *The Jefferson Image in the American Mind* (New York, 1960).

4. Charles A. Beard, *The Enduring Federalist* (Garden City, 1948), 10. "Seldom has any minister," wrote John Marshall in his *Washington,* V, 608, "excited in a higher or more extensive degree than Colonel Hamilton the opposite passions of love and hate."

5. S. E. Morison, "Faith of a Historian," *AHR,* LVI (1951), 261, 272.

6. Henry S. Randall, *The Life of Thomas Jefferson* (New York, 1858), esp. I, 640–645; Peterson, *Jefferson Image,* 112–113, 149 ff. See also George Tucker, *The Life of Thomas Jefferson* (Philadelphia, 1837), which is not, to be sure, quite so hard on a man Tucker later came to admire.

7. May 15, 1876, W. C. Ford, ed., *Letters of Henry Adams* (Boston, 1930–1938), I, 284; Henry Adams, *History of the United States,* I, 85, 277; II, 168 ff.; Peterson, *Jefferson Image,* 280 ff. Jefferson himself set this style for latter-day Jeffersonians by writing to John Breckinridge about "our Buonaparte," Jan. 29, 1800, *Jefferson* (Ford), VII, 417–418. In his *Life of Albert Gallatin* (Philadelphia, 1879), 267, Adams showed his respect for Hamilton as an administrator of great affairs by recommending him and Gallatin as the two "perfect models, not perhaps in all respects for imitation, but for study" to those "persons who wish to understand what practical statesmanship has been under an American system."

8. See again the treatment of Hamilton in Malone, *Jefferson and the Rights of Man,* xx–xxii, 286, 305, 314, 329, 341, 352, and *Jefferson and the Ordeal of Liberty,* 11, 43, 68, which are dotted with words like "aggressiveness," "imperiousness," "lust for power," "intrigue," "potential dictator," "officious," "natural prima donna," and "egotism." Jefferson, to the contrary, was "a true and sure symbol of the rights of man." The Manichean interpretation of Jefferson and Hamilton is stated explicitly by James Truslow Adams, *The Epic of America* (Boston, 1932), 111–113; Wiltse, *Jeffersonian Tradition,* 99–101, for whom their whole conflict is simply another chapter in the "age-old controversy between authority and liberty"; and Stuart Gerry Brown, "The Mind of Thomas Jefferson," *Ethics,* LXXIII (1963), 79, 82–83.

9. Above, pp. 162, 317; Dixon Wecter, *The Hero in America* (New York, 1941), 483–484, and references there noted; Merle Curti, *The Growth of American Thought,* 2nd ed. (New York, 1951), 192; John D. Hicks, *The Federal Union* (Boston, 1937), 218; David S. Muzzey, *Thomas Jefferson* (New York, 1918), 161; Vernon L. Parrington, *Main Currents in American Thought* (New York, 1930), I, 307; Paul P. Van Riper, *History of the United States Civil Service* (Evanston, 1958), 18; James MacGregor Burns, *The Deadlock of Democracy* (Englewood Cliffs, N.J., 1963), 335, who writes with true Jeffersonian contempt of Hamilton's "famous malediction on the people."

10. I base these judgments on a careful reading of all references to Hamilton and Jefferson in the following standard college texts in American history: John M. Blum *et. al., The National Experience* (New York, 1963), chap. 6 (by Edmund S. Morgan); Thomas A. Bailey, *The American Pageant,* 2nd ed. (Boston, 1961); Harry J. Carman and Harold C. Syrett, *A History of the American People* (New York, 1958); Oliver P. Chitwood, R. W. Patrick, Frank L. Owsley, and H. C. Nixon, *The American People: A History,* 3rd ed. (New York, 1962); Richard N. Current, T. Harry Williams, and Frank Freidel, *American History: A Survey* (New York, 1961); Dumas Malone and Basil Rauch, *Empire for Liberty* (New York, 1960); Harold U. Faulkner, *American Political and Social History* (New York, 1937); John D. Hicks, *The Federal Union;* Richard Hofstadter, William Miller, and Daniel Aaron, *The American Republic* (Englewood Cliffs, N.J., 1959); Samuel E. Morison and Henry S. Commager, *The Growth of the American Republic,* 5th ed. (New York, 1962); Dexter Perkins and Glyndon Van Deusen, *The United States of America: A History* (New York, 1962); R. A. Billington, B. J. Loewenberg, and S. H. Brockunier, *The United States* (New York, 1947); Charles A. Beard, *The Rise of American Civilization* (New York, 1930); Charles A. and Mary R. Beard, *A Basic History of the United States* (New York, 1944).

Not all these authors, to be sure, are blatantly unfair to Hamilton. Carman and Syrett, for example, speak warmly of the contributions of this "aristocrat" who "despised democracy and republicanism" to the "survival of the world's most democratic nation" (*History,* 229, 236); Morison and Commager concede that his "genius" enabled the new government to "function successfully" (*Growth of the Republic,* I, 323); Current and friends acknowledge that he had a decisive and largely "positive" influence on the policies of Washington's administration. Yet even the least Jeffersonian of them is guilty to some degree of the doubtless petty crime of portraying a great man as a somewhat smaller (or perhaps simply slightly more ridiculous) figure than he was in his own day and ought to be in ours. Perkins and Van Deusen, *United States of America,* I, 208, 210, express the standard Jeffersonian view of Hamilton more accurately than they probably realize in describing him as the "brilliant, profound and intolerant architect of the federal economic system," and in making him primarily a foil to the "shy and gentle" Jefferson, who "never engaged in a personal quarrel."

Hamilton is treated rather more blandly, and thus just as unsatisfactorily, in such standard high-school texts as Mabel G. Planer and W. L. Neff, *Freedom under Law* (Milwaukee, 1962), 136–139, 196–197; L. H. Canfield and H. B. Wilder, *The Making of Modern America* (Boston, 1958), chap. 7, which is kinder than usual to him; Merle Curti and L. P. Todd, *The Rise of the American Nation* (New York, 1961), 210, 218; Samuel Steinberg, *The United States* (New York, 1958), 145 ff.; H. W. Bragdon and S. P. McCutchen, *History of a Free People* (New York, 1961), 161 ff.

11. Arthur N. Holcombe, in Jones, ed., *Chief Justice John Marshall,* 34; Faulkner, *American Political and Social History,* 129; Morison and Commager, *Growth of the Republic,* I, 319; Hofstadter *et al., American Republic,* I, 237; Arthur M. Schlesinger, *New Viewpoints in American History* (New York, 1923), 26, 80, 81.

12. Randall, *Life of Jefferson,* I, 641.

13. Koch, *Power, Morals, and the Founding Fathers,* 59, 67; Monaghan, *Jay,* 342.

14. The implicit distinction between Hamilton as a major spur to American nationalism and Hamilton as an American patriot of questionable standing is made in Merle Curti, *The Roots of American Loyalty* (New York, 1946), 99, 109, 115.

15. The temptation to write Hamilton off as a clever plutocrat is evident in Harold J. Laski, *The American Democracy* (London, 1953), 211, 434. For a Marxist interpretation, see Herbert M. Morais, *The Struggle for Freedom* (New York, 1944), 250, 259 ff., 295, for whom Hamilton is (and deserves to be) the "patron saint of American reaction."

16. Ralph Barton Perry, *Characteristically American* (New York, 1949); Carl Becker, *Freedom and Responsibility in the American Way of Life* (New York, 1945); Dexter Perkins, *The American Approach to Foreign Policy,* rev. ed. (Cambridge, 1962); Hans Kohn, *American Nationalism* (New York, 1961). See also the neglect of Hamilton's ideas in Curti, *Growth of American Thought,* 190–192; Daniel J. Boorstin, *The Genius of American Politics* (Chicago, 1953), 96–97; David Potter, *People of Plenty* (Chicago, 1954). On the other hand, an unusual appreciation of Hamilton may be found in Stephen Vincent Benét, *America* (New York, 1944), 37.

17. Peterson, *Jefferson Image,* 343–344, reveals Wilson as a man perhaps a little too fond of this formula. In 1894 he disposed of Jefferson, of whom he then had a low opinion, in exactly the same words. See the interesting references to Hamilton in R. S. Baker and W. E. Dodd, eds., *The Public Papers of Woodrow Wilson* (New York, 1925), I, 33, 330, 427; II, 132; III, 7.

18. *World Almanac* (1962), 235.

19. Richard Hildreth, *The History of the United States of America* (New York, 1856), III, 430, 435, 491–494, 538; IV, 297–299, 357–373, 527; John Bach McMaster, *A History of the People of the United States* (New York, 1883–1913), I, 37, 51, 125, 528; Hermann von Holst, *The Constitutional History of the United States* (Chicago, 1876–1892), I, 104 ff. See also George Ticknor Curtis, *History of the Origin, Formation, and Adoption of the Constitution* (New York, 1854), I, 406–419, who later described the Civil War as a "vindication" of Hamilton; C. J. Riethmuller, *The Life and Times of Alexander Hamilton* (London, 1864). A fascinating picture of Hamilton as "monarchist," but also as a giant of the early years, was drawn in Martin Van Buren's post-humously published *Inquiry into the Origin and Course of Political Parties in the United States* (New York, 1867), esp. chaps. 2–4. The family's loyal retort was fired in James A. Hamilton, *Mr. Van Buren's Calumnies Repudiated* (New York, 1870).

20. John C. Hamilton, *History of the Republic of the United States of America, as Traced in the Writings of Alexander Hamilton and of His Cotemporaries,* 7 vols. (New York, 1857–1864); James A. Hamilton, *Reminiscences of James A. Hamilton* (New York, 1869), esp. chap. 1. See generally the interesting foot-notes in Douglass Adair, "Hamilton on the Louisiana Purchase," *WMQ,* 3rd ser., XII (1955), 268, 278–279. On the loyal efforts of Mrs. Hamilton, see Alice C. Desmond, *Alexander Hamilton's Wife* (New York, 1952). Whatever doubts others may have had, his "saucy little charmer" Betsy had none. In 1853 she was still telling skeptical visitors to her house in Washington: "He *made* your Government! He made your Bank." Carrol Perry, *A Professor of Life* (Boston, 1923), 78–79.

21. March 10, 1831, *The Works of Daniel Webster* (Boston, 1853), I, 200.

22. On the influence of Hamilton as political economist in the nineteenth century, see Dorfman, *Economic Mind,* II, 566, 574, 577, 631, 633, 650, 722, 752, 770, 887, 908–909. Dorfman, to be sure, rather overworks the description "Hamil-tonian" when he applies it to Lincoln. See also K. W. Rowe, *Matthew Carey* (Baltimore, 1933), 114.

23. Allan Nevins, ed., *The Diary of John Quincy Adams* (New York, 1928), 477–478. For the view of Hamilton as financier extraordinary, and as several other things as well, see Adams, *Jubilee of the Constitution,* 107–112. The son, of course, found it easier to be kind to Hamilton than did the father, whose tart opinions may be sampled in *Adams,* IX, 273, 277, 289–290, 294–295, 299–300; X, 127–128, 155; Malone, *Jefferson and the Ordeal of Liberty,* 330; P. Smith, *John Adams,* 1085. It is pleasant to learn that Adams, despite all his complaints against this "bastard brat of a Scotch peddler," was ready to meet him in heaven. *Adams,* X, 314.

24. In the one clear reference to Hamilton in Roy P. Basler, ed., *The Collected Works of Abraham Lincoln* (New Brunswick, 1953), III, 531–532, he is de-scribed in the course of the Cooper Union Address as one of several "noted anti-slavery men" of the early Republic who understood that the federal govern-ment could control slavery in the federal territories. It is interesting to note that his argument in *The Federalist,* number 23 for the limitless nature of the power to make war was used effectively in the highly influential work by William Whiting, *War Powers Under the Constitution,* 43rd ed. (Boston, 1871).

On Southern hostility to Hamilton, see Peterson, *Jefferson Image,* 214–215; Alexander Hamilton Stephens, *A Constitutional View of the Late War Between the States* (Philadelphia, 1868), I, 41–48, 127, 145, 218–285, 502; II, 25–29, in which the Vice-President of the Confederacy with the incongruous name tries to use Hamilton and to attack him as the arch-nationalist at the same time; Albert T. Bledsoe, "Alexander Hamilton," *Southern Review,* Oct., 1867, and July, 1869, a scathing view of Hamilton as a combined consolidationist-monarchist. The consensus of the South was stated in a letter of J. R. O'Sullivan to Jefferson Davis, August 10, 1879, D. Rowland, ed., *Jefferson Davis, Constitutionalist* (Jackson, Miss., 1923), VIII, 407: "The germ of the Civil War was in the Constitution of 1787. And it was Alexander Hamilton who, more than any other man, planted it there."

25. Jan. 26, 1865, B. A. Hinsdale, ed., *The Works of James Garfield* (Boston, 1882), I, 71.

26. Robert McCloskey, *American Conservatism in the Age of Enterprise* (Cambridge, 1951), 23–24. William Graham Sumner solved the dilemma presented to conservative Spencerians in Hamilton's record as a public man by playing up his loathing of repudiation and playing down his confidence in the guiding hand of government, in *Alexander Hamilton* (New York, 1890), esp. 13, 102.

27. E. Merrill Root, *Brainwashing in the High Schools* (New York, 1958), 58–60, 97–98, 101–103. See also the sharp treatment of Hamilton in Kirk, *The Conservative Mind,* 65–70, and the neglect of him as a suitable hero in the literature of modern business, as chronicled in F. X. Sutton *et al., The American Business Creed* (Cambridge, 1956). For a more sophisticated conservative approach to Hamilton, see "The Reluctant Democrat," *Fortune,* Dec., 1943, and Katherine Hamill, "Was Hamilton the First Keynesian?," *Fortune,* Aug., 1957, and for a more admiring ultra-conservative approach, see the testimony of J. Harvie Williams of the American Good Government Society, June 3, 1954, before a subcommittee of the Senate Committee on the Judiciary, *Establishment of a Commission to Celebrate the Two Hundredth Anniversary of the Birth of Alexander Hamilton,* 83rd Congr., 2nd sess. Mr. Williams did so well, apparently, that he was named to direct the Commission, and responded with an ultra-conservative exhortation called "Alexander Hamilton: His Spirit Is Alive Today," *American Bar Association Journal,* XLV (1959), 155.

28. James Bryce, *The American Commonwealth* (London, 1891), II, 639 n. See also Bryce's *The Predictions of Hamilton and De Tocqueville* (Baltimore, 1887), 13 ff., as well as the earlier admiring testimony of François Guizot, *The Character and Influence of Washington* (Boston, 1840), 126–127.

29. Lodge, *Alexander Hamilton;* John T. Morse, *The Life of Alexander Hamilton* (Boston, 1876); L. H. Boutell, *Alexander Hamilton, the Constructive Statesman* (Chicago, 1890); Frederick Scott Oliver, *Alexander Hamilton.* See also George Shea, *The Life and Epoch of Alexander Hamilton,* 3rd ed. (Boston, 1881); M. W. Stryker, *Hamilton, Lincoln and Other Addresses* (Utica, 1896); Chauncey Depew, *Orations, Addresses, and Speeches* (New York, 1910), I,

43–49; Frank P. Stearns, *True Republicanism* (Philadelphia, 1904), 107–140; Elbert Hubbard, *Little Journeys to the Homes of American Statesmen* (New York, 1898). See the approving comments on plans to erect a statue of Hamilton in Washington in *Bankers Magazine,* XCV (1917), 4, 58.

30. See the many references in E. E. Morison, ed., *The Letters of Theodore Roosevelt* (Cambridge, 1954), I, 490; V, 351–352, 368, 407, 469; VI, 1527; VII, 48, 121, 175, 229; VIII, 1415. Roosevelt was doubtless pleased to hear Elihu Root describe himself as "a convinced and uncompromising nationalist of the school of Alexander Hamilton" and Henry L. Stimson salute Hamilton as a "doer" who "made the nation go." Root, *Addresses on Government and Citizenship* (New York, 1916), 251; Stimson to Roosevelt, Dec. 27, 1910, Roosevelt Papers, L of C, enclosing a memorandum entitled "The Re-Alignment of National Parties in America."

31. Gertrude Atherton, *The Conqueror* (New York, 1902); Nicholas Murray Butler, *Building the American Nation* (New York, 1923), 99 ff.; Edward Channing, *A History of the United States* (New York, 1905–1925), III, 463–464, 473; IV, 42, 66, 87, 88, 162, 163, 166, 463.

32. Croly, *The Promise of American Life* (New York, 1909), 29, 38–46, 169, 214, 293.

33. In Lewis, ed., *Great American Lawyers,* I, 422–425, 432.

34. Foremost among those stalwart Republicans who hailed the memory of Hamilton—as republican, capitalist, Whig constitutionalist, and isolationist—was Arthur H. Vandenberg of Michigan, later to be a ranking Senator. See his *Alexander Hamilton, the Greatest American* (New York, 1921); *If Hamilton Were Here Today* (New York, 1923); and *The Trail of a Tradition* (New York, 1926). See also Robert I. Warshow, *Alexander Hamilton, First American Business Man* (New York, 1931), appropriately dedicated to Andrew W. Mellon, "who has carried on with rare distinction the tradition of Hamilton." Yet the American Liberty League seems to have preferred Jefferson to Hamilton as an exemplar of its version of the American way of life. Peterson, *Jefferson Image,* 368–371, 509–510.

35. In addition to the biographies of Hamilton by Mitchell, Hacker, Miller, and Schachner, see David Loth, *Alexander Hamilton: Portrait of a Prodigy* (New York, 1939). Stanley D. Rose, "Alexander Hamilton and the Historians," *Vanderbilt Law Review,* XI (1958), 853, is a useful word of caution to people like the author of this book. (I mean *this* book.)

36. Croly, *Promise of American Life,* 214; *Progressive Democracy* (New York, 1914), 54–55. For other Progressive views of Hamilton, which ranged from the respectful to the disrespectful by way of perplexity, see Parrington, *Main Currents in American Thought,* I, 292–307; Beard, *Economic Origins of Jeffersonian Democracy,* and *Economic Interpretation of the Constitution,* 100–114, who saw in him "the colossal genius of the new system"; Algie M. Simons, *Social Forces in American History* (New York, 1911), 108 ff.; J. Allen Smith, *The Spirit of American Government* (New York, 1912), 73 ff.

37. S. I. Rosenman, ed., *The Public Papers and Addresses of Franklin D. Roosevelt* (New York, 1938–1950), IX, 29–30, as well as I, 629, 745. For a less charitable assessment, see Roosevelt's review of Bowers, *Jefferson and Hamilton* in the *New York Evening World,* Dec. 3, 1925, reprinted in *American Mercury,* Sept., 1945. And for the most perceptive and revealing of the New Deal interpretations of Hamilton, see the articles of Dorfman and Tugwell, above, p. 262, n. 20. Stow Persons has noted this appeal of Hamilton in his *American Minds* (New York, 1958), 437.

38. George Bancroft, *History of the United States of America,* "The Author's Last Revision" (New York, 1883–1885), IV, 443.

39. James Parton, *Life of Thomas Jefferson* (Boston, 1874); Peterson, *Jefferson Image,* 234.

40. See especially the interpretation of Joseph Charles, *Origins of the American Party System,* 38–53. One of the chief obstacles to the Hamilton family's efforts to secure justice for their hero in the nineteenth century was the fear of old Federalist leaders that Washington's reputation might suffer if too much were revealed about such questions as the authorship of the Farewell Address. See J. A. Hamilton, *Reminiscences,* 24–34; *King,* VI, 612–621; Troup to Pickering, Feb. 15, March 17, 1828, Hamilton Papers, L of C, who speaks of "a very general and very strong repugnance" among "our old federal friends" to the maneuvers of the Hamilton family, which, incidentally, extended into the courts; Marshall to Bushrod Washington, June 20, 1825, Marshall Papers, L of C, who expresses surprise—and just a hint of distaste—at learning at this late date "that a correspondence took place between General Washington and General Hamilton respecting the Farewell Address which shows perhaps . . . that it was written by General Hamilton." See also the interesting letter of Madison to Jefferson, June 27, 1823, *Madison* (1867), III, 323.

41. Wecter, *Hero in America,* 11, 176, 180. And see the more subtle analysis of Gerald W. Johnson, *American Heroes and Hero-Worship* (New York, 1943), chap. 3, which emphasizes the Romantic streak in Hamilton's make-up.

42. From an editorial on the Senate's vote in favor of establishing Hamilton's home as a national monument, *New York Times,* April 3, 1962.

43. To G. Morris, Feb. 27, 1802, *Works,* X, 425–426.

44. Broadus Mitchell, *Heritage from Hamilton* (New York, 1957), 44.

45. I make this statement on the basis of a painstaking and frustrating search through the published and unpublished papers of the following of Hamilton's associates: Ames, Bayard, Boudinot, Bradford, Cabot, Duane, Duer, Ellsworth,

Harper, Harison, Higginson, Jay, King, Knox, Marshall, McHenry, G. Morris, R. Morris, Otis, Pickering, Read, Sedgwick, Smith, Troup, Washington, Wilson, and Wolcott, not to forget Adams, the Madison of 1783–1790, and such lesser lights (in Hamilton's own career) as Carroll, Iredell, H. Lee, the Pinckneys, J. Rutledge, Benjamin Stoddert, Tracy, Webb, and Noah Webster.

46. (Philadelphia) *Aurora,* Jan. 1, May 9, 1799; *Journal of William Maclay,* 202–203, 206, 221, 252; "Tom Callender, Esq.," *Letters to Alexander Hamilton,* 6.

47. See the candid tributes to Hamilton's intellectual leadership in the following letters: Higginson to Hamilton, Feb. 23, 1791, J. F. Jameson, ed., "Letters of Stephen Higginson, 1783–1804," *American Historical Association, Annual Report* (1896), I, 782, 784, who confesses that the very fact that certain "measures and projections" emanate from Hamilton is enough in itself to persuade him of their merit; Henry Lee to Hamilton, Aug. 12, 1791, Hamilton Papers, L of C ("The superiority of your understanding I am not a stranger to and therefore am very often led to doubt the accuracy of my own conclusions"); Henry Lee to Hamilton, March 5, 1800, *Works* (JCH), VI, 430; Bayard to Hamilton, Aug. 11, 1800, Bayard Papers, NYPL; William Vans Murray to Hamilton, Oct. 9, 1800, *Works* (JCH), VI, 476 ("A letter from you is no affair of ceremony. It is an obligation on any man who flatters himself with the hope of your personal esteem"); John Rutledge to Hamilton, Jan. 10, 1801, *Works* (JCH) VI, 509–511; King to Hamilton, Jan. 12, 1802, *Works* (JCH), VI, 527, only one of many letters in which this faithful friend paid unstinting tribute to the "treasures" of Hamilton's mind; Bayard to Hamilton, April 12, 1802, *Works* (JCH), VI, 539–540 ("We beg your opinion. You know the value we set upon it, and the influence it will have on our determination."); McHenry to Pickering, Feb. 23, 1811, *McHenry,* 569.

48. King to Hamilton, April 24, 1793, Carrington to Hamilton, Dec. 12, 1794, *Works* (JCH), V, 553–554, 614–616; Higginson to Hamilton, Oct. 27, 1789, *Papers,* V, 466. See also John Lowell's salute to Hamilton's intellectual leadership in 1828, in T. W. Higginson, *Life and Times of Stephen Higginson* (Boston, 1907), 292.

49. E. Rutledge to Hamilton, May 27, 1795, *Works* (JCH), VI, 2–3; John Wynkoop to Hamilton, March 25, 1789, *Papers,* V, 308. That Hamilton could seek as well as give advice on constitutional problems (in this instance, on the power to pardon) is plain in an exchange with Richard Harison, April 26, May 24, 1791, Harison Papers, NYHS, as well as the exchanges in *Papers,* V, 410, 413–414, 504–506, 521–522; VI, 296, 300, 480, 492. That he may also have been tutored in his deepening suspicions of democracy is plain in such letters as Ames to Hamilton, Jan. 26, 1797, Wolcott to Hamilton, April 5, 1798, Sedgwick to Hamilton, Jan. 27, 1803, *Works* (JCH), VI, 198, 278, 552.

50. Jan. 18, 1802, *Jefferson* (Ford), VIII, 127.

51. Gallatin to Gales and Seaton, Feb. 5, 1835, *Gallatin,* II, 501–503.

52. L. D. White, *The Jeffersonians* (New York, 1951), 134 ff.; Henry Adams, *Gallatin*, 276 ff.; Monroe to Jefferson, Oct. 1, 1813, S. M. Hamilton, *Writings of Monroe*, V, 273–274; Raymond Walters, *Albert Gallatin* (New York, 1957), 247, 262–264; Alexander Balinky, *Albert Gallatin. Fiscal Theories and Policies* (New Brunswick, 1958), 41 ff., 144, 149, a highly useful survey of the similarities and dissimilarities of the purposes and methods of the two men.

53. Henry Adams, *Gallatin*, 268.

54. Veto of "an act to incorporate the subscribers to the Bank of the United States of America," Jan. 30, 1815, *Madison* (Hunt), VIII, 327. As Madison's great champion Brant points out: "In 1791 he denied that the power of Congress to borrow money included the power of creating the ability to borrow it. But he vetoed this Second Bank because it had been stripped of that very function." *Madison*, VI, 349–350.

55. Dec. 5, 1815, *Madison* (Hunt), VIII, 335–344. Madison salved his own constitutional conscience by vetoing Calhoun's "bonus bill" for internal improvements on March 3, 1817. *Madison* (Hunt), VIII, 386–388. See also *Madison* (1867), III, 436, 507; IV, 136 n., 148, for some Madisonian observations on Hamilton's construction of the Constitution.

56. Brant, *Madison*, VI, 403.

57. March 9, 1816, *Annals*, XIV, 1189, 1191–1194; J. F. Hopkins, ed., *The Papers of Henry Clay* (Lexington, Ky., 1959–), II, 201–204. This was in fact a report of a speech to his constituents in Kentucky in which he gave the "substance" of his unreported speech in the Committee of the Whole in the House.

58. *Proceedings of the American Philosophical Society*, CII (1958), 127; Brant, *Madison*, VI, 403; *Annals*, XIV, 684–688.

59. Lodge, *Hamilton*, 276–277; *Gallatin*, III, 319–333, in which Gallatin (in 1831) accepts Hamilton's reading of the words "necessary and proper" but not "general welfare." One old Jeffersonian who refused to give an inch in the rearguard action against Hamiltonian constitutionalism was John Taylor of Caroline, especially in his *Construction Construed, and Constitutions Vindicated* (Richmond, 1820), and *New Views of the Constitution* (Washington, 1823).

60. Still the most judicious assessment is Edward S. Corwin, *John Marshall and the Constitution* (New Haven, 1920). I mean no disrespect to Senator Beveridge's justly celebrated *Life of John Marshall* (Boston, 1916–1919), when I say that the time has long since come for a major new biography of Marshall. Although Beveridge described Hamilton as a "colossus" of "courage and constructive genius," the "foremost creative mind in American statesmanship," and a man "transcendently great" (*Marshall*, I, 397 n.; III, 277 n.), he gives him no credit in the shaping of Marshall's ideas, indeed fails almost completely to forge any link, political or intellectual, between the two men.

61. See the testimony of Jefferson himself, who, learning in 1792 that Hamilton was pushing Marshall to run for Congress, wrote to Madison: "I am told that Marshall has expressed half a mind to come. Hence I conclude that Hamilton has plied him well with flattery and solicitation." And then he added, in a burst of unthinking prophecy he would have cause to regret: "I think nothing better could be done than to make him a judge." June 29, 1792, *Jefferson* (Ford), VI, 95.

62. See the note on Hamilton in the Pickering Papers, MHS, dated Washington, Feb. 13, 1811, in which Marshall is recorded as expressing "astonishment" over the quantity and quality of Hamilton's letters in the papers of Washington, as well as other notes of June 2, 1827, and Dec. 12, 1851 (Octavius Pickering), and the undated memoranda in vol. 51, pp. 233–234, 314, vol. 52, p. 85.

63. Marshall doubtless saw Hamilton's Opinion of 1791 in the Washington papers, which had been bequeathed to Bushrod Washington and made available to him in 1800 or 1801. The Opinion did not become available for public inspection until several years after Hamilton's death, when it was printed, first, in a pamphlet of which all extant copies lack the title page and thus cannot be dated exactly, and, second, in *Works of Alexander Hamilton* (1810), I, 111–155. Entry No. 23424 in Charles Evans, *American Bibliography* (Chicago, 1903–1955) was made with misgivings, and there is no evidence for the suggestion that the Opinion was printed in 1791. Hamilton would have been happy to have had it printed immediately, but Washington certainly had no intention of letting it go. On the Hamilton-Marshall relationship, see generally William McDonald, "The Indebtedness of John Marshall to Alexander Hamilton," *Massachusetts Historical Society, Proceedings,* XLVI (1912–1913), 412. Marshall, a jealous guardian of the secrets put in his hands by Bushrod Washington, "declined complying with a request of General Hamilton's to send him copies of some papers." Marshall to William Paterson, May 3, 1802, Paterson Papers, NYPL.

64. For interesting references to Hamilton, see Marshall, *Washington,* V, 131–132, 146–147, 213, 234 ff., 293 ff., 306, 352–353, 608–610.

65. For judicial echoes of *The Federalist,* number 78, during and just after Hamilton's life, see *Van Horne's Lessee* v. *Dorrance,* 2 Dallas 304, 308–310 (1795); *Calder* v. *Bull,* 3 Dallas 386, 387–388 (1798); *Fletcher* v. *Peck,* 6 Cranch 87, 137–138 (1810); *Dartmouth College* v. *Woodward,* 4 Wheaton 518, 625 (1819). The argument for judicial independence in this number of *The Federalist* was pressed on the attention of the Court by Charles Lee, counsel for Marbury, in *Marbury* v. *Madison,* 1 Cranch 137, 149 (1803).

66. Above, p. 330, n. 153.

67. Francis N. Thorpe, "Hamilton's Ideas in Marshall's Decisions," *Boston University Law Review,* I (1921), 8; B. H. Levy, *Our Constitution: Tool or Testament?* (New York, 1941), 29–33, 36–42.

68. *Speeches by Oliver Wendell Holmes* (Boston, 1934), 89–90. Later in this speech he ties together the heroes of the Union by remarking that "the theory for which Hamilton argued, and he [Marshall] decided, and Webster spoke, and Grant fought, and Lincoln died, is now our corner-stone." Perhaps the most positive statements of any scholar on the influence of Hamilton over Marshall have been made by Benjamin F. Wright, *Contract Clause of the Constitution,* 21, 28, and *The Growth of American Constitutional Law* (Boston, 1942), 23, 37, 42, 47, 244. See also Charles G. Haines, *The Role of the Supreme Court in American Government and Politics, 1798–1835* (Berkeley, 1944), 199, 356, 621, 639 ff., 657–658.

69. *Papers,* IV, 650.

70. Elliot, III, 553. See Edmond Cahn, ed., *Supreme Court and Supreme Law* (Bloomington, Ind., 1954), 13–19, for the thesis that Marshall must have become acquainted with the concept of judicial review in the course of the excitement over *Commonwealth* v. *Caton,* 4 Call (Va.) 5 (1782).

71. *McCulloch* v. *Maryland,* 4 Wheaton 316, 415 (1819).

72. Marshall to Hamilton, April 25, 1796 (in which Marshall seems to be trying to take both sides in the fight over the right of the House of Representatives to judge for itself whether to appropriate money for executing Jay's Treaty); Aug. 23, 1800 (a perfunctory note); Jan. 1, 1801 (a gem of a letter on the relative merits—or, rather, demerits—of Jefferson and Burr), all in *Works* (JCH), VI, 108, 460, 501; Hamilton to Marshall, Oct. 2, 1800, cited above, p. 313, n. 170, in which Hamilton discusses the military powers of the President and the necessity of an "accomodating course" toward France, and ends: "I will make no apology for intimations dictated by my solicitude for the public weal and offered to one whom I always place among the number of my friends." All three of Marshall's letters were written in reply to letters of Hamilton that have, alas, been lost.

73. *Massachusetts Historical Society, Proceedings,* 2nd ser., XIV (1900–1901), 324–360 (in a letter of Dec. 25, 1832, he gives all credit for crushing the Whiskey Rebellion to Washington); J. S. Adams, ed., *An Autobiographical Sketch by John Marshall* (Ann Arbor, 1937), 14.

74. 6 Wheaton 264, 418–420 (1821); *Federalist,* 493–494. See also *Weston* v. *Charleston,* 2 Peters 449, 469 (1829), in which Marshall referred obliquely to Hamilton as a "great statesman," as well as Marshall's deft handling of an attempt by counsel for Maryland to use *The Federalist* against the Bank in *McCulloch* v. *Maryland,* 4 Wheaton 316, 433–435 (1819). "Had the authors of those excellent essays been asked," he wrote, "whether they contended for that construction of the Constitution, which would place within the reach of the States those measures which the government might adopt for the execution

of its powers; no man, who has read their instructive pages, will hesitate to admit that their answer must have been in the negative"—which was certainly true of Marshall's favorite among the three authors.

75. "I have always expressed freely," Marshall wrote to James A. Hamilton, March 9, 1822, Hamilton Papers, L of C, "the very high respect I felt for your father while living, and for his memory since his decease, a respect which was certainly increased by his correspondence with General Washington." One wishes that a few of Marshall's free expressions of respect had been preserved for the instruction of posterity. In the Marshall Papers, L of C, there is a satirical reference in a letter of Marshall to C. C. Pinckney, April 21, 1798, to his having booked passage from Bordeaux on "a very excellent vessel but for the sin of the name which makes my return in her almost as criminal as if I had taken England in my way"—the name of the vessel being the *Alexander Hamilton.*

76. Corwin, *Marshall*, 230.

77. In Jones, ed., *Chief Justice Marshall*, xiii.

78. In a letter to Story, Sept. 22, 1832, *Massachusetts Historical Society, Proceedings*, 2nd ser., XIV (1900–1901), 352, Marshall echoes one strain of the long-dead Hamilton's hymn to the Union: "I yield slowly and reluctantly to the conviction that our constitution cannot last. . . . The union has been prolonged thus far by miracles. I fear they cannot continue."

79. Livingston also did important legal work for Hamilton, as witness the letters of March 30, April 4, 1790, *Papers*, VI, 329, 347.

80. 6 Wheaton 204, 225–226 (1821); 9 Wheaton 1, 229–230 (1824); Donald G. Morgan, *Justice William Johnson, the First Dissenter* (Columbia, S.C., 1954), esp. chaps. 7, 13.

81. For some uses of *The Federalist* by counsel (often by both sides in the case), see *McCulloch* v. *Maryland*, 4 Wheaton 316, 323, 332 ff., 372; *Cohens* v. *Virginia*, 6 Wheaton 264, 352 (1821); *Gibbons* v. *Ogden*, 9 Wheaton 1, 34, 48, 61, 64, 86, 109, 128–129, 141, 146, 164 (1824); *Osborn* v. *Bank*, 9 Wheaton 738, 808 (1824); *Brown* v. *Maryland*, 12 Wheaton 419, 430, 432, 434, 435 (1827). Joseph Hopkinson, one of counsel for Maryland in *McCulloch* v. *Maryland*, reminded Marshall rather vividly that "General Hamilton" was the "father and defender" of the doctrine of implied powers. 4 Wheaton 332.

82. John T. Horton, *James Kent: A Study in Conservatism* (New York, 1939), 56, 285, describes Hamilton as Kent's "idol." Kent's description of Hamilton is written on the flyleaf of his MS. record of the Croswell case in NYPL. See also his *Anniversary Discourse . . . December 6, 1828* (New York, 1829), 34.

83. *Commentaries on American Law*, 4 vols. (New York, 1826–1830), which had its fourteenth and final edition in 1896. Writing to Joseph Story Dec. 18, 1824,

about one of his lectures on American law, Kent made clear that he had "paid just homage to the argument of Hamilton and of the Ch. J. in favor of the right to institute a bank, and I was astonished at the folly of the court in Virginia in objecting to the validity of the carriage tax." *Massachusetts Historical Society, Proceedings,* 2nd ser., XIV (1900–1901), 414.

84. Warren, *Supreme Court,* I, 415–422; Brant, *Madison,* V, 167–172. Jefferson, to his credit as Jeffersonian, warned Madison against this potential "tory" who was much "too young," but Madison seems to have had more faith—a misplaced faith if ever there was one—in Story's Republicanism. Jefferson to Madison, October 15, 1810, *Jefferson* (Ford), IX, 283.

85. To H. G. Otis, Dec. 27, 1818, S. E. Morison, *The Life and Letters of Harrison Gray Otis* (Boston, 1913), I, 122–123.

86. To Samuel Fay, May 18, 1807, to Mrs. Story, Feb. 7, 1810, in W. W. Story, ed., *Life and Letters of Joseph Story* (Boston, 1851), I, 144, 195–196.

87. To James Kent, Dec. 22, 1836, to Ezekiel Bacon, April 30, 1842, in Story, *Life and Letters of Story,* II, 258, 420. And see the testimony recorded in Charles R. Williams, *The Life of Rutherford Birchard Hayes* (Columbus, Ohio, 1922–1926), I, 42, which has Story saying to his class in Harvard Law School in 1844 (which included Hayes): "I have heard Samuel Dexter, John Marshall, and Chancellor Livingston say that Hamilton's reach of thought was so far beyond theirs that by his side they were schoolboys—rush tapers before the sun at noon day."

88. Williams, *Life of Hayes,* I, 42.

89. Story, *Commentaries,* 3rd ed. (1858), secs. 906 ff., 977 ff., 1236–1258, 1259–1272 (to which Story adds, in the form of a footnote, a large chunk of "Mr. Hamilton's celebrated argument on the constitutionality of the Bank"), 1442–1449, 1573 ff. This is only a sampling of Story's dependence upon Hamilton's ideas and phrases, for one finds him used or cited or quoted on fully half of the 1,500 pages of the *Commentaries.* For an important commentary of the time that made considerably less direct use of Hamilton, see William Rawle, *A View of the Constitution,* 2nd ed. (Philadelphia, 1829), 37, 57, 148, 178, 207, 211, 212, 289. Other such works that followed the Hamiltonian line were Nathaniel Chipman, *Principles of Government* (Burlington, Vt., 1833); W. A. Duer, *A Course of Lectures on the Constitutional Jurisprudence of the United States,* 2nd ed. (Boston, 1856); and Nathan Dane, *A General Abridgment and Digest of American Law,* 9 vols. (Boston, 1823–1824). John N. Pomeroy, *An Introduction to the Constitutional Law of the United States* (New York, 1868), is an interesting example of the way in which Hamilton could get swallowed up in Marshall, Story, Webster, and the rest of his own intellectual descendants. See generally Elizabeth K. Bauer, *Commentaries on the Constitution, 1790–1860* (New York, 1952).

90. Story, *Commentaries,* I, v–vi (which dedicates the whole work to Marshall, whose achievements are likened to a "mighty river"), vii–viii (which acclaims the way his "masterly reasoning" has brought the prophecies of *The Federalist* to life).

91. Tiedeman, *A Treatise on State and Federal Control of Persons and Property* (St. Louis, 1900); Cooley, *A Treatise on the Constitutional Limitations etc.,* 6th ed. (Boston, 1890), and *The General Principles of Constitutional Law,* 4th ed. (Boston, 1931). See also the gingerly way in which Joseph H. Choate handled the dynamic aspects of Hamilton's constitutionalism in his *Alexander Hamilton* (London, 1904), 60 ff., and the interesting thoughts on "Jefferson and Hamilton" of Melville W. Fuller, several years before he became Chief Justice, in *The Dial,* IV (1883–1884), 4. H. St. G. Tucker, *Limitations on the Treaty-Making Power* (Boston, 1915), 83–84, describes those who adopt the extreme nationalist point of view as the "Hamiltonian School of Statesmen." On the laissez-faire jurists, see generally Benjamin R. Twiss, *Lawyers and the Constitution* (Princeton, 1942).

92. For an amusing view of the confusion in the 1930's over Hamilton and Jefferson as constitutionalists, see Irving Brant, *Storm over the Constitution* (Indianapolis, 1936), chap. 2.

93. See the respectful yet rather offhand (and sometimes off-target) references to Hamilton in such well-known works as A. C. McLaughlin, *A Constitutional History of the United States* (New York, 1935), 150–151, 200, 208, 213, 225–233, 241, 254–255; Carl B. Swisher, *American Constitutional Development* (Boston, 1943), 64 ff., 151–152, 837, 953; C. Herman Pritchett, *The American Constitution* (New York, 1959); B. F. Wright, *Growth of American Constitutional Law,* 23–25, 37, 42 ff., 244–245, 254, in which Hamilton is a figure of substance; Bernard Schwartz, *American Constitutional Law* (Cambridge, England, 1955), 32, 89, 140, 143, in which he is a shadow; Crosskey, *Politics and the Constitution,* I, 193 ff., 217 ff., 401 ff.; II, 711–712, 963–965, 1026–1028; H. C. Hockett, *The Constitutional History of the United States* (New York, 1939), I, 178 ff., 260 ff., which depicts early American constitutional development as a struggle between Hamilton and Jefferson; Alfred H. Kelly and W. A. Harbison, *The American Constitution* (New York, 1955), 105, 116, 154–156, 180, 183, 187–188, 229–230, 276, 289, 709, 839; Robert K. Carr, *The Supreme Court and Judicial Review* (New York, 1942), 51, perhaps the most offhand treatment of all.

94. W. W. Willoughby, *The Constitutional Law of the United States* (New York, 1910), I, 2, 58–62, 65–66; II, 1150, in which Hamilton gets almost completely swallowed up in Marshall and Story; C. K. Burdick, *The Law of the American Constitution* (New York, 1922), 15, 117–118, 144–149; David K. Watson, *The Constitution of the United States* (Chicago, 1910), references at II, 1863–1865; James Parker Hall, *Constitutional Law* (Chicago, 1917); J. M.

Mathews, *The American Constitutional System* (New York, 1932); Bernard Schwartz, *A Commentary on the Constitution of the United States* (New York, 1963–), references (most of them to *The Federalist*) at II, 482. The casebooks I have sampled—in most of which Hamilton is not even a shadow—are Noel T. Dowling, *Cases on Constitutional Law,* 6th ed. (Brooklyn, 1959); Dudley O. McGovney, *Cases on Constitutional Law,* 2nd ed. (Indianapolis, 1935); Henry Rottschaefer, *Cases on Constitutional Law* (New York, 1932); James Parker Hall, *Cases on Constitutional Law* (St. Paul, 1926); Walter F. Dodd, *Cases and Materials on Constitutional Law,* 5th ed. (St. Paul, 1954); Ray Forrester, *Constitutional Law: Cases and Materials* (St. Paul, 1959), 67–71, 257–259, 478–479.

See also, as a sampling, the references in the special studies of such scholars as Arthur N. Holcombe, *Our More Perfect Union* (Cambridge, 1950), 59–60, 318, which makes more of Hamilton's theory of "social dichotomy" (above, pp. 138–139) than of his constitutional interpretations; T. R. Powell, *Vagaries and Varieties of Constitutional Interpretation* (New York, 1956), 15, 26; Charles P. Curtis, Jr., *Lions Under the Throne* (Boston, 1947), 10, 126; Robert G. McCloskey, *The American Supreme Court* (Chicago, 1960), 9, 13, 29, 36, 66–67; Haines, *American Doctrine of Judicial Supremacy,* 137–140, an admiring view of Hamilton's argument in *The Federalist,* number 78; William B. Munro, *The Makers of the Unwritten Constitution* (New York, 1930), 27–50; H. L. McBain, *The Living Constitution* (New York, 1927), 158–159; and the essay on Amendment X by Walter Berns in R. A. Goldwin, ed., *A Nation of States* (Chicago, 1963).

The most eminent of twentieth-century writers on the Constitution had a thorough respect for the mind of Hamilton, yet his vision, too, was dazzled by the sight of Marshall: Edward S. Corwin, *The Constitution and What It Means Today,* 12th ed. (Princeton, 1958), 64, 100, 125, 142, 197, 245; *The Twilight of the Supreme Court* (New Haven, 1934), 60, 131, 148, 177; *Court over Constitution* (Princeton, 1938), 184; *The Commerce Power versus States Rights* (Princeton, 1936), 175 ff., 215–221; *Constitution Annotated,* 112 ff., 307, 335, 378–381, 554 ff.; *President's Control of Foreign Relations,* 8–15, 94–97, 133–135; *Doctrine of Judicial Review,* chap. 1; *The President,* 17, 179, 195, 199.

95. 272 U.S. 52, 118, 136–137 (1927); 299 U.S. 304, 316–317 (1936), with which must be read Sutherland's *Constitutional Power and World Affairs* (1919), 51–52; 297 U.S. 1, 65–66 (1936); 301 U.S. 619, 640 (1937). For an implicit blessing of Hamilton's argument about the difference between the opening words of Articles I and II, see Justice Brewer's remarks on "the judicial power of the United States" in *Kansas* v. *Colorado,* 206 U.S. 46, 81–83 (1907). And for an echo of the doctrine of resulting powers, see Marshall's opinion in *American Insurance Co.* v. *Canter,* 1 Peters 511, 542 (1828). See

also *Penhallow* v. *Doane,* 3 Dallas 54, 74, 76, 80, 81 (1795); *Holmes* v. *Jennison,* 14 Peters 540, 575, 576 (1840).

The influence of Chief Justice Hughes in securing a Hamiltonian interpretation of the "general welfare" clause is chronicled in Merlo J. Pusey, *Charles Evans Hughes* (New York, 1951), I, 387; II, 743.

I base my opinion of the Supreme Court's perhaps understandable failure to make much use of Hamilton—or, indeed, to give him even an occasional loud salute—on a careful survey of the 1,100-odd cases listed in Corwin's authoritative *The Constitution and What It Means Today,* 311–337. Most references to Hamilton are attempts to invoke the shade of Publius or to explain away one of his assertions. The case in which Hamilton was perhaps most heavily used (and used by both sides) was *Pollock* v. *Farmers' Loan and Trust Co.,* 157 U.S. 429 (1895), 158 U.S. 601 (1895).

In none of the roughly eighty cases of judicial review of acts of Congress is Hamilton cited as an authority in support of this power. In addition to the cases listed in *Constitution Annotated,* 1241–1254, see *U.S.* v. *Cardiff,* 344 U.S. 174 (1952); *Bolling* v. *Sharpe,* 347 U.S. 497 (1954); *U.S. ex rel. Toth* v. *Quarles,* 350 U.S. 11 (1955); *Reid* v. *Covert,* 354 U.S. 1 (1956); *Trop* v. *Dulles,* 356 U.S. 86 (1958); *Kinsella* v. *U.S. ex rel. Singleton,* 361 U.S. 925 (1960); *Kennedy* v. *Mendoza-Martinez,* 372 U.S. 144 (1963).

For representative citations of Hamilton as an authority (for the most part to his opinions in *The Federalist*), see *Dred Scott* v. *Sanford,* 19 Howard 393, 537 (1857); *Ex parte Garland,* 4 Wallace 333, 365, 388 (1867); *The Justices* v. *Murray,* 9 Wallace 274, 279–282 (1870); *Knox* v. *Lee,* 12 Wallace 457, 640–642, 665–666 (1871); *Myers* v. *U.S.,* 272 U.S. 52, 118, 136–140, 208, 293; *Newberry* v. *U.S.,* 265 U.S. 232, 248–249, 255–256, 283 (1921); *Evans* v. *Gore,* 253 U.S. 245, 249, 250, 252–253, 265 (1920); *Perry* v. *U.S.,* 294 U.S. 330, 351, 379–380 (1935); *U.S.* v. *Lovett,* 328 U.S. 303, 314 (1946). See also *Brown* v. *Maryland,* 12 Wheaton 419, 456 (1827); *Kendall* v. *U.S.,* 12 Peters 524, 643–645 (1838); *Fox* v. *Ohio,* 5 Howard 410, 439 (1847); *License Cases,* 5 Howard 504, 606–607 (1847); *Luther* v. *Borden,* 7 Howard 1, 53 (1849); *Cooley* v. *Port Wardens,* 12 Howard 299, 318–319 (1851); *Cummings* v. *Missouri,* 4 Wallace 277, 330-332 (1867), in which Justice Field makes excellent use of Phocion on the iniquity of oaths; *Veazie Bank* v. *Fenno,* 8 Wallace 533, 545, 550, 553 (1869); *Scholey* v. *Rew,* 23 Wallace 331, 348 (1895); *Claflin* v. *Houseman,* 93 U.S. 130, 138–139 (1876); *Sinking Fund Cases,* 99 U.S. 700, 731, 736–737, 759 (1879), in which Field referred to Hamilton as "the great conservative statesman"; *Ex parte Clarke,* 100 U.S. 399, 417–419 (1880); *Springer* v. *U.S.,* 102 U.S. 586, 596–598 (1881); *Hans* v. *Louisiana,* 134 U.S. 1, 12–14 (1890); *Leisy* v. *Hardin,* 135 U.S. 100, 109 (1890); *Capital Traction Co.* v. *Hof,* 174 U.S. 1, 6–7 (1899); *Smith* v. *Reeves,* 178 U.S. 436, 447 (1900); *U.S.* v. *Gradwell,* 243 U.S. 476, 484 (1917); *Frohwerk* v. *U.S.,* 249 U.S. 204, 206 (1919); *Massachusetts* v. *Mellon,* 262 U.S. 447, 480–481 (1923);

Home Building and Loan Association v. *Blaisdell*, 290 U.S. 398, 464 (1934); *Monaco* v. *Mississippi*, 292 U.S. 313, 322–326, 328, 329 (1934); *U.S.* v. *South-Eastern Underwriters Association*, 322 U.S. 533, 539, 550, 552 (1944); *Youngstown Sheet and Tube Co.* v. *Sawyer*, 343 U.S. 579, 634–635, 682 (1952), in which Justice Jackson rightly points out that in the game of quoting "respected sources on either side" of any question of executive power, "a Hamilton may be matched against a Madison." Most of these citations are to secondary, even tertiary principles of Hamilton's constitutional law.

For an example of the way in which a court will clutch happily at the Hamilton (or, for that matter, the Madison or Jay) of *The Federalist* for support, see *U.S.* v. *Allocco*, 305 F. 2d 704 (2nd Cir. 1962), in which Judge Irving R. Kaufman makes the maximum use of Hamilton's few words on the President's power to make recess appointments in number 67 (*Federalist*, 408–411).

96. The citations of all phrases in this paragraph may be found above, pp. 322–323, nn. 14–32.

97. See the dispatch by Anthony Lewis in the *New York Times*, April 14, 1963; C. L. Black, Jr., "The Proposed Amendment of Article V: A Threatened Disaster," *Yale Law Journal*, LXXII (1963), 957.

98. 299 U.S. 304 (1936); 301 U.S. 1 (1937); 301 U.S. 548 (1937); 312 U.S. 100 (1941); 317 U.S. 111 (1942); 327 U.S. 92 (1946); 349 U.S. 294 (1954); 351 U.S. 12 (1956); 369 U.S. 186 (1962). Perhaps the longest (if in some ways prudent) step to the rear in recent years was taken by the Court itself in *Erie Railroad* v. *Tompkins*, 304 U.S. 64 (1938), overruling *Swift* v. *Tyson*, 6 Peters 1 (1842).

99. *Federalist*, 153–154; *Works*, IV, 151–152; III, 452–453.

100. And "the modern conception of the presidential office" to be "the contribution primarily of Andrew Jackson and his times." *Constitution Annotated*, 381.

101. *Works*, IV, 439.

102. 350 U.S. 497 (1956); 352 U.S. 12 (1956); 355 U.S. 155 (1957).

103. 297 U.S. 1 (1936), and other cases listed in *Constitution Annotated*, 1252–1254.

104. Above, n. 95.

105. Coleman, 184. For guidance to references to Hamilton in the standard texts, see above, p. 263, n. 33.

106. Coleman, 123–124.

107. See the judicious assessment of a staunch Hamiltonian, Louis Hacker, in his *Hamilton*, 22. And for a much older attempt to have the best of both men, see J. G. Baldwin, *Party Leaders* (New York, 1858), 129–134.

108. For evidence of the persistent truth of this proposition, and for some variations on it, see the reviews of Sidney Kingsley's sentimentally Jeffersonian play *The Patriots* (New York, 1943), in *Current History,* new ser., IV (1943), 88, and *Saturday Review of Literature,* April 17, 1943; Peterson, *Jefferson Image,* 278, 310, 323, 339, 348, 351, 449; Hart, *American Presidency in Action,* 53.

A. Whitney Griswold, "Jefferson's Republic," *Fortune,* April, 1950, Louis Hartz, *The Liberal Tradition in America* (New York, 1955), 146, who speaks of "the silent unity of Hamilton and Jefferson," and Richard Hofstadter, *The American Political Tradition* (New York, 1948), are, in effect, heroic efforts to break out of the old mold. The preference for Jefferson is nonetheless plain, especially in the case of Hofstadter.

109. June 27, 1787, *Papers,* IV, 220.

110. A Book of Americans, 43.

111. On this particular point, it is hard to disagree with Hammond, *Banks and Politics,* 122, that "Americans still maintain a pharisaical reverence for Thomas Jefferson, but they have in reality little use for what he said and believed— save when, on occasion and out of context, it appears to be of political expediency. What they really admire is what Alexander Hamilton stood for, and his are the hopes they have fulfilled." See also Herbert Agar, *The Price of Union* (Boston, 1950), 51–52, 143.

112. Let it be duly recorded that I dissent from the pairing suggested by James Truslow Adams (and to which T. R. would have shouted his approval): "The contributions made by each of these men may be exemplified in a broad way by those made by man and woman respectively in the home or the nation." *The Living Jefferson* (New York, 1936), 12. Walter Lippmann, in a column of April 13, 1943, reprinted in *State Government,* XVI (1943), 139, asserts that "to be partisan today as between Jefferson and Hamilton is like arguing whether men or women are more necessary to the procreation of the race."

INDEX

Aaron, Daniel, 332
Acton, Lord, 264
Adair, Douglass, 54, 281, 308, 314, 334
Adams, Henry, 162, 228, 238, 265, 298, 331
Adams, James Truslow, 331, 348
Adams, John, 27, 50, 180, 181, 229, 238, 338
    reputation, 4, 235
    patriotism, 13–14
    as President, 26, 30, 36, 101, 144, 210, 241, 292
    as constitutionalist, 160, 170, 186, 199
    political science, 12, 16, 114, 117, 126, 129, 138, 139, 140, 157, 183, 187, 250
    on Hamilton, 14, 30, 50, 264, 268, 270, 334
Adams, John Quincy, 232, 266, 282, 286, 334
Agar, Herbert, 348
Alexander, E. P., 272
Alien and Sedition Acts, 100–101, 105, 170, 177, 207, 244, 299, 302, 320
Althusius, 56
Aly, Bower, 263, 321
American Liberty League, 336
American political thought, 12, 183–184, 263–264
American political tradition, 185, 250–252
Ames, Fisher, 25, 26, 76, 78, 192, 237, 267, 269, 289, 294, 304, 312, 324, 337, 338
anarchy, 158, 165–166, 176, 251
Angoff, Charles, 303
Annapolis Convention, 41–43
aristocracy, 139, 145, 181, 251
Aristotle, 119, 124
Articles of Confederation, 36–40, 42–43, 56–57, 65, 76, 96, 194, 202, 272, 274, 329
assumption of state debts, 76, 137

349

Atherton, Gertrude, 233
authority, 166–167, 176, 178–179, 187

Bailey, Thomas A., 262, 332
Baker v. *Carr,* 247
Baldwin, J. G., 347
Balinky, Alexander, 339
Bancroft, George, 234–235
Bank of the United States, 36, 39, 78–80, 238–239
Barck, Oscar T., 262
Bauer, Elizabeth K., 343
Bayard, James A., 113, 134, 302, 305, 308, 337, 338
Beard, Charles A., 228, 261, 269, 286, 296, 331, 332, 336–337
Becker, Carl, 230
Beckley, John, 225, 330
Beckwith, George, 264
Bein, Alex, 306
Bemis, Samuel F., 262
Benét, Stephen Vincent, 253–254, 259, 332
Benson, Egbert, 38, 43, 54, 73, 74
Benton, Thomas Hart, 277
Berns, Walter, 345
Beveridge, Albert J., 339
Billington, R. A., 332
Bingham, William, 260
Black, C. L., Jr., 347
Blackstone, William, 118, 307, 317
Blake, Nelson M., 262
Bledsoe, Albert T., 335
Blum, John M., 332
Boorstin, Daniel J., 333
Borden, Morton, 305
Boudinot, Elias, 73, 74, 78, 121, 237, 293, 337
Bourne, Edward G., 54, 281, 306
Boutell, L. H., 335
Bowers, Claude G., 259
Bowman, A. H., 261
Boyd, G. A., 287
Boyd, Julian P., 305
Bradford, William, 16, 94, 264–265, 292, 337
Brant, Irving, 267, 268, 271, 279, 281, 298, 339, 344
Brockunier, S. H., 332
Brown, Stuart Gerry, 331

Brown v. *Board of Education,* 247, 342
Bryce, James, 232–233, 335
Burdick, C. K., 344
Burke, Aedanus, 267
Burke, Edmund, 114, 150, 180, 181, 264
Burlamaqui, J. J., 118, 121
Burnett, E. C., 37, 272
Burns, E. M., 266
Burns, James MacGregor, 331
Burr, Aaron, 17, 109, 113, 115, 144, 226, 231
Butler, Nicholas Murray, 233

Cabot, George, 91, 267, 268, 337
Cahn, Edmund, 341
Caldwell, Lynton K., 6, 261, 263
Calhoun, John C., 12, 140, 183, 250
Callender, James T., 102
Camden, Lord, 118
Carman, Harry J., 332
Carosso, Vincent P., 263
Carpenter, W. S., 300
Carr, Robert K., 344
Carrington, Colonel Edward, 20, 156, 237, **288**, **338**
Case v. *Bowles,* 247
change, social, 139–140, 181, 321
Channing, Edward, 233
Charles, Joseph, 271, 337
Chase, Samuel, 94, 279
Cheetham, James, 298
Childs, Francis, 283
Chipman, Nathaniel, 343
Chitwood, Oliver P., 332
Choate, Joseph H., 344
Churchill, Winston, 152
Cicero, 118, 119, 296
Claiborne, William C. C., 302
classes, social, 138–139, 181, 311, 345
Clay, Henry, 239, 339
Clinton, George, 43, 47, 146, 171, 278, 279
    in Poughkeepsie Convention, 51, 60–70, 280
    as antinationalist, 41, 43–44
    on Hamilton, 61–62, 156
    Hamilton on, 143, 159

Cohens v. *Virginia,* 241, 242, 243, 342
Coit, Joshua, 292
Coke, Sir Edward, 118, 119, 296
Coker, F. W., 263, 320
Colbert, Jean-Baptiste, 119, 179
Cole, A. H., 262
Coleman, William, 54, 97, 298
Commager, Henry S., 332
commerce power, 202, 204–205, 325
common law, 100, 299
community, 16, 137–138, 142, 145, 172, 178–179
Congress, Confederation, 36–40, 70, 72, 200, 322
Congress, powers of, 199–211, 223–224, 225, 247–248
    commerce, 202, 204–205, 325
    "general welfare," 81–82, 203–204, 346
    taxation, 80, 81, 93–95, 203–204
    war, 23, 191, 205–207, 334
conservatism, 178, 180–182
Constitution, viii, 71, 189, 193, 242, 247, 249–250
contract, social, 122
Convention (Philadelphia) of 1787, 43–50, 276–279
    preliminaries, 37, 39–40, 41–43, 272–274
Convention (Poughkeepsie) of 1788, 10, 51, 56, 60–70, 283–285
Cooke, Jacob E., 280, 281, 316
Cooley, Thomas M., 102, 245
Cooper, Thomas, 303
Corwin, Edward S., 242, 296, 297, 339, 345
Coxe, Tench, 31, 260–261, 325
Croly, Herbert, 233–234
Crosskey, W. W., 58, 282, 296, 297, 298, 299, 344
Croswell, Harry, 102–106, 108, 109, 301, 303, 304
Culbertson, W. S., 264
Current, Richard N., 332
Curti, Merle, 331, 333
Curtis, Charles P., Jr., 345
Curtis, George T., 333

Dane, Nathan, 343
Dangerfield, George, 283
Dartmouth, 123
Dartmouth College v. *Woodward,* 340
Dauer, Manning, 302
Davis, Joseph S., 263

Dawson, H. B., 280–281
Dayton, Jonathan, 198
De Conde, Alexander, 262
demagoguery, 158–159, 251
democracy, 44, 143, 151, 157–162, 185, 188, 235, 250, 253, 332
Demosthenes, 29, 118
Depew, Chauncey, 335
De Riencourt, Amaury, 320
Desbrulons, Jacques Savary, 306
Destler, C. M., 292
Dewey, D. R., 260
Dickinson, John, 176
Dillon, C. Douglas, 6, 307
Dillon, Dorothy R., 307
diplomacy, conduct of, 7–9, 171–172, 173, 261
Dodd, Walter F., 345
Dorfman, Joseph, 260, 262, 334, 337
Dowling, Noel T., 345
Duane, James, 42, 62, 96, 280, 337
    in Confederation Congress, 36–38
Duane, William, 102
Duer, William, 31, 131, 280, 337
Duer, W. A., 343
Dunbar, Louise, 314

economic growth, 9–10, 21–23, 24, 81, 179–180, 182, 192, 252–253
Elkins, Stanley, 276
Ellsworth, Oliver, 11, 25, 49, 73, 297, 299, 337
emergency powers, 144, 215–216
energy, political, 21, 82–83, 93, 162–163, 168–169, 189–190, 197, 225, 246, 252
English, Raymond, 180
equality and inequality, 122, 140–142, 158
Erie Railroad v. Tompkins, 347
Erskine, Thomas, 302
executive power, 44, 45, 132–133, 156, 208–218, 248, 326–327
    as repository of energy, 82–83, 169, 252
    unity in, 210
experience, as guide to men, 124–125, 195

faction, 148–149, 158, 166
Fainsod, Merle, 268
Farewell Address, 14, 117, 123, 131, 147, 167, 177, 271, 337
Faulkner, Harold U., 332

federalism, 56–57, 187, 194–199, 221
Federalist, The, 6, 12, 51–60, 183
    Hamilton's part in, 52–60, 109, 116
    Madison's part in, 12, 53–60, 98, 203, 281, 282, 315
    authorship, problem of, 53–54, 280–281
    contents, 56
    "contradictions" in, 58, 86
    defects, 58–59
    prestige, 51–52, 56
    reprinting of, 55, 279, 282
    use of, 52, 57, 68, 86, 98, 212, 241, 279, 295, 297, 329, 341, 342, 347
    as commentary on Constitution, 52, 57
    as treatise in political science, 57–58
    Jefferson on, 52, 282
    Marshall on, 242, 341
    Washington on, 52
    number 9, 165
    number 10, 58
    number 23, 23, 110, 191, 206, 248, 334
    number 51, 58
    number 70, 58, 209–210
    number 72, 211
    number 78, 57, 95–96, 98, 219, 221–225, 240, 241, 244, 329, 340, 345
Federalists, 99, 102–103, 107, 298, 300
    as political force, 98, 148
    Hamilton's leadership of, 75, 78, 90, 92, 237–238, 288, 294
    interpretation of Constitution, 109–110
    in Poughkeepsie Convention, 62–69
Farrand, Max, 276, 279, 297, 300
Ferrell, Robert H., 262
Field, Stephen J., 245, 346
Fiske, John, 272
Fletcher v. *Peck,* 224, 240, 242
Foner, P. S., 273
Ford, Henry Jones, 308
Ford, P. L., 304, 316
Forrester, Ray, 345
Fox, Charles James, 302
Framers, 4, 43–50, 193, 213
    "intent" of, 91, 191, 323
Frankfurter, Felix, 300
Franklin, Benjamin, 4, 13, 49, 158, 233
Freeman, D. S., 275, 293

Freer, Samuel, 106
Freidel, Frank, 332
French Revolution, 14–15, 114, 124, 181–182
Fuller, Melville W., 344

Gallatin, Albert, 108, 238, 287, 331, 339
Garfield, James A., 232
Garosci, A., 279
"general welfare" clause, 81–82, 203–204, 346
Gettell, R. G., 263
Gibbons v. *Ogden,* 202, 243
Gibbs, Caleb, 267
Gilbert, Felix, 261, 271
Giles, William Branch, 33, 82, 88, 159, 290, 293
Goebel, Julius, Jr., 300
Gordon, Lincoln, 268
Gore, Christopher, 267, 287
Govan, Thomas P., 309
government:
    forms, 154–157, 162, 174, 315
    role, 22–24, 81, 163–165, 179–180, 188, 206, 207, 252
    desirable features, 18, 163, 172–175, 186, 251
    undesirability of weakness in, 57, 162–163, 165–168, 172, 251, 318
Great Britain, 14–15, 44, 118–119, 121, 264, 323
    constitution, 154–155
Greene, Nathanael, 37, 38, 273
Griffin v. *Illinois,* 247, 249
Grimes, A. P., 263
Griswold, A. Whitney, 348
Grotius, 119, 121
groups, 134, 137–138
Guizot, François, 335
Gunn, James, 293

Hacker, Louis, 179, 180, 261, 336, 347
Haines, Charles G., 296, 341, 345
Hall, James Parker, 344
Hall of Fame, 231
Hamill, Katherine, 335
Hamilton, Alexander:
    career, 15, 35–36, 188–189, 237
        early years, 13
        in Revolution, 14, 17, 30, 31, 36, 270

Hamilton, Alexander: career (cont.)
      in Confederation Congress, 23, 38–40, 41, 70, 274, 286
      1783–1787, 40–43
      in Philadelphia Convention, 17, 43–50, 196, 210, 222, 276–279
      in struggle over ratification, 17–18, 50–51, 60–70, 203, 279–285
      as Secretary of the Treasury, 5–6, 9, 22, 28, 30, 72–86, 86–90, 175, 194,
         210, 237, 286–292, 319, 325–326
      in "retirement," 30, 32, 90–101, 192, 300
      in crisis of 1798–1800, 10, 23–24, 32, 86, 152, 269
      in Croswell case, 101–108, 301–304
      death, 108, 304
      as leader of Federalists, 75, 78, 90, 92, 237–238, 288, 294
      relations with Washington, 11, 26, 30, 31–33, 47, 65, 75, 80, 83–84, 87,
         110–111, 133, 190–191, 193, 209, 217, 270–271, 301
      relations with Madison, 38–39, 68–69, 72, 73, 75, 78, 86, 193, 288
      relations with Jefferson, 26, 27, 88, 193, 227
      long-range purposes, 15–18, 19–21, 71–72, 149, 188, 225, 236
    character, 6, 14, 25–31, 61, 165, 180, 218, 228, 245
      appealing aspects, 26, 230
      unattractive aspects, 24, 26, 87–88, 236, 268
      attitude toward power, 28, 131, 268, 269
      attitude toward wealth, 27–29, 130–131, 236
      love of fame, 27–29, 130, 230, 268, 269
      military renown, desire for, 23–24, 266, 268
      sense of honor, 28–29, 172
      officiousness, 6, 30, 48, 87, 269
      supposed ambition for Presidency, 268–269
      as "public man," 15–16, 27, 171
      as Romantic, 11, 17, 142, 147, 149, 189, 268, 337
      instances of misbehavior, 26–27, 192
    constitutional law, 32, 249
      rules of construction, 83, 89, 94, 144, 189–193, 211, 213–214, 337
      on "intent" of Framers, 91, 191, 323
      commerce power, 202, 204–205, 325
      Congress, powers of, 81, 199–211, 223–224, 225, 247–248
      due process, 330
      emergency powers, 144, 215–216
      "executive power" clause, 212–214, 245, 248, 327, 345
      federalism, 187, 194–199, 221
      "general welfare" clause, 81–82, 203–204, 346
      "implied" powers, 39, 79–80, 200–202, 211, 342
      judicial review, 219, 221–225, 241, 248–249, 296–298, 329
      national supremacy, 77, 110, 194–199, 205, 219, 221, 224, 225, 247, 249

Hamilton, Alexander: constitutional law (cont.)

    "necessary and proper" clause, 200–202

    Presidency, powers and status of, 82–86, 92–93, 169, 208–218, 225, 248, 291, 326, 327

    "resulting" powers, 207–208, 325, 345

    states' rights, 197–198, 247, 253

    "supremacy" clause, 196–197

    taxing power, 203–204

    treaty-making power, 207, 216–218

    veto power, 143, 212

    war powers, 23, 191, 205–207, 334

  as constitutionalist, 11, 24–25, 57, 79, 135, 160, 170, 176, 185–189, 192, 225, 245, 253, 322

    influence on Constitution, 11–12, 25, 31, 34–36, 84, 87, 95–98, 102, 109–112, 189–190, 218, 229, 236–246

    relevance for Constitution of today, 246–250

    early ideas, 26–27

    indictment of Articles of Confederation, 36–38, 194, 274, 329

    call for convention, 40, 43, 274

    in Annapolis Convention, 41–42

    in Philadelphia Convention, 43–50, 109, 222

    speech and plan of June 18, 1787, 45–46, 59–60, 101, 199, 210, 216, 222, 232, 277–279, 282

    plan of September, 1787, 48, 155, 158–159, 196, 199–200, 210, 222

    in Poughkeepsie Convention, 50–51, 60-70

    responsibility for *The Federalist,* 51–53

    interpretations as Secretary of the Treasury, 25, 75–90

    before Supreme Court, 93–95, 190–191, 296

    on separation of powers, 160, 186

    on checks and balances, 187

    expectations of national government, 20–25, 81, 164, 179–180, 198, 207

    states, attitude toward, 13, 20, 43–46, 194–199, 218, 324, 328

    and Amendment X, 197

    and Amendment XI, 197–198, 224

    and Amendment XII, 218

    opinion on Yazoo lands, 224, 240, 330

  ideas and opinions:

    sources of ideas, 5, 29, 115, 118–125, 127, 130, 165, 182–184, 260–261, 296, 306–307, 315

    respect for ideas, 113–115

    economic views, 9, 10, 22, 24, 119, 136, 163–164, 179, 180, 206, 252–253, 260, 266, 268

    religious views, 18, 124, 175, 176, 177, 181, 308

Hamilton, Alexander: ideas and opinions (cont.)

   summary of political principles, 250–252

   on causes of war, 23, 128, 161

   on conduct of diplomacy, 7–9, 171–172, 173, 261

   on problem of economic growth, 9–10, 21–23, 24, 81, 179–180, 182, 192, 252–253

   on French Revolution, 14–15, 114, 124, 181–182

   on Great Britain, 14–15, 44, 118–119, 121, 154, 264, 323

   on Negroes, 141–142, 312

   dislike of oaths, 177, 320, 346

   on taxation, 169–170

   as "conservative," 29, 33, 140, 180–182, 229–230, 321, 346

   as Whig, 105, 119–125, 129, 140, 158, 160, 169, 170, 178, 182, 186, 193, 222

   as man ahead of his time, 7, 9–10, 22, 24, 33, 182, 229–230, 262

major roles in life, 15, 35, 229

   administrator, 6–7, 238, 331

   "diplomat," 7–9, 261, 274

   financier, 5–6, 170, 172–173, 202, 231–232, 234, 236, 238, 260, 334

   lawyer, 10, 102–108, 119, 192, 217, 233, 238, 291, 301

   leader of men, 30–31, 72–73, 75, 78, 90, 92, 110–111, 199, 237–238, 270, 288, 338

   molder of Constitution, 11–12, 25, 31, 34–36, 84, 87, 95–98, 102, 109–112, 189–190, 193, 218, 229, 236–246

   nationalist, 13–15, 16–17, 24, 39, 43–46, 101, 149–150, 194–199, 221, 333

   patriot, 13–15, 154, 162, 171, 176, 195, 230, 253, 264, 333

   politician, 10, 27, 48, 51, 64, 65

   prophet of industry, 9–10, 22, 24, 182, 262

   Revolutionist, 11, 14, 17

   rhetorician, 10, 67, 94, 296, 301

   soldier, 10–11, 23–24, 206, 266, 268, 274

   Unionist, 19–21, 41, 110, 137, 141, 194–196, 225, 232, 247, 253, 265, 304, 340, 342

political science, 12, 32, 45, 46, 57–58, 59, 67, 114–115, 116–117, 118, 123–124, 125, 126–127, 145–147, 152, 154, 180, 183, 184, 188, 192, 250–252, 253, 263–264

   anarchy, dislike of, 158, 165–166, 176, 251

   aristocracy, 139, 145, 181, 251

   authority, 166–167, 176, 178–179, 187

   change, 139–140, 181, 321

   classes, social, 138–139, 181, 311, 345

   community, 16, 137–138, 142, 172, 178–179

Hamilton, Alexander: political science (cont.)

    constitutionalism, 160, 176, 225

    demagoguery, dislike of, 158–159, 251

    democracy, 44, 143, 151, 157–162, 188, 250, 338

    energy, political, 21, 82–83, 93, 162–163, 168–169, 189–190, 197, 225, 246, 252

    equality and inequality, 122, 140–142, 158

    executive, role of, 44, 45, 82–83, 132–133, 156, 169, 208–218, 248, 252

    experience, as guide to men, 124–125, 195

    faction, 148–149, 158, 166

    government, forms of, 154–157, 162, 174, 315

    government, role of, 22–24, 81, 163–165, 179–180, 188, 206, 207, 252

    good government, qualities of, 18, 163, 172–175, 186, 251

    groups, 134, 137–138

    individualism and collectivism, 16, 164–165, 178–180

    interests, 132, 135–137, 145–147, 148–149, 151, 165, 251, 311

    law, 176, 181, 197

    legislature, role of, 169–170, 171, 208

    liberty, 16, 104, 140, 170, 175–178, 179, 200, 319

    majority rule, 187–188

    monarchy, 14, 153–157, 166, 278, 314

    morality, importance of, 122–124, 171, 172, 176

    national honor, importance of, 8–9, 171–172, 318

    natural law, 119, 121, 122, 123, 125, 186, 224, 307–308

    natural rights, 112, 175, 178

    nature of man, 15, 118, 125–137, 145, 161, 163, 167–168, 179, 181, 186, 196, 216, 251, 308–310

    obedience, importance of, 177, 181

    "passions," 133–135, 251, 310

    people, role of, 160–162, 187, 199, 218, 222–225, 250

    political parties, 147–149, 313

    power, abuse of, 131–132, 186

    power, uses of, 21, 163–164, 168, 246, 251–252

    popular assembly, 135, 157–158, 160, 186

    property, 140, 159, 163, 177, 316, 320

    public administration, 6–7, 174–175, 251, 319, 325

    public good, 16, 27, 142–147, 158, 179, 203, 251

    public opinion, 4, 149–152, 251, 313

    reason, importance of, 122, 123, 124–125, 133–135

    representation, 143

    republicanism, 46, 60, 153–157, 162

    resistance, right of, 122, 307

    society, 16, 137–142, 145, 161, 171, 175, 178, 251

Hamilton, Alexander: political science (cont.)
    tyranny, road to, 158, 165–167, 168, 251
    weak government, danger of, 57, 162–163, 165–168, 172, 251, 318
  reputation, 73, 272
    as seen by his friends, 16, 26, 43, 250, 267, 269, 287, 338
    as seen by his enemies, 24, 92, 127, 153, 154, 155, 225, 278, 330
    after death, 67, 108–109, 226–227, 304, 342
    in nineteenth century, 231–233, 244, 334–335, 344
    revival, 230–231, 233–234, 336–337
    in modern America, vii–viii, 4, 11–12, 13, 154, 227–230, 234–236, 245–246, 253, 335, 348
    treatment by historians, viii, 4, 26, 227–230, 231, 259, 263–264, 270, 331–334, 344–345
  writings, 7, 26, 116, 126, 257, 261, 277–278
    style, 117, 121
    use of pseudonyms, 150, 314
    early writings, 121
    letters, 116, 243, 299, 341
    public resolutions, 39, 116
    Caesar (inaccurately ascribed to Hamilton), 280, 316
    Camillus, 7, 91, 119, 160, 294
    Catullus, 159–160
    The Continentalist, 19, 21, 39, 275, 317
    Lucius Crassus, 97, 101, 137, 198, 220, 223
    Metellus, 209
    Pacificus, 7, 85–86, 110, 119, 213, 222, 245, 248, 292, 326
    Phocion, 17, 129, 132, 135–136, 207, 314, 320, 346
    Publius (The Federalist), 12, 59–60, 86, 95, 109, 116, 128, 139, 168, 196, 237, 326, 329
    in New York Evening Post, 97–98, 314
    Opinion on the Constitutionality of the Bank, 32–33, 79–80, 110, 190, 200–202, 205, 207–208, 222, 240, 244, 248, 290, 340, 343
    Report on Manufactures, 9, 22, 24, 81, 111, 163, 179, 203–204, 248, 262, 266, 288, 314
    Reports on the Public Credit, 74, 76, 77, 111, 172–173, 266, 306
Hamilton, Alexander, and Thomas Jefferson, 253–254
  their relations, 26, 27, 88, 193, 227
  Jefferson on Hamilton, 24, 30, 154, 238, 264, 271–272, 331
  Hamilton on Jefferson, 113, 212, 317, 324
  Hamilton versus Jefferson in American mythology, 227–228, 234–236, 246, 336
  Hamilton versus Jefferson in American historiography, viii, 227–230, 231, 259, 331–332, 344, 348

Hamilton, Alexander, and Thomas Jefferson (cont.)
summary of their differences, 235, 254
Hamilton, Elizabeth Schuyler, 103, 104, 116, 231, 308, 334
Hamilton, James A., 334, 337, 342
Hamilton, J. C., 231, 257, 306, 334
Hamilton, M. W., 301
Hammond, Bray, 260, 286, 348
Hammond, George, 262, 293
Hammond, Jabez, 301
Hancock, John, 31
Harbison, W. A., 344
Harison, Richard, 62, 103, 338
Harnett, Bertram, 303
Harper, Robert Goodloe, 243, 292, 301, 302, 330, 338
Hartz, Louis, 348
Harvard, 87
Harvey, Marvin, 308
Hayes, Rutherford Birchard, 343
Helvering v. *Davis,* 245
Henry, Patrick, 286
Hicks, John D., 331, 332
Higginson, Stephen, 237, 292, 338
Hildreth, Richard, 231, 233
Hobart, John Sloss, 62
Hobbes, Thomas, 119–120, 122, 127, 131, 133, 148, 182–183, 186, 310, 321
influence on Hamilton, 45, 118, 125
Hockett, H. C., 344
Hofstadter, Richard, 332, 348
Holcombe, Arthur, 332, 345
Holt, W. S., 278
Holmes, O. W., Jr., 217, 240, 341
Homes, Isaac, 307, 323
Hopkinson, Joseph, 342
Horton, John T., 342
House of Representatives, 88–89, 92–93, 158, 216, 295, 328, 329
Howe, Mark de Wolfe, 299
Hubbard, Elbert, 336
Hughes, Charles Evans, 204, 246
Hughes, James M., 61, 283
Hume, David, 45, 127, 128, 132, 133, 135, 142, 306, 310, 314
influence on Hamilton, 115, 120–121, 121–125, 126, 130, 138–139, 148, 174, 182–183
Hunter, David, 295

Hylton v. *United States,* 93–95, 237, 295–296
Hyneman, Charles S., 291

"implied" powers, 37, 79–80, 200, 211, 342
individualism and collectivism, 16, 164–165, 178–180
Independent Reflector, 307
interests, 132, 135–137, 145–147, 148–149, 151, 165, 251, 311
Iredell, James, 94, 296, 297, 299, 338

Jackson, Andrew, 210, 218, 347
Jackson, Jonathan, 306
Jackson, Robert H., 347
Jacobinism, 114, 124, 181, 241
Jacobson, J. M., 263
Jameson, J. F., 277
Jay, John, 31, 50, 118, 141, 192, 272, 299, 338
    as Chief Justice, 76–77, 89–90, 220, 294
    as nationalist, 38, 43
    and *The Federalist,* 53–54
    in Poughkeepsie Convention, 62, 64, 280
Jay's Treaty, 7, 9, 30, 83, 90–92, 262, 265, 291, 313
Jefferson, Thomas, 4, 24, 50, 111, 119, 124, 140, 280, 305, 343
    as symbol of American democracy, 227–228, 229, 231, 234–235, 253, 348
    reputation, 4, 233, 234, 331
    treatment by historians, viii, 227–229, 234–235, 236, 331–332
    as constitutionalist, 186, 189, 199, 249
    interpretation of Constitution, 25, 33, 76, 79–80, 81, 82, 83, 85, 88–89, 91–
        92, 99, 100–101, 110, 192, 194, 201, 203, 214, 221, 247, 275, 289, 291,
        293, 294, 298–299, 327
    political science, 12, 16, 21, 33, 114, 117, 121, 128, 133
    as Secretary of State, 30, 75, 84–86, 261, 288, 294
    as President, 34, 95, 98–100, 102, 106, 155, 159, 198, 212, 220, 238, 324
    and Kentucky Resolutions, 81, 100
    and Louisiana Purchase, 95, 98–100, 239, 298–299
    and civil liberties, 102, 178
    on Hamilton, 24, 30, 154, 238, 264, 271–272, 331
    Hamilton on, 113, 212, 317, 324
    relations with Hamilton, 26, 27, 88, 193, 227
    opinion of *The Federalist,* 52, 282
    preference for France, 15
    as nationalist, 18
    on Marshall, 344
Jensen, Merrill, 272, 276

Johnson, Gerald, 337
Johnson, William, 243
Johnson, William Samuel, 46, 48
Jones, Samuel, 62, 69
Jones, W. M., 300
judicial review, 93–95, 95–98, 219, 221–225, 241, 248–249, 296–298, 329, 341, 346
judiciary, 218–225, 248–249, 329–330
    independence, 101, 219–220, 221, 248
Judiciary Act of 1789, 96–97
Judiciary Act of 1801, 101, 220
juries, role of, 105

Kaufman, Irving R., 347
Kelly, Alfred H., 344
Kennan, George, 7
Kent, James, 64, 243, 263, 281
    on Hamilton, 10, 104, 116, 243, 342
    in Croswell trial, 103–104, 106–107, 301–303
    Commentaries, 243, 342–343
Kenyon, Cecelia, 142, 284, 312
King, Rufus, 14, 15, 17, 181, 276, 338
    in Philadelphia Convention, 48, 49, 277
    relations with Hamilton, 71, 92, 237, 294
Kingsley, Sidney, 348
Kirk, Russell, 180, 320, 335
Kirkland, E. C., 260
Klein, Milton, 307
Knox, Henry, 30, 38, 294, 338
Koch, Adrienne, 7, 261, 268, 290, 316
Kohn, Hans, 230, 264
Krout, John A., 42, 276, 286
Kurtz, Stephen G., 270, 292, 313

Lamb, John, 64–65, 155, 283
Landis, James, 300
Lansing, John, Jr., 42, 44–49, 60, 62, 69, 276, 278
Laski, Harold, 333
Laurens, Henry, 37, 273, 312
Laurens, John, 141, 268
law, 176, 181, 197
Leach, R. H., 263
Le Boutillier, Cornelia, 307
Lee, Charles, 340

Lee, Henry, 94, 267, 269, 388
legislature, role of, 169–170, 171, 208
Levy, B. H., 340
Levy, Leonard, 301
Lewis, Anthony, 347
Lewis, Morgan, 103, 105–106
libel, law of, 100, 101–108, 302–303
liberty, 16, 104, 140, 170, 175–178, 179, 200, 319
Lincoln, Abraham, 6, 12, 19–20, 205, 232, 250, 334
    reputation, 4, 183, 234
Lincoln, Benjamin, 289
Lippmann, Walter, 348
Livingston, Edward, 295
Livingston, Gilbert, 62, 64, 69, 283
Livingston, John C., 180
Livingston, R. R., 42, 98, 272, 273, 298
    in Poughkeepsie Convention, 62, 66, 68, 288
Livingston, William, 121, 307
Locke, John, 45, 119, 121–125, 127, 182–183, 306
Lodge, Henry Cabot, 14–15, 233, 257, 264, 268, 270, 290, 321, 335
Loewenberg, B. J., 332
Lossing, B. J., 273
Loth, David, 336
Louisiana Purchase, 95, 98–100, 214, 239, 298–299
Lowell, John, 338

Machiavelli, 117, 119, 122, 125, 172, 182–183, 306, 321
Maclay, William, 55, 75, 288
Madison, James:
    reputation, 4, 235
    in Confederation Congress, 38–40, 282
    and Annapolis Convention, 41–42
    in Convention of 1787, 45, 48–50
    in Congress, 25, 73, 79–80, 212, 286, 288–294, 295
    as President, 239, 244, 339, 343
    as constitutionalist, 50, 111, 160, 170, 186, 189, 199
    interpretation of Constitution, 11, 33, 76, 78–80, 82, 83, 85–86, 91–92, 203,
        213, 214, 239, 289, 290–291, 295, 297, 339
    political science, 12, 114, 117, 162, 167, 183, 187, 250
    and The Federalist, 12, 53–60, 78, 98, 162, 203, 281, 282, 315
    as nationalist, 18, 38, 39, 42, 78, 200, 338
    on Hamilton, 111–112, 190, 265, 276, 278, 323, 337
    Hamilton on, 281, 317

Madison, James (cont.)
    early relations with Hamilton, 38–39, 68–69, 72, 73, 288
    later hostility to Hamilton, 75, 78, 86, 88, 193, 288, 293
    as Helvidius, 86, 292, 327
Main, Jackson T., 283
majority rule, 187–188
Malone, Dumas, 259, 268, 331, 332
Mansfield, Lord, 103, 118, 119, 305
Marbury v. *Madison,* 95–98, 240, 242, 296, 298, 340
Marshall, John, 186, 297, 313, 324, 338, 339
    reputation, 4, 235, 244, 245
    as Chief Justice, 86, 95, 97–98
    on Hamilton, 75, 240, 241, 331, 337, 340, 341, 342
    on *The Federalist,* 242, 341–342
    debt to Hamilton, 240–242, 340
    correspondence with Hamilton, 241, 341
    Jefferson on, 340
Martin, Luther, 45, 243
Mason, Alpheus T., 58, 263, 282
Mason, Jeremiah, 97
Mason, John M., 67
McBain, H. L., 345
McCloskey, Robert, 335, 345
McCulloch v. *Maryland,* 200, 203, 239, 240, 242, 243, 341, 342
McDonald, Forrest, 269
McGovney, Dudley O., 345
McHenry, James, 30, 217, 267, 270, 275, 278, 287, 338
McKean, Thomas, 102
McKee, Samuel, Jr., 261
McKesson, John, 283
McKitrick, Eric, 276
McLaughlin, A. C., 297, 304, 344
McMaster, John Bach, 231, 233
Mellon, Andrew W., 336
mercantilism, 119, 179–180
Merriam, C. E., 263
middle class, 138–139
militia, 23, 267
Miller, John C., 97, 118, 139, 259, 261, 274–275, 316, 336
Miller, William, 332
Miner, C. E., 276, 280
Mission, American, 17–18, 265–266
Missouri v. *Holland,* 217

Mitchell, Broadus, 27, 180, 236, 259, 270, 275, 280, 316, 321, **336**

Monaghan, Frank, 272

Monroe, James, 98, 291

Montesquieu, 56, 119, 121, 154, 156, 187, 307

Moore v. *Michigan,* 249

Morais, Herbert M., 333

morality, importance of, 122–124, 171, 172, 176, 307

Morgan, Donald G., 342

Morgan, Edmund S., 332

Morgenthau, Hans, 7, 8, 261

Morison, Samuel Eliot, 228, 332

Morris, Gouverneur, 14, 34, 43, 118, 218, 280, 338
    and Constitution, 38, 48, 272
    on Hamilton, 49, 279, 300, 304, 315

Morris, Richard B., 10, 62, 261, 271, 296

Morris, Robert, 19, 39, 73, 181, 260, 275, 338
    as financier, 5, 31, 38, 87

Morse, John T., 233

Mosteller, Frederick, 280, 281, 316

Munro, William B., 345

Murray, William Vans, 267, 338

Myers v. *United States,* 245

N.L.R.B. v. *Jones and Laughlin Steel Corp.,* 204, 247

national honor, 8–9, 171–172, 318

national purpose, 18

natural law, 119, 121, 122, 123, 125, 186, 224, 307–308

natural rights, 119, 121, 122, 123, 125, 186, 224, 307–308

nature of man, 15, 118, 125–137, 145, 161, 163, 167–168, 179, 181, 186, 196, 216, 251, 308–310

"necessary and proper" clause, 78, 200–202

Necker, Jacques, 315

Negroes, 141–142, 312

Nelson v. *Pennsylvania,* 249

Nettels, Curtis P., 261

Neutrality Crisis (1793), 7–8, 84–86, 89, 213

Nevins, Allan, 272, 298

New Deal, 232, 234, 245, 337

New Jersey Plan, 45, 94

New York Evening Post, 97–98, 150, 298, 299, 314

Nicholas, John, 268

Nicholas, Wilson Cary, 299

Niebuhr, Reinhold, 7

Nixon, H. C., 332
North, Douglass C., 263
Nott, Eliphalet, 252

obedience, importance of, 177, 181
Oliver, F. S., 14, 175, 233, 259, 270
Osborn v. *Bank,* 342
O'Sullivan, J. R., 335
Otis, Harrison Gray, 87, 213, 263, 266, 267, 269, 299, **338**
Owsley, Frank L., 332

Padover, Saul K., 321
Paine, Tom, 37, 108, 272–273
Palamountain, J. C., 268
Paltsits, V. H., 271
Panagopoulos, E. P., 269, 306, 308
Parrington, Vernon L., 331, 336
Parsons, Theophilus, Jr., 162, 316
Parton, James, 235
"passions," 133–135, 251, 310
Paterson, Samuel, 302
Paterson, William, 45, 94, 299
Patrick, R. W., 332
Patterson, Jonathan, 285
People v. *Croswell,* 10, 102–106, 108, 177, 301–304
people, role of, 160–162, 187, 199, 218, 222–225, 250
Perkins, Bradford, 264
Perkins, Dexter, 230, 332
Perry, Ralph Barton, 230
Persons, Stow, 337
Peterson, Merrill, 331, 333
Pickering, Timothy, 27, 30, 92, 155, 270, 287, 308, **338**
Pierce, William, 43
Pinckney, Charles, 45, 159
Pinkney, William, 243
Pitt, William, 260
Plato, 182
Platt, Zephaniah, 64, 69
Plumer, William, 299
Plutarch, 118, 156
political parties, 147–149, 313
Pollock v. *Farmers' Loan and Trust Co.,* 346
Pomeroy, John N., 343

Pope, Alexander, 133, 155, 174
Postlethwayt, Malachy, 119, 125, 306
Potter, David, 333
Powell, T. R., 345
power:
    love of, 28, 131, 268, 269
    abuse of, 131–132, 186
    uses of, 21, 163–164, 168, 246, 251–252
Pratt, Julius W., 262
Presidency, 208–218, 248, 291, 327
    leadership of Congress, 208, 213, 216
    power of removal, 212, 326
    power to withhold papers from Congress, 92–93, 295
    veto power, 143, 212
    problem of re-eligibility, 210–211
press, freedom of, 104–105, 107, 177, 301–303
Pritchett, C. Herman, 344
property, 140, 159, 163, 177, 316, 320
public administration, 6–7, 174–175, 251, 319, 325
public good, 16, 27, 142–147, 158, 179, 203, 251
public opinion, 4, 149–152, 251, 313
Pufendorf, Baron, 119, 121, 125
Pusey, Merlo J., 346

Quincy, Josiah, 239

Randall, Henry S., 228, 229–230
Randolph, Edmund, 30, 33, 42, 79–80, 83, 88–89, 289, 291
Randolph, John, 239
Rauch, Basil, 332
Rawle, William, 343
Read, George, 46, 73, 277, 338
reason, importance of, 122, 123, 124–125, 133–135
religion, 18, 124, 175, 176, 177, 181, 308
Repeal Act of 1802, 98, 190, 220, 300
representation, 143
Republican party (modern), 232, 234
Republican party (under Jefferson), 98, 99, 101, 102, 107
republicanism, 46, 60, 153–157, 162
resistance, right of, 122, 307
"resulting" powers, 207–208, 325, 345
Reynolds, Maria, 26–27, 29
Riethmuller, C. J., 333

Roberts, Owen J., 245
Roche, John P., 279
Rogers, G. C., 290
Rolt, Richard, 306
Roosevelt, Franklin D., 234, 337
Roosevelt, Theodore, 228, 233, 234, 248, 336, 348
Root, Elihu, 336
Root, E. Merrill, 232, 335
Rose, Stanley D., 336
Rostow, E. V., 330
Rottschaefer, Henry, 345
Rousseau, J. J., 118, 119, 127, 142, 182, 183
Rush, Richard, 6, 261
Rutgers v. *Waddington*, 10, 41, 95, 106, 243, 275, 296, 297, 306, 323, 329
Rutledge, Edward, 37, 238, 273
Rutledge, John, 31, 49, 293, 338

Schachner, Nathan, 259, 263, 298, 316, 336
Schlesinger, Arthur, 333
Schneider, Herbert W., 282
Schuyler, Philip, 13, 37, 38, 39, 44, 103, 195, 267, 273, 275
Schuyler, Robert L., 286
Schwartz, Bernard, 344, 345
Scott, A. M., 263
Scott, James Brown, 293
Scott, John Morin, 307
Sedgwick, Theodore, 17, 73, 78, 150, 237, 265, 267, 292, 304, 314, 338
separation of powers, 74–75, 160, 186, 322
Seton, William, 191
Shakespeare, William, 133
Shays, Daniel, 109
Shays Rebellion, 43
Shea, George, 335
Sherman, Roger, 45, 49
Shields, C. V., 320
Simons, Algie M., 337
slavery, 289, 334
Smith, Adam, 119, 130, 133, 165, 179, 182, 306
Smith, H. R., 260
Smith, J. Allen, 337
Smith, James M., 299, 302, 320
Smith, Maynard, 319
Smith, Melancton, 62, 64–69, 70, 283, 285

Smith, Page, 260, 268, 279
Smith, William, Jr., 307
Smith, William L., 78, 80, 173, 212, 237, 269, 287, 290, 312, 338
society, 16, 137–142, 145, 161, 171, 175, 178, 251
Society for establishing Useful Manufactures, 9, 262
Soule, George, 263
Spaight, R. D., 297
Sparks, Jared, 270
Spaulding, E. W., 272, 279, 283
Spencer, Ambrose, 102, 239, 301
Spinoza, 119
state of nature, 122
states' rights, 197–198, 247, 253
Stearns, Frank P., 336
Stephens, Alexander Hamilton, 334–335
Stevens, Edward, 268
Steward Machine Co. v. *Davies,* 247
Stimson, Henry L., 336
Stoddert, Benjamin, 338
Story, Joseph, 241, 243–244, 299, 343
    debt to Hamilton, 244
    Commentaries, 100, 244–245, 299, 300, 325, 343–344
    on Hamilton, 244
    on Marshall, 344
Strayer, J. R., 276
Stuart v. *Laird,* 98, 101
Sullivan, John, 37, 273, 274, 284
Sumner, William Graham, 335
"supremacy" clause, 196–197
Supreme Court, 77, 101, 218–225, 248–249
    independence, 89–90, 95, 219–220, 221, 248
    use of Hamilton, 245, 346–347
Sutherland, George, 208, 245, 325, 345
Sutton, F. X., 335
Swisher, Carl B., 344
Syrett, Harold C., 275, 281, 290, 304, 332

Taft, William Howard, 204, 245
Talleyrand, viii, 259
tariff, 81, 290
taxation, 169–170
    power of Congress, 80, 81, 93–95, 203–204
Taylor, John, 93, 99, 140, 295, 339

Thach, C. C., 278, 322
Thomas, Charles M., 291
Thompson, Smith, 106
Thomson, Charles, 282
Thorton, John V., 303
Thorpe, Francis N., 340
Tiedeman, Christopher G., 245
Tillinghast, Charles, 64–65, 155
Tracy, Uriah, 265, 338
Treasury Act of 1789, 286, 287
treaty-making power, 207, 216–218
Troup, Robert, 28, 42, 263, 269, 276, 287, 301, 337, 338
Trumbull, John, 265
Tucker, George, 331
Tucker, H. St. George, 344
Tugwell, R. G., 262, 337
Turner, L. W., 265
Twiss, Benjamin R., 344
tyranny, road to, 158, 165–167, 168, 251

Union, viii, 19–21, 41, 51, 110, 137, 141, 194–196, 225, 232, 247, 253, 265, 304, 340, 342
United States v. *Butler,* 245, 249
United States v. *Curtiss Wright Corp.,* 208, 245, 247
United States v. *Darby,* 247
United States v. *Hudson and Goodwin,* 299

Van Buren, Martin, 333
Van Deusen, Glyndon, 332
Vandenberg, Arthur H., 336
Van Ness, William W., 103, 106, 303
Van Riper, Paul P., 331
Vattel, Emmerich de, 119
Ver Steeg, Clarence L., 260
veto power, 143, 212
Virginia and Kentucky Resolutions, 81, 97, 198, **299**
Virginia Plan, 45
Von Holst, Hermann, 231

Walters, Raymond, 339
war, causes of, 23, 128, 161
Ware v. *Hylton,* 97
Warren, Charles, 274, 276, 281, 298, 300

Warren, Earl, 20, 242

Washington, Bushrod, 243, 340

Washington, George, 23, 38, 49, 128, 280, 338
    reputation, 4, 234, 235, 337
    as President, 11, 36, 72, 78–80, 83–86, 218, 220, 286, 288, 293, 324, 341
    relations with Hamilton, 11, 26, 30, 31–33, 47, 65, 72, 75, 80, 83–90, 133,
        139, 190, 191, 217, 270–271, 301
    reliance on Hamilton, 31–33, 87, 111, 209, 286, 294, 295, 337
    on Hamilton, 26, 31, 32
    Hamilton on, 32, 302–303
    interpretation of Constitution, 25, 32, 78–79, 83–84, 88–89, 110, 291
    patriotism, 13–14, 18, 195
    on *The Federalist,* 52, 282

Watson, David K., 344

Webb, Samuel Blachley, 64, 280, 283, 338

Webster, Daniel, 19–20, 231, 243

Webster, Noah, 269, 273, 338

Webster, Peletiah, 273

Wecter, Dixon, 236, 331

Weigley, R. F., 267

Whiggery, 119–125, 129, 140, 158, 160, 169, 170, 178, 186, 193, **222**

Whiskey Rebellion, 148, 341

White, Leonard D., 6, 174–175, 261, 319, 339

Wickard v. *Filburn,* 247

Willard, Joseph, 293

Williams, J. Harvie, 335

Williams, John, 62

Williams, T. Harry, 332

Willoughby, W. W., 344

Wilson, Francis G., 263

Wilson, James, 11, 38, 49, 97, 200, 260, 297, 299, 338

Wilson, Woodrow, 7, 13, 230, 264, 333

Wiltse, C. M., 321, 331

Wirt, William, 243

Wolcott, Oliver, 30, 31, 92, 117, 170, 269, 270, 281, 295, 304, 338

Wright, B. F., 281, 330, 341, 344

Wythe, George, 45

Yates, Robert, 42, 44–49, 60, 62, 69, 276, **278**